Accounting for Managers

Authors

**Christopher D. Burnley • Donald C. Cherry • Maureen R. Fizzell •
Robert E. Hoskin**

ISBN 9781119236108

List of Titles

Understanding Financial Accounting, Canadian Edition
by Christopher D. Burnley, Robert E. Hoskin, Maureen R. Fizzell, and Donald C. Cherry
Copyright © 2015, ISBN: 978-1-118-84938-5

Table of Contents

Understanding FINANCIAL ACCOUNTING

Understanding FINANCIAL ACCOUNTING

CANADIAN EDITION

Christopher D. Burnley

Vancouver Island University

With contributions by

Julia A. Scott

McGill University

Peggy Wallace

Trent University

Based on *Financial Accounting: A User Perspective, Sixth Canadian Edition*

Robert E. Hoskin

University of Connecticut

Maureen R. Fizzell

Simon Fraser University

Donald C. Cherry

Dalhousie University (Retired)

WILEY

Library and Archives Canada Cataloguing in Publication

Burnley, Christopher D., 1966–, author
Understanding financial accounting / Christopher D. Burnley, Robert E. Hoskin, Maureen R. Fizzell, Donald C. Cherry. — Canadian edition.

Issued in print and electronic formats.
ISBN 978-1-118-84938-5 (bound).—ISBN 978-1-119-04857-2 (loose-leaf).—ISBN 978-1-119-04855-8 (pdf)

1. Accounting—Textbooks. I. Fizzell, Maureen, author II. Hoskin, Robert E., 1949–, author III. Cherry, Donald C., author IV. Title.

HF5636.B87 2014 657′.044 C2014-906821-2
C2014-906822-0

Production Credits

Acquisitions Editor: Zoë Craig
Vice President and Publisher: Veronica Visentin
Director of Marketing: Joan Lewis-Milne
Marketing Manager: Anita Osborne
Editorial Manager: Karen Staudinger
Developmental Editor: Daleara Jamasji Hirjikaka
Media Editor: Luisa Begani
Editorial Assistant: Maureen Lau
Cover and Interior Design: Joanna Vieira
Cover Image: Christopher Burnley
Typesetting: Aptara®, Inc.

Printing & Binding: Quad/Graphics

Printed and bound in the United States of America
1 2 3 4 5 QG 18 17 16 15 14

John Wiley & Sons Canada, Ltd.
5353 Dundas Street West, Suite 400
Toronto, ON, M9B 6H8 Canada
Visit our website at: www.wiley.ca

CHAPTER 1 Overview of Corporate Financial Reporting

CORE QUESTIONS

If you are able to answer the following questions, then you have achieved the related learning objectives.

LEARNING OBJECTIVES

After studying this chapter, you should be able to:

INTRODUCTION

- What is financial accounting?

1. Define financial accounting and understand its relationship to economic decision-making.

- Who needs to have an understanding of financial accounting and why?

2. Identify the main users of financial accounting information and explain how they use this information.

FORMS OF BUSINESS ORGANIZATION

- What is a corporation?
- What differentiates a corporation from other forms of business?

3. Describe the major forms of business organization and explain the key distinctions between them.

ACTIVITIES OF A BUSINESS

- What are the three categories of business activities?
- What are examples of financing activities?
- What are examples of investing activities?
- What are examples of operating activities?

4. Explain the three categories of business activities and identify examples of transactions related to each category.

FINANCIAL REPORTING

- What information is included in a set of financial statements?
- What is the reporting objective of the statement of income? What does it include?
- What is the reporting objective of the statement of changes in equity? What does it include?
- What is the reporting objective of the statement of financial position? What does it include?
- What is the reporting objective of the statement of cash flows? What does it include?
- What type of information is in the notes to a company's financial statements?

5. Identify and explain the content and reporting objectives of the four basic financial statements and the notes to the financial statements.

Are Higher Profits in the Bag?

Danier Leather Inc. was founded in 1972 as Royal Leather Goods Limited, and through the 1980s it amalgamated with various other leather manufacturers. Danier is now one of the largest publicly traded leather apparel retailers in the world. Headquartered in Toronto, Danier designs and manufactures women's and men's leather clothing, bags, and other goods. Some goods are manufactured in Canada while others are made overseas. Danier has more than 90 stores across Canada in malls, power centres ("big-box" stores), and streetfronts.

If you had a leather craft business and wanted to expand, you might finance this by using your savings or borrowing from family members. But how do large companies such as Danier finance growth? Like many companies that reach a certain size, Danier became a public company, issuing shares that trade on the Toronto Stock Exchange (TSX). The company's initial public offering, in 1998, raised $68 million, which was used to ramp up production and open new stores. In recent years, Danier seems to have taken a steady approach to growth, not needing to borrow to finance it. The company has had no long-term debt since 2007 and at the end of its 2014 fiscal year it had $13.5 million in cash.

Danier has been able to finance its growth through its operating profits and its cash reserves. Company management is continually looking for ways to increase sales, especially of those items that generate higher profits. A big focus for the company is to increase its higher-margin accessories business. Management believes that this focus on accessories will enable the company to attract new and younger customers, make sales less seasonal, generate higher margins, and reduce issues caused by needing to have the correct sizes on hand to fit customers.

One accessories area that Danier plans to expand is its handbag business. "Currently, we see a gap in the market for stylish leather handbags priced under $200," wrote Danier President and CEO Jeffery Wortsman in the company's 2013 annual report. "We believe there are tremendous opportunities for Danier in this under-served niche in the market."

Shareholders and others use a company's financial statements to see how the company has performed and what its future prospects might be. Shareholders use them to make informed decisions about things such as whether to sell their shares, hold onto them, or buy more. Creditors use financial statements to assess a company's ability to service its debts (pay interest and repay principal), while suppliers may use them to determine whether to allow the company to purchase on credit. Companies communicate all this information through financial reporting and the tool used to prepare financial information is accounting.

Whether or not Danier achieves the increased revenues and profits it hopes for by increasing its accessories business will be reported in the company's future financial statements. These financial statements will tell the story of whether higher profits for Danier really were "in the bag."[1]

INTRODUCTION

LEARNING OBJECTIVE 1
Define financial accounting and understand its relationship to economic decision-making.

The opening story describes how a large company grows and how accounting assists in that development. Whether a business is borrowing money for a start-up or expansion, restructuring the organization, or deciding to purchase or lease, it needs to have accounting information to make the best decisions. You, too, will use accounting information to help you make decisions, whether it's determining if you should buy a company's shares, apply for a job there, or make a large purchase from it.

What is financial accounting?

Financial accounting is the process by which information on the transactions of an organization is captured, analyzed, and used to report to decision makers outside of the organization's management team. These decision makers are often referred to as **financial statement users** and include the owners (normally referred to as **investors**) and those who have lent money to the organization (normally referred to as **creditors**). The primary purpose of financial accounting information is to aid these users in their economic decision-making relative to the organization. As these users are generally outside of the organization and are not involved in its day-to-day operations, the financial accounting information they receive is often their only "window" into the organization.

Users inside the organization (**management**) also use financial accounting information, but they generally require the information at a different level of detail. For example, managers in a national retail chain may need information for a particular store rather than for the organization as a whole. Managers may need different information altogether, such as information needed to develop forward-looking budgets rather than to report on past transactions. It is important to note that management has access to all of the organization's financial information, including information that is never shared outside of the organization. This information is known as **managerial accounting** and will be the basis for another course in your business studies.

Financial accounting, the focus of this textbook, can be as simple as determining the daily sales of a food truck or as complex as recording and reporting on the economic condition of your university, a multinational corporation, or the Government of Canada. All of these entities need to know economic information in order to continue to operate efficiently and effectively. Financial accounting provides the vital financial information that enables people and organizations to make decisions. Because it is very likely that you will be a financial statement user in some way, it is important that you have at least a basic understanding of what financial accounting is (and is not), what it is trying to accomplish, and how it does so.

The focus of this book is the financial accounting information produced by profit-oriented organizations, although we will occasionally refer to not-for-profit organizations or governments. We will concentrate mainly on the **financial statements**, which are management's reports to the company's owners that are produced at the end of each accounting period, such as every quarter or every year. They are included in the company's **annual report** together with **management's discussion and analysis (MD&A)** of the company's results for the year. The annual report is made available to the company's owners, but many other parties, such as lenders, financial analysts, credit-rating agencies, securities regulators, and taxing authorities, also use it.

LEARNING OBJECTIVE 2
Identify the main users of financial accounting information and explain how they use this information.

Who needs an understanding of financial accounting and why?

Before we answer these questions, let's take some time to think a little about the game of hockey. (Yes, hockey. After all, what's a Canadian textbook without a hockey reference?) Whether you have lived in Canada your whole life or you are here studying from some other part of the world, chances are good that you have seen a professional hockey game on television or perhaps even in person. During the game, the TV commentary or the conversations of those around you would have included terms like *icing*, *charging*, *slashing*, *five-hole*, *hash marks*, *neutral zone*, and so on. These would have been confusing terms the first time you heard them, but once they were explained to you, your ability to follow the game and understand it at a deeper level would have improved. This is the same with financial accounting. Through the text's 12 chapters we will learn the language of financial accounting and how to interpret financial accounting information so you can come away with a deeper understanding of the subject.

So, let's rephrase our opening question and think about "who needs to understand the rules of professional hockey?" Many groups likely come to mind fairly quickly, including:

- players (including their agents and players' union)
- coaches and general managers
- referees, linesmen, and off-ice officials
- fans
- TV commentators, arena announcers, and sports journalists
- league officials
- team owners
- suppliers, sponsors, and advertisers

We can call these people *stakeholders* because they have a stake in understanding hockey. Now, let's take this list of hockey stakeholders and find the parallel business stakeholders who would have a similar stake in a business, as shown in Exhibit 1-1.

Exhibit 1-1 Similarities between Hockey Stakeholders and Business Stakeholders

Hockey Stakeholders	Parallel Business Stakeholders
Players, including their agents and players' union	Employees, unions
Coaches and general managers	Management
Referees, linesmen, off-ice officials	Auditors, federal and provincial government departments, legislators
Fans	Potential investors, customers
Announcers, TV analysts, sports journalists	Stock analysts, brokers, financial advisors, business reporters
League officials	Stock exchange regulators
Team owners	Shareholders, board of directors
Suppliers, sponsors, advertisers	Creditors, suppliers

Now, let's consider some of the questions that each of the stakeholders in a business may be trying to answer about that business that would require an understanding of financial accounting, as shown in Exhibit 1-2.

Exhibit 1-2 Questions That Stakeholders in a Business May Be Asking

Business Stakeholders	**Potential Questions They May Be Trying to Answer About the Business**
Employees, unions	Is the business profitable? Will I earn a bonus this year? Could the company afford to negotiate increased wages? Is the company pension plan in decent shape?
Management	How do this year's sales compare with last year's? How do they compare with the budget? Are we maintaining our profit margins on certain product lines? How much do we owe our employees and suppliers?
Auditors, federal and provincial government departments, legislators	Has the company presented its financial information fairly? How does the company's financial information compare with the information submitted for taxation or payroll purposes?
Potential investors, customers	What are the long-term prospects for this company? Has the management team done a reasonable job? Will this company be around to honour its warranties?
Stock analysts, brokers, financial advisors, business reporters	What are the company's trends? What are the prospects for this company? How has this company performed relative to expectations?
Stock exchange regulators	Has the company complied with the financial reporting standards and listing requirements?
Shareholders, board of directors	Has the company generated a sufficient return on our investment? How effectively has management used the resources at their disposal? Does the company generate enough income to be able pay dividends?
Creditors, suppliers	Should we extend credit to this company? Is this a credible and successful company that we want to attach our brand to?

These groups of business stakeholders are often known as *financial statement users*. Throughout this book, we will be looking at the information needs of many of these users and discussing how they use financial accounting information in making a variety of decisions. The breadth of this list of users illustrates that no matter which path you take in your business studies, having a basic understanding of accounting information will be essential to business success or could be a job requirement. As we move through the chapters, try to see yourself in one or more of these roles and think about the ways in which you can make use of the accounting information that you will no doubt come across.

The primary goal of this book is to help you become an intelligent user of accounting information by enhancing your ability to read and understand corporate financial statements. You may become a manager, accountant, banker, or financial analyst, and even if you do not end up working directly in the finance industry, you will invest in the shares or bonds of a company at some point in your life. If you work in a company, whether in sales, human resources, or other areas, your decisions will likely have an impact on what is reported to owners. Whatever your business role, you will make decisions about companies, such as whether to invest in their shares, lend them money, or sell them goods or services on credit. In making these decisions, it will be important for you to understand the information that is presented in corporate financial statements. You must know not only what each piece of information tells you about the company, but also what it does not tell you. You should also have an understanding that some important information is not contained in the financial statements, yet could be useful in making certain decisions.

We have written this book for a broad readership, understanding that many of you will play multiple roles as owners (shareholders), creditors, and managers of companies. We have assumed that you know little or nothing about accounting. We have not assumed that you are training to be an accountant, although that may be your objective. Therefore, this book does not emphasize accounting procedures. Instead, it emphasizes the underlying concepts of accounting and the analysis of financial statements. However, it is not really possible to have a knowledgeable understanding of the end result of the accounting process without first having an overall view of how the accounting system works. For this reason, the first three chapters present the basic mechanics of the accounting system. The remaining chapters are then devoted to more detailed accounting issues and concepts, and to a more in-depth analysis of financial statements.

We will now explore the financial statement users in more detail. Exhibit 1-3 lists the various financial statement users, categorizing them as either internal or external users.

Exhibit 1-3 Users of Financial Statement Information

Internal users:
Management
External users:
Shareholders, the board of directors, and potential investors
Creditors (for example, bankers and suppliers)
Regulators (for example, a stock exchange)
Taxing authorities (for example, the Canada Revenue Agency)
Other corporations, including competitors
Securities (stock) analysts
Credit-rating agencies
Labour unions
Journalists

Since the focus of financial accounting is reporting to external users, let's look at these users and their information needs in greater details.

Shareholders, the Board of Directors, and Potential Investors

A company is owned by its **shareholders**. There may be a single shareholder in the case of a **private company** or many thousands of shareholders in the case of a **public company**. We will discuss the distinctions between private and public companies a little later in the chapter, so for now it is just important to understand that companies are owned by their shareholder(s). In situations where there are numerous shareholders, they elect a **board of directors** to represent their interests. The board of directors is given the responsibility of overseeing the management team that has been hired to operate the company.

The board of directors, individual shareholders, and potential investors all require information to enable them to assess how well management has been running the company. Just like hockey fans look at the arena scoreboard to see how their team is doing in terms of the score, shots on goal, and so on, stakeholders in a business look at a company's financial reports to determine how it's doing in a number of areas. Business stakeholders want to make decisions about buying more shares or selling some or all of the shares they already own. (Similar to a hockey team's general manager deciding whether to acquire a star player or trade an underperforming one.) They will analyze the current share price (as reflected on the stock exchange) and compare it with the original price that they paid for the shares. Are the shares now worth more or less? They will also be comparing the share price with the company's underlying value, which is reflected in the financial statements and other sources of information they have about the company.

Individual shareholders will also want to assess whether the current board of directors have effectively carried out their oversight role. They will seek to answer questions such as:

- Is the company heading in the right direction (that is, has the strategic direction approved by the board resulted in increased sales, profits, and so on)?
- Is it making decisions that result in increased value to the shareholders?
- Is the company generating a sufficient return on the resources invested in it by the shareholders?

Creditors

Creditors are those who lend money or otherwise extend credit to a company rather than invest in it directly as investors do. There are two major groups of creditors:

1. Financial institutions and other lenders
2. Suppliers, employees, and the various levels of government

Financial institutions, such as banks and credit unions, lend money to companies. They do so seeking to generate a return on these loans in the form of **interest**. Of course, the lenders also want to ensure that the money they lend out will eventually be repaid (that is, they will get back their **principal**). The loans can either be short-term or extend over several years. These lenders need financial accounting information to assess the company's ability to service the loan. One of the ways this is done is by looking at the cash flows the company generates through its operations. They are also generally interested in the amount of the company's inventory, equipment, buildings, or land, because these may be pledged as security by the borrowing company in the event that it cannot repay the loan. Large companies enter into long-term borrowing arrangements by issuing corporate bonds. Rather than borrowing from a single lender, companies that issue bonds borrow from many lenders. Nevertheless, these lenders are also concerned about the company's ability to service the debt (pay interest and repay principal) over the term of the bond and their financial accounting information needs are similar to those of other lenders.

The other group of creditors includes suppliers, employees, and various levels of government. These groups often sell goods or provide services prior to receiving payment. For example, a supplier may agree to sell goods or provide services to a company and agree to wait 30 days for payment. Employees are another common creditor as they normally work for the company and then receive payment after the fact, such as at the end of every two weeks or at the end of a month. Different levels of government may also be creditors of a company as they wait to receive tax payments or payroll deduction amounts. These users normally focus on the short-term cash level in the company because they are concerned about being paid.

Regulators

The regulators who are interested in financial statements are numerous. For example, the federal and provincial governments have regulations related to how companies report their financial information and are interested in ensuring that these regulations are followed. The stock exchanges, on which the shares of public companies are traded, have regulations about the timing and format of information that companies must convey to them and to investors. Companies not complying with these regulations can be delisted, meaning their shares cease to trade on the exchange, which greatly affects their ability to raise capital.

Taxing Authorities

The **Canada Revenue Agency (CRA)** is the federal taxing authority in Canada and is responsible for federal tax collection. Corporate taxes are primarily based on taxable income, which is calculated based on accounting net income. As such, the CRA is another key user of a company's financial accounting information.

Other Users

Additional users of financial statement information include other companies, securities analysts, credit-rating agencies, labour unions, and journalists. Other companies may want information about the performance of a company if they are going to enter into contracts with it. If it is a direct competitor, they may seek information that will help assess the competitor's strength and future plans. Securities analysts and credit-rating agencies use the financial statements to provide information about the strengths and weaknesses of companies to people who want to invest. Labour unions need to understand the company's financial health in order to negotiate labour contracts with management. Companies often give journalists news releases that disclose financial information such as expected earnings. The journalists may refer to the actual financial statements to validate the information they were given and to supplement the original information.

It is important to understand that all of these users are using the same set of financial statements in spite of their various information needs. The bodies that establish the international and domestic standards for financial reporting are aware of all of these users, but have taken the position that they will emphasize the needs to investors and creditors in the determination of standards. As such, many pieces of information that particular users may want cannot be found in the financial statements and these users must look to other sources of information as well.

The types of financial information gathered and made available to stakeholders vary depending on the form of organization a business has, which we discuss next.

FORMS OF BUSINESS ORGANIZATION

LEARNING OBJECTIVE 3
Describe the major forms of business organization and explain the key distinctions between them.

What is a corporation?

Businesses can be operated in a number of different forms, including as a corporation, as a proprietorship, or as a partnership. Most businesses of any significant size operate as corporations and, as such, this text will focus on the accounting information related to that form of business. However, most of the accounting issues that we will identify in the text also apply in some degree to the other forms of business. If you have a good understanding of corporate accounting, it is not a big challenge to understand the nuances of accounting for proprietorships or partnerships.

As previously mentioned, corporations are owned by shareholders, with the initial shareholders having provided cash or other assets to a corporation in exchange for share certificates. These shares are called **common shares**. One of the key distinctions between corporations and other forms of business is that corporations are separate legal entities; that is, they are legally distinct from their owners. This is where the "Limited" or "Ltd." that you see in the names of many corporations comes from; it refers to the fact that the company has limited legal liability. Since the corporations are separate legal entities, they can enter into contracts and be sued. In the event the company fails, the liability of shareholders is limited to their investment in the corporation.

There are two main types of corporations: public companies (which are also known as *publicly traded companies*) and private companies (which are also known as *privately held companies*). The distinction between the two is that the shares of public companies trade on public stock exchanges such as the Toronto Stock Exchange (TSX) while the shares of private companies trade privately and are not available through public exchanges. The shares of public companies are often widely held, meaning that they are owned by a large number of individuals or entities. Some portion of their ownership will usually change hands every day. On the other hand, shares of a private company are often narrowly held, meaning that they are owned by a relatively small number of people. It is not as easy to transfer ownership in a private company.

Shareholders are not typically involved in the day-to-day operations, except in small private corporations. Given that public companies have a large number of shareholders who are not involved in day-to-day activities, the shareholders typically elect a board of directors to represent them. The board of directors has the authority to hire (and fire if necessary) the management team who will manage the company's day-to-day operations. These senior executives, along with the other managers they hire, are known as *management*. To keep shareholders informed of the performance of their investment in the company, management reports periodically to the shareholders. Financial statements are normally prepared for shareholders quarterly (every three months). Annual financial statements are also produced and are included in the company's annual report. It is these annual financial statements that we will be focusing on.

What differentiates a corporation from other forms of business?

There are a number of key distinctions between corporations and the other forms of business: partnerships and proprietorships. Exhibit 1-4 outlines a number of the key distinctions to help you understand them. It is important to be aware of these differences, but also to understand that there are circumstances in which it makes sense to organize a business using each one of these three main forms of business.

Exhibit 1-4 Key Distinctions between the Forms of Business

Distinguishing Feature	Corporation	Proprietorship	Partnership
Number of owners	Can be a single owner or multiple owners	Single owner	Multiple owners
Separate legal entity?	Yes, personal assets of shareholders *are not* at risk in the event of legal action against company	No, personal assets of owner *are* at risk in the event of legal action	No, partners' personal assets *are* at risk in the event of legal action
Owner(s) responsible for debts of the business?	Only to extent of investment	Yes	Yes
Taxed?	Yes, taxed separately	No, profits taxed in hands of owner	No, profits taxed in hands of owners
Costs to establish	Most expensive	Least expensive	Moderately expensive
Cost to maintain	Most expensive	Least expensive	Moderately expensive

ACTIVITIES OF A BUSINESS

What are the three categories of business activities?

■ **LEARNING OBJECTIVE 4**
Explain the three categories of business activities and identify examples of transactions related to each category.

To understand the information in financial statements, it is useful to think about the fundamental types of activities that all businesses engage in and report on. As illustrated in Exhibit 1-5, all of the activities of businesses can be grouped into three categories: (1) **financing activities**, (2) **investing activities**, and (3) **operating activities**. Each of these involves inflows and outflows of cash into and out of the company.

TAKE5

Exhibit 1-5 The Three Categories of Business Activities

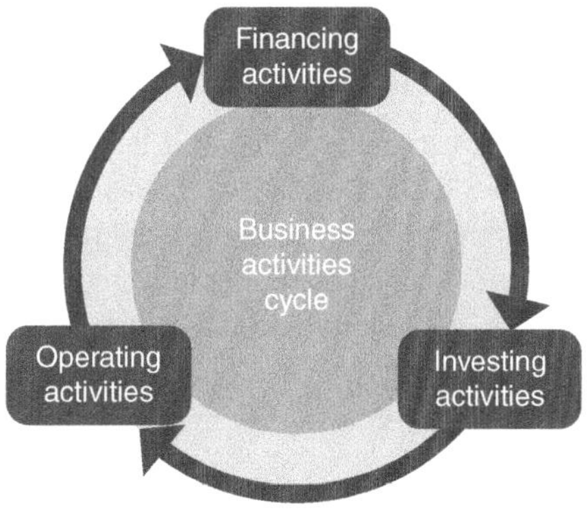

Now, let's explore each category.

What are examples of financing activities?

The first activities of all companies involve obtaining the funding (or *financing*) needed to purchase the equipment and/or buildings they require to start operations. At the outset of the business, funding may also be required to pay for things such as the initial purchase of goods for resale or to pay a landlord a deposit on rented space. While these activities are a necessity for new companies, they also continue as companies grow and expand. Companies obtain funding from two primary sources: (1) investors and (2) creditors.

KEY POINT
A company's financing comes from two sources:
- investors, through the issuance of shares;
- creditors, through taking out loans or making purchases on credit.

Companies obtain funding from investors by issuing them shares (common shares) in the company in exchange for cash or other assets. These shares represent the investor's ownership interest in the company. For example, if the investor owns 10% of the shares issued by the company, they normally own 10% of the company. Since investors own shares in the company, we normally refer to them as *shareholders*. Shareholders purchase shares seeking to generate a return, which may be realized in two different ways. First, they hope to receive **dividends**. These are payments made by a company that distribute profits to shareholders. The other way shareholders seek to make a return is by being able to sell their shares to other investors for more than they paid for the shares. This gain or increase in value is known as **capital appreciation**. Of course, when the sale occurs, investors may also experience a loss if they receive less than the initial amount paid for the shares. The funds that flow into the company from its shareholders form part of what is called **shareholders' equity**.

Once a company has some shareholders' equity, it is then able to seek funding from the second primary financing source, creditors. Creditors are entities that lend money to a company rather than buying shares of the company. Banks are the most common example of a creditor. Creditors also seek a return from the money they lend to a company. This return is the interest they receive for the time they have allowed the company to use their money. Of course, creditors also expect to get their money back. This is known as a *return of principal*.

If a company is operating profitably, it has an internal source of new funding because those profits are not being paid out to shareholders as dividends. Any profits that are kept or retained by the company are known as **retained earnings**. If a company's retained earnings are less than the funding it requires to grow (such as purchasing additional equipment or carrying new lines of inventory), the only way it can expand is to obtain more funds from investors (existing shareholders or new investors) or to borrow from creditors. How much to borrow from creditors and how much funding to obtain from investors are important decisions that the company's management must make. Those decisions can determine whether a company grows, goes bankrupt, or is bought by another company. Examples of financing activities follow:

TYPICAL FINANCING ACTIVITIES	
Inflows:	Borrowing money
	Issuing shares
Outflows:	Repaying loan principal
	Paying dividends

What are examples of investing activities?

KEY POINT
A company's investing activities are related to two things:
- buying and selling property, plant, and equipment;
- buying and selling the shares of other companies.

Once a company obtains funds, it must invest them to accomplish its goals. Most companies make both long-term and short-term investments in order to carry out the activities that help them achieve their goals. Most short-term investments (such as the purchase of raw materials and inventories) are related to the day-to-day operations of the business and are therefore considered operating activities. Many long-term investments are related to the purchase of property, plant, and equipment that can be used to produce goods and services for sale. Companies can also consider investing in the shares of other companies either long-term or short-term.

Examples of investing activities follow:

TYPICAL INVESTING ACTIVITIES	
Inflows:	Proceeds from the sale of property, plant, and equipment
	Proceeds from the sale of shares of other companies
Outflows:	Purchase of property, plant, and equipment
	Purchase of shares of other companies

What are examples of operating activities?

Operating activities are all of the activities associated with developing, producing, marketing, and selling the company's products and/or services. While financing and investing activities are necessary to conduct operations, they tend to occur on a more sporadic basis than operating activities. The day-to-day ongoing activities of a company are generally classified as operating activities.

Examples of operating activities follow:

TYPICAL OPERATING ACTIVITIES	
Inflows:	Sales to customers
	Collections of amounts owed by customers
Outflows:	Purchases of inventory
	Payments of amounts owed to suppliers
	Payments of expenses such as wages, rent, and interest
	Payments of taxes owed to the government

KEY POINT

A company's operating activities are related to the company's revenues and expenses, which fall into two basic categories:

- inflows from sales to and collections from customers;
- outflows related to payment of the expenses of the business.

Of the three categories of activities, operating activities are considered the most critical to the long-run success or failure of a company. If the company is not successful at generating cash flows from its operations, it will ultimately run out of cash as financing sources will dry up because it will be unable to attract new investors or lenders. It will have to sell the property, plant, and equipment it uses to generate its revenues.

Exhibit 1-6 illustrates the principal inflows and outflows associated with the three categories of business activities.

Exhibit 1-6 The Three Categories of Business Activities: Key Inflows and Outflows

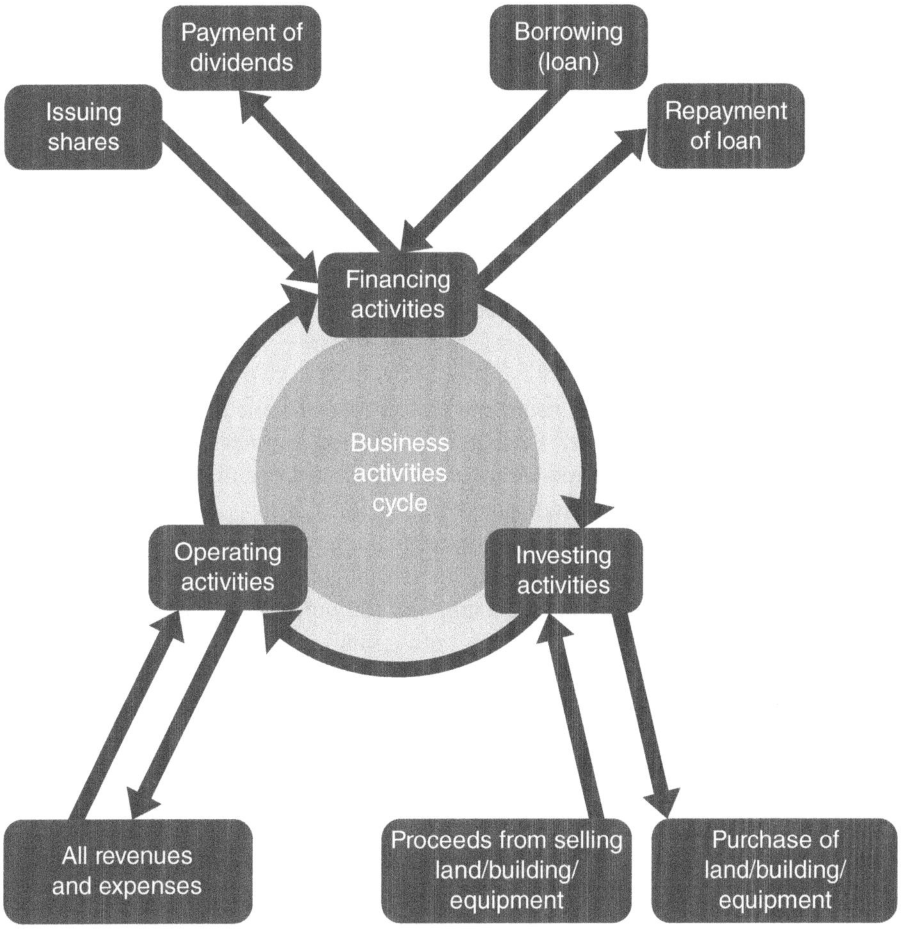

TAKE5

The financial statements provide information about a company's operating, financing, and investing activities. By the end of this book, you should be able to interpret financial statements as they relate to these activities. To help you become a successful user of financial statement information, in Appendix A at the back of the book, we present the financial statements of **Danier Leather Inc.**, which were included in the company's 2014 annual report. As noted in the feature story, Danier is a Canadian manufacturer and retailer of leather clothing and accessories. Let's walk through the various types of information contained in this part of Danier's annual report.

FINANCIAL REPORTING

LEARNING OBJECTIVE 5
Identify and explain the content and reporting objectives of the four basic financial statements and the notes to the financial statements.

What information is included in a set of financial statements?

The components of the financial statements are shown below.

COMPONENTS OF THE FINANCIAL STATEMENTS
Statement of income
Statement of changes in equity
Statement of financial position
Statement of cash flows
Notes to the financial statements

Let's look at each component of the financial statements in detail, including what it sets out to do and what information it includes.

What is the reporting objective of the statement of income? What does it include?

The objective of the **statement of income** is to measure the company's performance by the results of its operating activities for a month, a quarter, or a year. The sum of these operating activities is known as the company's **profit**, which is determined by subtracting the **expenses** incurred in the period from the **income** earned during the same time period. Profit, which is also known as **net income**, **net earnings**, or **earnings**, is a standard measure of corporate performance. Of course, it is possible to have a **net loss**, which would mean that the expenses for the period exceeded the income earned.

Income (which is also known as **revenues**) is defined as increases in economic benefits, but this is more commonly thought of as the money or other resources that flow into the company as a result of its ordinary activities, such as sales of goods and services. Income also includes **gains** that a company generates from sales that are outside its normal course of operations. An example is when a company sells some of its equipment that it has finished using and the proceeds of sale are greater than the amount the equipment is recorded at by the company. Expenses are defined as decreases in economic benefits, but are more commonly thought of as the money or other resources that flow out of the company in the course of it generating its revenues. Expenses include things like the cost of the goods that are sold in sale transactions or the wages that are paid to the employees making these sales. Expenses also include **losses** that a company can incur on sales that are outside its normal course of operations. An example is when a company sells equipment that it has finished using, but the proceeds of sale are less than the amount the equipment is recorded at by the company. As both gains and losses are outside of the company's normal operations, they are presented separately from revenues and expenses on the statement of income, so that the users of the financial statements are able to make this distinction.

THE STATEMENT OF INCOME IS ALSO KNOWN AS THE . . .
Statement of operations
Statement of earnings
Statement of profit or loss

Refer to the consolidated statements of earnings (loss) and comprehensive earnings (loss) for Danier in Appendix A. It is called a **consolidated financial statement** because it includes the financial information for the main or **parent company** plus the financial information of all the other companies that it controls (known as the **subsidiary companies**). The time period of the statement is indicated at the top, where it reads "Years Ended June 28, 2014 (52 weeks), and June 29, 2013 (52 weeks)." Companies are required to provide **comparative information** (the results of both the current period and preceding period) so that users can assess the changes from the previous period. As noted above, this statement reports on the company's operating performance for the year ended June 28, 2014. This period is also known as the company's **fiscal year**. You may be wondering why Danier's fiscal years ended on different days in 2014 and 2013 (that is, June 28 in 2014 and June 29 in 2013). This is because the company has established that its fiscal year ends on the last Saturday in June each year. Having a fiscal year end on a Saturday is common among retailers, but it means that every fifth or sixth year, the year includes 53 weeks rather than 52 weeks. Finally, it is also important to note that the numbers in the Danier financial statements are presented in thousands of Canadian dollars. Some Canadian companies, whose shares trade on U.S. stock exchanges, report in U.S. dollars instead of Canadian dollars.

Revenue

From the statement, we can see that Danier generated revenues of almost $142 million during its 2013 fiscal year. This would be the sales from all 90 stores that the company owns. From the comparative information, we can see that the company's sales decreased 8% over the prior period. This trend is negative, so we would need to read the management discussion and analysis (MD&A) section of the company's annual report to get additional details regarding the change in revenues. As the name implies, the MD&A section is where senior management discusses and analyzes its financial statements. (We will explore more aspects of an MD&A later in the chapter.) A look at Danier's MD&A tells us that 39% of the company's revenues resulted from sales of accessories and that the sales in the company's stores in all regions declined, with the decreases in Quebec and Atlantic Canada being the most significant. The MD&A also explains that the company's sales are very seasonal, with 44% of total sales occurring in the three-month period between October and December. As you can see, while the information presented in the statement of income is useful, it often needs to be supplemented with other information in order to carry out meaningful analysis.

Further down on the statement, we can see that the company earned interest income of $118,000 during the year. Since this income did not come from the sale of goods to customers, Danier has presented it separately from its revenues. This helps users of the financial statements to have a clearer picture of the results of the company's operations.

Expenses

Costs and expenses are also listed under various categories, including cost of goods sold (or cost of sales, or cost of merchandise sold); selling, general, and administrative expenses (or operating expenses); interest expense; and income tax expense (or provision for income taxes). As you would expect, cost of sales is a significant expense for a company like Danier. As a manufacturer, it purchases raw materials like leather from which it manufactures clothing to sell in its retail locations. The company also purchases finished goods, like the accessories it also sells in its stores. The other significant cost would be the wage costs for all of the company's employees, whether they work at the retail locations, manufacturing operations, or at the company's head office. These costs are included in selling, general, and administrative expenses. Danier provides some additional information on the makeup of cost of sales and selling, general, and administrative expenses in Notes 13, 21 and 22 to the financial statements. This is another example of providing information in addition to that presented in the statement itself so users can fully understand the financial information.

Gross Profit

Gross profit (or *gross margin*) is another very important number presented on the statement of income for all companies that sell goods. It is equal to the difference between the revenue received from the sale of the goods and the amount these goods cost the seller. From Danier's statement of income, we can see that this amounted to $68.2 million in 2014. It is often more meaningful to express gross profit as a percentage of revenue rather than as a dollar figure. For Danier, the gross profit percentage was 48.1% in 2014. This means that for every dollar in sales revenue, the company had just over $0.48 after paying for its products. This gross profit must then be used to cover the rest of the company's operating costs, such as wages, rent, and advertising. Another way of looking at this is to consider that Danier, on average, was able to sell its products for just about double the price they cost to manufacture or purchase.

Net Earnings

Net earnings (*net income* or *profit*) is the amount of the company's revenue that remains after all of its expenses, such as product costs, wages, rents, interest, and income taxes. In the case of Danier, the company had a net loss of $7,663,000 for 2013. If we reflect this as a percentage of sales, we can see that for every $1 in sales revenue, Danier lost about $0.05 in net earnings. In other words, all of Danier's expenses represented about $1.05 of every $1 in sales revenue.

Earnings per Share

At the bottom of the statement of income is an **earnings per share** disclosure. Basic earnings per share is the company's net income divided by the average number of common shares that are outstanding (owned by shareholders of the company) during the year. Shareholders find this calculation useful since it puts the performance of their investment into perspective. In other words, a shareholder who holds 10,000 shares of Danier can determine his or her share of the earnings during the period. In the fiscal year ending June 28, 2014, Danier's earnings per share was a loss of $2.00. Therefore, that investor's share of the loss for 2014 would be $20,000. The board of directors determines how much of the company's earnings, if any, will be paid to shareholders as dividends. Given the loss, no dividends were declared by Danier's board in 2014.

On some statements of income, there will also be a diluted earnings per share amount, which is normally lower than the basic earnings per share. Danier has indicated that its diluted earnings (loss) per share was $2.00. Diluted earnings per share reflects the earnings per share figure that would have been determined if all of the securities that can be converted into shares had actually been converted. More advanced financial accounting courses discuss diluted earnings per share in more detail.

Below is a list of some of the items you can expect to see on the statement of income.

COMMON STATEMENT OF INCOME ITEMS	
Sales revenues	The total amount of sales of goods and/or services for the period.
Other income	Various types of revenues or income to the company other than sales, including interest or rental income.
Cost of goods sold	The cost of the inventory that was sold during the period.
Selling, general, and administrative expense	The total amount of other expenses (such as salaries and rent) during the period that do not fit into any other category.
Depreciation expense (Amortization expense)	The allocation of part of the cost of long-lived items such as equipment or a patent.
Interest expense	The amount of interest incurred on the company's debt during the period.
Income tax expense (provision for taxes)	The taxes levied on the company's profits during the period.

Ethics in Accounting

Accounting standards allow companies to choose among different measurement methods. These choices can impact the information on financial statements and provide management with the opportunity to select methods that can raise or lower income and report revenues and/or expenses at different times. When management selects accounting methods to achieve a specific reporting objective, it is called **earnings management**. Most times, managers will use earnings management legitimately, but as a user of the financial statement information, it is important that you recognize the circumstances that make it possible for earnings to be managed in an unethical way.

What is the reporting objective of the statement of changes in equity? What does it include?

The **statement of changes in equity** provides details on how each component of shareholders' equity changed during the period. As we begin thinking about the concept of **equity**, it can help to use the example of home ownership to illustrate that equity is a "net" number. For example, if we were trying to determine the equity that a person had in their home, we would calculate it as the value of their home (what they could sell it for) less the amount of any mortgage(s) that would have to be paid off if the home were sold. This difference would be the person's equity in the home, also known as homeowner's equity. Continuing with this example, we can see that the initial equity of the homeowner in the home would be equal to their down payment. We can also see that their equity would be increased by both increases in the value of the home and repayments of the mortgage. As the shareholders of a company are its owners, we can use a similar approach when thinking about their equity in the company. It includes the amount put into the company by shareholders when the company *initially* issued shares and any income generated by the company that has not been distributed to shareholders as dividends. We call these amounts **share capital** and retained earnings, which are the earnings or income that have been "retained" by the company and reinvested into the business. There are a couple of other components to equity that can appear in the statement of equity, including contributed surplus and accumulated other comprehensive income. We will ignore these in the early part of the book in order to concentrate on share capital and retained earnings. These other components will be discussed in later chapters.

THE STATEMENT OF CHANGES IN SHAREHOLDERS' EQUITY IS ALSO KNOWN AS THE . . .
Statement of shareholders' equity Statement of changes in equity Statement of equity

The objective of the statement of changes in equity is to illustrate the changes to a number of different components of equity. For example, this statement will explain changes to each class of shares issued by the company if the company issued additional shares during the year or repurchased and cancelled others. The statement will also explain the changes in the company's retained earnings during the year, which will be equal to the net income for the period less any dividends that the company's board of directors declared during the period; that is, the amount of earnings that have been retained rather than distributed.

If we refer to Danier's consolidated statements of changes in shareholders' equity in Appendix A, we can see the changes to the company's share capital. During the year ended June 28, 2014, the company received $350,000 when it issued shares as a result of stock options being exercised. We can also see that the company repurchased some of its shares during the year and cancelled them. The company had received $111,000 when it had initially issued the repurchased shares, so this amount was removed from share capital. The notes to the financial statements explained that 47,000 shares were issued during the year and 25,000 shares were repurchased and cancelled.

Looking at the changes to Danier's retained earnings, we can see that the company had a net loss of $7,663,000 during the most recent year, which we knew by looking at the company's statement of income. We can also see that the company did not declare any dividends during the year but did use some of its retained earnings when it repurchased and cancelled the 25,000 shares discussed above. When these shares were repurchased, the company paid the shareholders more than it received when the shares were initially issued. This difference, which is a distribution to shareholders, is treated like a dividend and is therefore reflected on the statement of changes in equity as a reduction to retained earnings. We will come back to the changes in retained earnings frequently throughout the book, so it will be important for you to understand that the retained earnings of a company are determined as follows:

RETAINED EARNINGS =
Opening Retained Earnings + Net Income − Dividends Declared Ending Retained Earnings

As previously mentioned, the two components of shareholders' equity that we will be focusing on throughout the early parts of the textbook are:

COMMON SHAREHOLDERS' EQUITY COMPONENTS	
Share capital	Represents the shares issued by the company, usually stated at an amount equal to what the company received from investors on the initial issuance of the shares. There can be different types of shares (common shares and preferred shares). There can also be different classes of shares; in other words, shares that have different rights and privileges.
Retained earnings	The company's earnings (as measured on the statement of income) that have been kept (retained) and not paid out as dividends.

What is the reporting objective of the statement of financial position? What does it include?

The **statement of financial position** is also known as the *balance sheet*. The term *financial position* indicates that this statement presents the company's financial status at a particular point in time. The consolidated statement of financial position for Danier is shown in Appendix A. In the case of Danier, the information presented is as at June 28, 2014, and June 29, 2013, which are the dates the company's fiscal year ended, also known as its *year end*. This means that the amounts in the statement are those that existed on those dates, which are considered to be the beginning and end points of the current accounting period. In the transition from one accounting period to the next, the ending balances of one accounting period become the beginning balances of the next accounting period. The statement of financial position is often described as a snapshot of a company's financial position at a particular point in time.

The format of this statement of financial position is known as a **classified statement of financial position** and is typical of most Canadian statements of financial position, which present information in order of **liquidity**. Liquidity refers to how soon something will be received, realized, or consumed, or else settled or paid. Canadian companies use a 12-month period to distinguish between items that are **current** and those that are **non-current**. Current items are those that will be received, realized, or consumed, or else settled or paid within 12 months from year end. Those are that are non-current will *not* be received, realized, consumed, or settled or paid within 12 months from the year end. It is important to note that other formats can be used to present a company's financial position, but all of them will reflect this notion of liquidity because it is critical for financial statement users to be able to assess a company's liquidity.

Throughout the book, we will learn about a number of ways that liquidity is commonly assessed. One of the most common measures of liquidity is **working capital**. This is quantified as the difference between a company's **current assets** (assets that are cash or will become cash within the next 12 months) and its **current liabilities** (liabilities that must be settled within the next 12 months). It measures a company's ability to meet its short-term obligations using its short-term assets. The working capital equation is shown below.

WORKING CAPITAL
Working Capital = Current Assets − Current Liabilities

So what makes up the company's financial position? Individuals, if asked about their own financial position, would probably start by listing what they own, such as a car, a computer, or a house, and then listing what they owe to others, such as bank loans and credit card balances. What is owned less what is owed would be a measure of an individual's net worth (wealth or equity) at a particular point in time. A company lists exactly the same types of things in its statement of financial position. They are referred to as **assets**, **liabilities**, and shareholders' equity. These are the three components of the **accounting equation**, which provides the structure to the statement of financial position:

THE ACCOUNTING EQUATION
Assets = Liabilities + Shareholders' Equity

Assets

When asked for a simple definition of an asset, many people reply that it is something of value that the company either owns or has the right to use. In fact, the accounting definition of an asset is very similar. Assets must meet three criteria, shown in the box below:

CHARACTERISTICS OF AN ASSET

1. It is a resource controlled by an entity.
2. The company expects future economic benefits from the use or sale of the resource.
3. The event that gave the company control of the resource has already happened.

The assets that Danier lists on its statement of financial position include:

- cash, accounts receivable, income taxes recoverable, inventories, and prepaid expenses
- property and equipment (often called *capital assets*)
- computer software (considered part of *intangible assets* as it lacks physical form)
- deferred income tax asset

While later chapters discuss in more detail how each of these assets meets the criteria of control and future economic benefits, we can look at Danier's inventory as an example for now. Control of the inventory is proven either by possession of the goods or by legal documentation. The inventory has future economic benefits because the company can later sell it and receive cash in the amount of the selling price. The presence of the inventory or the underlying documents of the purchase indicates that the event that gave the company control has already happened.

The total assets of Danier as at June 29, 2013, were $60,629 thousand. A list of assets normally found on a statement of financial position is below.

COMMON ASSETS	
Cash	The amount of currency that the company has, including amounts in bank accounts.
Short-term investments	Short-term investments in shares of other companies.
Accounts receivable	Amounts owed to the company by its customers as a result of credit sales.
Inventory	Goods held for resale to customers.
Prepaid expenses and deposits	Amounts that have been paid by the company but the underlying service has not yet been used. Common examples include insurance premiums or rent paid in advance.
Property, plant, and equipment	Land, buildings, equipment, vehicles, and so on that the company purchases to use to generate revenues in the future; they are *not* purchased to resell.
Intangible assets	Licences, patents, trademarks, copyrights, computer software, and other assets that lack physical form. These are also acquired to generate revenues in the future.
Goodwill	A premium that has been paid on the acquisition of another company related to factors such as management expertise and corporate reputation that will result in higher future earnings.

Liabilities

A simple definition of liabilities might be amounts that the company owes to others. (They are also known as *debt* and *obligations*.) The accounting definition of liabilities encompasses this concept and refers to items that will require the outflow or sacrifice of economic resources in the future to settle an obligation that exists as a result of a transaction that has already taken place. In most cases, the economic resource that will be sacrificed is cash, but a company can also settle liabilities by providing services or goods. For example, most of you will pay your university the full amount of the semester's tuition before or at the beginning of the semester. The university has a liability to you for this amount, which it will settle by providing the related course instruction over the semester. Alternatively, a warranty liability for a washing machine could be satisfied with a new part or by providing the services of a repair person. Liabilities must meet three criteria, as shown in the box below.

CHARACTERISTICS OF A LIABILITY

1. It is a present obligation of the entity.
2. The company expects to settle it through an outflow of resources that represent future economic benefits.
3. The obligation results from an event that has already happened.

The liabilities that Danier lists on its statement of financial position include:

- payables and accruals (representing amounts owed to suppliers, unpaid wages, unpaid taxes, or estimates of warranty obligations)
- deferred revenue (often called *unearned revenue*, which represents customer *deposits* or amounts paid in advance of the company providing the related goods or service)
- sales return provision (representing an estimate of the sales to customers that may have to be negated as a result of the customer returning the purchased goods in accordance with the company's return policy)
- deferred lease inducements and rent liability (representing amounts received from landlords at some of the company's leased store locations that will be used to offset future rent expense)

The total liabilities of Danier as at June 28, 2014, were $12,222 thousand. The following list includes some of the more common liabilities found on the statement of financial position.

COMMON LIABILITIES	
Bank indebtedness	Amounts owed to the bank on short-term credit.
Accounts payable (Trade payables)	Amounts owed to suppliers from the purchase of goods on credit.
Deferred revenue (Unearned revenue)	Amounts owed to customers for advance payments until the related goods or services have been provided.
Dividends payable	Amounts owed to shareholders for dividends that have been declared by the board of directors.
Accrued liabilities	Amounts owed related to expenses that are not yet due, such as interest and warranty expense.
Income taxes payable	Amounts owed to taxing authorities.
Notes payable	Amounts owed to a creditor (bank or supplier) that are represented by a formal agreement called a *note* (sometimes called a *promissory note*). Notes payable often have an interest component, whereas accounts payable usually do not.
Long-term debt	Amounts owed to creditors due beyond one year.
Deferred income taxes	Amounts representing probable future taxes the company will have to pay.

Shareholders' Equity

The last major category in the statement of financial position is the section called *shareholders' equity*. This section captures the amount of the company's shareholders' interest in the assets of the company. Shareholders' equity is often referred to as the **net assets** of the company. This is the amount of assets that would remain after all of the company's liabilities were settled. If the accounting equation is rearranged, you can see that shareholders' equity is equal to the company's assets less its liabilities:

THE ACCOUNTING EQUATION (REARRANGED)
Assets − Liabilities = Shareholders' Equity (Net Assets)

It is important to understand that this amount is determined using the values of the assets and liabilities as they are reflected on the statement of financial position. These values will often differ from those in the current market. Throughout the text, we will explore the reasons why these values differ. For now, let's consider a company's inventory. It is reflected on the company's statement of financial position at its cost to the company, but this amount will differ from what the company would sell it for. The selling price would also differ if it were an urgent or distress sale (that is, if the company desperately had to sell the goods) rather than a sale in the ordinary course of its operations.

Based on Danier's statement of financial position, shareholders' equity at June 28, 2014, was $48,407 thousand.

Assets − Liabilities = Shareholders' Equity
$60,629 thousand − $12,222 thousand = $48,407 thousand

Note that the market value of the shares held by a company's shareholders is another measure of the shareholders' wealth in the company. By **market value**, we mean the price at which the shares are trading in the stock market. This value is likely very different from the book value of shareholders' equity because it reflects the market's expectations of future earnings and events.

One of the objectives of the statement of financial position is to enable financial statement users to assess the relative proportions of liabilities and shareholders' equity to better understand a company's financing strategy. For Danier as at June 28, 2014, total liabilities were $12,222 thousand and total shareholders' equity was $48,407 thousand, relative to total assets of $60,629 thousand. The proportion of liabilities is 20% ($12,222 ÷ $60,629), which is slightly less than one fifth of the total financing. This means that Danier has financed its assets using significantly more shareholders' equity than debt. Specifically, it gets about 80% of its financing from shareholders' equity. This low percentage of debt to equity demonstrates that the company has grown its operations using internal financing rather than through the use of debt. While the use of debt can be a good thing, generally the higher the proportion of debt to equity, the greater the financial risk facing the company. We will discuss the concept of leverage—using other people's money to make money—in a later chapter of the text.

As discussed in the section on the statement of changes in shareholders' equity, equity is usually composed of a number of components. For now, we will focus on two components: share capital and retained earnings. The first component, share capital (some companies use the term *common shares*), records the amount that the investors originally paid (invested) for the shares that the company issued. The second component, retained earnings, keeps track of the company's earnings less any amounts that the company pays to the shareholders in dividends. As mentioned previously, we will ignore the other components of shareholders' equity until later in the text.

Exhibit 1-7 illustrates how information flows between the first three financial statements. The statement of income is generally prepared first in order to determine net income. This statement is then used when preparing the statement of changes in equity. Finally, the share capital and retained earnings balances are used when preparing the statement of financial position.

Exhibit 1-7 Information Flows between the First Three Financial Statements

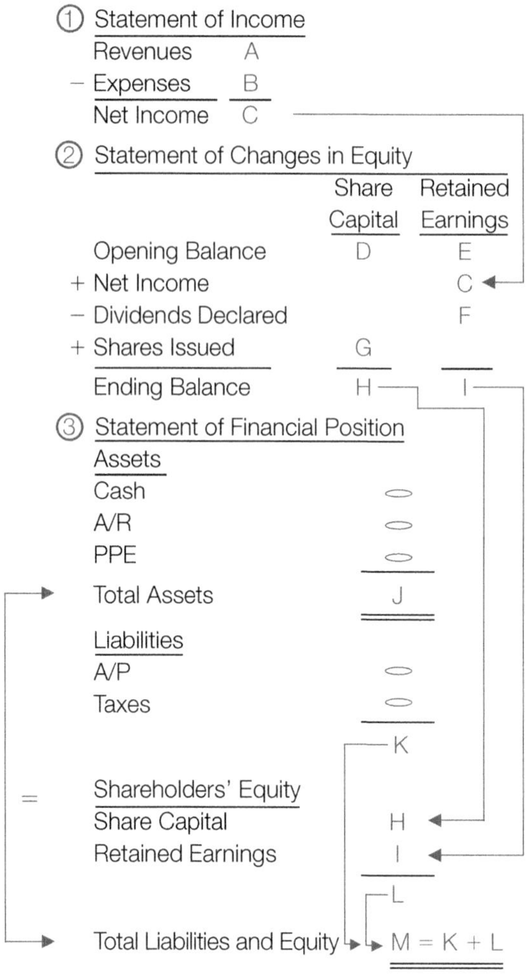

What is the reporting objective of the statement of cash flows? What does it include?

The **statement of cash flows** (sometimes called the *cash flow statement*) presents the flows of cash related to the three categories of business activities, which we discussed earlier in the chapter. The reporting objective of this statement is to enable financial statement users to assess the company's inflows and outflows of cash related to each of these activities, so they can see where the company's cash came from and how it was used.

Danier's consolidated statement of cash flow in Appendix A presents the company's inflows and outflows of cash for the years ending June 28, 2014, and June 29, 2013. This statement differs from the statement of income in that it measures cash flows during the period rather than the revenues and expenses for the period, which may not be received or paid in cash. Cash is very important to the company's operations and this statement is critical to a user's evaluation of a company. Given the importance of this statement, Chapter 5 of the text is focused on how the statement is prepared and used. For now, we will review the basic content of the statement.

The cash flow statement has three sections that report the sources and uses of cash and cash equivalents for the three categories of business activities described earlier: operating, financing, and investing.

SUBSECTIONS OF THE STATEMENT OF CASH FLOWS
Cash flow from operating activities Cash flow from financing activities Cash flow from investing activities

Operating activities include all inflows and outflows of cash related to the sale of goods and services. They are the activities that the company provides in its normal operations. The starting point in this section is frequently net earnings (or net income or profit) from the statement of income. There are adjustments to this number because the recognition (recording) of revenues and expenses does not necessarily coincide with the receipt and payment of cash, as we will see in future chapters. For instance, sales could be either cash sales or sales on account. That is, customers can pay at a later date, resulting in an account receivable rather than cash. Expenses may also be paid later if the company is given credit by its suppliers, which would result in an account payable. Because operating activities are the backbone of the company, a positive cash flow from operations is essential to the company's long-term health. Due to its loss in the current year, Danier had an out-flow of cash of $4,907 thousand from its operating activities in the fiscal year ending June 28, 2014, as compared to an in-flow of $6,752 thousand in the previous year.

Financing activities are transactions that either resulted from new funds being received from investors or creditors or from the return of funds to these two groups. Typical activities in this category are the issuance of shares, the proceeds of new borrowings, the repayment of debt, or the payment of dividends. Danier's cash flow from financing activities was an outflow of $48 thousand for the year ended June 28, 2014. We can see from this that the company did not obtain any new funding from either shareholders or creditors during the period and actually returned funds to shareholders through the repurchase of the company's shares from shareholders.

Investing activities generally involve the purchase and sale of long-term assets such as property, plant, and equipment, and investments in other companies. In the case of Danier, we can see the company purchased property, equipment, and computer software during the year ended June 28, 2014. It did not sell any long-term assets during the period. This resulted in cash outflows of $6,079 thousand for the period. Companies that are growing, and even those that are just maintaining their current operations, normally have negative cash flows from investing activities. This results from them spending more cash to purchase new long-term assets than they are receiving as proceeds from the sale of long-term assets that they have finished using in their operations.

Overall, we can see that Danier had a net decrease in cash of $11,034 million during the year ended June 28, 2014. This is the sum of the cash flows from the categories of business activities ($4,907 + $48 + $6,079 = −$11,034). This explains why the company's cash balance decreased from $24,541 thousand at the start of the year to $13,507 thousand at the end of the year.

SUMMARY OF THE FINANCIAL STATEMENTS

Statement of income	Measures the operating performance of a company over a period of time.
Statement of changes in equity	Measures the changes in the equity of the company over a period of time, differentiating between changes that result from transactions with shareholders and those resulting from the company's operations.
Statement of financial position	Measures the resources controlled by a company (assets) and the claims on those resources (by creditors and investors) at a given point in time.
Statement of cash flows	Measures the change in cash flow through operating, financing, and investing activities over a period of time.

What type of information is in the notes to a company's financial statements?

You may have noticed that some of the items in the financial statements directed the user to specific notes. These **notes to the financial statements** are a critical part of the financial statements. In them, management gives more detail about specific items such as the various types of inventory held by the company and details on its long-term assets. By including additional explanations in notes rather than in the financial statements, management keeps the company's statements simple and uncluttered. Note disclosures help to increase the usefulness of the financial statements and enhance the user's understanding of the various components of the statements.

A full discussion of notes will be left to succeeding chapters, but some attention should be paid to two of the notes that normally appear at the beginning of the notes to the financial statements. These are the note explaining the basis on which the financial statements have been prepared and the note outlining the significant accounting policies used in the preparation of the statements. Danier presented this information in the second and third of 22 notes that were included with the company's financial statements.

From these two notes, we can see that Danier's financial statements were prepared using **International Financial Reporting Standards (IFRS)**, which are the accounting standards that must be followed by Canadian public companies. From these notes, we can also learn more about the choices and judgements made by management in applying these reporting standards. As you progress through the book, you will learn that these choices have important implications for how to interpret the statements. Comparing two companies that have made two different choices and judgements would pose difficulties. To help users compare various companies, management must therefore disclose in this note the major accounting principles that it uses.

While not part of the notes to the financial statements, all publicly traded companies are required to include a management discussion and analysis (MD&A) section in their annual reports. The MD&A section provides readers with senior management's perspective on the information contained in the financial statements. While it is not part of the financial statements, it provides very useful context for users of the financial statements.

In addition to management's perspectives on the company's financial results for the prior year, the MD&A also provides a discussion of the risks facing the company and information about future plans. Often information is presented from the perspective of the company's various divisions. It also includes information on significant events and about sales, profits, and cash flow during the year. The discussion focuses on the financial aspects of the business, including pricing strategies, expenses, earnings, liquidity, environmental and corporate social responsibility, expansion and future development, taxes, events after the end of the current year, and executive compensation policies.

Ethics in Accounting

The management of a company, through the direction given to it by the board of directors, has both a moral and a legal obligation to safeguard the investment that shareholders have made in the company and entrusted to the care of management. To ensure that management fulfills this stewardship function over the company's resources, shareholders typically provide some incentives for and controls over management. You have probably heard about stock option plans and bonuses given to top management. These additional compensation arrangements are often tied to the company's financial performance and provide incentives for management to make decisions that are in the best interests of the shareholders. Danier has provided information about the remuneration, including salaries and share-based compensation, of senior executives and members of the board of directors in note 20 to the financial statements. This information is intended to show shareholders and others that the company is open and accountable for its decisions.

For a number of years, the Canadian Coalition for Good Governance, which represents institutional investors and asset managers, has been advocating for public companies to voluntarily implement annual shareholder "Say on Pay" votes. These votes involve shareholders approving the executive compensation programs implemented by the company's board of directors. These are non-binding votes (that is, the board is not required to make changes as a result of these votes) and are meant to advise the board on the perspective of shareholders. As of March 2014, 127 Canadian public companies had voluntarily adopted "Say on Pay" votes, including more than three quarters of the 60 largest companies listed on the TSX. This trend is not unique to Canada, as annual "Say on Pay" votes are required for public companies in the U.K. and Australia, while a vote must be held at least every three years for U.S. public companies.

To date, the vast majority of "Say on Pay" votes have indicated a high level of shareholder support for the executive compensation practices, with average overall support of close to 90%. Shareholders have only voted "no" at three Canadian companies. Barrick Gold Corporation was the largest of the three, with its institutional shareholders protesting the $17 million in compensation paid to the company's vice-chairman in 2012. In Barrick's case, only 15% of shareholders supported the company's "Say on Pay" vote.

The "Say on Pay" movement illustrates the importance of boards' ensuring that the executive compensation packages they approve are aligned with corporate performance. It also reflects the growing influence of institutional shareholders in overseeing governance of public companies.[2]

Now that you know what corporate financial reporting involves and what the main financial statements contain, in the next chapter we'll look at how users can analyze them.

Ethics in Accounting

Shareholders hire an independent external **auditor** to review the financial statements presented to them by the company's management. The auditor must maintain their independence from the company's management team throughout the audit.

In order to ensure their independence and encourage ethical behaviour, the accounting profession has developed codes of professional conduct.

CHAPTER END REVIEW PROBLEM

The Chapter End Review Problems reinforce your understanding of major sections in the chapter. One or more questions have been created to illustrate the topics and demonstrate how you can use the information. Answers are provided so that you can check your knowledge. You can use these questions as examples when working on other questions assigned by your instructor.

The major financial statements of **High Liner Foods Incorporated** from its 2013 annual report are included in Exhibits 1-8 A, B, and C. Nova Scotia–based High Liner is a leading processor and marketer of frozen seafood. Note that its fiscal year is a 52-week period ended December 28, 2013. We will refer to these as the 2013 financial statements and use them to answer a series of questions.

Exhibit 1-8A High Liner Foods Incorporated's 2013 Consolidated Statement of Income

FINANCIAL STATEMENTS

CONSOLIDATED STATEMENT OF INCOME

(in thousands of U.S. dollars, except per share amounts)	Notes	Fifty-two weeks ended **December 28, 2013**	Fifty-two weeks ended December 29, 2012
Revenues		**$ 947,301**	$ 942,631
Cost of sales		**731,884**	735,970
Gross profit		**215,417**	206,661
Distribution expenses		**53,368**	44,511
Selling, general and administrative expenses		**98,902**	100,862
Impairment of property, plant and equipment		**—**	13,230
Business acquisition, integration and other expenses		**3,256**	10,741
Results from operating activities		**59,891**	37,317
Finance costs		**16,329**	36,585
(Income) loss from equity accounted investee, net of income tax		**(86)**	196
Income before income taxes		**43,648**	536
Income taxes			
Current	20	**12,378**	5,442
Deferred	20	**(86)**	(7,109)
Total income tax expense (recovery)		**12,292**	(1,667)
Net income		**$ 31,356**	$ 2,203
PER SHARE EARNINGS			
Earnings per common share			
Basic	17	**$ 2.07**	$ 0.15
Diluted	17	**$ 2.01**	$ 0.14
Weighted average number of shares outstanding			
Basic	17	**15,183,747**	15,118,752
Diluted	17	**15,593,166**	15,460,417

FINANCIAL STATEMENTS

Exhibit 1-8B High Liner Foods Incorporated's 2013 Consolidated Statement of Financial Position

CONSOLIDATED STATEMENT OF FINANCIAL POSITION

(in thousands of U.S. dollars)	Notes	**December 28, 2013**	December 29, 2012
ASSETS			
Current:			
Cash		**$ 1,206**	$ 65
Accounts receivable	9	**91,334**	73,947
Income taxes receivable		**3,509**	5,145
Other financial assets	22	**1,524**	533
Inventories	8	**254,072**	222,313
Prepaid expenses		**2,952**	2,991
Total current assets		**354,597**	304,994
Non-current:			
Property, plant and equipment	6	**97,503**	89,268
Deferred income taxes	20	**4,656**	7,207
Other receivables and miscellaneous assets		**1,906**	2,035
Intangible assets	5	**105,253**	110,631
Goodwill	5	**111,999**	112,873
Total non-current assets		**321,317**	322,014
Assets classified as held for sale	7	**542**	4,819
Total assets		**$ 676,456**	$ 631,827
LIABILITIES AND SHAREHOLDERS' EQUITY			
Current:			
Bank loans	12	**$ 97,227**	$ 59,704
Accounts payable and accrued liabilities	10	**103,215**	101,441
Provisions	11	**240**	1,614
Other current financial liabilities	22	**459**	550
Income taxes payable		**2,543**	1,165
Current portion of long-term debt	13	**—**	34,237
Current portion of finance lease obligations	13	**979**	1,039
Total current liabilities		**204,663**	199,750
Non-current:			
Long-term debt	13	**226,929**	213,359
Other long-term financial liabilities	22	**5,597**	1,130
Other long-term liabilities		**1,044**	1,532
Long-term finance lease obligations	13	**1,647**	2,181
Deferred income taxes	20	**43,998**	45,126
Future employee benefits	14	**7,929**	13,791
Total non-current liabilities		**287,144**	277,119
Liabilities directly associated with the assets held for sale	7	**—**	1,604
Total liabilities		**491,807**	478,473
Shareholders' equity:			
Common shares	16	**80,260**	75,169
Contributed surplus		**13,781**	7,719
Retained earnings		**90,792**	66,373
Accumulated other comprehensive (loss) income		**(184)**	4,093
Total shareholders' equity		**184,649**	153,354
Total liabilities and shareholders' equity		**$ 676,456**	$ 631,827

Exhibit 1-8C High Liner Foods Incorporated's 2013 Consolidated Statement of Cash Flows

FINANCIAL STATEMENTS

(in thousands of U.S. dollars)	Fifty-two weeks ended **December 28, 2013**	Fifty-two weeks ended December 29, 2012
Cash provided by (used in) operations:		
Net income for the period	**$ 31,356**	$ 2,203
Charges (credits) to income not involving cash from operations:		
Depreciation and amortization	**15,159**	19,381
Share-based payment expense	**6,704**	10,255
(Gain) loss on asset disposals, and impairment	**(126)**	13,589
Payments of future employee benefits in excess of expense	**(948)**	(1,728)
Finance costs	**16,329**	36,585
Income tax expense (recovery)	**12,292**	(1,667)
(Income) loss from equity accounted investee, net of income taxes	**(86)**	196
Unrealized foreign exchange loss	**700**	683
Cash flow provided by operations before changes in non-cash working capital, interest and income taxes paid:	**81,380**	79,497
Net change in non-cash working capital balances:		
Accounts receivable	**(15,157)**	4,958
Inventories	**(3,162)**	35,258
Prepaids	**841**	(423)
Provisions	**(1,237)**	904
Accounts payables and accrued liabilities	**(7,407)**	(14,535)
Net change in non-cash working capital balances	**(26,122)**	26,162
Interest paid	**(16,786)**	(19,145)
Income taxes paid	**(11,161)**	(7,530)
Net cash flows provided by operating activities	**27,311**	78,984
Cash provided by (used in) financing activities:		
Increase (decrease) in current working capital facilities	**37,771**	(59,673)
Repayment of finance lease obligations	**(1,052)**	(1,009)
Repayment of long-term debt	**(15,406)**	(1,875)
Finance costs	**(1,423)**	—
Common share dividends paid	**(10,305)**	(6,379)
Share repurchase	**—**	(497)
Stock options exercised	**1,395**	650
Net cash flows provided by (used in) financing activities	**10,980**	(68,783)
Cash provided by (used in) investing activities:		
Purchase of property, plant and equipment, net of investment tax credits (note 6)	**(14,734)**	(12,709)
Net proceeds on disposal of assets	**7,124**	232
Acquisition of business, net (note 4)	**(30,312)**	—
Change in other receivables and miscellaneous assets	**249**	(247)
Net cash flows used in investing activities	**(37,673)**	(12,724)
Foreign exchange (decrease) increase on cash	**(182)**	88
Change in cash during the period	**436**	(2,435)
Add-back: cash directly associated with assets held for sale (note 7)	**705**	(705)
Cash, beginning of period	**65**	3,205
Cash, end of period	**$ 1,206**	$ 65

STRATEGIES FOR SUCCESS

- Start by reviewing High Liner's three financial statements. Refresh your understanding of the kinds of information found in each statement.
- As you work through the list of items in question 1, try to remember which financial statement to look at by linking in your mind the name of the item identified and the financial statement on which it is included. As you work through more problems like this, you will become more familiar with what is on each statement.
- To answer question 2, first reread the section in the statement of financial position discussion in this chapter that explains shareholders' equity. The discussion of Danier's use of liabilities and shareholders' equity to finance its operations should be helpful.

Required:

1. Find the following amounts in the statements:
   a. Total revenues for fiscal year 2013
   b. Total cost of sales for fiscal year 2013
   c. Total selling, general, and administrative expenses for fiscal year 2013
   d. Finance costs for fiscal year 2013
   e. Income tax expense (recovery) (current and deferred) for fiscal year 2013
   f. Net income (earnings) for fiscal year 2013
   g. Inventories at the end of fiscal year 2013
   h. Accounts payable and accrued liabilities at the beginning of fiscal year 2013
   i. Shareholders' equity at the end of fiscal year 2013
   j. Retained earnings at the beginning of fiscal year 2013
   k. Cash provided from operating activities in fiscal year 2013
   l. Cash payments, net of investment tax credits, to acquire property, plant, and equipment in fiscal year 2013
   m. Cash used in the repayment of long-term debt in fiscal year 2013
   n. Cash used in the payment of dividends in fiscal year 2013
   o. Cash provided from (used for) investing activities in fiscal year 2013
2. Does High Liner Foods finance its business primarily with debt or with shareholders' equity? Support your answer with appropriate data.
3. List the two largest sources of cash and the two largest uses of cash in fiscal year 2013. (Consider operating activities to be a single source or use of cash.)
4. Does High Liner Foods use a classified statement of financial position? Explain.

Suggested Solution to the Chapter End Review Problem

To find the answers to the above questions, you will need to examine closely the three financial statements that have been provided.

1. The following answers are found on the financial statements included in Exhibits 1-8A, B, and C:
   a. Total revenues in 2013: $947,301 thousand. Revenues are reported on the statement of income.
   b. Total cost of sales in 2013: $731,884 thousand. The cost of sales is a type of expense. Expenses are reported on the statement of income.
   c. Total selling, general, and administrative expenses in 2013: $98,902 thousand. Expenses are reported on the statement of income.
   d. Finance costs in 2013: $16,329 thousand. Expenses are reported on the statement of income.
   e. Income tax expense (current and deferred) in 2013: $12,292 thousand ($12,378 + ($86)). Expenses are reported on the statement of income.
   f. Net income (earnings) in 2013: $31,356 thousand. The earnings are reported on the statement of income.
   g. Inventories at the end of 2013: $254,072 thousand. Inventories are assets, which are reported on the statement of financial position.
   h. Accounts payable and accrued liabilities at the beginning of 2013: $101,441 thousand (the end of 2012 is the same as the beginning of 2013). Liabilities are reported on the statement of financial position.
   i. Shareholders' equity at the end of 2013: $184,649 thousand. Shareholders' equity is reported on the statement of financial position.
   j. Retained earnings at the beginning of 2013: $66,373 thousand. (Again, you need to look to the end of 2012 to find the beginning of 2013.) The retained earnings are a part of shareholders' equity that is reported on the statement of financial position.
   k. Cash provided from operating activities in 2013: $27,311 thousand. The cash provided by various business activities is reported on the statement of cash flows. Operating activities are shown in the first section of this statement.
   l. Cash payments, net of investment tax credits, to acquire property, plant, and equipment in 2013: ($14,734 thousand). The net addition of capital assets is reported under the investing section on the statement of cash flows. Putting the amount in parentheses indicates that it is a negative number. In other words, cash was used.
   m. Cash used in the repayment of long-term debt in fiscal year 2013: ($15,406 thousand). The cash used for various business activities is reported on the statement of cash flows. The repayment of debt is a financing activity.

n. Cash used in the payment of dividends in 2013: ($10,305 thousand). The cash used for various business activities is reported on the statement of cash flows. Paying dividends is a financing activity.
o. Cash provided from (used for) investing activities in 2013: ($37,673 thousand). The cash provided by various business activities is reported on the statement of cash flows. Investing activities are one of the three main sections on this statement.

2. High Liner uses substantially more liabilities than shareholders' equity to finance its business. You can see this when you compare the total liabilities with the total liabilities plus shareholders' equity (on the statement of financial position as at December 28, 2013) as follows:

   Total liabilities: $491,807 thousand
   Total shareholders' equity: $184,649 thousand
   Total liabilities and shareholders' equity: $676,456 thousand

   Total liabilities are, therefore, 73% (($491,807 ÷ $676,456) × 100) of High Liner's total sources of financing. Because debt must be repaid, it is important for users to understand how much of the company's activities are being financed by debt. The greater the percentage of debt to total liabilities and shareholders' equity, the more risk there is that the company may not be able to repay its debt when it comes due. At December 28, 2013, 73% of High Liner's financing was debt financing.
3. The two largest sources of cash are proceeds from the operating activities, $27,311 thousand, and the increase in current working capital facilities, $37,771 thousand. The two largest uses are the acquisition of business (net) ($30,312 thousand) and the repayment of long-term debt ($15,406 thousand).
4. High Liner does use a classified statement of financial position. It has labelled a section for current assets and current liabilities and for the non-current assets and non-current liabilities. It has included the non-current assets and non-current liabilities in separate sections after the totals of the current assets and current liabilities. It has also given you a separate total for the non-current assets and non-current liabilities.

SUMMARY

1. **Define financial accounting and understand its relationship to economic decision-making.**
   - Financial accounting is the process by which information on the transactions of an organization is captured, analyzed, and reported to external decision makers.
   - These decision makers are referred to as *financial statement users* and include investors and creditors.
   - The primary purpose of financial accounting information is to aid these users in making economic decisions related to the reporting organization, such as whether to invest in it or lend it money.

2. **Identify the main users of financial accounting information and explain how they use this information.**
   - The main users of financial accounting information include shareholders, the board of directors, potential investors, creditors (bankers and suppliers), regulators (stock exchanges), taxing authorities (governments), securities analysts, and others.
   - Shareholders, the board of directors, and potential investors will use financial accounting information to enable them to assess how well management has run the company; determine whether they should buy, sell, or continue to hold shares in the company; assess the company's share price relative to the financial accounting information; and so on.
   - Creditors will use financial accounting information to determine whether they should lend funds to the company, establish credit terms for it, assess a company's ability to meets its obligations, and so on.
   - Regulators will use financial accounting information to determine whether a company has met its listing requirements.
   - Taxing authorities will use this information in assessing the taxes owed by the organization.

3. **Describe the major forms of business organization and explain the key distinctions between them.**
   - There are three major forms of business organization: (1) proprietorships, (2) partnerships, and (3) corporations.
   - There are public corporations (whose shares trade on a public stock exchange and are widely held) and private corporations (whose shares do not trade on a public exchange and are generally owned by a small number of people).
   - Corporations are separate legal entities, whereas proprietorships and partnerships are not. This means the personal assets of owners are protected in the event of legal action against corporations, whereas they are at risk in the case of proprietorships and partnerships. It also means corporations file separate tax returns, whereas the income from proprietorships and partnerships is reported on the personal tax returns of their owners.

4. **Explain the three categories of business activities and identify examples of transactions related to each category.**
   - The three categories of business activities are: (1) operating, (2) investing, and (3) financing activities.
   - Operating activities are related to the company's revenues and expenses, such as sales to customers, collections from customers, purchases of inventory, and payments of wages and other expenses.
   - Investing activities include buying and selling property, plant, and equipment and buying and selling the shares of other companies.
   - Financing activities include borrowing money, issuing shares, repaying loan principal, and paying dividends.
5. **Identify and explain the content and reporting objectives of the four basic financial statements and the notes to the financial statements.**
   - There are four basic financial statements: (1) the statement of income, (2) the statement of changes in equity, (3) the statement of financial position, and (4) the statement of cash flows.
   - The objective of the statement of income is to measure the company's operating performance (its profit) for a period of time. This is measured by subtracting the expenses incurred during the period from the income earned (revenues) in the same period.
   - The objective of the statement of changes in equity is to provide details on how each component of shareholders' equity changed during the period. The components of shareholders' equity include share capital (the shares issued by the company) and retained earnings (the company's earnings that have been kept and not distributed as dividends).
   - The objective of the statement of financial position is to present information on a company's assets, liabilities, and shareholders' equity at a specific date. Assets must be controlled by the company and embody a future benefit. Examples include cash; accounts receivable; inventory; property, plant, and equipment; land; and so on. Liabilities are obligations of a company that will result in an outflow of resources. Examples include accounts payable, deferred revenue, long-term debt, and so on. Shareholders' equity represents the shareholders' interest in the assets of the company and is referred to as *net assets*. Examples include common shares and retained earnings.
   - The objective of the statement of cash flows is to enable financial statement users to assess the company's inflows and outflows of cash related to its operating, investing, and financial activities for a period of time.
   - The notes to a company's financial statements are used to provide additional detail and context for items in the financial statements. They enable the financial statements themselves to remain uncluttered, while increasing their usefulness.

KEY TERMS

Accounting equation (16)
Annual report (4)
Assets (16)
Auditor (23)
Board of directors (6)
Canada Revenue Agency (CRA) (7)
Capital appreciation (10)
Classified statement of financial position (16)
Common shares (8)
Comparative information (13)
Consolidated financial statement (12)
Creditors (3)
Current (16)
Current assets (16)
Current liabilities (16)
Dividends (10)
Earnings (12)
Earnings management (14)
Earnings per share (14)
Expenses (12)
Equity (15)
Financial accounting (3)
Financial statement users (3)
Financial statements (4)
Financing activities (9)
Fiscal year (13)
Gains (12)
Gross profit (13)
Income (12)
Interest (7)
International Financial Reporting Standards (IFRS) (22)
Investing activities (9)
Investors (3)
Liabilities (16)
Liquidity (16)
Losses (12)
Management (3)
Management discussion and analysis (MD&A) (4)
Managerial accounting (3)
Market value (19)
Net assets (19)
Net earnings (12)
Net income (12)
Net loss (12)
Non-current (16)
Notes to the financial statements (21)
Operating activities (9)
Parent company (12)
Principal (7)
Private company (6)
Profit (12)
Public company (6)
Retained earnings (10)
Revenues (12)
Share capital (15)
Shareholders (6)
Shareholders' equity (10)
Statement of cash flows (20)
Statement of changes in equity (15)
Statement of financial position (16)
Statement of income (12)
Subsidiary companies (12)
Working capital (16)

ABBREVIATIONS USED

CRA	Canada Revenue Agency
IFRS	International Financial Reporting Standards
MD&A	Management discussion and analysis

SYNONYMS

Accounts payable | Trade payables
Depreciation | Amortization
Gross profit | Gross margin
Liabilities | Debt | Obligations
Net earnings | Net income | Net profit
Property, plant, and equipment | Capital assets
Share capital | Common shares
Shareholders | Investors
Shareholders' equity | Net assets
Statement of cash flows | Cash flow statement
Statement of changes in shareholders' equity | Statement of shareholders' equity | Statement of changes in equity | Statement of equity
Statement of income | Statement of operations | Statement of earnings | Statement of profit or loss | Statement of comprehensive income
Statement of financial position | Balance sheet
Unearned revenue | Deferred revenue | Deposits

ASSIGNMENT MATERIAL

Discussion Questions

DQ1-1 Describe the role that accounting plays in the management of a business.

DQ1-2 Describe the owner's legal liability and the taxation of income in the following forms of business: corporation, proprietorship and partnership.

DQ1-3 Explain the difference between a public corporation and a private corporation.

DQ1-4 Identify at least three major users of corporate financial statements, and briefly state how these users might use the information from the statements.

DQ1-5 Explain how investors expect to receive a return on the investment they make in a corporation.

DQ1-6 What is capital appreciation and how can an investor realize this type of return?

DQ1-7 Creditors are ultimately concerned with receiving two streams of cash in relation to the loans they make. Explain each of them.

DQ1-8 Describe and illustrate the three major types of activities in which all companies engage.

DQ1-9 Describe and illustrate the three major categories of items that appear in a typical statement of financial position.

DQ1-10 How do the activities that are considered to be operating activities differ from those considered to be investing activities?

DQ1-11 How do the activities that are considered to be operating activities differ from those considered to be financing activities?

DQ1-12 Would we normally expect a company to have an overall inflow or an overall outflow of cash from its operating activities? Explain why.

DQ1-13 Would we normally expect a company to have an overall inflow or an overall outflow of cash from its investing activities? Explain why.

DQ1-14 How is the statement of income related to the three major types of business activities?

DQ1-15 How does the statement of changes in equity relate to the statement of income? Which of these statements would need to be prepared first?

DQ1-16 Describe the purpose of the four main financial statements that are contained in annual reports.

DQ1-17 Explain the purpose behind the notes to the financial statements.

DQ1-18 What role does the management discussion and analysis section of an annual report play in informing users about a company?

Application Problems

AP1-1 (Characteristics of assets and liabilities)

Required:
Using the characteristics of assets and liabilities discussed in the chapter, explain whether the following items would be considered to be an asset or a liability. Be sure to apply the criteria in your response:

a. A one-year insurance policy covering the company's delivery vehicles, paid in advance.
b. Gift cards sold to customers.

AP1-2 (Identify financing, investing, and operating transactions)

Required:
For a company like **Canadian Tire Corporation**, provide two examples of transactions that you would classify as financing, investing, and operating activities.

AP1-3 (Identify financing, investing, and operating transactions)

Required:
For a company like Hudson's Bay Company, provide two examples of transactions that you would classify as financing, investing, and operating activities.

AP1-4 (Identify financing, investing, and operating transactions)

Required:
For a company like Bank of Nova Scotia, provide two examples of transactions that you would classify as financing, investing, and operating activities.

AP1-5 (Compare statement of income and statement of cash flows)

Required:
Compare and contrast the purpose of the statement of income and the purpose of the statement of cash flows. Outline how they are similar.

AP1-6 (Compare statement of income and statement of financial position accounts)

Required:
a. On what financial statement would you expect to find sales revenue, and what does it represent?
b. On what financial statement would you expect to find accounts receivable, and what does it represent?
c. What is the connection between sales revenue and accounts receivable?

AP1-7 (Compare statement of income and statement of financial position accounts)

Required:
a. On what financial statement would you expect to find wages payable, and what does it represent?
b. On what financial statement would you expect to find wage expense, and what does it represent?
c. What is the connection between wages payable and wage expense?

AP1-8 (Classify items on financial statements)

Use the following abbreviations to answer this question:

CA	Current assets
NCA	Non-current assets
CL	Current liabilities
NCL	Non-current liabilities
SC	Share capital
RE	Retained earnings
SI	Statement of income item
SCF	Statement of cash flows item
SCE	Statement of changes in equity item

Required:
Classify the following items according to where they would appear in the financial statements:
a. Accounts payable
b. Rent revenue
c. Unearned revenue
d. Property, plant, and equipment
e. Short-term investment in the shares of another company
f. Sales to customers
g. Repayment of the principal of a loan owed to a financial institution
h. Payment of interest on a loan owed to a financial institution
i. Common shares
j. Cash
k. Loan payable (debt due in 10 years)

AP1-9 (Classify items on financial statements)

Use the same abbreviations as in AP1-8 to answer the following question.

Required:

Classify the following items according to where they would appear in the financial statements:

a. Rent payable
b. Amounts owed by customers of the company
c. Administrative expense
d. Proceeds received from taking out a long-term bank loan
e. Office supplies
f. Net earnings for the year
g. Cash proceeds from the sale of old equipment
h. Increase in the cash balance for the year
i. Income taxes expense
j. Cost to the company of inventory sold to customers this year
k. Proceeds from issuing common shares during the year

AP1-10 (Classify items on financial statements)

Use the same abbreviations as in AP1-8 to answer the following question.

Required:

Classify the following items according to where they would appear in the financial statements:

a. Intangible assets
b. Interest revenue
c. Cash collections from amounts owed by customers on account
d. Cost of developing a new advertising campaign
e. Earnings over the years that have not been paid to shareholders as dividends
f. Revenue from the provision of services to customers
g. Dividends paid
h. Increase in a bank loan (additional borrowings)
i. Supplies used this year
j. An investment in the shares of another corporation (the intent is not to sell the investment in the near future)
k. Amounts paid to repurchase shares from shareholders

AP1-11 (Classify items on statement of cash flows)

Use the following abbreviations to answer this question:

O	Operating activities item
I	Investing activities item
F	Financing activities item

Required:

Classify each of the following transactions according to whether they are operating, financing, or investing activities:

a. Payment of employee wages
b. Cash collected from customers for sales
c. Payment of dividends
d. Purchase of land for an office building
e. Repayment of debt owed to a financial institution
f. Purchase of shares of another company
g. Cash received as rent payment from a tenant in a building owned by the company
h. Issuance of shares

AP1-12 (Classify items on statement of cash flows)

Required:

Use the same abbreviations as in AP1-11 to classify each of the following transactions according to whether they are operating, financing, or investing activities:

a. Proceeds from the sale of an investment in another company's shares
b. Net income

c. Cash paid to suppliers of inventory
d. Acquisition of a long-term bank loan
e. Depreciation of the factory building
f. Purchase of a truck used for deliveries
g. Payment of dividends

AP1-13 (Identify items on statement of financial position and statement of income)

Required:
Indicate whether each of the following items will be reported on the statement of financial position (SFP), statement of income (SI), both the statement of financial position and statement of income (B), or neither statement (N)—for example, it might appear only on the statement of cash flows.

a. Cash
b. Land acquired four years ago
c. Prepaid rent
d. Interest revenue
e. Sales of goods and services
f. Dividends paid to shareholders
g. Rent expense
h. Sales anticipated next period
i. Payment made to reduce the principal amount of a bank loan
j. Common shares issued when the company was organized five years ago

AP1-14 (Identify items on statement of financial position and statement of income)

Required:
Indicate whether each of the following items will be reported on the statement of financial position (SFP), statement of income (SI), both the statement of financial position and statement of income (B), or neither statement (N)—for example, it might appear only on the statement of cash flows.

a. Notes receivable
b. Interest revenue from a short-term investment
c. Common shares
d. Accounts payable
e. Depreciation expense on a building
f. Interest expense
g. Cash from the issuance of shares
h. Wages payable
i. Interest expense on a bank loan
j. Retained earnings

AP1-15 (Relationship of statement of financial position and statement of income)

Required:
In question AP1-13 or AP1-14, did you identify any items that appeared on both the statement of financial position and statement of income? Would you expect to? Explain by describing the nature of each financial statement.

AP1-16 (Determine missing statement of financial position amounts)

Required:
Calculate the missing statement of financial position amounts in each of the following independent situations:

	A	B	C	D
Current assets	$?	$ 600,000	$180,000	$ 990,000
Non-current assets	780,000	?	390,000	?
Total assets	?	1,335,000	?	1,650,000
Current liabilities	375,000	345,000	135,000	390,000
Non-current liabilities	?	330,000	?	225,000
Shareholders' equity	638,000	?	330,000	?
Total liabilities and shareholders' equity	1,350,000	?	?	?

AP1-17 (Determine missing statement of financial position amounts)

Required:
Calculate the missing statement of financial position amounts in each of the following independent situations:

	A	B	C	D
Current assets	$ 650,000	$?	$150,000	$320,000
Non-current assets	?	380,000	?	760,000
Total assets	1,800,000	?	360,000	?
Current liabilities	750,000	170,000	50,000	410,000
Non-current liabilities	500,000	?	120,000	?
Shareholders' equity	?	425,000	?	400,000
Total liabilities and shareholders' equity	?	800,000	?	?

AP1-18 (Determine missing statement of changes in equity amounts of retained earnings)

The change in retained earnings from the beginning of the year to the end of the year is the result of net earnings minus dividends for the year. These changes are part of the information presented on the statement of changes in equity.

Required:
Calculate the missing amounts in the reconciliation of retained earnings in each of the following independent situations:

	A	B	C	D
Retained earnings, Dec. 31, 2015	$100,000	$420,000	$?	$ 930,000
Net earnings	40,000	?	550,000	290,000
Dividends declared and paid	10,000	50,000	225,000	?
Retained earnings, Dec. 31, 2016	?	530,000	1,800,000	1,080,000

AP1-19 (Prepare simple statement of income)

Jason Chan operates a takeout pizza business called A Slice of Life Ltd. During the month of November, the following things occurred:

1. He paid $7,692 for pizza ingredients, $1,200 for rent, $220 for the telephone system, and $1,090 for utilities.
2. He took in $23,870 from selling pizzas.
3. He used up $7,130 worth of ingredients to make the pizzas.
4. His employees earned and were paid wages totalling $5,120 for the month.

Required:

a. Prepare a statement of income to determine how much A Slice of Life Ltd. earned in November.
b. Are there any other costs that might have been incurred in November but are not listed?

AP1-20 (Prepare simple statement of income)

Lydia Cravette operates a florist shop called Scents Unlimited Ltd. During the month of May, the following things occurred:

1. She spent $160 on the telephone system, $370 on utilities, and $1,500 on rent.
2. She took in $24,730 from selling flowers and plants. All of the shop's sales were cash sales.
3. She spent $10,733 on flowers from a local grower, she paid $329 for gas and repairs to the delivery vehicle, and she paid her employees $7,000 for wages earned during the month.

Required:

a. Prepare a statement of income to determine how much Scents Unlimited Ltd. earned in May.
b. Are there any other costs that might have been incurred in May but are not listed?

AP1-21 (Prepare simple statement of income)

Michelle Fontaine runs an outdoor adventure company called Call of the Wild Ltd. Her busiest months are June through September, although, if the weather holds, she extends her excursions into October and November. For the month of July, she recorded the following items:

1. She paid $49,860 for employee wages and she spent $14,610 on advertising.
2. Customers paid her $171,430 for excursions that took place in July and $21,000 in deposits for trips scheduled in August and September.

3. She used supplies in July that cost $25,629.
4. She spent $1,532 on the utilities for the office and $3,460 on gas and repairs on the vehicles.

Required:

a. Prepare a statement of income to determine how much Call of the Wild Ltd. earned in July.
b. Are there any other costs that might have been incurred in July but were not listed?

AP1-22 (Prepare simple statement of financial position)

AP1-19 introduced Jason Chan and his pizza business, A Slice of Life Ltd. At the end of November, the following items were in his records:

Supply of ingredients	$ 670
Wages owed to employees	1,460
Loan owed to the bank	11,000
Cash held in a chequing account	3,490
Cost of ovens and refrigerators	14,300
Prepaid rent for December	1,200
Common shares	5,000
Retained earnings	2,200

Required:

a. Identify each of the items in his records as an asset, liability, or shareholders' equity item.
b. Prepare a statement of financial position for A Slice of Life Ltd. at the end of November.
c. Jason Chan does not have accounts receivable in his records. Explain why it is unlikely that he will record accounts receivable. Under what business circumstances would it be necessary for him to record accounts receivable?

AP1-23 (Prepare simple statement of financial position)

AP1-20 introduced Lydia Cravette and her florist shop, Scents Unlimited Ltd. At the end of May, the following items were in her records:

Inventory	$ 1,100
Wages owed to employees	950
Loan owed to the bank	8,000
Cash held in a chequing account	8,361
Cost of refrigerator used to store the flowers	18,695
Prepaid rent for June	1,500
Common shares	18,000
Retained earnings	2,706

Required:

a. Identify each of the items in her records as an asset, liability, or shareholders' equity item.
b. Prepare a statement of financial position for Scents Unlimited Ltd. at the end of May.
c. Lydia Cravette does not have accounts receivable in her records. Explain why it is unlikely that she will record accounts receivable. Under what business circumstances would it be necessary for her to record accounts receivable?

AP1-24 (Prepare statement of financial position)

AP1-21 introduced Michelle Fontaine and her outdoor adventure company, Call of the Wild Ltd. At the end of July, the following items were in her records:

Loan owed to the bank	$24,000
Supplies on hand to be used in August	13,420
Cash in bank accounts	33,670
Common shares	20,000
Cost of tents and rafts	34,100
Retained earnings	56,450
Amounts prepaid by customers for trips to be taken in August	19,140
Vehicles	38,400

Required:

a. Identify each of the items in her records as an asset, liability, or shareholders' equity item.
b. Prepare a statement of financial position for Call of the Wild Ltd. at the end of July.
c. Does Michelle Fontaine have any inventory? Explain.
d. Michelle Fontaine does not have accounts receivable in her records. Explain why it is unlikely that she will record accounts receivable. Under what business circumstances would it be necessary for her to record accounts receivable?

AP1-25 (Identify assets and liabilities)

Required:

For each of the following companies, list at least two types of assets and one type of liability that you would expect to find on its statement of financial position. Try to include at least one item for each company that is unique to its type of business.

a. **Bombardier Inc.** This Quebec-based company manufactures transportation equipment and other industrial products.
b. **Sobeys Inc.** This company operates grocery stores across Canada.
c. **McCain Foods Limited.** This New Brunswick company prepares frozen vegetables.
d. **Royal Bank of Canada.** This is a major commercial bank.
e. **Suncor Energy Inc.** This is an energy company.
f. **WestJet.** This is an airline company.
g. **Danier Leather Inc.** This company designs and sells leather goods.

AP1-26 (Identify statement of income items)

Required:

For each of the companies listed in Problem AP1-25, list at least two line items that you would expect to find on its statement of income. Try to include at least one item for each company that is unique to its type of business.

AP1-27 (Identify statement of cash flows items)

Required:

For each of the companies listed in Problem AP1-25, list at least two line items that you would expect to find on its statement of cash flows. Try to include at least one item for each company that is unique to its type of business.

User Perspective Problems

UP1-1 (Information for decision-making)

Suppose that you started your own company that assembles and sells laptop computers. You do not manufacture any of the parts yourself. The computers are sold through orders received over the Internet and through mail orders.

Required:

Make a list of the information that would be relevant to running this business. Then discuss the information you would need to gather if you were going to approach a bank for a small business loan.

UP1-2 (Information for decision-making)

Suppose that you own and operate a company. You need to raise money to expand your operation, so you approach a bank for a loan. The loan officer has asked you for your company's financial statements.

Required:

a. What items on your financial statements would be of the most interest to the loan officer?
b. Develop four questions that you think the loan officer would be trying to answer by looking at your financial statements.

UP1-3 (Form of business)

Taylor Leblond just graduated from university and is planning to start a software development company to develop and market a mapping program he has developed. He is debating whether to operate the business as a proprietorship or incorporate.

Required:

a. What advantages are there to operating as a proprietorship?
b. What advantages are there to operating as a corporation?
c. Which form of business organization would his customers likely prefer? Why?

d. Which form of business organization would his creditors likely prefer? Why?
e. Which form of business will be most advantageous to Taylor if he expects the business to grow rapidly? Why?

UP1-4 (Raising new capital)

Suppose that your best friend wants to start a new company that provides website development services to customers. Your friend has some savings to start the company but not enough to buy all the equipment that she thinks she needs. She has asked you for some advice about how to raise additional funds.

Required:
Give your friend at least two alternatives and provide the pros and cons for each alternative.

UP1-5 (Distribution of dividends to shareholders)

The board of directors of a public company is having its monthly meeting. One of the items on the agenda is the possible distribution of a cash dividend to shareholders. If the board decides to issue a cash dividend, the decision obliges the company to issue cash to shareholders based on the number of shares each shareholder owns.

Required:
Before making its decision, what information about the company should the board consider? Think of the items on the financial statements that you saw in this chapter.

Reading and Interpreting Published Financial Statements

RI1-1 (Financial statements of Dollarama)

Base your answers to the following questions on the financial statements for Dollarama Inc. in Exhibits 1-9A to D.

EXHIBIT 1-9A DOLLARAMA INC.'S 2014 CONSOLIDATED STATEMENT OF FINANCIAL POSITION

Dollarama Inc.
Consolidated Statement of Financial Position as at
(Expressed in thousands of Canadian dollars)

	Note	February 2, 2014 $	February 3, 2013 $
Assets			
Current assets			
Cash and cash equivalents		71,470	52,566
Accounts receivable		5,963	5,798
Deposits and prepaid expenses		5,382	5,756
Merchandise inventories		364,680	338,385
Derivative financial instruments	15	11,455	3,710
		458,950	406,215
Non-current assets			
Property and equipment	7	250,612	197,494
Intangible assets	8	129,436	122,201
Goodwill	8	727,782	727,782
Total assets		1,566,780	1,453,692
Liabilities and shareholders' equity			
Current liabilities			
Accounts payable and accrued liabilities	9	128,857	101,286
Dividend payable		9,823	8,099
Income taxes payable		22,102	23,636
Derivative financial instruments	15	—	185
Current portion of finance lease obligations	11	1,022	604
Current portion of long-term debt	10	3,017	—
		164,821	133,810

continued

EXHIBIT 1-9A **DOLLARAMA INC.'S 2014 CONSOLIDATED STATEMENT OF FINANCIAL POSITION (continued)**

	Note	February 2, 2014 $	February 3, 2013 $
Non-current liabilities			
Long-term debt	10	395,446	262,071
Finance lease obligations	11	1,484	–
Deferred rent and tenant inducements	12	51,592	45,327
Deferred income taxes	14	89,271	80,994
Total liabilities		702,614	522,202
Commitments	11		
Shareholders' equity			
Share capital	13	493,602	517,306
Contributed surplus		10,884	8,157
Retained earnings		346,478	403,266
Accumulated other comprehensive income	13	13,202	2,761
Total shareholders' equity		864,166	931,490
Total liabilities and shareholders' equity		1,566,780	1,453,692

EXHIBIT 1-9B **DOLLARAMA INC.'S 2014 CONSOLIDATED STATEMENT OF INCOME**

Dollarama Inc.
Consolidated Statement of Net Earnings and Comprehensive Income for the years ended
(Expressed in thousands of Canadian dollars, except share and per share amounts)

	Note	52-weeks February 2, 2014 $	53-weeks February 3, 2013 $
Sales		2,064,676	1,858,818
Cost of sales		1,299,092	1,163,979
Gross profit		765,584	694,839
General, administrative and store operating expenses		363,182	339,662
Depreciation and amortization	18	47,898	39,284
Operating income		354,504	315,893
Net financing costs	18	11,673	10,839
Earnings before income taxes		342,831	305,054
Provision for income taxes	14	92,737	84,069
Net earnings for the year		250,094	220,985
Other comprehensive income			
Items to be reclassified subsequently to net earnings			
Unrealized gain on derivative financial instruments, net of reclassification adjustment		14,249	1,093
Income taxes relating to component of other comprehensive income		(3,808)	(308)
Total other comprehensive income, net of income taxes		10,441	785
Total comprehensive income for the year		260,535	221,770

EXHIBIT 1-9C **DOLLARAMA INC.'S 2014 CONSOLIDATED STATEMENT OF CASH FLOWS**

Dollarama Inc.
Consolidated Statement of Cash Flows for the years ended
(Expressed in thousands of Canadian dollars)

	Note	52-weeks February 2, 2014 $	53-weeks February 3, 2013 $
Cash flows			
Operating activities			
Net earnings for the year		250,094	220,985
Adjustments for:			
Depreciation and amortization	18	47,898	39,284
Interest accrual long-term debt	10	3,017	(216)
Amortization of debt issue costs		592	1,133
Excess of receipts over amount recognized on derivative financial instruments	15	6,319	1,272
Recognition of deferred leasing costs		465	295
Recognition of deferred tenant allowances	12	(3,543)	(2,871)
Deferred lease inducements	12	3,750	5,328
Deferred tenant allowances	12	6,058	6,832
Share-based compensation	13	4,053	1,558
Deferred income taxes	14	4,469	6,921
Loss on disposal of assets		1,017	716
		324,189	281,237
Changes in non-cash working capital components	19	(15,811)	(24,198)
Net cash generated from operating activities		308,378	257,039
Investing activities			
Additions to property and equipment	7	(96,303)	(69,577)
Additions to intangible assets	8	(11,095)	(8,210)
Proceeds on disposal of property and equipment		552	256
Net cash used by investing activities		(106,846)	(77,531)
Financing activities			
Proceeds from senior unsecured notes	10	400,000	–
Disbursements on long-term debt		(264,420)	(10,361)
Proceeds from bank indebtedness		166,000	–
Repayment of bank indebtedness		(166,000)	–
Payment of debt issue costs		(2,797)	(837)
Repayment of finance leases		(985)	(695)
Dividends paid		(38,418)	(30,972)
Repurchase and cancellation of shares	13	(277,438)	(155,942)
Issuance of common shares		1,430	1,594
Net cash used by financing activities		(182,628)	(197,213)
Increase (decrease) in cash and cash equivalents		18,904	(17,705)
Cash and cash equivalents – Beginning of year		52,566	70,271
Cash and cash equivalents – End of year		71,470	52,566
Cash payment of interest		6,025	7,639
Cash payment of income taxes		89,801	75,090

EXHIBIT 1-9D DOLLARAMA INC.'S 2014 CONSOLIDATED STATEMENTS OF CHANGES IN SHAREHOLDERS' EQUITY

Dollarama Inc.
Consolidated Statement of Changes in Shareholders' Equity for the years ended
(Expressed in thousands of Canadian dollars except share amounts)

	Note	Number of common shares	Share capital $	Contributed Surplus $	Retained earnings $	Accumulated other comprehensive income $	Total $
Balance – January 29, 2012		73,807,542	525,024	15,659	352,287	1,976	894,946
Net earnings for the year		—	—	—	220,985	—	220,985
Other comprehensive income							
Unrealized gain on derivative financial instruments, net of reclassification adjustment and income tax of $308	13	—	—	—	—	785	785
Repurchase and cancellation of shares	13	(2,583,264)	(18,372)	—	(137,570)	—	(155,942)
Dividends declared		—	—	—	(32,436)	—	(32,436)
Issuance of common shares	13	1,866,192	1,594	—	—	—	1,594
Share-based compensation	13	—	—	1,558	—	—	1,558
Reclassification related to exercise of stock options	13	—	9,060	(9,060)	—	—	—
Balance – February 3, 2013		73,090,470	517,306	8,157	403,266	2,761	931,490
Net earnings for the year		—	—	—	250,094	—	250,094
Other comprehensive income							
Unrealized gain on derivative financial instruments, net of reclassification adjustment and income tax of $3,808	13	—	—	—	—	10,441	10,441
Repurchase and cancellation of shares	13	(3,720,418)	(26,460)	—	(266,741)	—	(293,201)
Dividends declared		—	—	—	(40,141)	—	(40,141)
Issuance of common shares	13	108,817	1,430	—	—	—	1,430
Share-based compensation	13	—	—	4,053	—	—	4,053
Reclassification related to exercise of stock options	13	—	1,326	(1,326)	—	—	—
Balance – February 2, 2014		69,478,869	493,602	10,884	346,478	13,202	864,166

In the questions below, the year 2014 refers to Dollarama's fiscal year that ends February 2, 2014, and the year 2013 refers to the prior fiscal year ending February 3, 2013.

Required:

a. Determine the amount of dividends that Dollarama declared in 2014. On which financial statement(s) did you find this information?
b. Find the following amounts in the statements:
   i. Revenues from the sale of merchandise in 2014
   ii. Cost of sales and general, administrative, and store operating expenses in 2014
   iii. Net financing costs in 2014
   iv. Income tax expense in 2014
   v. Net earnings in 2013
   vi. Merchandise inventories at the end of 2013
   vii. Accounts payable and accrued liabilities at the beginning of the 2014 fiscal year
   viii. Retained earnings at the end of 2014
   ix. Long-term debt at the beginning of 2014 (include the current portion long-term debt)
   x. Cash flows generated from operating activities in 2014
   xi. Cash payments to purchase property, plant, and equipment in 2014
   xii. Cash proceeds from the issuance of common shares in 2014

xiii. Cash flows generated from (used for) financing activities in 2013
xiv. Cash payments to reduce long-term debt in 2014

c. List the two largest sources of cash and the two largest uses of cash in 2014. (Consider operations to be a single source or use of cash.)
d. Suggest two reasons why net earnings were $250,094 thousand in 2014, yet cash flows generated from operations were $308,378 thousand.
e. During 2014, total sales revenue was approximately $205,858 thousand higher than in 2013. However, net earnings in 2014 were only $29,109 thousand higher than in 2013. Examine the consolidated statement of net earnings and comprehensive income and explain where the additional revenue went.

RI1-2 (Financial statements of Le Château Inc.)

Base your answers to the following questions on the 2014 financial statements for Le Château Inc. in Exhibits 1-10A to C.

EXHIBIT 1-10A **LE CHÂTEAU INC.'S 2013 CONSOLIDATED BALANCE SHEETS**

CONSOLIDATED BALANCE SHEETS
As at January 25, 2014 and January 26, 2013
[in thousands of Canadian dollars]

	2014 $	2013 $
ASSETS		
Current assets		
Cash	1,446	1,783
Accounts receivable *[note 6]*	1,476	1,906
Income taxes refundable	6,663	3,211
Derivative financial instruments	418	215
Inventories *[notes 6 and 7]*	124,878	123,218
Prepaid expenses	2,292	1,890
Total current assets	137,173	132,223
Property and equipment *[notes 8 and 12]*	69,870	83,315
Intangible assets *[note 9]*	3,815	4,672
	210,858	220,210
LIABILITIES AND SHAREHOLDERS' EQUITY		
Current liabilities		
Bank indebtedness *[note 6]*	30,767	13,034
Trade and other payables *[note 10]*	19,553	20,718
Deferred revenue	3,712	3,558
Current portion of provisions *[note 11]*	265	228
Current portion of long-term debt *[note 12]*	7,987	9,844
Total current liabilities	62,284	47,382
Long-term debt *[note 12]*	7,843	14,290
Provisions *[note 11]*	391	530
Deferred income taxes *[note 14]*	1,829	2,298
Deferred lease credits	13,412	15,912
Total liabilities	85,759	80,412
Shareholders' equity		
Share capital *[note 13]*	42,960	42,740
Contributed surplus	3,581	2,664
Retained earnings	78,253	94,239
Accumulated other comprehensive income	305	155
Total shareholders' equity	125,099	139,798
	210,858	220,210

EXHIBIT 1-10B **LE CHÂTEAU INC.'S 2013 CONSOLIDATED STATEMENTS OF LOSS**

Years ended January 25, 2014 and January 26, 2013
[in thousands of Canadian dollars, except per share information]

	2014 $	2013 $
Sales *[note 20]*	274,840	274,827
Cost of sales and expenses		
Cost of sales *[note 7]*	101,770	92,565
Selling *[note 8]*	155,859	155,561
General and administrative *[notes 8 and 9]*	36,218	35,847
	293,847	283,973
Results from operating activities	(19,007)	(9,146)
Finance costs	2,714	3,063
Finance income	(13)	(23)
Loss before income taxes	(21,708)	(12,186)
Income tax recovery *[note 14]*	(5,722)	(3,469)
Net loss	(15,986)	(8,717)
Net loss per share *[note 17]*		
Basic	(0.59)	(0.34)
Diluted	(0.59)	(0.34)
Weighted average number of shares outstanding	27,288,766	25,658,585

EXHIBIT 1-10C **LE CHÂTEAU INC.'S 2013 CONSOLIDATED STATEMENTS OF CASH FLOWS**

CONSOLIDATED STATEMENTS OF CASH FLOWS
Years ended January 25, 2014 and January 26, 2013
[in thousands of Canadian dollars]

	2014 $	2013 $
OPERATING ACTIVITIES		
Net loss	(15,986)	(8,717)
Adjustments to determine net cash from operating activities		
Depreciation and amortization *[notes 8 and 9]*	18,723	19,574
Write-off and net impairment of property and equipment and intangible assets *[notes 8 and 9]*	1,897	2,142
Loss on disposal of property and equipment *[note 8]*	–	108
Amortization of deferred lease credits	(2,539)	(1,285)
Deferred lease credits	39	1,088
Stock-based compensation	978	336
Provisions	(102)	338
Finance costs	2,714	3,063
Finance income	(13)	(23)
Interest paid	(2,436)	(2,863)
Interest received	13	28
Income tax recovery	(5,722)	(3,469)
	(2,434)	10,320

continued

EXHIBIT 1-10C **LE CHÂTEAU INC.'S 2013 CONSOLIDATED STATEMENTS OF CASH FLOWS (continued)**

	2014 $	2013 $
Net change in non-cash working capital items related to operations *[note 21]*	(3,030)	(6,340)
	(5,464)	3,980
Income taxes refunded	2,108	2,056
Cash flows related to operating activities	(3,356)	6,036
FINANCING ACTIVITIES		
Increase in bank indebtedness	17,482	13,600
Repayment of long-term debt	(8,304)	(16,323)
Issue of share capital upon exercise of options	159	—
Cash flows related to financing activities	9,337	(2,723)
INVESTING ACTIVITIES		
Additions to property and equipment and intangible assets *[notes 8 and 9]*	(6,318)	(9,237)
Proceeds from disposal of property and equipment *[note 8]*	—	514
Cash flows related to investing activities	(6,318)	(8,723)
Decrease in cash	(337)	(5,410)
Cash, beginning of year	1,783	7,193
Cash, end of year	1,446	1,783

In the questions below, the year 2014 refers to Le Château's fiscal year ended January 25, 2014, and the year 2013 refers to the prior year ended January 26, 2013.

Required:

a. Le Château has issued consolidated financial statements. What does the word *consolidated* at the top of a financial statement tell you about the company's structure?

b. Le Château prepared a classified statement of financial position. Calculate the difference between current assets and current liabilities at the end of 2014, and at the end of 2013.This amount is referred to as *working capital*. Did the company's working capital improve in 2014? Explain.

c. Find the following amounts in Le Château's statements (note that the amounts are in thousands of Canadian dollars):
   i. Sales revenues in 2014
   ii. Cost of sales in 2014
   iii. Finance costs (cost of debt) in 2013
   iv. Income tax expense (recovery) in 2014
   v. Net income (loss) in 2013
   vi. Intangible assets at the end of 2014
   vii. Trade receivables (accounts receivable) at the beginning of 2014
   viii. Share capital at the end of 2014
   ix. Property, plant, and equipment at the end of 2014
   x. Cash flows from operating activities in 2014
   xi. Cash payments to acquire intangibles and property, plant, and equipment in 2013
   xii. Cash used for the payment of dividends in 2013
   xiii. Cash produced from or used for financing activities in 2014

d. Did Le Château finance the company's assets mainly from creditors (total liabilities) or from shareholders (shareholders' equity) in 2014? Support your answer with appropriate calculations.

e. List the two largest sources of cash and the two largest uses of cash in 2014. (Consider cash generated from operating activities to be a single source or use of cash.)

f. Suggest some reasons why there was a loss of approximately $15,986 thousand in 2014, yet cash generated from operating activities was only a negative (or outflow of) $3,356 thousand.

RI1-3 (Financial statements of Ten Peaks Coffee Company Inc.)

The major financial statements of Ten Peaks Coffee Company Inc. from its 2013 annual report are included in Exhibits 1-11A to C. Note that its fiscal year end is December 31, 2013.

EXHIBIT 1-11A **TEN PEAKS COFFEE COMPANY INC.'S 2013 CONSOLIDATED STATEMENTS OF FINANCIAL POSITION**

TEN PEAKS COFFEE COMPANY INC.
CONSOLIDATED STATEMENTS OF FINANCIAL POSITION
(Tabular amounts in thousands of Canadian dollars, except per share and number of shares figures)

	December 31 2013	**December 31 2012**
Assets		
Current assets		
Inventories	$ 6,463	$ 9,494
Accounts receivable	4,972	3,962
Prepaid expenses and other receivables	236	169
Derivative assets	152	227
Cash	2,594	1,304
Total current assets	14,417	15,156
Non-current assets		
Plant and equipment	12,508	13,298
Intangible assets	2,465	2,724
Deferred tax assets	1,578	2,058
Derivative assets	—	37
Total non-current assets	16,551	18,117
Total assets	$ 30,968	$ 33,273
Liabilities and shareholders' equity		
Current liabilities		
Bank indebtedness	$ 4,786	$ 6,983
Accounts payable	916	1,559
Accrued liabilities	1,100	1,066
Dividend payable	417	417
Derivative liabilities	119	11
Current income tax liabilities	18	—
Current portion of other liabilities	219	—
Total current liabilities	7,575	10,036
Non-current liabilities		
Derivative liabilities	131	—
Other liabilities	28	69
Asset retirement obligation	725	705
Total non-current liabilities	884	774
Total liabilities	8,459	10,810
Shareholders' equity		
Share capital	24,631	24,631
Share-based compensation reserve	106	45
Deficit	(2,228)	(2,213)
Total equity	22,509	22,463
Total liabilities and shareholders' equity	$ 30,968	$ 33,273

EXHIBIT 1-11B **TEN PEAKS COFFEE COMPANY INC.'S 2013 CONSOLIDATED STATEMENTS OF INCOME**

TEN PEAKS COFFEE COMPANY INC.
CONSOLIDATED STATEMENTS OF INCOME AND COMPREHENSIVE INCOME
(Tabular amounts in thousands of Canadian dollars, except per share and number of shares figures)
for the years ended

	Note	December 31 2013	December 31 2012
Revenue		$ 53,873	$ 59,713
Cost of sales		(47,662)	(55,050)
Gross profit		6,211	4,663
Sales and marketing expenses		(1,415)	(1,292)
Occupancy expenses		(50)	(63)
Administration expenses		(3,034)	(2,847)
Finance income		92	117
Finance expenses		(149)	(258)
Realized gain on derivative financial instruments		1,614	1,678
Unrealized loss on derivative financial instruments		(1,045)	(197)
(Loss) gain on foreign exchange		(68)	223
Loss on disposal of plant and equipment		(4)	—
Income before tax		2,152	2,024
Income tax expense	11	(498)	(520)
Net income and comprehensive income for the year		$ 1,654	$ 1,504
Earnings per share			
Basic and Diluted (per share)	20	$ 0.25	$ 0.23

EXHIBIT 1-11C **TEN PEAKS COFFEE COMPANY INC.'S 2013 CONSOLIDATED STATEMENTS OF CASH FLOWS**

TEN PEAKS COFFEE COMPANY INC.
CONSOLIDATED STATEMENTS OF CASH FLOWS
(Tabular amounts in thousands of Canadian dollars, except per share and number of shares figures)
for the years ended

	December 31 2013	December 31 2012
Cash flows from operating activities		
Net income for the period	$ 1,654	$ 1,504
Items not affecting cash		
Depreciation and amortization	1,415	1,396
Unrealized loss on derivative financial instruments	1,045	197
Loss on disposal of plant and equipment	4	—
Share-based compensation	238	100
Foreign exchange gain on cash held	(102)	(149)
Foreign exchange loss on debt	315	—
Income taxes recognized in profit and loss	498	520
Finance income	(92)	(117)
Finance expenses	149	258
	5,124	3,709

continued

EXHIBIT 1-11C

TEN PEAKS COFFEE COMPANY INC.'S 2013 CONSOLIDATED STATEMENTS OF CASH FLOWS (continued)

	December 31 2013	December 31 2012
Movements in working capital:		
Accounts receivable	$ (1,010)	$ 236
Inventory	3,031	1,767
Prepaid expenses	(67)	(10)
Accounts payable and accrued liabilities	(608)	(396)
Derivative assets at fair value through profit or loss	112	(16)
Derivative liabilities at fair value through profit or loss	(806)	(315)
Change in non-cash working capital relating to operating activities	652	1,266
Cash generated from operations	5,776	4,975
Interest received	92	117
Interest paid	(129)	(240)
Net cash generated from operating activities	5,739	4,852
Cash flows from investing activities		
Additions to plant and equipment	(370)	(499)
Net cash used in investing activities	(370)	(499)
Cash flows from financing activities		
Dividends paid	(1,669)	(1,669)
Repayments of bank indebtedness	(2,512)	(2,029)
Net cash used in financing activities	(4,181)	(3,698)
Effects of foreign exchange rate changes on cash held	102	149
Net increase in cash	1,290	804
Cash, beginning of period	1,304	500
Cash, end of period	$ 2,594	$ 1,304

Required:

a. Find the following amounts in the statements:
   i. Total sales for fiscal year 2013
   ii. Total cost of sales for fiscal year 2013
   iii. Sales and marketing expenses for fiscal year 2012
   iv. Finance expenses for fiscal year 2013
   v. Income tax expense for fiscal year 2013
   vi. Net income for fiscal year 2013
   vii. Inventories at the end of fiscal year 2013
   viii. Accounts payable at the beginning of fiscal year 2013
   ix. Shareholders' equity at the end of fiscal year 2013
   x. Deficit at the beginning of fiscal year 2013
   xi. Cash provided from operating activities in fiscal year 2013
   xii. Cash payments to acquire plant and equipment in fiscal year 2013
   xiii. Cash used in the repayment of debt in fiscal year 2013
   xiv. Cash used to pay dividends in fiscal year 2013

b. Does Ten Peaks finance its business primarily with debt or with shareholders' equity? Support your answer with appropriate data.

c. Did Ten Peaks have a net inflow or a net outflow of cash from financing activities in 2013? What about from its investing activities?

d. Does Ten Peaks use a classified statement of financial position? Explain.

RI1-4 (Financial statements of Gildan Activewear Inc.)

Excerpts from the 2013 financial statements of Gildan Activewear Inc. are in Exhibits 1-12A to C.

EXHIBIT 1-12A **GILDAN ACTIVEWEAR INC.'S 2013 CONSOLIDATED STATEMENTS OF EARNINGS**

GILDAN ACTIVEWEAR INC.
CONSOLIDATED STATEMENTS OF EARNINGS AND COMPREHENSIVE INCOME
Years ended September 29, 2013 and September 30, 2012
(in thousands of U.S. dollars, except per share data)

	2013	**2012**
Net sales	**$2,184,303**	$1,948,253
Cost of sales	**1,550,266**	1,552,128
Gross profit	**634,037**	396,125
Selling, general and administrative expenses (note 17(a))	**282,563**	226,035
Restructuring and acquisition-related costs (note 18)	**8,788**	14,962
Operating income	**342,686**	155,128
Financial expenses, net (note 15(c))	**12,013**	11,598
Equity earnings in investment in joint venture	**(46)**	(597)
Earnings before income taxes	**330,719**	144,127
Income tax expense (recovery) (note 19)	**10,541**	(4,337)
Net earnings	**320,178**	148,464
Other comprehensive income (loss), net of related income taxes (note 15(d)):		
Cash flow hedges	**6,419**	(6,399)
Actuarial gain on employee benefit obligations	**436**	323
	6,855	(6,076)
Comprehensive income	**$ 327,033**	$ 142,388

EXHIBIT 1-12B **GILDAN ACTIVEWEAR INC.'S 2013 CONSOLIDATED STATEMENTS OF FINANCIAL POSITION**

GILDAN ACTIVEWEAR INC.
CONSOLIDATED STATEMENTS OF FINANCIAL POSITION
(in thousands of U.S. dollars)

	September 29, 2013	**September 30, 2012**
Current assets:		
Cash and cash equivalents (note 6)	**$ 97,368**	$ 70,410
Trade accounts receivable (note 7)	**255,018**	257,595
Income taxes receivable	**700**	353
Inventories (note 8)	**595,794**	553,068
Prepaid expenses and deposits	**14,959**	14,451
Assets held for sale (note 18)	**5,839**	8,029
Other current assets	**11,034**	8,694
Total current assets	**980,712**	912,600
Non-current assets:		
Property, plant and equipment (note 9)	**655,869**	552,437
Intangible assets (note 10)	**247,537**	259,981
Goodwill (note 10)	**150,099**	143,833
Investment in joint venture	**—**	12,126
Deferred income taxes (note 19)	**1,443**	4,471
Other non-current assets	**7,991**	10,989
Total non-current assets	**1,062,939**	983,837
Total assets	**$2,043,651**	$1,896,437
Current liabilities:		
Accounts payable and accrued liabilities	**$ 289,414**	$ 256,442
Total current liabilities	**289,414**	256,442

continued

EXHIBIT 1-12B

GILDAN ACTIVEWEAR INC.'S 2013 CONSOLIDATED STATEMENTS OF FINANCIAL POSITION (continued)

	September 29, 2013	September 30, 2012
Non-current liabilities:		
Long-term debt (note 11)	**—**	181,000
Employee benefit obligations (note 12)	**18,486**	19,612
Provisions (note 13)	**16,325**	13,042
Total non-current liabilities	**34,811**	213,654
Total liabilities	**324,225**	470,096
Commitments, guarantees and contingent liabilities (note 24)		
Equity:		
Share capital	**107,867**	101,113
Contributed surplus	**28,869**	25,579
Retained earnings	**1,583,346**	1,306,724
Accumulated other comprehensive income	**(656)**	(7,075)
Total equity attributable to shareholders of the Company	**1,719,426**	1,426,341
Total liabilities and equity	**$2,043,651**	$1,896,437

EXHIBIT 1-12C

GILDAN ACTIVEWEAR INC.'S 2013 CONSOLIDATED STATEMENTS OF CASH FLOWS

GILDAN ACTIVEWEAR INC.
CONSOLIDATED STATEMENTS OF CASH FLOWS
Years ended September 29, 2013 and September 30, 2012
(in thousands of U.S. dollars)

	2013	2012
Cash flows from (used in) operating activities:		
Net earnings	**$ 320,178**	$ 148,464
Adjustments to reconcile net earnings to cash flows from operating activities (note 22(a))	**109,023**	94,221
	429,201	242,685
Changes in non-cash working capital balances:		
Trade accounts receivable	**2,986**	(36,660)
Income taxes	**(392)**	2,440
Inventories	**(38,092)**	77,111
Prepaid expenses and deposits	**(1,098)**	(1,828)
Other current assets	**(1,896)**	(2,368)
Accounts payable and accrued liabilities	**36,447**	(61,798)
Cash flows from operating activities	**427,156**	219,582
Cash flows from (used in) investing activities:		
Purchase of property, plant and equipment	**(162,643)**	(71,316)
Purchase of intangible assets	**(4,315)**	(5,439)
Business acquisitions (note 5)	**(8,027)**	(87,373)
Proceeds on disposal of assets held for sale and property, plant and equipment	**2,849**	600
Dividend received from investment in joint venture	**—**	1,509
Cash flows used in investing activities	**(172,136)**	(162,019)
Cash flows from (used in) financing activities:		
Decrease in amounts drawn under revolving long-term bank credit facility	**(181,000)**	(28,000)
Dividends paid	**(43,723)**	(36,615)
Proceeds from the issuance of shares	**6,014)**	1,501
Share repurchases for future settlement of non-Treasury RSUs (note 14(e))	**(9,621)**	(5,990)
Cash flows used in financing activities	**(228,330)**	(69,104)
Effect of exchange rate changes on cash and cash equivalents denominated in foreign currencies	**268**	(74)
Net increase (decrease) in cash and cash equivalents during the year	**26,958**	(11,615)
Cash and cash equivalents, beginning of year	**70,410**	82,025
Cash and cash equivalents, end of year	**$ 97,368**	$ 70,410
Cash paid during the period (included in cash flows from operating activities):		
Interest	**$ 4,278**	$ 8,101
Income taxes	**9,340**	4,331

In the questions below, the year 2013 refers to Gildan's fiscal year ended September 29, 2013, and the year 2012 refers to the prior year ended September 30, 2012.

Required:

a. Find the following amounts in the statements:
    i. Net sales in 2013
    ii. Total selling, general, and administrative expenses in 2013
    iii. Income tax expense (recovery) in 2012
    iv. Net income (earnings) in 2013
    v. Inventories at the beginning of 2013
    vi. Trade accounts receivable at the end of 2012
    vii. Retained earnings at the end of 2013
    viii. Long-term debt at the end of 2012
    ix. Cash flows from operating activities in 2013
    x. Cash payments to acquire property, plant, and equipment in 2013
    xi. Dividends paid in 2013
    xii. Cash produced or used for investing activities in 2013
b. Did Gildan Activewear finance its business primarily from creditors (total liabilities) or from shareholders (shareholders' equity) in 2013? Support your answer with appropriate calculations.
c. List the two largest sources of cash and the two largest uses of cash in 2013. (Consider operating activities to be a single source or use of cash.)
d. Did Gildan Activewear prepare a classified statement of financial position? How can you tell?
e. Calculate the difference between the current assets and current liabilities at the end of 2013, and at the end of 2012. This amount is referred to as *working capital*. Did the company's working capital improve in 2013? Explain.

RI1-5 (Use sources other than the textbook to find company information)

The SEDAR website (www.sedar.com) contains most securities-related information required by the Canadian securities regulatory authorities. It is probably your best source for financial statements of Canadian companies on the Internet. In addition, most companies that have a website have a section on investor information. In this section, they often include their most recent financial reports and news releases.

Required:

Choose a Canadian publicly traded company. Collect several articles about the company that cover the most recent two-year period. Try to find at least three longer articles. If the company has a website (most companies do), it will probably have useful news releases there. Finally, go to the SEDAR website and find the company's most recent financial statements filed there.

Answer the following questions:

a. What are the products (or product lines) and/or services that it sells? Be as specific as possible.
b. Who are the company's customers?
c. In what markets, domestic and global, does the company sell its products and/or services?
d. Who are the company's major competitors?
e. What are the major inputs that the company needs in order to produce its product? Who are the suppliers of these inputs?
f. Are any of the items listed in the questions above changing substantially? Use a two-year time span to answer this question.

RI1-6 (Find information about a new company)

Required:

Go to a publicly traded company's website and find the company's most recent annual report. Answer the following questions:

a. What are the major sections of the annual report?
b. What are the three most important points in the letter to the shareholders?
c. What are the titles of the major financial statements in the report?
d. What are the company's total assets, total liabilities, and total shareholders' equity? What percentage of the company's total assets is financed through liabilities?
e. Is the statement of financial position classified or unclassified? If it is classified, what are the major categories?
f. What are the net sales in the most recent year? Are they up or down from the previous year? (Answer in both dollar and percentage amounts.)
g. What is the net income and earnings per share in the most recent year? Are these amounts up or down from the previous year? (Answer in both dollar and percentage amounts.)
h. What is the net cash provided (used) by operating, financing, and investing activities for the most recent year?
i. What is the last day of the company's fiscal year?

Case

C1-1 Enticing Fashions Ltd.

Enticing Fashions Ltd. designs and manufactures upscale women's clothing. The company's early customers were small boutiques in Toronto, Montreal, and Vancouver. Customers liked the colours and fabrics used and enjoyed the unique styling of the garments. Demand for the company's clothing rose to the point where they are looking at opening a number of their own stores in various retail locations across Canada. The company has approached its bank seeking additional financing so that the company can proceed with its plan to develop retail locations and hire more people to assist with various aspects of the business. The bank wants to see the company's financial statements.

You are an accountant employed by a local accounting firm and Enticing Fashions Ltd. has been your client for several years. In previous years, you have prepared the company's financial statements and corporate tax returns. Enticing Fashion's CEO has approached you because he wants to have an understanding about how the bank may use the company's financial statements in determining whether or not to grant the loan.

Required:

Prepare a memo to Enticing Fashion's CEO addressing his question regarding how banks use financial statements to determine whether or not to grant loans to companies.

ENDNOTES

1. Ian McGugan, "Share Buybacks Put a Shine on Danier," *The Globe and Mail*, October 8, 2010; Danier Leather Inc. 2013 and 2014 annual reports; Danier corporate website, www.danier.com.
2. Canadian Coalition for Good Governance, *Model "Say on Pay" Policy for Issuers*, September 2010? www.ccgg.ca; Blakes Bulletin; *Say on Pay: Is the Canadian Future Voluntary?*; 03/27/2014; www.blakes.com; Theresa Tedesco, "Say-on-Pay Movement on the Rise in Canada, but Is It Changing Anything?", *The Financial Post*. March 12, 2014; Janet McFarland, "Shareholders Increasingly Draw Line in Sand on Executive Pay," *The Globe and Mail*, July 28, 2013.

CHAPTER

3 Double-Entry Accounting and The Accounting Cycle

CORE QUESTIONS

If you are able to answer the following questions, then you have achieved the related learning objectives.

LEARNING OBJECTIVES

After studying this chapter, you should be able to:

INTRODUCTION

- How does the double-entry accounting system work and how does it overcome the limitations of the template method?

1 Explain how the double-entry accounting system works, including how it overcomes the limitations of the template approach.

- What is the normal balance concept and how is it used?

2 Explain the normal balance concept and how it is used within the double-entry accounting system.

UNDERSTANDING THE ACCOUNTING CYCLE

- What are the steps in the accounting cycle?

3 Identify and explain the steps in the accounting cycle.

THE CHART OF ACCOUNTS

- What is the chart of accounts?
- Can companies change their chart of accounts and what are the implications if they do?

4 Explain the significance of a company's decisions regarding its chart of accounts and the implications of subsequent changes.

OPENING BALANCES

- What is the difference between permanent and temporary accounts?

5 Explain the difference between permanent and temporary accounts.

TRANSACTION ANALYSIS AND RECORDING

- How are transactions identified?
- How are transactions recorded in the general journal?
- Why are transactions also recorded in the general ledger?
- What is the purpose of preparing a trial balance?

6 Identify and record transactions in the general journal and general ledger.

ADJUSTING ENTRIES

- What are adjusting entries and why are they necessary?
- What is the purpose of preparing an adjusted trial balance?

7 Explain why adjusting entries are necessary and prepare them.

PREPARING FINANCIAL STATEMENTS AND CLOSING ENTRIES

- What are closing entries and why are they necessary?

8 Explain why closing entries are necessary and prepare them.

Balancing the Books when Bartering

When the Hudson's Bay Company (HBC) was established under a royal charter from King Charles II in 1670, it had 18 shareholders who invested a total of £10,500. The company's fur-trading operations, which would eventually span the upper half of North America, were complicated by the lack of any monetary system. Instead, the company largely worked by bartering, trading things like blankets and kettles for furs.

For over 150 years, HBC valued items in units equivalent to one prime beaver pelt, called a "made beaver" (MB), and this became the standard of currency used in trading. For example, trappers could trade 11 MB for a gun, 3 MB for a yard of cloth, and 6 MB for a 3-gallon kettle. Even other furs were translated into MB. An otter or a fox pelt was worth two MB, whereas a marten was worth one third of an MB.

HBC required its chief factors, who commanded the company's trading posts, to record these transactions and maintain a complete set of accounts. Across the various trading posts, the company used standardized accounting practices, many of which are similar to those still in use 350 years later. The company required a journal and a ledger to be maintained at each post, together with inventory records and a reconciliation between the goods traded and the MBs received in exchange. These records were sent to HBC's London headquarters for review and to inform the company's decision-making for the next trading period.

Coming back to the company's earlier practice of bartering, it is worth noting that barter transactions should not result in profits, because goods of equivalent values are being exchanged. In spite of this, the accounting records of virtually all of HBC's trading posts reported an amount known as "overplus." This represented profits that resulted from traders altering the standard of trade in the company's favour, such as requiring 8 MB in exchange for a kettle rather than 6 MB. Overplus added to the company's profits from the eventual sale of the furs. Between 1670 and 1857, HBC produced profits of at least £20 million, some of which it returned to shareholders. While those initial 18 shareholders had to wait 15 years for their first dividend, on the strength of its profits, HBC paid dividends in 249 of the 314 years between its inception in 1670 and 1984!

HBC is the world's oldest commercial enterprise that still carries on its original line of business, operating over 300 stores under banners such as Hudson's Bay, Saks Fifth Avenue, Lord & Taylor, and Home Outfitters in Canada and the United States. Its sales in 2013 were $5.2 billion—equal to an untold number of made beavers. You can bet that keeping good accounting records has contributed to its success over nearly 350 years.[1]

INTRODUCTION

LEARNING OBJECTIVE 1
Explain how the double-entry accounting system works, including how it overcomes the limitations of the template approach.

Now that you understand the basic accounting equation and can work through the analysis of some transactions, we are going to take you further into the practical side of accounting. We are going to show you how data are recorded in an accounting system so that organizations can easily extract information and summarize it into financial statements and other reports. Of course, today's technology makes financial record-keeping far easier than in the early days of the **Hudson's Bay Company**.

How does the double-entry accounting system work and how does it overcome the limitations of the template method?

As we discussed in Chapter 2, recording transactions in a template or spreadsheet, with columns reflecting the basic accounting equation, is adequate for small entities with few transactions to record. However, it is cumbersome when large numbers of accounts and transactions are involved. To address this, accountants developed the **double-entry accounting system**. It is called this because it requires that each transaction be recorded in a way that affects at least two accounts, with the transaction amount recorded in *each* account. (In other words, the transaction amount is recorded twice, which is the "double" in the term *double-entry accounting*.) The total effects of these entries will be equal and offsetting. This is similar to what we did in the template method, which required that each line balance.

The most significant limitation of the template method is the number of columns that can be manageably used. This significantly limits the information that management can capture and analyze in managing the business. For example, an organization may have multiple types of inventory that it wishes to track and would need specific accounts (or columns) for each. Think of the bookstore at your university or college. At a minimum, management would want to track the major categories of inventory separately (such as new textbooks, digital textbooks, used textbooks, clothing, office supplies, and information technology). They may also want some of this information further broken down by program or faculty. Obviously, the number of accounts (or columns) would quickly become too large for a workable spreadsheet.

The double-entry accounting system overcomes this limitation by enabling companies to uses hundreds or even thousands of accounts to capture information at the level of detail required to manage the business effectively. It enables businesses to capture transaction details while making it easy to summarize information by account.

For Example

The level of detail required to manage the operations of a major Canadian university is significant. According to the director of financial services at Vancouver-based Simon Fraser University, the university has "8,500 cost centres that have detailed object accounts below them, so that translates into more than 100,000 general ledger accounts." Imagine trying to work with a spreadsheet having 100,000 columns![2]

■ LEARNING OBJECTIVE 2
Explain the normal balance concept and how it is used within the double-entry accounting system.

What is the normal balance concept and how is it used?

Before discussing the double-entry accounting system further, we have to learn about the **normal balance** concept. First, picture yourself as a crew member on a sailboat out on a local lake or bay. Your duties include working with the sails, hoisting them up and down and moving them from one side of the boat to the other. Your friend, the captain, loves to shout out orders referring to "port" or "starboard." If you aren't a regular sailor, you would likely be confused by these terms. Is the captain referring to the left side of the boat or the right side? If you don't understand, you probably can't follow the captain's orders and may even get knocked out of the boat by a sail boom that you had no idea was coming!

Just as sailors have invented their own terms for left (*port*) and right (*starboard*), so have accountants. Understanding what these mean is one of the keys to the double-entry accounting system. While you will not literally get hit by a sail boom while working with accounting information, it may feel as though you have been figuratively knocked overboard if you don't understand what the terms *debit* and *credit* mean.

While these terms are the accounting equivalent of left and right, you are likely wondering "left and right of what?" The easiest way to explain this is to revisit the accounting equation, through which we will draw a big "T" to divide it in half as follows:

TAKE5

ASSETS	LIABILITIES + SHAREHOLDERS' EQUITY
"LEFT"	"RIGHT"
DEBIT	CREDIT
DR	CR

KEY POINTS
- Asset accounts normally have a debit balance.
- Liabilities and shareholders' equity accounts normally have a credit balance.

This illustrates the normal balance concept. Basically, accountants say that accounts on the left side of the T (asset accounts) *normally* have a **debit** balance, while accounts on the right side of the T (liabilities and shareholders' equity accounts) *normally* have a **credit** balance.*

Using the normal balance concept, we can determine whether an account normally has a debit or a credit balance. Once we know this, we will use the account's normal balance to increase it and do the opposite to decrease it. Let's look at a couple of examples.

- Cash is an asset. It is on the left side of the T and, therefore, it normally has a debit balance. Therefore, to record an increase in the Cash account, we would debit it. To record a decrease, we would do the opposite: we would credit it. At the end of a period, when we tally up the debits and credits, we would expect there to be more debits than credits, because this account normally has a debit balance.
- Accounts payable is a liability. It is on right side of the T and, therefore, it normally has a credit balance. Therefore, to record an increase in the Accounts Payable account, we would credit it. To record a decrease, we would do the opposite: we would debit it. At the end of a period, when we tally up the debits and credits, we would expect there to be more credits than debits, because this account normally has a credit balance.

Under the template system, each account had its own column in which the transactions affecting it were recorded. These columns were organized just like the accounting equation; that is, asset accounts came first, then the liability accounts, and finally the shareholders' equity accounts. When thinking about the structure of the double-entry accounting system further, it helps to picture a box of playing cards, organized by suit (hearts, clubs, spades, and diamonds) and order (such as 2, 3, 4, 5 or Jack, Queen, King, Ace). If you were looking for a specific card, say the 8 of clubs, it is easy to find it within the organized box

*Accountants use *DR* to abbreviate for debit and *CR* to abbreviate for credit. These abbreviations stem from the first and last letters of the old English terms *debitor* and *creditor* (much like *Mr.* is used as an abbreviation for *Mister*). While the term *debitor* is seldom used any more, *creditor* is still commonly used, as are the abbreviations for both.

of cards. Continuing with this analogy, picture each account in the double-entry accounting system having its own card, with the box of cards organized by type of account; that is, asset cards coming first, followed by the cards for the liability accounts and then the cards for the shareholders' equity accounts. Within each type of account, the cards will also be in order of **liquidity**. That is, the most current assets will come before the non-current assets and the current liabilities will come before the non-current liabilities. Just as with the deck of cards, if we know which account we are looking for, it is easy to find it within the box of cards. The box of cards is known as the **general ledger** (or **G/L**), so each account is referred to as a **general ledger account**. Each card will have the account name written on top of a big T as follows:

CASH

All of the transactions affecting that account are recorded as debits or credits on that particular card. For example, since cash is an asset that normally has a debit balance, transactions increasing the account are recorded on the debit side (or left side), while transactions that decrease the account are recorded on the credit side (or right side). After all of the transactions for the period are recorded, each side is totalled, but the account is expected to end up with a net debit balance (that is, with more debits than credits).

> **HELPFUL HINT**
> Remember that increases in accounts *are recorded in the same way as the account balances:*
> - Asset accounts normally have debit balances; increases in assets are also recorded as debits.
> - Liability and shareholders' equity accounts normally have credit balances; increases in liabilities and shareholders' equity are also recorded as credits.

Another key difference between the template method and the double-entry accounting system is that there are cards for revenue accounts, expense accounts, and the Dividends Declared account. You will recall that transactions affecting these accounts were recorded in the retained earnings column in the template method. This is not the case under the double-entry accounting system. Instead, we will use specific accounts for them. At the end of each accounting period, we will transfer the balances of the Revenues, Expenses, and Dividends Declared accounts to the Retained Earnings account. This is the closing entry process, which we will discuss later in the chapter. For now, it is important to understand that we can no longer make entries directly to the Retained Earnings account. The ability to easily track revenues and expenses is essential for managing any business and this is one of the significant advantages of the double-entry accounting system.

Given that each revenue account, expense account, and dividends declared account will have its own card, it is important to understand what their normal balances are. The easiest way to think of this is to reflect on the impact each of these has on retained earnings. In Chapter 2, we discussed the following:

RETAINED EARNINGS =
Opening Retained Earnings
\+ Net Income
− Dividends Declared
Ending Retained Earnings

\+ Revenues
− Expenses
Net Income

From this we can deduce the following:

- Revenues ultimately increase Retained Earnings because they increase net income, which increases retained earnings.
- Expenses ultimately decrease Retained Earnings because they decrease net income and a lower net income means lower retained earnings.
- Dividends declared decrease Retained Earnings because they are a distribution of retained earnings.

If we know the above and we know that Retained Earnings normally has a credit balance (that is, it is on the right side of the "T"), then we also know the following.

> **KEY POINTS**
> - Revenue accounts normally have a credit balance.
> - Expense accounts normally have a debit balance.
> - The Dividends Declared account normally has a debit balance.

- Revenue accounts will normally have a credit balance. This is because revenue accounts increase Retained Earnings and Retained Earnings normally has a credit balance, so it must be credited to increase it.
- Expense accounts will normally have a debit balance. This is because expense accounts decrease Retained Earnings and Retained Earnings normally has a credit balance, so it must be debited to decrease it.
- Dividends Declared will normally have a debit balance. This is because Dividends Declared decreases Retained Earnings and Retained Earnings normally has a credit balance, so it must be debited to decrease it.

Exhibit 3-1 presents a visual summary of the normal balance rules.

Exhibit 3-1 Normal Balance Illustration

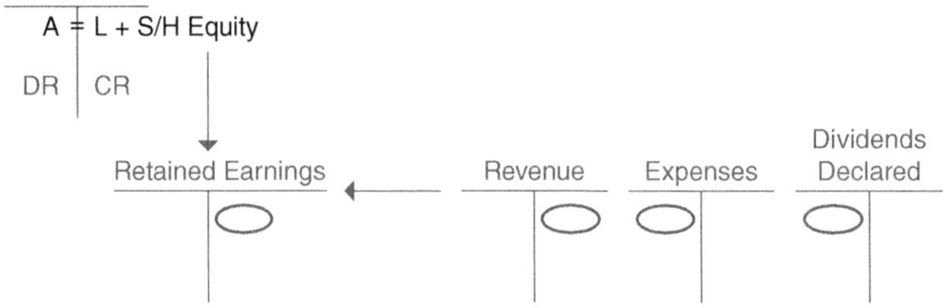

Exhibit 3-2 presents an expanded version of the normal balance illustration, with the specific rules for each type of account, including Revenues, Expenses, and Dividends Declared.

Exhibit 3-2 Expanded Normal Balance Illustration

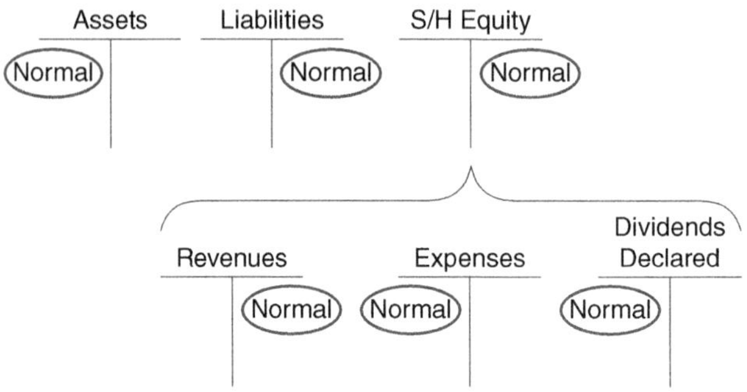

UNDERSTANDING THE ACCOUNTING CYCLE

LEARNING OBJECTIVE 3
Identify and explain the steps in the accounting cycle.

What are the steps in the accounting cycle?

We are now ready to look at the whole system by which transactions are first measured, recorded, and summarized, and then communicated to users through financial statements. This system is called the **accounting cycle** because it is repeated each accounting period.

Exhibit 3-3 illustrates the complete cycle. Each of the steps will be discussed in the subsections that follow.

Exhibit 3-3 The Accounting Cycle

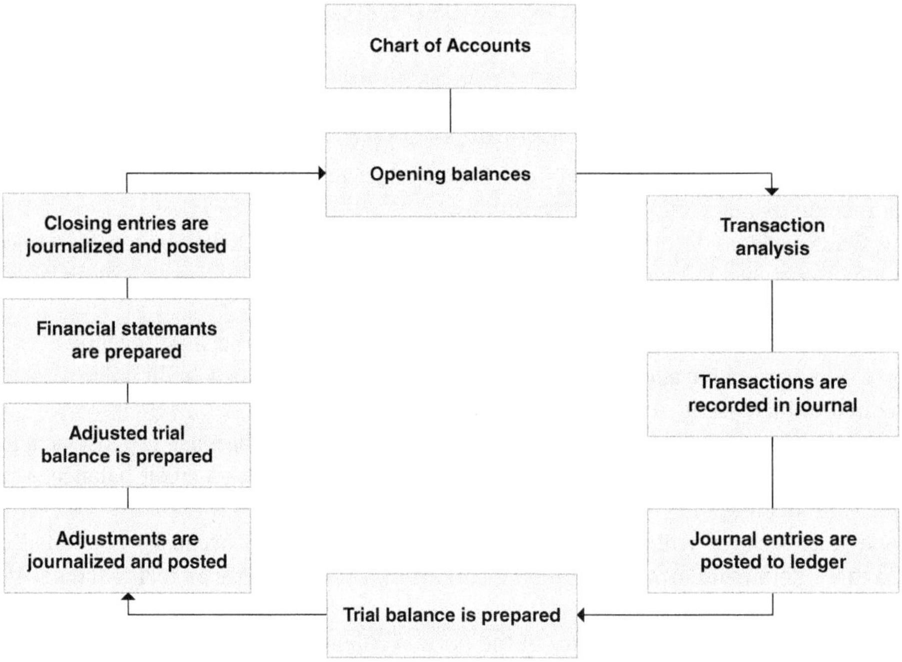

As we proceed through a discussion of the accounting cycle, we will demonstrate each stage by revisiting the Sample Company Ltd. ("SCL") example that we used in Chapter 2. In that chapter, we analyzed and recorded SCL's January transactions using the template method and then prepared the company's financial statements for the month of January. In this chapter, we will use these same transactions to explain how they are recorded within the double-entry accounting system and to illustrate each of the steps in the accounting cycle. You can refer back to the transaction analysis in Chapter 2 for any of the transactions if needed as we learn how to record them within the double-entry accounting system.

A system for maintaining accounting records can be as simple as a notebook, in which everything is processed by hand, or as sophisticated as a computerized system. We will use a simple manual system to illustrate the accounting cycle. However, the same underlying processes apply to any accounting system, no matter how simple or sophisticated it is.

THE CHART OF ACCOUNTS

What is the chart of accounts?

■ LEARNING OBJECTIVE 4
Explain the significance of a company's decisions regarding its chart of accounts and the implications of subsequent changes.

Accounting systems are information systems. When a company is formed, one of the most critical initial decisions management makes as they set up the accounting system is to determine what information they need to manage the business. They would ask themselves the following questions:

- What information is needed to make well-informed decisions?
- What information is needed by outside users?
- What information is needed to satisfy the applicable financial reporting standards?

The information needs of managers differ, so companies in the same type of business will develop their own unique information systems and capture different information or summarize information in different ways.

Each type of information that management wishes to capture requires its own account in which it can be recorded. In Chapter 2, each column within the template was considered an account and all of the transactions affecting that account were recorded in that column. As we discussed above, the double-entry accounting system also uses accounts, but rather than columns, there are cards (although they are generally virtual), one for each account.

The list of all of a company's accounts is known as its **chart of accounts**. Establishing the chart of accounts is the starting point for a company's initial accounting cycle. However, the chart of accounts is dynamic and can be changed. As a company grows, management may need to add different types of accounts, such as when different types of capital assets are purchased or when new types of products and services are offered to customers. Although there are certain account titles that are commonly used, an account can be given any name that makes sense to the company and describes the account's purpose. In most accounting systems, each of the accounts in the chart of accounts would also be identified by a number that indicates the sequence of the accounts and makes it easier to record transactions. In this textbook, accounts are designated by their names and not by account numbers.

Exhibit 3-4 shows the chart of accounts for Sample Company Ltd. It consists of all the accounts that were used to record SCL's transactions in Chapter 2. There is an account for each column that was used in the template method. There are also accounts for Revenues, Expenses, and Dividends Declared because transactions affecting these accounts will no longer be recorded directly to Retained Earnings.

Notice that the accounts are listed in the chart of accounts in the order in which they will appear on the financial statements. Accounts are kept in this order so that it is easy to locate them in the general ledger and easier to prepare the financial statements. If account numbers are assigned to the accounts, a different set of account numbers will usually be assigned to each section of the financial statements. For example, many companies using four-digit account numbers will assign numbers between 1000 and 1999 to assets, 2000–2999 to liabilities, 3000–3999 to shareholders' equity, 4000–4999 to revenues, 5000–5999 to expenses, and so on.

Exhibit 3-4 Sample Company Limited's Chart of Accounts

Assets
- Cash
- Accounts Receivable
- Inventory
- Prepaid Expenses
- Equipment
- Land

Liabilities
- Accounts Payable
- Interest Payable
- Bank Loan Payable

Shareholders' Equity
- Common Shares
- Retained Earnings

Revenue Account
- Sales Revenue

Expense Account
- Cost of Goods Sold
- Wages Expense
- Rent Expense
- Utilities Expense
- Depreciation Expense
- Insurance Expense
- Interest Expense

Dividends Declared

Can companies change their chart of accounts and what are the implications if they do?

Yes, companies can and do make changes to their chart of accounts. Companies can add new accounts when they enter into new types of operations, open new locations, wish to capture information at a different level of detail, and so on. They can also delete accounts that are no longer required. Changes to permanent accounts (assets, liabilities, and shareholders' equity accounts) within the chart of accounts can be made anytime. However, changes to temporary accounts (revenue and expense accounts) are generally made only at the beginning of an accounting period. This is because management normally wants to capture annual data related to the company's revenues and expenses. Introducing new revenue and expense accounts during a cycle would require the company to go back and adjust the accounting for any such revenues or expenses already recorded in the period or else it would have incomplete information. Of course, if the revenue or expense account being added is related to a new activity, this is not a problem.

OPENING BALANCES

LEARNING OBJECTIVE 5
Explain the difference between permanent and temporary accounts.

What is the difference between permanent and temporary accounts?

When a company begins operations, none of its accounts will have an opening balance. This will not be the case once a company completes its first accounting cycle because all of the accounts on its statement of financial position (its assets, liabilities, and shareholders' equity) will have balances at the end of the cycle. These ending balances will become the opening balances for the next cycle; that is, the cash that the company had at the end of its accounting cycle will be the cash it begins the next cycle with. Accounts with balances that carry over from one period to the next are known as **permanent accounts**.

KEY POINTS
- Asset, liabilities, and shareholders' equity accounts are permanent accounts.
- Revenue, expense, and dividends declared accounts are temporary accounts.

Management normally wants to track its revenues and expenses each period (such as each year) in order to assess things such as the profitability of operations and the outcome of their decisions. They are less interested in cumulative numbers, such as sales revenues earned or total wages paid during the life of the company. As a result, it is necessary for the balances in all the accounts that appear on the statement of income (that is, all revenues and expenses) to be "reset" at the end of each accounting cycle or period. Accounts with balances that are closed at the end of each accounting period are known as **temporary accounts**. The amount of dividends declared is also tracked period to period and the Dividends Declared account is also a temporary account. The balance in each temporary account is transferred to retained earnings, so that it starts each accounting cycle with zero or nil balances. This transfer/reset process is accomplished through closing entries. These entries are discussed a little later in the chapter.

TRANSACTION ANALYSIS AND RECORDING

How are transactions identified?

LEARNING OBJECTIVE 6
Identify and record transactions in the general journal and general ledger.

The next step in the accounting cycle is transaction analysis. This involves identifying whether an event or transaction has occurred and, if so, determining its effects on the company's accounts.

Evidence of a transaction or event is usually some sort of "source document"—a document that is received or created by the company indicating that a transaction that needs to be recorded has happened. Examples of source documents include invoices, cheques, cash register tapes, bank deposit slips, and shipping documents.

When a transaction or event has occurred, the accountant must analyze it to determine what accounts have been affected and how the transaction should be recorded in the accounting system. We introduced this phase of the process in Chapter 2, where we analyzed the effects of various transactions on the basic accounting equation and recorded the results by entering positive and negative amounts in the template columns. In this chapter—and throughout the remainder of this book—we will analyze the effects of transactions to see how they should be recorded as debits and credits in a company's accounts.

How are transactions recorded in the general journal?

KEY POINTS

- Transactions are initially recorded in the general journal.
- Subsequently, they are posted to the general ledger.

After an accountant has decided how to record transactions, appropriate entries must be made in the accounting system. The initial entries are usually made in the **general journal**. The journal is a chronological listing of all the events that are recorded in the accounting system. It is similar to the diary or travel journal that many people keep of their daily life or travels. A journal could be as simple as a book in which a chronological list of transactions is recorded, but most organizations' journals are computerized. Each entry in the journal shows the effects of a transaction on the company's accounts and is called a **journal entry**.

Journal entries are always dated and are normally numbered sequentially. Then, the names of the accounts affected by the transaction, and the amounts involved, are listed. The accounts being debited are listed first, followed by the accounts being credited. The credit portions are indented. Finally, an explanation of the transaction is generally included for future reference.

In this book, we will not include explanations with each journal entry because they would just repeat the wording in the question. As such, the format for presenting journal entries is:

BASIC JOURNAL ENTRY FORMAT		
Date and/or entry number	DR Name of Account CR Name of Account	Amount debited Amount credited

As illustrated above, when journal entries are made, the customary practice is to list the accounts that are being debited before the accounts that are being credited, and to indent the accounts that are being credited. Of course, each journal entry must keep the accounting system balanced. As such, the total debits must equal the total credits. Also, the dollar signs are omitted from journal entries; in this text, assume all amounts in journal entries are in dollars.

We will now illustrate the process of analyzing transactions and recording them as journal entries by working through SCL's January transactions (see Exhibit 3-5). Each transaction will be presented and analyzed to determine what accounts are affected and whether they should be debited or credited. Then the journal entry to record the transaction will be presented. You should study this material carefully to ensure that you understand how debits and credits are applied and how journal entries are used to record transactions in an accounting system.

Exhibit 3-5 SCL's Transactions for January 2016

#	Date	Description
1	Jan. 1	SCL issued 10,000 common shares in exchange for $250,000 cash.
2	Jan. 1	To raise additional financing, SCL borrowed $100,000 from its bank. The loan principal is due in three years, while the interest rate on the loan is 6% per year. The interest is payable every three months.
3	Jan. 1	The company rented a retail location, paying $1,100 in rent for the month of January.
4	Jan. 1	The company paid $65,000 to purchase equipment.
5	Jan. 1	SCL paid $1,800 cash for a one-year insurance policy covering the new equipment for the period January 1–December 31.
6	Jan. 6	SCL purchased some land for $180,000 on which it plans to build a warehouse in the future.
7	Jan. 10	The company bought $23,000 of inventory from suppliers on account. (That is, SCL will pay for the goods at a later date.)
8	Jan. 12	SCL sold products to customers for $34,000, of which $21,000 was received in cash and the balance was on account. (That is, SCL's customers will pay at a later date.) The products that were sold had cost SCL $17,000.
9	Jan. 20	SCL received $11,000 from its customers as payments on their accounts that originated from the sale on January 12.
10	Jan. 22	The company made payments of $13,500 to its suppliers, settling part of the account that originated from the purchase on January 10.
11	Jan. 25	SCL paid monthly utility costs of $1,900.
12	Jan. 26	SCL paid advertising costs for the month of $2,200.
13	Jan. 28	SCL paid $2,900 in wages to its employees for the month of January.
14	Jan. 31	Dividends in the amount of $400 were declared by SCL's board of directors and paid.
15	Jan. 31	SCL's accountant determined that the depreciation expense on the company's equipment was $850 per month.
16	Jan. 31	SCL's insurance expense was recorded for January.
17	Jan. 31	SCL recorded the interest expense on the bank loan for the month. Although the principal of the loan does not have to be repaid for three years, the company is incurring interest expense each month that the loan is outstanding.

Transaction 1: Issuing Shares for Cash

SCL issued 10,000 common shares in exchange for $250,000 cash.

ANALYSIS OF TRANSACTION
Assets (specifically, Cash) **increased** by $250,000 **Shareholders' Equity** (specifically, Common Shares) **increased** by $250,000

This analysis must be translated into debits and credits. As we have learned, asset accounts normally have a debit balance; therefore, an increase to the Cash account is recorded as a debit. Shareholders' equity accounts normally have a credit balance; therefore, the increase to the Common Shares account is recorded as a credit.

Jan. 1	DR Cash	250,000	
	CR Common Shares		250,000

From this transaction, we can see that the total amount debited in the transaction equals the total amount credited. This is required in order to keep the accounting records in balance.

Transaction 2: Taking Out a Bank Loan

To raise additional financing, SCL borrowed $100,000 from its bank. The loan principal is due in three years, while the interest rate on the loan is 6% per year. The interest is payable every three months.

ANALYSIS OF TRANSACTION
Assets (specifically, Cash) **increased** by $100,000 **Liabilities** (specifically, Bank Loan Payable) **increased** by $100,000

As asset accounts normally have a debit balance, the increase to the Cash account is recorded as a debit. Liability accounts normally have a credit balance; therefore, the increase to the Bank Loan Payable account is recorded as a credit.

Jan. 1	DR Cash	100,000	
	CR Bank Loan Payable		100,000

Transaction 3: Paying Rent for the Month

The company rented a retail location, paying $1,100 in rent for the month of January.

ANALYSIS OF TRANSACTION
Assets (specifically, Cash) **decreased** by $1,100 **Expenses** (specifically, Rent Expense) **increased** by $1,100

As asset accounts normally have a debit balance, a decrease to the Cash account is recorded as a credit. Since they ultimately reduce retained earnings, expense accounts normally have a debit balance. Therefore, the increase to the Rent Expense account is recorded as a debit.

Jan. 1	DR Rent Expense	1,100	
	CR Cash		1,100

Transaction 4: Purchasing Equipment

The company paid $65,000 to purchase equipment.

ANALYSIS OF TRANSACTION
Assets (specifically, Equipment) **increased** by $65,000 **Assets** (specifically, Cash) **decreased** by $65,000

Asset accounts normally have a debit balance. Therefore, the Equipment account must be debited to record the increase (the new equipment) and the Cash account must be credited (that is, the opposite of its normal balance) to record the decrease.

Jan. 1	DR Equipment	65,000	
	CR Cash		65,000

Transaction 5: Purchasing Insurance Coverage

SCL paid $1,800 cash for a one-year insurance policy covering the new equipment for the period January 1 to December 31.

ANALYSIS OF TRANSACTION
Assets (specifically, Cash) **decreased** by $1,800
Assets (specifically, Prepaid Expenses) **increased** by $1,800

Asset accounts normally have a debit balance. Therefore, the Prepaid Expenses account must be debited to record the increase and the Cash account must be credited (that is, the opposite of its normal balance) to record the decrease.

Jan. 1	DR Prepaid Expenses	1,800	
	CR Cash		1,800

Transaction 6: Purchasing Land

SCL purchased some land for $180,000 on which it plans to build a warehouse in the future.

ANALYSIS OF TRANSACTION
Assets (specifically, Cash) **decreased** by $180,000
Assets (specifically, Land) **increased** by $180,000

Asset accounts normally have a debit balance. Therefore, the Land account must be debited to record the increase (the new land) and the Cash account must be credited (that is, the opposite of its normal balance) to record the decrease.

Jan. 6	DR Land	180,000	
	CR Cash		180,000

Transaction 7: Purchasing Inventory

The company bought $23,000 of inventory from suppliers on account. (That is, SCL will pay for the goods at a later date.)

ANALYSIS OF TRANSACTION
Assets (specifically, Inventory) **increased** by $23,000
Liabilities (specifically, Accounts Payable) **increased** by $23,000

Asset accounts normally have a debit balance. Therefore, the Inventory account must be debited to record the increase (the additional inventory). Liabilities normally have a credit balance. Therefore, the Accounts Payable account must be credited to record the increase.

Jan. 6	DR Inventory	23,000	
	CR Accounts Payable		23,000

Transaction 8: Selling Products to Customers

SCL sold products to customers for $34,000, of which $21,000 was received in cash and the balance was on account. (That is, SCL's customers will pay at a later date.) The products that were sold had cost SCL $17,000.

ANALYSIS OF TRANSACTION	
Part 1	**Assets** (specifically, Cash and Accounts Receivable) **increased** by $34,000 **Revenues** (specifically, Sales Revenue) **increased** by $34,000
Part 2	**Assets** (specifically, Inventory) **decreased** by $17,000 **Expenses** (specifically, Cost of Goods Sold) **increased** by $17,000

As discussed in Chapter 2, when a company sells products to customers, it is useful to separate the transaction into two parts. Part one is to account for the sales revenue and the cash and/or accounts receivable that flow into the company as a result. Part two is to account for the inventory that has been provided to the customer and has become an expense (known as cost of goods sold) to the company.

For part one, because asset accounts normally have a debit balance, the Cash and Accounts Receivable accounts must each be debited to record the increases in both accounts. Revenue accounts normally have a credit balance because they ultimately increase retained earnings. Therefore, the Sales Revenue account must be credited.

For part two, expense accounts, like Cost of Goods Sold, normally have a debit balance because they ultimately reduce retained earnings. Asset accounts like Inventory normally have a debit balance, so this account must be credited to reduce it to reflect the cost of the goods that have been removed from inventory and provided to customers.

Jan. 6	DR Cash	21,000	
	DR Accounts Receivable	13,000	
	CR Sales Revenue		34,000
Jan. 6	DR Cost of Goods Sold	17,000	
	CR Inventory		17,000

Notice that the journal entry for part one affects three accounts. However, the total of the two debits (21,000 and 13,000) is equal to the amount of the credit entry (34,000), so the entry as a whole balances. This illustrates the fact that, although every journal entry must have at least one debit and one credit, a journal entry can have any number of debit and credit parts, as long as the sum of the amounts debited is equal to the sum of the amounts credited. The term **compound journal entry** is used for a journal entry that has more than two parts.

Transaction 9: Collecting Payments from Customers

SCL received $11,000 from its customers as payments on their accounts that originated from the sale on January 12.

ANALYSIS OF TRANSACTION
Assets (specifically, Cash) **increased** by $11,000 **Assets** (specifically, Accounts Receivable) **decreased** by $11,000

Asset accounts normally have a debit balance. Therefore, the Cash account must be debited to record the increase. The opposite must be done to the Accounts Receivable account to reduce it. Therefore, the account must be credited.

Jan. 12	DR Cash	11,000	
	CR Accounts Receivable		11,000

Transaction 10: Paying Suppliers

The company made payments of $13,500 to its suppliers, settling part of the account that originated from the purchase on January 10.

ANALYSIS OF TRANSACTION
Assets (specifically, Cash) **decreased** by $13,500
Liabilities (specifically, Accounts Payable) **decreased** by $13,500

Asset accounts normally have a debit balance. Therefore, to reduce the Cash account, it must be credited to record the decrease. Liabilities normally have a credit balance, so the opposite must be done to the Accounts Payable account to reduce it. Therefore, the account must be debited.

Jan. 22	DR Accounts Payable	13,500	
	CR Cash		13,500

Transaction 11: Paying Utility Costs

SCL paid monthly utility costs of $1,900.

ANALYSIS OF TRANSACTION
Assets (specifically, Cash) **decreased** by $1,900
Expenses (specifically, Utilities Expense) **increased** by $1,900

Asset accounts normally have a debit balance. Therefore, to reduce the Cash account, it must be credited to record the decrease. Expenses normally have a debit balance because they reduce retained earnings. As such, the Utilities Expense account must be debited.

Jan. 25	DR Utilities Expense	1,900	
	CR Cash		1,900

Transaction 12: Paying Advertising Costs

SCL paid advertising costs for the month of $2,200.

ANALYSIS OF TRANSACTION
Assets (specifically, Cash) **decreased** by $2,200
Expenses (specifically, Advertising Expense) **increased** by $2,200

Asset accounts normally have a debit balance. Therefore, to reduce the Cash account, it must be credited to record the decrease. Expenses normally have a debit balance because they reduce retained earnings. As such, the Advertising Expense account must be debited.

Jan. 26	DR Advertising Expense	2,200	
	CR Cash		2,200

Transaction 13: Paying Wages to Employees

SCL paid $2,900 in wages to its employees for the month of January.

ANALYSIS OF TRANSACTION
Assets (specifically, Cash) **decreased** by $2,900
Expenses (specifically, Wages Expense) **increased** by $2,900

Asset accounts normally have a debit balance. Therefore, to reduce the Cash account, it must be credited to record the decrease. Expenses normally have a debit balance because they reduce retained earnings. As such, the Wages Expense account must be debited.

Jan. 28	DR Wages Expense	2,200	
	CR Cash		2,200

Transaction 14: Declaring and Paying Dividends

Dividends in the amount of $400 were declared by SCL's board of directors and paid.

ANALYSIS OF TRANSACTION
Assets (specifically, Cash) **decreased** by $400
Shareholders' Equity (specifically, Dividends Declared) **decreased** by $400

Asset accounts normally have a debit balance. Therefore, to reduce the Cash account, it must be credited to record the decrease. The declaration of dividends reduces retained earnings, so this account normally has a debit balance. As such, the Dividends Declared account must be debited.

Jan. 31	DR Dividends Declared	400	
	CR Cash		400

Transaction 15: Recording Depreciation of Equipment

SCL's accountant determined that the depreciation expense on the company's equipment was $850 per month.

ANALYSIS OF TRANSACTION
Contra-asset accounts (specifically, Accumulated Depreciation, Equipment) **increased** by $850
Expenses (specifically, Depreciation Expense) **increased** by $850

As discussed in the previous chapter, companies allocate the cost of capital assets to those periods in which the asset is expected to help generate revenues. We learned about the straight-line depreciation method, which allocates a consistent portion of the asset's cost each period. In Chapter 2, the depreciation expense for the period was recorded directly to the Capital Asset account as a reduction in that column. While the net effect of doing this is correct, it is not what is done in practice. Instead of reducing the Equipment account, accountants use an account called **Accumulated Depreciation**. This is a **contra-asset account**, which is an asset account, but its normal balance is contrary or opposite to what an asset account would normally have. As such, a contra-asset account normally has a credit balance rather than a debit balance. Using this account to record the cumulative portion of the asset's costs that have been expensed allows accountants to leave the asset's original cost intact in the Equipment account. This enables financial statement users to assess the relative age of a company's capital assets by comparing the asset's costs with the amount recorded in its related contra-asset account. We will explore this concept further in Chapter 8. For now, it is important to know that we will make entries in a capital asset account only when an asset is purchased or sold, but not when recording depreciation.

Capital assets are carried on the statement of financial position at their **carrying value**. Carrying value is the cost of the capital asset less the accumulated depreciation on that asset. It represents the portion of the asset's cost that has yet to be expensed. It does *not* represent the asset's market value (the amount for which it could be sold). It is useful to view carrying value as shown in Exhibit 3-6.

KEY POINTS

- Accumulated Depreciation is a contra-asset account.
- Its normal balance is credit.
- A capital asset's carrying value is its cost less accumulated depreciation.

Exhibit 3-6 Carrying Value

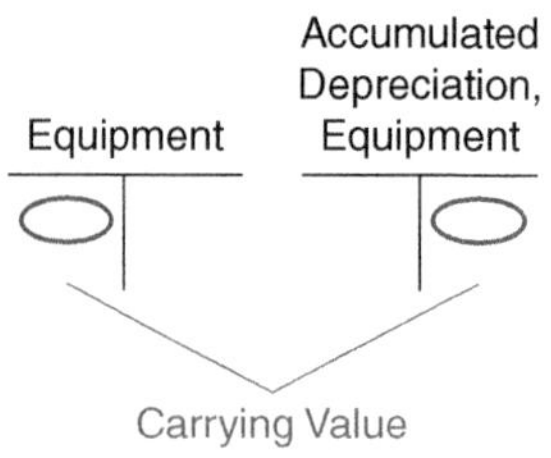

In terms of recording the journal entry for depreciation expense, we will debit the Depreciation Expense account because expense accounts normally have a debit balance. The normal balance of a contra-asset account is a credit, so we will credit the Accumulated Depreciation, Equipment account.

Jan. 31	DR Depreciation Expense	850	
	CR Accumulated Depreciation, Equipment		850

Transaction 16: Recording Insurance Expense

SCL's insurance expense was recorded for January.

ANALYSIS OF TRANSACTION
Assets (specifically, Prepaid Expenses) **decreased** by $150
Expenses (specifically, Insurance Expense) **decreased** by $150

Asset accounts normally have a debit balance. Therefore, to reduce the Prepaid Expenses account, it must be credited. Expenses normally have a debit balance because they reduce retained earnings. As such, the Insurance Expense account must be debited.

Jan. 31	DR Insurance Expense	150	
	CR Prepaid Expenses		150

Transaction 17: Recording Interest Expense

SCL recorded the interest expense on the bank loan for the month. Although the principal of the loan does not have to be repaid for three years, the company is incurring interest expense each month that the loan is outstanding.

ANALYSIS OF TRANSACTION
Liabilities (specifically, Interest Payable) **increased** by $500
Expenses (specifically, Interest Expense) **decreased** by $500

Liabilities normally have a credit balance. Therefore, to increase the Interest Payable account, it must be credited. Expenses normally have a debit balance because they reduce retained earnings. As such, the Interest Expense account must be debited.

Jan. 31	DR Interest Expense	500	
	CR Interest Payable		500

This completes the journal entries required to record SCL's transactions for January 2015 in the company's general journal. These journal entries are an example of how companies initially record their transactions. While companies need the detailed information that is captured in the general journal, they also require information at a summary level.

Let's continue to think of a company's general journal as being similar to a tourist's travel journal. We can visualize how the entries in the travel journal would provide the details of each art gallery or museum visited during the trip. However, if the traveller wanted to know how many galleries or museums they had visited during their trip, they would need to flip through the journal and count up the number of entries in which visits to galleries and museums were recorded. This may not be too difficult on a short trip, but the longer their travels, the longer it would take to obtain the information. This is exactly the same for companies when they require summary information. For example, while they want to record the details of each individual sale, they also want to know their total sales number. Summarizing the information from the general journal is known as posting to the general ledger (or *posting*) and is the next step in the accounting cycle.

Why are transactions also recorded in the general ledger?

While the general journal provides an important chronological record of the effects of each transaction, companies require summarized information. For example, if a manager wanted to know the balance in the Cash account, the accountant would have to take the beginning balance of Cash and add or subtract all the journal entries that affected Cash. To prepare financial statements, the accountant would have to go through this process for all of the accounts in order to determine their ending balances. If the company had hundreds or thousands of journal entries, this would be extremely time-consuming and inefficient. Therefore, to provide more efficient access to information about the cumulative effects of transactions on individual accounts, the next step in the accounting cycle transfers or posts the data in the journal to the accounts in the general ledger.

Earlier in the chapter, we discussed using the analogy of a box of cards for the general ledger. We noted that each account would have its own card and that the debits and credits affecting an account would be recorded on its card. These would then be totalled at the end of each period and an ending debit or credit balance would be determined for each account. The process of transferring the information from the journal entries to the ledger accounts is known as **posting**.

KEY POINTS

- The general journal contains *detailed* information on each *transaction*.
- The general ledger contains *summary* information for each *account*.

Each account in the ledger represents a separate, specific T account, and includes the account name (and its number, if applicable), its beginning balance, all of the postings that affected the account during the period, and its ending balance. Each posting includes the transaction date and number, as well as the amount debited or credited. Including the date and transaction number enables users to trace the amount posted to the related journal entry and, thus, to the transaction details.

The posting process itself is very mechanical and, while we will not focus on it, it is important that you have a basic understanding of it. As such, let's look at how the January transactions affecting SCL's Cash account are posted to the company's Cash account. This is shown in Exhibit 3-7.

As Cash is an asset, it normally has a debit balance. To determine the ending balance of the Cash account, we would add all of the debits posted to the account to its opening balance and subtract all of the credits posted to the account. Because SCL began operations in January, the account had no opening balance. The total debits posted to the account amounted to $382,000, while the total credits posted to the account amounted to $268,800. The difference between these two amounts gives us the account's ending balance of $113,200.

Exhibit 3-7 SCL's Cash Account after the January Transactions have been Posted

Cash					
Opening Bal.	Jan. 1	-			
Entry #1	Jan. 1	250,000			
Entry #2	Jan. 1	100,000			
			1,100	Jan. 1	Entry #3
			65,000	Jan. 1	Entry #4
			1,800	Jan. 1	Entry #5
			180,000	Jan. 6	Entry #6
Entry #8a	Jan. 12	21,000			
Entry #9	Jan. 20	11,000			
			13,500	Jan. 22	Entry #10
			1,900	Jan. 25	Entry #11
			2,200	Jan. 26	Entry #12
			2,900	Jan. 28	Entry #13
			400	Jan. 31	Entry #14
Ending Bal.		113,200			

As a result of the posting references, a user can determine the details for any of the postings to the account. For example, if they want to determine what the $180,000 cash payment on January 6 was related to, they can go to the general journal and look at entry 6. Then they can see the cash was spent to purchase land.

Posting to the ledger can be done daily, weekly, monthly, or at any frequency desired. The timing of the postings is determined to some extent by management's (or the shareholders') need for up-to-date information. If managers need to know the balance in a particular account, say Cash, on a daily basis, then the postings have to be done at least daily. If management needs to know the amount of cash available on an hourly basis, then the postings have to be done at least hourly. Computerized accounting systems can post journal entries instantly, so that the information in the company's general ledger is always up to date. Other computer systems collect journal entries in batches and post them all at the same time (for example, twice a day, after they have been reviewed by management).

At this point, it is important to note that a system consisting only of journal entries would make it difficult for managers to know the balances in the accounts. On the other hand, a system of only ledger accounts, without the original journal entries, would make it difficult to understand the sources of the amounts in the accounts. Accounting systems need both journal entries and ledger accounts in order to collect information in a way that makes it readily accessible and as useful as possible.

HELPFUL HINT
Do not confuse a *trial balance* with a *statement of financial position*. A trial balance lists the balances in *all* the accounts, while a statement of financial position (balance sheet) includes only the asset, liability, and shareholders' equity accounts.

What is the purpose of preparing a trial balance?

The **trial balance** is a listing of all the account balances in the general ledger at a specific point in time. The final balances of each account are listed, with the accounts having final debit balances in one column and accounts having final credit balances in another. A check can then be done to ensure that the total of all accounts with debit balances equals the total of all accounts with credit balances. If these amounts are not equal, an error has been made in the journal entries or the posting process. It must be found and corrected before proceeding.

SCL's trial balance as at January 31, 2016, is presented in Exhibit 3-8.

Exhibit 3-8 SCL's Trial Balance as at January 31, 2016

Account Names	Debit Balances	Credit Balances
Cash	$113,200	
Accounts receivable	2,000	
Inventory	6,000	
Prepaid expenses	1,650	
Equipment	65,000	
Accumulated depreciation, equipment		$ 850
Land	180,000	
Accounts payable		9,500
Interest payable		500
Bank loan payable		100,000
Common shares		250,000
Retained earnings		0
Dividends declared	400	
Sales revenue		34,000
Cost of goods sold	17,000	
Wages expense	2,900	
Utilities expense	1,900	
Rent expense	1,100	
Advertising expense	2,200	
Insurance expense	150	
Depreciation expense	850	
Interest expense	500	
Totals	$394,850	$394,850

Notice that the accounts are presented in the trial balance in the same order that they appear in the ledger. The permanent accounts are presented first (in the same order as they will appear on the statement of financial position), followed by the temporary accounts (the dividends declared, revenues, and expenses). This makes it easier to prepare the financial statements.

The purpose of a trial balance is to assist in detecting errors that may have been made in the recording process. Something is wrong if the ledger does not balance; that is, if the total of all the accounts with debit balances does not equal the total of all the accounts with credit balances. In such cases, there is no point in proceeding until the errors have been found and corrected. This makes the preparation of a trial balance a useful step in the accounting cycle. However, it is important to realize that, because a trial balance only checks whether the total of the debit balances in the ledger accounts equals the total of the credit balances, it cannot detect all types of errors. For example:

- The trial balance will still balance if the correct amount was debited or credited, but to the wrong account. An example is if a purchase of equipment was debited to the Inventory account, rather than to the Equipment account.
- The trial balance will still balance if an incorrect amount was recorded. An example is if a $450 transaction was recorded as a $540 transaction, for both the debit and credit portions of the entry.
- The trial balance will also not detect the complete omission of an entire journal entry. If neither the debit nor the credit portions of a journal entry were posted, the totals on the trial balance will still be equal.

Despite these limitations, preparing a trial balance is very helpful in detecting many other types of common errors in the recording process, and is an important step in the accounting cycle.

HELPFUL HINT

If you prepare a trial balance that does not balance, here are some tips for finding your error.

- First, calculate the difference between the total debits and the total credits, and look for a transaction for this amount that may have been recorded or posted incorrectly.
- Divide the difference from the first step by 2, and check to see whether a debit for this amount has been recorded as a credit, or vice versa.
- Divide the difference from the first step by 9. If it divides evenly—with no decimals—check for a *transposition error:* two digits that have been reversed. An example is 765 written as 756, or 432 written as 234.

ADJUSTING ENTRIES

What are adjusting entries and why are they necessary?

LEARNING OBJECTIVE 7

Explain why adjusting entries are necessary and prepare them.

Most of a company's transactions are easy to identify because there are obvious indications that a transaction has taken place. For example, cash is received or paid, receipts are issued, invoices are received, and so on. However, there are other events that lack any obvious indications that a transaction has taken place. At the end of each accounting period, a number of additional journal entries are normally required to adjust the company's accounts to reflect these transactions. These entries are known as **adjusting entries** and are classified into two broad categories: accruals and deferrals.

Accruals are required when a company needs to recognize a revenue or expense *before* the receipt or payment of cash. A common example of an adjusting entry for an accrued revenue is where a company has made interest-bearing loans to a customer or an employee that involve the interest being paid sometime in the future. Each month, the company would need to accrue the interest revenue earned on these loans. Common examples of adjusting entries for accrued expenses are the entry to recognize the wages expense for employees who have worked but have not yet been paid or the entry to record interest expense that had been incurred during the period on borrowed funds.

Deferrals are required when a company needs to recognize a revenue or expense in an accounting period *after* the cash has been received or paid. For example, when a customer or client has prepaid for goods or services, a deferral adjusting entry is required to recognize the revenue that had been earned during the period between prepayment and the end of the accounting period. For example, your university or college would normally require you to prepay tuition for your semester within the first few weeks of the term. At that time, the institution would record the receipt of cash and a related liability (unearned revenue). Over the course of the semester, the institution would use adjusting entries each month to recognize the revenues earned in that period and the reduction of the unearned revenue liability. An example of a deferral adjusting entry related to expenses is the entries necessary to recognize insurance or rent expense. Both of these are normally paid in advance (that is, they are prepaids) and an adjusting entry is required each month to recognize rent expense or insurance expense and reduce the amount of the prepaid expense. Another example of a deferral adjusting entry related to expenses is the depreciation of capital assets. The capital asset may be paid for years before the accounting period in which it is depreciated (expensed). Some accountants consider depreciation entries to be a third category of adjusting entries. However, as they are really a form of deferral, we will consider them to be part of that category of adjusting entries.

KEY POINTS

- There are two types of adjusting entries: accruals and deferrals.
- Accrual entries are required when a revenue or expense needs to be recognized before cash is received or paid.
- Deferral entries are required when a revenue or expense needs to be recorded after it has been received or paid.

KEY POINTS

Adjusting journal entries:

- never involve cash.
- are made at the end of each accounting period (such as each month, quarter, or year end).

It is important to understand that adjusting entries *never* involve cash. This is because whenever cash is paid or received, companies would account for it at that time. They would not wait until the end of the accounting period, which is when adjusting entries are made. Notice also that the types of items that need to be adjusted generally relate to the passage of time: the depreciation of capital assets, the expiration of prepaid expenses, the accrual of interest, and the consumption of supplies all occur daily. However, they are typically updated only at the end of the accounting period, through adjusting entries. In most situations, there is no external transaction at the end of a period to signal that an adjustment needs to be made. Only the passage of time triggers an adjustment. As a result, the ending balances in the accounts have to be carefully reviewed to determine those that need to be adjusted.

The Conceptual Framework

COMPARABILITY AND ADJUSTING ENTRIES

Comparability is one of the enhancing qualitative characteristics included in the conceptual framework. Accounting standard setters have concluded that financial information is more useful when it can be compared with financial information from a previous period prepared on a comparable basis. Preparing adjusting entries each period to accrue expenses such as interest and wages helps to enhance the period-to-period comparability of financial information.[3]

HELPFUL HINT

Notice that each of these adjusting entries involves both a statement of financial position account and a statement of income account. That is, one half of each adjusting entry (either the debit or the credit) is an asset or liability account, while the other half of the entry is a revenue or expense account.

Adjusting entries are very important. They ensure that all events and transactions related to the period have been accounted for, and thus make the financial statements as accurate as possible. While we did not initially identify them as adjusting entries, transactions 15, 16, and 17 for SCL were just that. Transaction 15 recorded the depreciation of SCL's equipment for the month of January and transaction 16 was the recognition of the company's monthly insurance expense for which premiums for one year's coverage had been paid in advance. These transactions were both examples of deferral entries. Transaction 17 recorded SCL's interest expense on its bank loan for the month of January. This was an example of an accrual entry.

Ethics in Accounting

Many adjusting entries require management to make estimates and exercise judgement, providing opportunities for managers to manipulate earnings or balances on the statement of financial position. For other adjusting entries, there is no obvious evidence that a transaction has taken place and should be recorded.

For example, suppose that you, as an accountant for a company, are asked by your manager to postpone making the adjusting entry to accrue the interest on a company bank loan. Your manager has proposed this because it will increase net income, enabling the company to meet the earnings target it had forecast. The manager has said that the underaccrual of interest can be corrected in the next period and no one will be harmed by your actions. What should you do?

As you consider your response to this, or any, ethical question, it is sometimes helpful to think about who will be affected by your decision (including yourself), and how it will help or hurt them. Particularly, think of who the users or potential users of the financial statements are, and how they might be affected by your action or inaction. This should help you better understand the situation and make an ethical decision.

It is essential that financial statements not be presented in a way that could mislead, or potentially harm, a user—such as creditors and investors, in this case.

The next step in the accounting cycle is the preparation of another trial balance. This one includes the effects of posting all of the adjusting entries to the related accounts.

What is the purpose of preparing an adjusted trial balance?

After all the adjusting entries have been recorded and posted, an **adjusted trial balance** is prepared. This is done to ensure that the total debits in the accounts still equal the total credits. Any imbalance must be corrected before the financial statements are prepared. Since we had already included the effects of
8 SCL's three adjusting entries (transactions 15, 16, and 17) in the company's trial balance (Exhibit 3-8), the adjusted trial balance in Exhibit 3-9 is exactly the same.

Exhibit 3-9 SCL's Adjusted Trial Balance as at January 31, 2016

Account Names	Debit Balances	Credit Balances
Cash	$113,200	
Accounts receivable	2,000	
Inventory	6,000	
Prepaid expenses	1,650	
Equipment	65,000	
Accumulated depreciation, equipment		$ 850
Land	180,000	
Accounts payable		9,500
Interest payable		500
Bank loan payable		100,000
Common shares		250,000
Retained earnings		0
Dividends declared	400	
Sales revenue		34,000
Cost of goods sold	17,000	
Wages expense	2,900	
Utilities expense	1,900	
Rent expense	1,100	
Advertising expense	2,200	
Insurance expense	150	
Depreciation expense	850	
Interest expense	500	
Totals	$394,850	$394,850

PREPARING FINANCIAL STATEMENTS AND CLOSING ENTRIES

What are closing entries and why are they necessary?

▪ **LEARNING OBJECTIVE 8**
Explain why closing entries are necessary and prepare them.

After the adjusted trial balance has been prepared, the financial statements for the period can be prepared. As discussed in Chapters 1 and 2, the statement of income (Exhibit 3-10) is the first statement prepared, using the information related to the revenue and expense accounts in the adjusted trial balance. The next statement is

Exhibit 3-10 Statement of Income

SAMPLE COMPANY LIMITED
Statement of Income
For the month ended January 31, 2016

Sales revenue	$34,000	
Cost of goods sold	17,000	
Gross profit	17,000	50%
Wages expense	2,900	
Utilities expense	1,900	
Rent expense	1,100	
Advertising expense	2,200	
Insurance expense	150	
Depreciation expense	850	
Interest expense	500	
Net income	$ 7,400	

the statement of changes in equity (Exhibit 3-11) and then the statement of financial position (Exhibit 3-12). The final major financial statement to be prepared is the statement of cash flows. However, because we prepared the statement of cash flows for SCL in Chapter 2 and because Chapter 5 is devoted entirely to this topic, we will defer any further discussion of the statement until Chapter 5.

Exhibit 3-11 Statement of Changes in Equity

SAMPLE COMPANY LIMITED
Statement of Changes in Equity
For the month ended January 31, 2016

	Number of Common Shares	Share Capital— Common Shares	Retained Earnings	Total
Balance - Jan. 1	–	$ –	$ –	$ –
Net income	–	–	7,400	7,400
Declaration of dividends	–	–	(400)	(400)
Issuance of common shares	10,000	250,000	–	250,000
Balance - Jan. 31	10,000	$250,000	$ 7,000	$257,000

Exhibit 3-12 Statement of Financial Position

SAMPLE COMPANY LIMITED
Statement of Financial Position
As at January 31, 2016

ASSETS		
Current assets		
Cash	$113,200	
Accounts receivable	2,000	
Inventory	6,000	
Prepaid expenses	1,650	
		$122,850
Non-current assets		
Equipment (net)		64,150
Land		180,000
		244,150
Total assets		$367,000
LIABILITIES		
Current liabilities		
Accounts payable	$ 9,500	
Interest payable	500	
		$ 10,000
Non-current liabilities		
Bank loan payable		100,000
Total liabilities		110,000
SHAREHOLDERS' EQUITY		
Common shares		250,000
Retained earnings		7,000
Total shareholders' equity		257,000
Total liabilities and shareholders' equity		$367,000

You will recall from Chapter 2 that dividends declared are reflected on the statement of changes in equity as a reduction to retained earnings. The sum of opening retained earnings plus net income less dividends declared gives us the company's ending retained earnings balance. This amount must be determined before preparing the company's statement of financial position.

As discussed earlier in the chapter, all of the accounts on a company's statement of financial position are permanent accounts. That is, their balances carry over from one period to the next. Meanwhile, all of the accounts on a company's statement of income are temporary. That is, the balance in each of these accounts is transferred to the Retained Earnings account at the end of each year, so that the temporary accounts start each accounting period with a nil balance. Dividends Declared is also a temporary account and its balance is also transferred to Retained Earnings at the end of each accounting period.

Once the financial statements have been prepared, the balances in the temporary accounts must be transferred to the Retained Earnings account. This resets these accounts so that they have a nil balance to start the next year. This is referred to as *closing the accounts* and the required entries are known as *closing entries*.

Closing entries are required to transfer the balances in the temporary accounts (revenues, expenses, and Dividends Declared) to retained earnings. By doing this, the temporary accounts will start each year with nil balances. Companies are then able to measure their revenues, expenses, and dividends declared for each year rather than having cumulative balances for multiple years. It is much more relevant for financial statement users to know the revenues or expenses of a period, so that this amount can be compared with prior periods, budgets, forecasts, and so on. Preparing closing entries is the last stage of the accounting cycle.

There are a few different ways to prepare closing entries. Some accountants use a two-entry approach, some use three entries, while others use four entries. Some accountants even prepare individual closing entries—one for each temporary account—which could mean hundreds of closing entries. We will use four closing entries to close the temporary accounts because this method most closely replicates the format used to show the changes to a company's retained earnings on the statement of changes in equity. On the statement of changes in equity, a company's ending retained earnings balance is determined as:

= Beginning Retained Earnings + Net Income − Dividends Declared

The first three closing entries will close the revenue and expense accounts while determining net income and transferring it to the Retained Earnings account. The fourth will close the Dividends Declared account. Therefore, the four closing entries are as follows:

1. Close all revenue accounts to the Income Summary account.
2. Close all expense accounts to the Income Summary account.
3. Close the Income Summary account to Retained Earnings.
4. Close the Dividends Declared account to Retained Earnings.

The first closing entry will close all revenue accounts to the Income Summary account. The **Income Summary account** is a temporary account that is opened and closed on the last day of a company's fiscal year. It is used only to determine the amount of the company's net income, which is then transferred to Retained Earnings. Using the Income Summary account minimizes the number of entries flowing through the Retained Earnings account. Because revenue accounts normally have a credit balance, a debit for the total account balance has to be made to each revenue account to reset the account balances to zero and a credit is made to the Income Summary account for the total revenue amount. If there were 100 revenue accounts, closing entry 1 would have 100 debits, but only a single credit transferring total revenues to the Income Summary account.

In the case of SCL, there was only a single revenue account, Sales Revenue, so closing entry 1 is:

Closing Entry 1

Year-end date	DR Sales Revenue	34,000	
	CR Income Summary		34,000

The second closing entry will close all expense accounts to the Income Summary account. Because expense accounts normally have a debit balance, a credit for the total account balance has to be made to each expense account to reset the account balances to zero and a debit is made to the income summary account for the total expense amount. Again, if there were 100 expense accounts, closing entry 2 would have 100 credits, but only a single debit transferring total expenses to the Income Summary account.

In the case of SCL, there were eight expense accounts, so closing entry 2 is:

Closing Entry 2

	DR Income Summary	26,600	
	CR Cost of Goods Sold		17,000
	CR Wages Expense		2,900
	CR Utilities Expense		1,900
Year-end date	CR Rent Expense		1,100
	CR Advertising Expense		2,200
	CR Insurance Expense		150
	CR Depreciation Expense		850
	CR Interest Expense		500

Preparing a T account for Income Summary after the first two closing entries enables us to easily determine net income:

INCOME SUMMARY	
	34,000 Closing Entry #1
Closing Entry #2 26,600	
	7,400 Net Income

It is also worth noting that, if a temporary account had a debit or a credit prior to the closing entries, it remains the same way in the Income Summary account. As such, the total revenue amount is reflected as a credit balance in the Income Summary account and the total expense amount is reflected as a debit balance in the Income Summary account. Because revenues normally exceed expenses for most companies, we would normally expect to have a net credit balance in the Income Summary account, meaning that the company has net income. It is possible to have a net debit balance in the Income Summary account if the company has a net loss for the period; that is, expenses exceed revenues. In the case of SCL, the company was profitable. We know that net income ultimately increases retained earnings. This is what is accomplished through closing entry 3, which in the case of SCL is:

Closing Entry 3

Year-end date	DR Income Summary	7,400	
	CR Retained Earnings		7,400

The final closing entry is required to close the Dividends Declared account to Retained Earnings. We know that dividends are a distribution to shareholders of retained earnings—a company's profits from current and prior years. If a company declared dividends in the year, then Retained Earnings must be reduced accordingly. The Dividends Declared account normally has a debit balance, so the account must be credited to close it. Retained Earnings, which normally has a credit balance, is debited to reflect the reduction in the account balance resulting from the declaration of dividends. In the case of SCL, the company declared dividends of $400 during the year, so closing entry 4 is as follows:

Closing Entry 4

Year-end date	DR Retained Earnings	400	
	CR Dividends Declared		400

If we prepared a T account for the Retained Earnings account after the four closing entries, it would be as follows:

RETAINED EARNINGS

		–	Opening Balance
		7,400	Net Income – Closing Entry #3
Closing Entry #4 – Dividends Declared	400		
		7,000	Ending Balance

This ending retained earnings balance equals the amount of retained earnings on SCL's statement of changes in equity (Exhibit 3-11) and the company's statement of financial position (Exhibit 3-12).

Exhibit 3-13 provides an overview of the four closing entries, including their effects on the Income Summary and Retained Earnings accounts.

Exhibit 3-13 Overview of Closing Entry Process

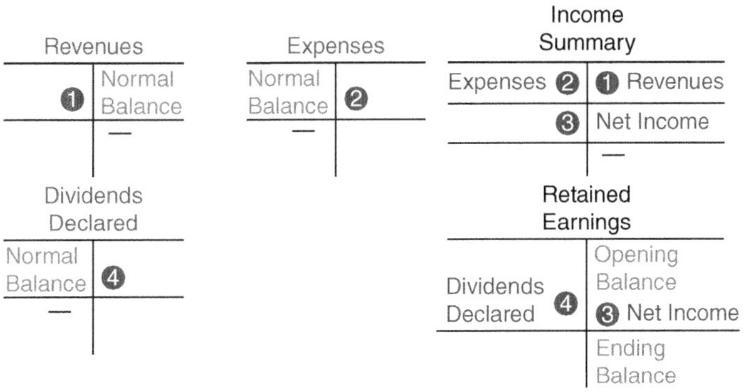

The closing entry process has achieved two key objectives:

- The balance in the Retained Earnings account has been brought up to date by adding the net income for the period and deducting the dividends declared during the period.
- The balances in all of the temporary accounts have been reset to zero, so that the accounts are ready to use at the start of the next accounting period.

This completes our review of the accounting cycle. As with any cycle, the ending of one cycle is the beginning of the next. With the exception of the closing entry process, which happens only once a year, most companies will have monthly cycles, meaning they will prepare adjusting entries and financial statements at the end of each month.

KEY POINTS

Closing entries:

- transfer the balances in all temporary accounts to Retained Earnings.
- reset all temporary account balances to zero.
- are made at the end of each year.

SUMMARY

1. **Explain how the double-entry accounting system works, including how it overcomes the limitations of the template approach.**
   - Every transaction must be recorded in a way that affects at least two accounts, with the effects of these entries being equal and offsetting.
   - The double-entry accounting system enables the use of a huge number of accounts and is not limited to a fixed number of columns as is the case with the template approach. This allows the company to capture information at the level of detail required to manage the business, yet make it easy to summarize the information for reporting purposes.
2. **Explain the normal balance concept and how it is used within the double-entry accounting system.**
   - The normal balance concept is used to determine whether an account *normally* has a debit or credit balance.
   - To determine an account's normal balance, a "T" is drawn through the middle of the accounting equation. Accounts on the left side of the "T" (assets) normally have a debit (DR) balance, while accounts on the right side of the "T" (liabilities and shareholders' equity) normally have a credit (CR) balance.
   - An account's normal balance illustrates what needs to be done to increase that account. The opposite is done to decrease it.
   - As Retained Earnings is a shareholders' equity account, it normally has a credit balance. Therefore, to increase it, we would credit it, and to decrease it, we would debit it.
   - Following this, revenue accounts, which ultimately increase retained earnings, normally have a credit balance. Expense and dividends declared accounts, which ultimately decrease retained earnings, normally have a debit balance.
3. **Identify and explain the steps in the accounting cycle.**
   - The steps in the accounting cycle are: (1) start with opening balances, (2) complete transaction analysis, (3) record transactions in the general journal, (4) post transactions to the general

ledger, (5) prepare a trial balance, (6) record and post adjusting entries, (7) prepare an adjusted trial balance, (8) prepare financial statements, and (9) prepare closing entries.

- At a minimum, this cycle is repeated annually, but parts of it repeat much more frequently (quarterly, monthly, weekly, or even daily).

4. **Explain the significance of a company's decisions regarding its chart of accounts and the implications of subsequent changes.**
   - The chart of accounts outlines the type of information management wishes to capture to assist them in managing the business.
   - The chart of accounts is dynamic and can be changed when the company enters into new types of operations, opens new locations, requires more detailed information, or requires less detailed information.
   - Changes to the chart of accounts are most often introduced at the beginning of a fiscal year.

5. **Explain the difference between permanent and temporary accounts.**
   - Permanent accounts have balances that are carried over from one accounting period to the next.
   - Temporary accounts have balances that are closed to retained earnings at the end of each accounting period. That is, they are reset to zero.
   - All of the accounts on the statement of financial position (assets, liabilities, and shareholders' equity accounts) are permanent accounts.
   - All of the accounts on the statement of income (revenues and expenses) and Dividends Declared are temporary accounts.

6. **Identify and record transactions in the general journal and general ledger.**
   - The general journal is a chronological listing of all transactions. It contains detailed information on each transaction.
   - Each journal entry must affect two or more accounts and the total dollar amount of debits in the entry must be equal to the total dollar amount of credits. In other words, total DR = total CR.
   - On a periodic basis (such as daily, weekly, or monthly), the information recorded in the general journal is posted to the general ledger.
   - The general ledger is used to prepare summary information for each account. The detail from each journal entry affecting a specific account is recorded in the general ledger account for that specific account.
   - A trial balance is prepared to ensure that the total of all debits posted to the general ledger is equal to the total credits posted.

7. **Explain why adjusting entries are necessary and prepare them.**
   - Adjusting entries are required at the end of each accounting period to record transactions that may have been missed.
   - There are two types of adjusting entries: accruals and deferrals.
   - Accrual entries are used to record revenues or expenses before cash is received or paid.
   - Deferral entries are used to record revenues or expenses after cash has been received or paid.
   - Depreciation is a type of deferral entry.
   - Adjusting entries never involve cash.

8. **Explain why closing entries are necessary and prepare them.**
   - Closing entries are used to close temporary accounts and transfer the balances in these accounts to Retained Earnings.
   - There are four closing entries: (1) close all revenue accounts to the Income Summary account, (2) close all expense accounts to the Income Summary account, (3) close the Income Summary Account to Retained Earnings, and (4) close Dividends Declared to Retained Earnings.

KEY TERMS

Accounting cycle ( )
Accruals ( )
Accumulated Depreciation ( )
Adjusted trial balance ( )
Adjusting entries ( )
Carrying value ( )
Chart of accounts ( )
Closing entries ( )
Compound journal entry ( )
Contra-asset account ( )
Credit ( )
Debit ( )
Deferrals ( )
Double-entry accounting system ( )
General journal ( )
General ledger (G/L) ( )
General ledger account ( )
Income Summary account ( )
Journal entry ( )
Liquidity ( )
Normal balance ( )
Permanent accounts ( )
Posting ( )
Temporary accounts ( )
Trial balance ( )

ABBREVIATIONS USED

CR	Credit
DR	Debit
G/L	General ledger

SYNONYMS

Carrying Value | Net Book Value

CHAPTER END REVIEW PROBLEM I

This problem will reinforce and extend what you have learned in this chapter about transaction analysis, journal entries, and adjusting entries. You should carefully work through the following problem and then check your work against the suggested solution.

Exhibit 3-14 shows the trial balance of Matchett Manufacturing Ltd. ("MML") at November 30, 2016.

STRATEGIES FOR SUCCESS:

- As you record transactions, remember that the total dollar value of the debits must equal the total dollar value of the credits. In other words, the entry must balance.
- When analyzing each transaction, think about:
  - What accounts are being affected?
  - What kind of accounts are they (asset, liability, and so on)?
  - Are they increasing or decreasing? If so, by what amount?
  - What is the normal balance of each account (see Exhibit 3-1)?
- While not all transactions will affect the Cash account, many do. It is often easiest to "think cash first," as it is usually straightforward to think about whether cash is increasing or decreasing. This can provide you with half of the journal entry right away.

EXHIBIT 3-14 MML'S TRIAL BALANCE

MATCHETT MANUFACTURING LIMITED
Trial Balance
As at November 30, 2016

Account	Debit (DR)	Credit (CR)
Cash	$ 37,000	
Accounts receivable	298,900	
Inventory	108,000	
Prepaid expenses	8,400	
Equipment	76,000	
Accumulated depreciation, equipment		$ 16,000
Building	500,000	
Accumulated depreciation, building		75,200
Land	385,000	
Accounts payable		145,000
Wages payable		23,000
Bank loan payable		400,000
Common shares		250,000
Retained earnings		230,800
Dividends declared	30,000	
Sales revenue		1,650,000
Cost of goods sold	908,000	
Wages expense	375,000	
Insurance expense	12,000	
Depreciation expense	29,700	
Interest expense	22,000	
	$2,790,000	$2,790,000

MML has a December 31 year end and had the following transactions in December 2016:

1. Sales for the month totalled $155,000, all on account. The inventory sold had cost MML $70,000.
2. Payments received from customers during the month in relation to their accounts receivable were $215,900.
3. The company's employees earned wages of $37,300 during the month.
4. The company made wage payments of $41,700 to its employees during the month.
5. Purchases of inventory, all on account, amounted to $125,000.
6. During the month, the company made payments to suppliers totalling $98,000.
7. The company declared dividends of $10,000 on its 100,000 common shares. MML had a policy of declaring quarterly dividends of this amount. The dividends from the first three quarters had been paid on April 15, 2016; July 15, 2016; and October 15, 2016. The dividends from the last quarter will be paid on January 15, 2017.

MML also prepared adjusting entries for the following transactions:

A1. Interest on the company's bank loan was recorded for the month of December. The interest rate on the loan was 6% per year and was payable on the first day of each month. (That is, the interest for December 2016 will be paid on January 1, 2017.)

A2. Depreciation expense for the month of December was recorded on MML's equipment. The equipment, which had been purchased on January 1, 2015, for $76,000, was estimated to have a useful life of five years and a residual value of $10,000. MML uses the straight-line method to depreciate its equipment.

A3. Depreciation expense for the month of December was recorded on MML's building. The building had been purchased on January 1, 2013, at a cost of $500,000. Company management had determined that it had a useful life of 25 years and a residual value of $20,000. MML uses the straight-line method to depreciate the building.

A4. Insurance expense for the month of December was recorded. The company had renewed insurance coverage on its equipment and building on July 1, 2016, when its previous policy ended. The annual premiums of $14,400 were paid at that time.

Required:

a. Prepare journal entries for transactions 1 to 7.
b. Prepare adjusting entries for transactions A1 to A4.

CHAPTER END REVIEW PROBLEM 2

STRATEGIES FOR SUCCESS:

- Trial balances are normally prepared with accounts ordered by type (assets, liabilities, shareholders' equity, revenues, and expenses). This means that you can easily group the accounts into the categories needed to prepare the financial statements.
- Remember that the statement of income must be prepared first, so that net income can be used to prepare the statement of changes in equity. The statement of financial position can then be prepared.
- Only temporary accounts are closed at the end of an accounting period. This means that only revenue, expense, and dividends declared accounts are closed. When a trial balance has been prepared with the accounts ordered by type, it is helpful to draw a line under the Retained Earnings account. All accounts below the line are temporary and must be closed. All accounts above the line should remain open, so do not touch them.
- It is helpful to prepare the four closing entries in the same order each time.
- It is helpful to use a T account for both the Income Summary and Retained Earnings accounts when preparing closing entries.

This problem will reinforce and extend what you have learned in this chapter about closing entries. After the journal entries and adjusting entries for MML had been posted, the company prepared an adjusted trial balance (see Exhibit 3-15).

EXHIBIT 3-15 MML'S ADJUSTED TRIAL BALANCE

MATCHETT MANUFACTURING LIMITED
Adjusted Trial Balance
As at December 31, 2016

Account	Debit (DR)	Credit (CR)
Cash	$ 113,200	
Accounts receivable	238,000	
Inventory	163,000	
Prepaid expenses	7,200	
Equipment	76,000	
Accumulated depreciation, equipment		$ 17,100
Building	500,000	
Accumulated depreciation, building		76,800
Land	385,000	
Accounts payable		172,000
Wages payable		18,600
Dividends payable		10,000
Interest payable		2,000
Bank loan payable		400,000
Common shares		250,000
Retained earnings		230,800
Dividends declared	40,000	
Sales revenue		1,805,000
Cost of goods sold	978,000	
Wages expense	412,300	
Insurance expense	13,200	
Depreciation expense	32,400	
Interest expense	24,000	
	$2,982,300	$2,982,300

Required:

a. Prepare a statement of income for 2016, a statement of changes in equity, and a classified statement of financial position.
b. Prepare the closing entries required to ready MML's accounts for the beginning of 2017.

Suggested Solution To Chapter End Review Problem I

The journal entries and adjusting entries for MML are shown in Exhibit 3-16. Extended explanations are provided for transaction 1 and the four adjusting entries because they are the more complex transactions.

EXHIBIT 3-16 MML'S JOURNAL ENTRIES AND ADJUSTING ENTRIES FOR DECEMBER 2016

Journal Entries:		
1a. Accounts Receivable	155,000	
Sales Revenue		155,000
1b. Cost of Goods Sold	70,000	
Inventory		70,000
2. Cash	215,900	
Accounts Receivable		215,900
3. Wages Expense	37,300	
Wages Payable		37,300
4. Wages Payable	41,700	
Cash		41,700
5. Inventory	125,000	
Accounts Payable		125,000
6. Accounts Payable	98,000	
Cash		98,000
7. Dividends Declared	10,000	
Dividends Payable		10,000
Adjusting entries:		
A1. Interest Expense	2,000	
Interest Payable		2,000
A2. Depreciation Expense	1,100	
Accumulated Depreciation, Equipment		1,100
A3. Depreciation Expense	1,600	
Accumulated Depreciation, Building		1,600
A4. Insurance Expense	1,200	
Prepaid Expenses		1,200

Transaction 1: Sale of Goods

As we discussed in Chapter 2, when you see the word *sale*, you should think "two parts." Part 1 is to account for the sale and the related cash and accounts receivable. Part 2 is to account for the cost of goods sold and inventory. The information to prepare part 1 will always be provided because a company knows its selling price and whether the sale was for cash or on account. The information for part 2 may not be available, because some companies may not know the cost of the products being sold at the time of sale.

Adjusting Entry 1: Interest

MML has had an outstanding bank loan for the entire month. Even though the interest will not be paid until January 1, the expense was incurred in December. The interest rate on the loan is 6% and it is important to remember that interest rates are stated in annual terms. As such, the interest rate must be prorated to determine the monthly interest expense. The interest expense for the month is determined as follows:

$$\$400,000 \times 6\% \times 1/12 = \$2,000$$

Adjusting Entry 2: Depreciation Expense (Equipment)

Depreciation expense must be recorded to allocate a portion of a capital asset's cost to each period in which it is being used to generate revenue. As we have discussed, there are a number of different methods that can be used to depreciate capital assets, but for now, we will assume that companies use the straight-line method. This method allocates a consistent amount of the asset's cost each period. Most companies use a single account to record depreciation expense, because it is usually a single line on the statement of income. However, companies use separate accumulated depreciation accounts for each capital asset, because separate contra-asset accounts are required to report the carrying value of each asset category on the statement of financial position.

As we have discussed, an accumulated depreciation account is referred to as a contra-asset because its normal balance is contrary or opposite to the normal balance for that category of accounts. Assets normally have a debit balance, so a contra-asset account will normally have a credit balance. The balance in this account represents the portion of the asset's cost that has been expensed to date.

MML's depreciation expense on its equipment for the month of December is determined as follows:

$$\frac{\$76,000 - \$10,000}{5 \text{ years}} = \$13,200 \text{ per year}/12 = \$1,100 \text{ per month}$$

Adjusting Entry 3: Depreciation Expense, Building

MML's depreciation expense on its building for the month of December is determined as follows:

$$\frac{\$500,000 - \$20,000}{25 \text{ years}} = \$19,200 \text{ per year}/12 = \$1,600 \text{ per month}$$

Adjusting Entry 4: Insurance Expense

MML had purchased a one-year insurance policy covering its equipment and building on July 1, 2015. The total premiums of $14,400 were paid at that time and would have been recorded as an asset, Prepaid Expenses, at that time. With each month, the coverage is being used up and the monthly insurance expense must be recorded. The amount of the expense for December is as follows:

$$\$14,400/12 = \$1,200$$

Suggested Solution To Chapter End Review Problem 2

EXHIBIT 3-17 STATEMENT OF INCOME

MATCHETT MANUFACTURING LIMITED
Statement of Income
For the year ended December 31, 2016

Sales revenue	$1,805,000	
Cost of goods sold	978,000	
Gross profit	827,000	45.8%
Wages expense	412,300	
Insurance expense	13,200	
Depreciation expense	32,400	
Interest expense	24,000	
Net income	$ 345,100	

EXHIBIT 3-18 STATEMENT OF CHANGES IN EQUITY

MATCHETT MANUFACTURING LIMITED
Statement of Changes in Equity
For the year ended December 31, 2016

	Number of Common Shares	Share Capital, Common Shares	Retained Earnings	Total
Balance - Jan. 1	10,000	$250,000	$230,800	$480,800
Net income	–	–	345,100	345,100
Declaration of dividends	–	–	(40,000)	(40,000)
Issuance of common shares	–	–	–	–
Balance - Dec. 31	10,000	$250,000	$535,900	$785,900

EXHIBIT 3-19 STATEMENT OF FINANCIAL POSITION

MATCHETT MANUFACTURING LIMITED
Statement of Financial Position
As at December 31, 2016

ASSETS		
Current assets		
Cash	$113,200	
Accounts receivable	238,000	
Inventory	163,000	
Prepaid expenses	7,200	
		$ 521,400
Non-current assets		
Equipment (net)		58,900
Building (net)		423,200
Land		385,000
		867,100
TOTAL ASSETS		$1,388,500
LIABILITIES		
Current liabilities		
Accounts payable	$172,000	
Wages payable	18,600	
Dividends payable	10,000	
Interest payable	2,000	
		$ 202,600
Non-current liabilities		
Bank loan payable		400,000
TOTAL LIABILITIES		602,600
SHAREHOLDERS' EQUITY		
Common shares		250,000
Retained earnings		535,900
TOTAL SHAREHOLDERS' EQUITY		785,900
TOTAL LIABILITIES AND SHAREHOLDERS' EQUITY		$1,388,500

EXHIBIT 3-20 **MML'S CLOSING ENTRIES**

C1. Close all revenue accounts to the Income Summary account.		
Sales Revenue	1,805,000	
Income Summary		1,805,000
C2. Close all expense accounts to the Income Summary account.		
Income Summary	1,459,900	
Cost of Goods Sold		978,000
Wages Expense		412,300
Insurance Expense		13,200
Depreciation Expense		32,400
Interest Expense		24,000
C3. Close the Income Summary account to Retained Earnings.		
Income Summary	345,100	
Retained Earnings		345,100
C4. Close the Dividends Declared account to Retained Earnings.		
Retained Earnings	40,000	
Dividends Declared		40,000

Income Summary

Debit	Credit
C2 1,459,900	1,805,000 **C1**
	345,100 Net Income
C3 345,100	
	-

Retained Earnings

Debit	Credit
	230,800 Opening Balance
C4 Dividends Declared 40,000	345,100 Net Income **C3**
	535,900 Ending Balance

Note that, after posting the closing entries, all the revenue and expense accounts and the Dividends Declared account have zero balances. They are now ready to start the new accounting cycle for 2017. Also, the Retained Earnings account has been updated to reflect the cumulative amount as at the end of 2016.

ASSIGNMENT MATERIAL

Discussion Questions

DQ3-1 In general terms, explain the role of each of the two main financial statements for a business enterprise: the statement of income and the statement of financial position. Outline the type of information that each statement presents, and the basic difference between the types of items that appear on the statement of income versus those that appear on the statement of financial position.

DQ3-2 Indicate whether each of the following statements is true or false:

a. Under the accrual basis of accounting, when cash is collected on accounts receivable, revenue is recorded.
b. Cash receipts from customers are debited to Accounts Receivable.
c. The cash basis of accounting recognizes expenses when they are incurred.
d. Under the cash basis of accounting, there is no such thing as a Prepaid Expenses account.
e. Asset accounts and expense accounts normally have debit balances.
f. Credits increase asset accounts.
g. Revenues are recorded with credit entries.
h. Dividends are an expense of doing business and should appear on the statement of income.

DQ3-3 Indicate whether each of the following accounts normally has a debit balance or a credit balance:

a. Sales Revenue
b. Rent Expense
c. Prepaid Expenses
d. Bank Loan Payable
e. Common Shares -> Equity -> C
f. Accounts Receivable Asset -> D
g. Accounts Payable -> Liability -> C
h. Retained Earnings -> Equity -> C
i. Dividends Declared -> D

j. Dividends Payable
k. Depreciation Expense

DQ3-4 Indicate whether each of the following accounts normally has a debit balance or a credit balance:
a. Inventory
b. Cost of Goods Sold
c. Prepaid Expenses
d. Wages Expense
e. Wages Payable
f. Interest Revenue
g. Equipment
h. Accumulated Depreciation, Equipment
i. Notes Payable
j. Common Shares
k. Cash

DQ3-5 The Retained Earnings account has a credit balance and credit entries are used to record increases in this account. Why do expense accounts, which are transferred to Retained Earnings when they are closed, have debit balances? Why are debit entries used to record increases in these accounts?

DQ3-6 List the steps in the accounting cycle, and briefly explain each step.

DQ3-7 In the adjusted trial balance part of the accounting cycle, the Retained Earnings account has its beginning-of-period balance, whereas the rest of the permanent accounts have their end-of-period balances. Explain why this is so.

DQ3-8 Explain what is meant by the term *prepaid expense*, including how a prepaid expense arises and where it is reported in the financial statements.

DQ3-9 Explain what is meant by the term *accrued expense*, including how an accrued expense arises and where it is reported in the financial statements.

DQ3-10 Explain how a prepaid expense differs from an accrued expense.

DQ3-11 If a company fails to record an accrued expense at the end of an accounting period, what effect will this omission have on the current period's financial statements? On the next period's financial statements?

DQ3-12 Explain the meaning of *depreciation expense* and *accumulated depreciation*. How do they differ? Where does each of these items appear in the financial statements?

DQ3-13 Explain why closing entries are made. What are the two objectives that are accomplished by making closing entries?

DQ3-14 Discuss why one company might close its books monthly and another might close them quarterly.

Application Problems

AP3-1 (Determine effects of transactions on statement of financial position accounts)

Ann and Greg Fenway run a small art gallery and custom framing business.

Required:
Explain how the basic statement of financial position accounts of assets, liabilities, and shareholders' equity would be affected by each of the following transactions and activities:
a. Framing materials are purchased on credit.
b. Payment is made for the framing materials that were purchased previously.
c. Wages are paid to their assistant in the shop.
d. Pictures are purchased by the gallery for cash.
e. A picture is sold for cash, at a profit.
f. A receivable is collected on a framing project that was completed for a customer last month.
g. A loan from the bank is repaid, with interest.
h. Depreciation on the equipment is recognized.

AP3-2 (Determine effects of transactions on statement of financial position accounts)

Gagnon's Autobody Ltd. repairs and paints automobiles after accidents.

Required:
Explain how the basic statement of financial position accounts of assets, liabilities, and shareholders' equity would be affected by each of the following transactions and activities:
a. Gagnon's Autobody purchases new spray-painting equipment. The supplier gives the company 60 days to pay.
b. The company pays for the spray-painting equipment that was purchased above.
c. Supplies such as paint and putty are purchased for cash.
d. The company pays for a one-year liability insurance policy.
e. The company pays its employees for work done.
f. A car is repaired and repainted. The customer pays the deductible required by her insurance policy, and the remainder of the bill is sent to her insurance company.
g. Cash is collected from the customer's insurance company.

AP3-3 **(Prepare journal entries)**

Required:

For each of the following transactions, construct journal entries:

a. Inventory costing $3,100 was purchased on account.
b. A payment of $3,000 was made on accounts payable.
c. Inventory costing $1,800 was sold on account for $2,700. (Hint: Two journal entries are required.)
d. Accounts receivable of $2,000 were collected.
e. Supplies costing $1,400 were purchased on account.
f. Supplies costing $500 were consumed during the period.
g. New equipment costing $7,500 was purchased for cash.
h. The company borrowed $12,000 from a bank.
i. The company issued common shares for $20,000.
j. Wages totalling $6,300 were earned by employees and paid to them.
k. The company paid $2,000 on its bank loan, which included $150 of interest.
l. The company paid $2,500 for the monthly rent on its leased premises.
m. Land costing $23,000 was purchased. The company paid $3,000 in cash and the remainder was financed with a mortgage (a long-term loan).

AP3-4 **(Prepare journal entries)**

Chapati Company started business on January 1, 2016. Some of the events that occurred in its first year of operations follow:

1. An insurance policy was purchased on February 28 for $1,800.
2. During the year, inventory costing $140,000 was purchased, all on account.
3. Sales to customers totalled $200,000. Of these, $40,000 were cash sales.
4. Payments to suppliers for inventory that had been purchased earlier totalled $110,000.
5. Collections from customers on account during the year totalled $140,000.
6. Customers paid $25,000 in advance payments for goods that will be delivered later.
7. Equipment that cost $140,000 was purchased on October 1 for $40,000 cash plus a two-year, 10% note with a principal amount of $100,000.
8. Wages totalling $44,000 were paid to employees during the year.
9. The board of directors declared dividends of $12,000 in December 2016, to be paid in January 2017.
10. A year-end review revealed that the insurance policy (in item 1) was for one year of coverage that began on March 1, 2016.
11. The equipment that was purchased (in item 7) on October 1, 2016, is to be depreciated using the straight-line method, with an estimated useful life of 10 years and an estimated residual value of $20,000.
12. No interest was paid on the note during the year.
13. A physical count at year end revealed $20,000 of unsold inventory still on hand.
14. It was determined that 80% of the goods that were paid for in advance (in item 6) had been delivered to the customers by the end of the year.
15. In addition to the wages that were paid during the year, wages of $4,000 remained unpaid at the end of the year.

Required:

Prepare journal entries for each of the above transactions and adjustments.

AP3-5 **(Prepare journal entries)**

Le Petit Croissant Ltd. ("LPC") is a wholesale bakery that supplies flash frozen croissants to restaurants, hotels, and other commercial customers. LPC began operating in August 2016 and had the following transactions in its first month:

Aug. 1	LPC issued 30,000 common shares to its two founding shareholders in exchange for $250,000 in cash and equipment valued at $50,000.
1	The company borrowed $100,000 from the Commercial Bank at an interest rate of 6%. The borrowing agreement terms state that the loan is to be repaid at the end of each month in the amount of $2,500 per month plus interest.
3	In order to access a commercial kitchen, LPC leased the site of a former restaurant, paying $6,000, of which $3,000 represented the rent for August and the balance was a damage deposit.
8	LPC purchased flour and other ingredients costing $32,800 on account.
12	LPC paid $6,800 to a local marketing company for its logo design and media planning services.

14 LPC recorded its sales of the first two weeks of the month. Total sales (half in cash and half on account) amounted to $50,200 and the inventory related to these sales was determined to have a cost of $17,100.

19 Paid the suppliers $25,000 for goods previously purchased on account.

25 Collections from customers on account totalled $22,600.

26 LPC purchased additional inventory (flour and so on) on account for $23,000.

29 LPC received an invoice from its natural gas supplier for $2,700, which is payable on September 14.

31 LPC recorded the sales for the balance of the month. Sales for this period totalled $60,800, of which $20,000 was on account. The cost of the ingredients from inventory related to these sales amounted to $20,700.

31 LPC's six full-time employees were paid $3,900 each in wages for the month.

31 LPC made the loan payment required under the terms of the borrowing agreement.

31 LPC's board of directors declared a dividend of $1.00 per share to the holders of the company's common shares.

Required:
Prepare all necessary journal entries related to the above transactions.

AP3-6 (Journalize, post, and prepare trial balance)

Sweet Dreams Chocolatiers Ltd. began operations on January 1, 2016. During its first year, the following transactions occurred:

1. Issued common shares for $200,000 cash.
2. Purchased $475,000 of inventory on account.
3. Sold inventory on account for $640,000. The original cost of the inventory that was sold was $380,000.
4. Collected $580,000 from customers on account.
5. Paid $430,000 to suppliers for the inventory previously purchased on account.
6. Bought a delivery vehicle for $36,000 cash.
7. Paid $26,000 for rent, including $2,000 related to the next year.
8. Incurred $20,000 of operating expenses, of which $18,000 was paid.
9. Recorded $2,000 of depreciation on the vehicle.
10. Declared and paid dividends of $6,000.

Required:

a. Prepare journal entries to record each of the above transactions.
b. Create T accounts and post the journal entries to the T accounts.
c. Prepare a December 31, 2016, trial balance.

AP3-7 (Journalize, post, and prepare trial balance)

Sparkling Clean Dry Cleaners Inc. began operations on January 1, 2016. In its first year, the following transactions occurred:

1. Issued common shares for $150,000 cash.
2. Purchased dry cleaning equipment for $75,000 cash.
3. Purchased cleaning supplies, on account, for $9,600.
4. Used $8,400 of the supplies in cleaning operations.
5. Collected $124,000 from customers for dry cleaning services provided.
6. Borrowed $15,000 from the bank on July 1, 2015, at an interest rate of 8% per year.
7. Paid wages of $49,000 to employees. In addition to this, $1,000 of wages were owed to employees at the end of the year.
8. Depreciated the equipment by $3,000 for the year.
9. Paid $22,000 for utilities (telephone, electricity, and water).
10. On December 31, paid interest on the bank loan described in transaction 6.

Required:

a. Prepare journal entries to record each of the above transactions.
b. Create T accounts and post the journal entries to the T accounts.
c. Prepare a December 31, 2016, trial balance.

AP3-8 (Journal entries and adjusting entries)

Offcopy Ltd. ("OL") is an office supply company that also sells and services commercial office copiers. OL was founded in 2012 and has seen significant growth since then. OL's bookkeeper retired in August and her replacement has asked for your assistance in recording the following transactions from the month of September 2016:

Regular entries:

Sept. 1	OL purchased a new delivery truck for $80,000, paying $30,000 cash and financing the balance using a note payable at 9% per annum. The note payable is due in 12 months, and interest on the note must be paid on the first day of every month, beginning on October 1, 2016. OL's management has determined that the truck will have a useful life of six years and a residual value of $8,000.
1	OL paid $2,400 for an insurance policy on the new truck for the period September 1, 2016, to August 31, 2017.
5	The company purchased inventory on credit at a cost of $13,000.
12	Pinamalas University, one of OL's largest customers, signed a photocopy service contract with OL. The contract runs from October 1, 2016, to September 30, 2017, and will mean that OL services all of the university's photocopiers. In accordance with the contact terms, Pinamalas paid OL $7,500, representing the first month's service revenue under the contract.
18	OL sold $16,000 of office supplies, of which one quarter was on account and the balance was cash. The cost to OL of the products sold was $10,500.
30	OL paid dividends in the amount of $15,000, which had been declared by the board (and recorded) in August 2016.

Adjusting entries:

Sept. 30	OL made the necessary month-end adjusting entry related to the depreciation of the new delivery truck.
30	OL made the necessary month-end adjusting entry related to the interest on the note payable.
30	OL made the necessary month-end adjusting entry related to the insurance policy.

Required:
Prepare the journal entries for the above transactions.

AP3-9 (Journal entries and adjusting entries)

Aquarium World Ltd. ("AWL") was incorporated in 2013 and imports fish tanks and related supplies for the saltwater aquarium market. AWL primarily imports from Asian suppliers and is a wholesaler supplying independent retailers in Western Canada.

During the month of January 2016, AWL had the following transactions:

Regular entries:

Jan. 1	In order to better service its growing business and manage its inventory more effectively, AWL purchased new computer equipment to run its inventory system for $145,000, paying cash. AWL's management determined that the new computer equipment would have a useful life of five years and have a residual value of $10,000.
1	AWL also entered into an agreement to lease a warehouse. This would allow the company to import larger shipments from its Asian suppliers and reduce the impact of the long shipping times. In accordance with the lease terms, AWL paid $14,400, which represented the first six months' rent in advance.
13	A major hotel contacted AWL about supplying it with an 8-metre saltwater aquarium for the lobby. AWL agreed to this and received a $50,000 payment from the hotel. AWL ordered the tank the same day and it was scheduled to arrive on February 25. AWL has guaranteed that it will be installed before the end of February.
14	AWL paid its employees $9,000 for wages earned during the first two weeks of January.
15	AWL's board of directors declared dividends in the amount of $20,000, which will be paid on February 15.
19	AWL made sales totalling $62,000. Of this, half was cash and the balance was on account. The cost to AWL of the products sold was $36,000.

Adjusting entries:

Jan. 31	The company recorded the $9,000 in wages earned by employees during the last two weeks of the month. These wages will be paid on February 1, 2016.
31	AWL recorded the adjusting entry to depreciate the new computer equipment.
31	AWL recorded the adjusting entry for the warehouse lease.

Required:
Prepare the journal entries and adjusting entries for January 2016 based on the above transactions.

AP3-10 (Closing entries and ending retained earnings balance)

Presented below are the balances from Elsie's Electronics Ltd.'s general ledger as at September 30, 2016:

	DR	CR
Cash	28,000	
Accounts receivable	35,000	
Inventory	65,000	
Equipment	331,000	
Accumulated depreciation, equipment		150,000
Accounts payable		120,000
Bank loan payable		70,000
Unearned revenue		22,000
Common shares		10,000
Retained earnings		70,000
Dividends declared	18,000	
Sales revenue		488,000
Interest revenue		2,000
Cost of goods sold	316,000	
Wages expense	70,000	
Rent expense	26,000	
Depreciation expense	43,000	

Required:

a. Prepare the necessary closing entries for Elsie's Electronics at September 30.
b. Determine the closing Retained Earnings account balance.

AP3-11 (Closing entries and ending Retained Earnings balance)

Presented below are the balances from Zoë Developments Ltd.'s general ledger as at January 31, 2016:

	DR	CR
Cash	56,000	
Accounts receivable	135,000	
Inventory	124,000	
Prepaid expenses	5,000	
Equipment	361,000	
Accumulated depreciation, equipment		120,000
Accounts payable		32,000
Unearned revenue		5,000
Wages payable		11,000
Common shares		103,000
Retained earnings		88,000
Dividends declared	21,000	
Sales revenue		956,000
Interest revenue		19,000
Cost of goods sold	560,000	
Depreciation expense	10,000	
Wages expense	41,000	
Utilities expense	9,000	
Insurance expense	12,000	

Required:

a. Prepare the necessary closing entries for Zoë Developments at January 31.
b. Determine the ending Retained Earnings account balance.

AP3-12 (Journalize, post, and prepare trial balance and closing entries)

Singh Company started business on January 1, 2015. The following transactions occurred in 2015:

1. On January 1, the company issued 10,000 common shares for $250,000.
2. On January 2, the company borrowed $50,000 from the bank.
3. On January 3, the company purchased land and a building for a total of $200,000 cash. The land was recently appraised at a fair market value of $60,000. (Note: As the building will be depreciated in the future and the land will not, these two assets should be recorded in separate accounts.)
4. Inventory costing $130,000 was purchased on account.
5. Sales to customers totalled $205,000. Of these, $175,000 were sales on account.
6. The cost of the inventory that was sold to customers in transaction 5 was $120,000.
7. Payments to suppliers on account totalled $115,000.
8. Collections from customers on account totalled $155,000.
9. Payments to employees for salaries were $55,000. In addition, there was $2,000 of unpaid salaries at year end.
10. The interest on the bank loan was recognized and paid. The interest rate on the loan was 6%.
11. The building was estimated to have a useful life of 30 years and a residual value of $20,000. The company uses the straight-line method of depreciation.
12. The company declared dividends of $7,000 on December 15, 2015, to be paid on January 15, 2016.

Required:

a. Prepare journal entries for each of the transactions and adjustments listed in the problem.
b. Prepare the necessary T accounts and post the journal entries to them.
c. Prepare an adjusted trial balance.
d. Prepare the closing entries and post them to the T accounts.

AP3-13 (Journalize, post, and prepare trial balance and closing entries)

The Hughes Tools Company started business on October 1, 2015. Its fiscal year runs through to September 30 the following year. The following transactions occurred in the fiscal year that started on October 1, 2015, and ended on September 30, 2016.

1. On October 1, 2015, Jill Hughes invested $175,000 to start the business. Hughes is the only owner. She was issued 10,000 common shares.
2. On October 1, Hughes Tools borrowed $225,000 from a venture capitalist (a lender who specializes in start-up companies).
3. On October 1, the company rented a building. The rental agreement was a two-year contract requiring quarterly rental payments (every three months) of $15,000, payable in advance. The first payment was made on October 1, 2015 (covering the period from October 1 to December 31). Thereafter, payments were due on December 31, March 31, June 30, and September 30 for each three-month period that followed. All the rental payments were made as specified in the agreement.
4. On October 1, the company purchased equipment costing $220,000 for cash.
5. Initial inventory was purchased for $90,000 cash.
6. Additional purchases of inventory during the year totalled $570,000, all on account.
7. Sales during the year totalled $800,000, of which $720,000 was on account.
8. Collections from customers on account totalled $650,000.
9. Payments to suppliers on account totalled $510,000.
10. The cost of the inventory that was sold during the year was $560,000.
11. Selling and administrative expenses totalled $86,500 for the year. Of this amount, $4,000 was unpaid at year end.
12. Interest on the loan from the venture capitalist was paid at year end (September 30, 2016). The interest rate on the loan is 10%. In addition, $25,000 of the loan principal was repaid at that time.
13. The equipment was depreciated based on an estimated useful life of 10 years and a residual value of $20,000.
14. The company declared and paid a dividend of $7,000.

Required:

a. Prepare journal entries for each of the transactions and adjustments listed in the problem.
b. Prepare the necessary T accounts and post the journal entries to them.
c. Prepare an adjusted trial balance.
d. Prepare the closing entries and post them to the T accounts.

AP3-14 (Journalize, post, and prepare trial balance and closing entries)

A.J. Smith Company started business on January 1, 2015, and the following transactions occurred in its first year:

1. On January 1, the company issued 12,000 common shares at $25 per share.
2. On January 1, the company purchased land and a building from another company in exchange for $80,000 cash and 6,000 shares. The land's value is approximately one quarter of the total value of the transaction. (Hint: You need to determine a value for the shares using the information given in transaction 1, and the land and building should be recorded in separate accounts.)
3. On March 31, the company rented out a portion of its building to Frantek Company. Frantek is required to make quarterly payments of $7,500 on March 31, June 30, September 30, and December 31 of each year. The first payment, covering the period from April 1 to June 30, was received on March 31, and the other payments were all received as scheduled.
4. Equipment worth $120,000 was purchased on July 1, in exchange for $60,000 cash and a one-year note with a principal amount of $60,000 and an interest rate of 10%. No principal or interest payments were made during the year.
5. Inventory costing $250,000 was purchased on account.
6. Sales were $300,000, of which credit sales were $250,000.
7. The inventory sold had a cost of $190,000.
8. Payments to suppliers totalled $205,000.
9. Accounts receivable totalling $200,000 were collected.
10. Operating expenses amounted to $50,000, all of which were paid in cash.
11. The building purchased in transaction 2 is depreciated using the straight-line method, with an estimated useful life of 20 years and an estimated residual value of $30,000.
12. The equipment purchased in transaction 4 is depreciated using the straight-line method, with an estimated useful life of 10 years and an estimated residual value of $5,000. Because the equipment was purchased on July 1, only a half year of depreciation is recognized in 2015.
13. Dividends of $20,000 were declared during the year, of which $5,000 remained unpaid at year end.

Required:

a. Prepare journal entries for each of the transactions and adjustments listed in the problem.
b. Prepare the necessary T accounts and post the journal entries to them.
c. Prepare an adjusted trial balance.
d. Prepare the closing entries and post them to the T accounts.

AP3-15 (Determine statement of income amounts)

Jake Fromowitz owns and operates a tire and auto repair shop named Jake's Jack'em and Fix'em Shop. During the current month, the following activities occurred:

1. The shop charged $8,500 for repair work done during the month. All but one of Jake's customers paid in full. The one customer who had not yet paid owed Jake $500. Jake still has the car in the shop's parking lot and he intends to keep it until the customer pays the bill. The $500 is included in the $8,500.
2. The total cost of parts and oil purchased during the month was $2,900. Jake pays for the parts with cash, but the oil is purchased in bulk from a supplier on 30 days' credit. At the end of the month, he still owes $400 to this supplier.
3. The cost of the parts that were used in repair work during the month was $2,600.
4. Jake paid $750 monthly rent on the repair shop on the first day of the month, and since he had extra cash on hand at the end of the month, he paid another $750 to cover the next month's rent.
5. On the 10th of the month, Jake paid the previous month's utility bills of $250. At the end of the month, he received this month's utility bills, totalling $230, which he intends to pay on the 10th of next month.
6. Jake paid a friend $500 for helping him in the repair shop, and also gave him a new set of tires from the shop's stockroom. These tires had cost Jake $300, and could have been sold to customers for $400.
7. Utilities expenses related to operating the repair shop for the month totalled $875. All of these were paid during the month, as well as $125 that was owed from the previous month.
8. During the last week of the month, a customer dropped off her vehicle for repair work. Jake set aside $600 of parts to be used in these repairs, but he has not yet had time to do any work on this job.

Required:

Referring to the concepts discussed so far in this textbook:

a. Determine the amounts that would properly be reported in the statement of income for Jake's shop this month. If an item is excluded, explain why.
b. Calculate the net income for the month.

AP3-16 (Determine statement of income amounts)

Jan Wei owns a cycle store that sells equipment, clothing, and other accessories. During the month of June, the following activities occurred:

1. The business earned $30,000 from the sale of bicycles, clothing, and accessories. Half the sales were for cash and the other half was on account.
2. The merchandise that was sold originally cost $17,400.

3. Jan purchased additional merchandise on credit for $20,800.
4. Jan paid $18,000 to the suppliers of the merchandise purchased above.
5. The telephone, electricity, and water bills for the month came to $430. All but one of these bills, for $130, was paid by the end of the month.
6. Additional expenses for the month, including depreciation expense of $600, totalled $2,100. They were all paid in cash, except the depreciation expense, and were for repairs and maintenance done to the store.
7. At the end of May, Jan had an 8% loan for $5,000 outstanding with the bank. On the last day of June, Jan paid the monthly interest that was owed on the loan, and also paid $500 on the loan principal.
8. On the last day of June, a customer ordered a $1,300 bicycle. Jan did not have it in stock, so it was ordered and will be delivered in July. Since it was a special order, the customer paid a $300 deposit on it.

Required:
Referring to the concepts discussed so far in this textbook:

a. Determine the amounts that would properly be reported in the June statement of income for Jan's shop. If an item is excluded, explain why.
b. Calculate the net income for the month.

AP3-17 (Determine expenses)

The following are activities in a three-month period for Basiliadis Company:

1. A new lease for the business premises goes into effect on October 1 and increases the rent from $1,000 to $1,150 per month. The rent for the next month is always prepaid on the last day of the current month. Accordingly, rent of $1,000 was paid on August 31, and $1,150 was paid on September 30 and October 31.
2. The company borrowed $12,000 on September 1. The interest rate on the loan is 10% per year and interest is to be repaid quarterly.
3. Basiliadis Company purchased a large supply of lubricant for $2,000 on September 1. The lubricant is to be used in the company's operations and is expected to last for four months.
4. Employees work Monday through Friday and are paid each Monday for the previous week's work. The payroll for the week of Monday, September 29, to Friday, October 3 (paid on October 6), is $10,000. The payroll for the week of Monday, October 27, to Friday, October 31 (paid on November 3), is $10,500.

Required:
For each of the above independent cases, determine how much of the cost should be recognized as expense in each of the months of September, October, and November.

AP3-18 (Determine previous account balances)

Puzzle-Solver Consulting Services Ltd. has a December 31 year end. Selected items from the company's adjusted trial balance as at January 31, 2016, follow:

Partial Adjusted Trial Balance as at January 31, 2016

	Debit balances	Credit balances
Supplies	$ 800	
Prepaid expenses	2,400	
Wages payable		$2,600
Unearned revenue		1,000
Service revenue		7,000
Wages expense	4,100	
Insurance expense	400	
Supplies expense	300	

Required:

a. If supplies costing $1,000 were purchased in January, determine what the balance in the Supplies account must have been at the beginning of the month.
b. If the Prepaid Expenses and Insurance Expense amounts relate to an insurance policy with an original term of one year, determine the total premium that was paid and the date on which the policy was purchased.
c. If the amount paid for wages during the month was $3,000, determine what the balance in the Wages Payable account must have been at the beginning of the month.
d. If there are no accounts receivable, and the amount of fee payments received during the month was $3,000, determine what the balance in the Unearned Revenue account must have been at the beginning of the month. (Note: Customers are required to prepay for all services.)

AP3-19 (Journalize, post, prepare statement of income and statement of financial position, and prepare closing entries)

On December 31, 2015, Clean and White Linen Supplies Ltd. had the following account balances:

Cash	$ 90,000	Accumulated Depreciation, Equipment	$ 90,000
Accounts Receivable	96,000	Accounts Payable	60,000
Inventory	60,000	Wages Payable	8,000
Supplies	2,000	Bank Loan Payable	150,000
Long-Term Investment	80,000	Common Shares	250,000
Equipment	330,000	Retained Earnings	100,000

In 2016, the following transactions occurred:

1. On January 1, paid $3,900 for a three-year fire insurance policy.
2. Purchased additional uniform inventory on credit for $120,000.
3. Sold uniforms for $180,000 on account. The inventory that was sold had been purchased for $100,000.
4. Performed cleaning services for customers for $520,000. One quarter of this amount was paid in cash and the remainder was on account.
5. Paid $130,000 to suppliers to settle some of the accounts payable.
6. Received $246,000 from customers to settle amounts owed to the company.
7. Paid $12,000 for advertising.
8. At the end of 2016, paid the interest on the bank loan for the year at the rate of 7%, as well as $30,000 on the principal. The remaining principal balance is due in three years.
9. Received a $3,000 dividend from the long-term investment.
10. Paid $15,000 for utilities for the year.
11. Declared and paid dividends of $12,000 at the end of the year.
12. Paid $102,000 for wages during the year. At year end, the company still owed $2,000 to the employees for the last week of work in December.
13. Depreciated the equipment for the year. The company had bought its equipment at the beginning of 2013, and it was expected to last 10 years and have a residual value of $30,000.
14. Made an adjustment for the cost of the insurance that expired in 2016.

Required:

a. Prepare journal entries to record each of the above transactions and adjustments.
b. Create T accounts. Enter the beginning balances from 2015, post the 2016 journal entries, and determine the ending balances for 2016.
c. Prepare an adjusted trial balance, and ensure that the total of the debit balances is equal to the total of the credit balances.
d. Prepare a statement of income for 2016.
e. Prepare the closing entries and post them to the T accounts.
f. Prepare a statement of financial position for 2016.

AP3-20 (Prepare journal entries, trial balances, and closing entries)

Evergreen Retail Company, whose fiscal year end is December 31, had the following transactions in its first year of operations:

1. Issued common shares for $65,000 cash on January 1, 2016.
2. Borrowed $15,000 of additional financing from the bank on January 1, 2016.
3. Bought equipment for $25,000 cash, also on January 1, 2016.
4. Made $60,000 of inventory purchases on account.
5. Had total sales of $92,000, of which $28,000 were on account. The cost of the products sold was $44,000.
6. Bought supplies for $800 cash.
7. Collected payments of $24,000 from customers on their accounts.
8. Paid suppliers $25,000 for the inventory that had been purchased on account.
9. Paid employees $36,200.
10. Paid the interest on the bank loan on December 31, 2016. The interest rate was 8%.
11. Declared dividends of $2,000, which will be paid in 2017.

Information for adjusting entries:

12. The equipment purchased on January 1 has an estimated useful life of eight years and an estimated residual value of $1,000 at the end of its life.
13. Supplies costing $200 were still on hand at the end of the year.
14. Wages in the amount of $800 were owed to employees at the end of the year. These will be paid early in 2017.

Required:

a. Prepare journal entries for transactions 1 through 11.
b. Prepare adjusting journal entries for adjustments 12 to 14.
c. Set up T accounts, post the 2016 entries, and calculate the balance in each account.
d. Prepare a trial balance, and ensure that the total of the debit balances is equal to the total of the credit balances.
e. Prepare the closing entries, post them to the T accounts, and calculate the final balance in each account.

AP3-21 (Journalize, post, prepare statement of income and statement of financial position, and prepare closing entries)

Perfect Pizza had the following account balances at December 31, 2015:

Cash	$ 33,000	Vehicles	80,000
Accounts Receivable	15,000	Accumulated Depreciation, Vehicles	36,000
Inventory	10,000	Accounts Payable	7,000
Prepaid Expenses	3,000	Wages Payable	2,000
Equipment	60,000	Common Shares	110,000
Accumulated Depreciation, Equipment	30,000	Retained Earnings	16,000

During 2016, the following transactions occurred:

1. Purchases of ingredients and supplies (inventory) were $230,000, all on account.
2. Sales of pizzas for cash were $510,000, and sales of pizzas on account were $40,000.
3. The company paid $105,000 for wages and $25,000 for utilities expenses.
4. Payments for ingredients and supplies purchased on account totalled $220,000.
5. Collections from customers for sales on account totalled $50,000.
6. Ingredients and supplies valued at $225,000 were used in making pizzas.
7. A dividend of $15,000 was declared and paid at the end of the year.

Information for adjusting entries:

8. At the end of 2016, the amount of rent paid in advance was $1,500.
9. Wages owed to employees at the end of 2016 were $2,500.
10. The equipment had an estimated useful life of eight years, with no residual value.
11. The delivery vehicles had an estimated useful life of six years with a residual value of $8,000.

Required:

a. Prepare journal entries for transactions 1 through 7. Create new accounts as necessary.
b. Prepare adjusting journal entries for adjustments 8 to 11.
c. Set up T accounts, enter the beginning balances from 2015, post the 2016 entries, and calculate the balance in each account.
d. Prepare a trial balance, and ensure that the total of the debit balances is equal to the total of the credit balances.
e. Prepare a statement of income for 2016.
f. Prepare the closing entries, post them to the T accounts, and calculate the final balance in each account.
g. Prepare a statement of financial position for 2016.

AP3-22 (Prepare journal entries, trial balances, and closing entries)

Genesis Sportswear Ltd. is a wholesale company that buys sports clothing from manufacturers and sells it to retail stores. It had the following transactions in its first year of operations. The company's fiscal year end is December 31.

1. Common shares were issued for $60,000.
2. An insurance premium that provides coverage for the 12-month period starting March 1 was bought for $1,200 on February 15.
3. Clothing was purchased for $75,000 on account.
4. Employees were paid $46,900 in wages.
5. Utilities expenses totalled $10,000. Of this amount, $9,000 was paid during the year; the remainder was due to be paid early in the next year.
6. Sales recorded for the period totalled $105,000, all on credit.
7. The cost of the inventory sold during the year was $62,000.

8. Cash collections on customer accounts totalled $96,000.
9. Payments to suppliers for clothing purchased totalled $54,000.
10. New equipment was purchased for $15,000 cash.

Adjusting entries: (Hint: You may need to use information recorded in the first 10 transactions.)

11. Recognized the amount of insurance expense that was incurred during the period.
12. Recorded depreciation of $2,000 on the equipment.

Required:

a. Prepare journal entries to record transactions 1 through 10.
b. Prepare adjusting journal entries for adjustments 11 and 12.
c. Set up T accounts, post the 2016 entries, and calculate the balance in each account.
d. Prepare a trial balance, and ensure that the total of the debit balances is equal to the total of the credit balances.
e. Prepare the closing entries, post them to the T accounts, and calculate the final balance in each account.

AP3-23 (Determine amounts to appear in financial statements)

The following is the final trial balance (after the adjusting and closing entries had been made) for Hartman Company as at August 31, 2016. Hartman adjusts and closes its books at the end of each month.

	Debit balances	**Credit balances**
Cash	$ 6,000	
Accounts receivable	40,000	
Inventory	90,000	
Prepaid expenses	8,000	
Equipment	18,000	
Accumulated depreciation, equipment		$ 3,000
Accounts payable		32,000
Note payable		30,000
Interest payable		1,500
Common shares		50,000
Retained earnings		45,500
	$162,000	$162,000

Hartman's transactions in September 2016 and all relevant data for month-end adjustments follow:

1. Sales on account were $41,000.
2. Payments of $37,000 were collected from customers on their accounts.
3. Cash sales were $50,000.
4. Merchandise was purchased for $39,000 on account.
5. The cost of merchandise sold in September was $59,000.
6. Payments of $33,000 were made to suppliers for accounts owing.
7. Advertising costs of $3,000 were paid.
8. Employees were paid $15,000 in wages.
9. Wages of $1,000 were earned by employees but not yet paid.
10. Miscellaneous expenses of $9,000 were paid in cash.
11. The prepaid expense balance represented the rent paid in advance for the period from September 1 to December 31, 2016.
12. The equipment was purchased on September 1, 2015 (one year before the start of the current month), and is expected to have a total useful life of six years.
13. The note payable was dated March 1, 2015, and the principal is due to be repaid in two equal instalments on March 1, 2016 and 2017. Interest on the note, at a rate of 10% per year, is also to be paid on March 1, 2016 and 2017.

Required:

Based on the above information, answer the following questions:

a. What amount should Hartman report as revenue for September?
b. What amount should Hartman report as wages expense for September?
c. What amount should Hartman report as rent expense for September?

d. What amount should Hartman report as interest expense for September?
e. As at the end of September, what should the balance in Hartman's cash account be?
f. As at the end of September, what is the amount of Hartman's accounts receivable?
g. As at the end of September, what should the balance in Hartman's merchandise inventory account be?
h. As at the end of September, what is the amount of Hartman's accounts payable?
i. Is the equipment expected to have any value at the end of its useful life? If so, how much?
j. As at September 30, 2016, what is the carrying value of Hartman's equipment?
k. What amount should be shown under long-term liabilities on Hartman's statement of financial position as at September 30, 2016?

AP3-24 (Prepare adjusting entries)

The trial balance for Cozy Fireplaces Inc. for December 31, 2016, follows:

	Debit balances	Credit balances
Cash	$ 89,000	
Accounts receivable	38,000	
Inventory	95,000	
Supplies	5,000	
Prepaid expenses	46,000	
Land	80,000	
Building	150,000	
Accumulated depreciation, building		$ 19,500
Accounts payable		21,400
Salaries and wages payable		0
Interest payable		0
Income tax payable		0
Unearned revenue		12,400
Bank loan payable		40,000
Common shares		150,000
Retained earnings		16,700
Sales revenue		840,000
Cost of goods sold	482,000	
Wages expense	95,000	
Rent expense	0	
Supplies expense	0	
Depreciation expense	0	
Interest expense	0	
Miscellaneous expense	14,000	
Income tax expense	0	
Dividends declared	6,000	
Totals	$1,100,000	$1,100,000

Additional information for adjusting entries:

1. The deposits from customers were for future deliveries. As at December 31, three quarters of these goods had been delivered.
2. There is $2,000 in salaries and wages owed at year end.
3. Rent is paid in advance on the last day of each month. There was a balance of $3,000 in the Prepaid Expenses account on January 1, 2016. At the end of January, $3,000 was paid for the February rent and was debited to the Prepaid Expenses account. All the rent payments during the year were treated the same way. The rent for July to December increased to $4,000 per month. (Hint: Determine the amount of rent expense for 2016, as well as the correct amount that has been prepaid for 2017, and make an adjustment that will bring both these accounts to the correct balances.)

4. A count of the supplies at year end revealed that $500 of supplies were still on hand.
5. The building is being depreciated over 20 years with a residual value of $20,000.
6. The bank loan was taken out on April 1, 2016. The first interest payment is due on April 1, 2017. The interest rate is 9%.
7. Income tax for the year should be calculated using a tax rate of 30%. (Hint: After you finish the other adjusting entries, you will have to determine the *income before income tax* and then calculate the tax as 30% of this amount.)

Required:
Prepare the adjusting entries for the year 2016.

AP3-25 **(Prepare adjusting entries)**

The following trial balance before adjustments is for Snowcrest Ltd. on December 31, 2016:

	Debits	Credits
Cash	$ 10,000	
Inventory	24,000	
Advances to employees	2,000	
Supplies	3,000	
Equipment	56,000	
Accumulated depreciation, equipment		$ 4,000
Unearned revenue		6,000
Bank loan payable		20,000
Common shares		40,000
Retained earnings		9,000
Sales revenue		230,000
Cost of goods sold	130,000	
Wages expense	34,000	
Repairs and maintenance expense	25,000	
Rent expense	6,600	
Miscellaneous expense	15,000	
Dividends declared	3,400	
Totals	$309,000	$309,000

Data for adjusting entries:

1. As at December 31, 2016, 80% of the wages that had been paid in advance to the salespeople had been earned.
2. A count of the supplies at year end revealed that $600 of supplies were still on hand.
3. Depreciation on the equipment for 2016 was $1,000.
4. The unearned revenue was advance receipts for future deliveries of goods. By December 31, 2016, two thirds of these deliveries had been made.
5. The bank loan was a six-month loan taken out on October 1, 2016. The interest rate on the loan is 9%, but the interest is not due to be paid until the note is repaid on April 1, 2017.
6. Salaries owed at year end and not yet recorded were $500.
7. The rent expense figure includes $600 paid in advance for January 2017.
8. Income tax for the year should be calculated using a tax rate of 25%. (Hint: After you finish the other adjusting entries, determine the *income before income tax* and then calculate the tax as 25% of this amount.)

Required:
Prepare the adjusting entries for the year 2016.

AP3-26 **(Determine statement of income and statement of financial position values)**

The following information was available for Brilliant Consulting Company at its year end, December 31, 2016:

1. During the year, the company agreed to provide certain consulting services to a client for a fee of $10,000, which was received in advance. At the end of the year, it was estimated that 85% of the services had been provided.
2. The Supplies account had a balance of $350 at the beginning of the year and additional supplies costing $950 were purchased during the year. At the end of the year, a count of the supplies indicated that supplies costing $250 remained on hand.

3. A new "business occupancy" tax was introduced by the municipal government in 2016. The company was required to pay $1,800 to cover the period from April 1, 2016, to March 31, 2017. (Hint: Use the Property Tax Expense account.)
4. The company rents some surplus space in its building to a tenant for $1,500 per quarter, payable in advance. The agreement began on September 1, 2016, and the tenant paid $1,500 on that date and an additional $1,500 on December 1.
5. Another tenant rents space in the company's building for $750 per month, due on the first day of each month. The agreement began several years ago and the tenant has paid the rent as scheduled every month, except for the most recent one. At year end, the rent for December 2016 was still outstanding.
6. During the year, the company used an advertising agency and paid $3,000 for its services. In addition to this, there were unpaid advertising bills at year end totalling $450; these are due in January 2017.

Required:
For each of the items above, indicate what should appear on the statement of income for the year ended December 31, 2016, and on the statement of financial position as at that date.

AP3-27 (Determine statement of income and statement of financial position values)

The Great Graphics Group began operations on January 1, 2015. At the end of its *second* year of operations, and before any adjustments had been made, the trial balance was as follows:

	Debit balances	Credit balances
Cash	$ 8,600	
Accounts receivable	13,500	
Prepaid expenses	1,800	
Equipment	48,000	
Accumulated depreciation, equipment		$ 3,300
Accounts payable		11,000
Unearned revenue		7,500
Notes payable		18,000
Common shares		22,000
Retained earnings		7,200
Service revenue		45,500
Wages expense	33,000	
Supplies expense	3,300	
Advertising expense	1,700	
Rent expense	2,700	
Utilities expense	1,900	
	$114,500	$114,500

Analysis reveals the following additional data for adjustments to be made:

1. There were $2,000 of supplies on hand at year end.
2. The note payable was issued on October 1, 2016. It is a nine-month note, with an interest rate of 9% per year. The interest does not have to be paid until July 1, 2017, when the note is due to be repaid.
3. The balance in the Prepaid Expenses account is the insurance premium paid for a one-year policy that began March 1, 2016.
4. By year-end $4,500 of the amount recorded in the Unearned Revenue account had been earned. In addition, $3,000 of additional service fees had been earned, but not yet billed or recorded. The work was completed in December 2016, and the clients will pay for it in January 2017.
5. The equipment was acquired on April 1, 2015, and is being depreciated at a rate of $4,400 per year.

Required:
Calculate the amount that should appear (after adjustments) on the December 31, 2016, financial statements for each of the following items:

a. On the statement of income, related to supplies
b. On the statement of financial position, related to interest
c. On the statement of financial position, related to insurance

d. On the statement of income, related to service
e. On the statement of financial position, as the carrying value of the equipment

AP3-28 (Determine effects of omitted adjustment)

When it was preparing its financial statements for the year ended December 31, 2016, D'Amelio Ltd. failed to record $3,000 of accrued salaries. These salaries were paid, and recorded as an expense, in 2017.

Required:
State the effect (if any) that this error will have on each of the following financial statement items:

a. Net income for 2016
b. Total assets on December 31, 2016
c. Total liabilities on December 31, 2016
d. Total shareholders' equity on December 31, 2016
e. Net income for 2017
f. Total assets on December 31, 2017
g. Total liabilities on December 31, 2017
h. Total shareholders' equity on December 31, 2017

AP3-29 (Determine adjusted balances; prepare statement of income and statement of financial position)

On December 31, 2016, Information Inc. completed its third year of operations. Abdul Mukhtar is a student working part-time in the company's business office while taking his first accounting course. Abdul assembled the following list of account balances, which are not arranged in any particular order:

Accounts Receivable	$150,000	Advertising Expense	$ 76,000
Interest Expense	2,000	Cash	20,000
Notes Receivable	26,000	Inventory	140,000
Cost of Goods Sold	590,000	Dividends Declared	12,000
Common Shares	570,000	Unearned Revenue	6,000
Building	360,000	Insurance Expense	6,300
Accumulated Depreciation, Equipment	20,000	Retained Earnings (as at January 1, 2016)	177,000
Land	160,000	Equipment	200,000
Accumulated Depreciation, Building	40,000	Miscellaneous Expense	5,200
Sales	963,000	Accounts Payable	72,700
Utilities Expense	2,500	Wages Expense	125,000
Notes Payable	30,000	Supplies	3,700

These account amounts are correct, but Abdul did not consider the following information:

1. The amount shown as insurance expense includes $900 for coverage during the first two months of 2017.
2. The note receivable is a six-month note that has been outstanding for four months. The interest rate is 10% per year. The interest will be received by the company when the note becomes due at the end of February 2017.
3. As at December 31, 2016, the supplies still on hand had a cost of $600.
4. On November 1, 2016, the company rented surplus space in its building to a tenant for $1,000 per month. The tenant paid for six months in advance.
5. Depreciation for 2016 is $10,000 on the building and $20,000 on the equipment.
6. Employees earned $3,000 of salaries in December 2016 that will not be paid until the first scheduled payday in 2017.
7. Additional dividends of $50,000 were declared in December 2016, but will not be paid until January 2017.

Required:

a. Determine the amounts that would appear in an adjusted trial balance for Information Inc. as at December 31, 2016.
b. Prepare a statement of income for the year ended December 31, 2016.

c. Calculate the amount of retained earnings as at December 31, 2016.
d. Prepare a classified statement of financial position as at December 31, 2016.

AP3-30 (Calculate income and retained earnings; prepare statement of financial position)

Little Lads and Ladies Ltd. sells children's clothing. At the end of December 2016, it had the following adjusted account balances, which are listed in random order:

Cash	$ 3,000	Utilities Expense	$ 600
Wages Payable	500	Dividends Declared	1,200
Supplies Expense	4,200	Depreciation Expense	500
Equipment	23,000	Common Shares	20,000
Wages Expense	25,000	Telephone Expense	200
Prepaid Expenses	400	Interest Expense	300
Cost of Goods Sold	32,000	Accumulated Depreciation, Equipment	1,500
Sales Revenue	66,450	Retained Earnings	17,600
Accounts Receivable	10,000	Inventory	8,000
Rent Expense	4,800	Repairs and Maintenance Expenses	400
Bank Loan Payable	3,800	Supplies	800
Advertising Expense	750	Interest Payable	300
Accounts Payable	5,000		

Required:
a. Identify the statement of income accounts and calculate the net income (or loss) for the year.
b. Determine the amount of retained earnings at the end of 2016.
c. Prepare a classified statement of financial position as at December 31, 2016.

AP3-31 (Calculate income and retained earnings; prepare statement of financial position)

Your assistant prepared the following adjusted trial balance data for Commerce Company on December 31, 2016. The accounts are arranged in alphabetical order.

Accounts Payable	$ 36,000	Land	$ 70,000
Accounts Receivable	67,000	Long-Term Investment	12,000
Accumulated Depreciation, Buildings	20,000	Miscellaneous Expenses	13,000
Buildings	72,000	Mortgage Payable	48,000
Cash	24,000	Notes Payable	15,000
Common Shares	85,000	Prepaid Expenses	500
Cost of Goods Sold	110,000	Retained Earnings	31,500
Depreciation Expense	4,500	Sales Revenue	179,800
Dividends Declared	12,400	Selling Expenses	27,000
Dividends Payable	4,000	Service Revenue	93,100
Income Tax Expense	8,000	Supplies	800
Income Tax Payable	2,000	Supplies Expense	2,200
Insurance Expense	1,400	Unearned Revenue	1,200
Interest Expense	1,700	Utilities Expense	2,400
Interest Payable	300	Wages Expense	60,000
Inventory	30,000	Wages Payable	3,000

Required:

a. Calculate the net income for the year ended December 31, 2016.
b. Determine the Retained Earnings balance as at the end of the year.
c. Prepare a classified statement of financial position as at December 31, 2016. The note payable is due in 6 months.

AP3-32 (Prepare statement of financial position—manufacturing company)

The following adjusted trial balance data are for Novasco Manufacturing Corporation as at December 31, 2016. (Note: The accounts are listed in alphabetical order, first for debit balances, then for credit balances.)

	Debit balances	Credit balances
Accounts receivable	$ 77,000	
Administrative expenses	75,000	
Cash	30,000	
Cost of goods sold	430,000	
Dividends declared	35,000	
Equipment	280,000	
Income tax expense	21,700	
Interest expense	25,000	
Inventory	290,000	
Prepaid expenses	3,000	
Selling expenses	95,300	
Short-term investments	65,000	
Accounts payable		$ 65,000
Accumulated depreciation, equipment		65,000
Common shares		150,000
Dividends payable		7,000
Income tax payable		13,000
Interest revenue		10,000
Notes payable (current portion)		85,000
Notes payable (non-current portion)		250,000
Retained earnings		114,000
Sales revenue		650,000
Unearned revenue		18,000
	$1,427,000	$1,427,000

Required:

Prepare a classified statement of financial position for Novasco Manufacturing Corporation as at December 31, 2016.

AP3-33 (Determine missing amounts in financial statements)

Lee's Enterprises Ltd. suffered serious flood damage that destroyed most of its accounting records. The following statements were reconstructed from the records that were recovered, but many of the amounts are missing:

	2015	2016
Statement of Income		
Revenues	A	200,000
Expenses	B	K
Net income	15,000	L

continued

	2015	2016
Retained Earnings		
Opening balance	C	M
Net income	D	20,000
Dividends	5,000	N
Ending balance	E	O
Statement of Financial Position		
Current assets	F	30,000
Other assets	54,000	P
Total assets	G	80,000
Current liabilities	10,000	Q
Long-term liabilities	H	10,000
Total liabilities	40,000	R
Common shares	I	20,000
Retained earnings	20,000	S
Total shareholders' equity	34,000	55,000
Total equity and liabilities	J	T

The following information is also available, to help you determine the missing amounts:

1. The company's Retained Earnings balance at the end of 2014 was $10,000.
2. The company's profit margin ratio was 15% in 2015 and 10% in 2016.
3. In both 2015 and 2016, the company's current assets were twice the amount of the current liabilities.

Required:

For each of the letters above, determine the missing dollar amount that will complete the financial statements. (Hint: It might not be possible to find all the missing amounts in the order they are presented in. You may have to skip over some, initially, and come back to them after you have determined other items.)

AP3-34 (Determine missing amounts in financial statements)

Rao's Recycling Centre suffered a serious fire that destroyed most of the firm's accounting records. The following statements were reconstructed from the records that were recovered, but many of the amounts are missing:

	2015	2016
Statement of Income		
Revenues	A	180,000
Expenses	B	K
Net income	14,000	L
Retained Earnings		
Opening balance	C	M
Net income	D	18,000
Dividends	5,000	N
Ending balance	20,000	O
Statement of Financial Position		
Current assets	E	30,000
Other assets	54,000	P
Total assets	F	90,000
Current liabilities	10,000	Q
Long-term liabilities	G	20,000
Total liabilities	40,000	R
Common shares	H	25,000
Retained earnings	I	S
Total shareholders' equity	J	55,000
Total equity and liabilities	74,000	T

The following information is also available, to help you determine the missing amounts:

1. The company's profit margin ratio was 10% in both 2015 and 2016.
2. In both 2015 and 2016, the company's current assets were twice the amount of the current liabilities.

Required:
For each of the letters above, determine the missing dollar amount that will complete the financial statements. (Hint: It might not be possible to find all the missing amounts in the order they are presented in.)

User Perspective Problems

UP3-1 (Differences between the adjusted trial balance and a set of financial statements)

Assume that you are part of a commercial lending team for a bank. As part of the loan terms, one of the bank's clients must submit monthly financial statements for review. The client has just phoned and left your boss a message asking if it would be enough to just provide the bank with an adjusted trial balance. Your boss has asked you to prepare a brief memo outlining any differences between the information that would be provided by the financial statements and that provided by the adjusted trial balance. Your boss has also asked that you recommend the position the bank should take regarding this request.

Required:
Respond to your boss's requests.

UP3-2 (Purpose of closing entries)

A friend came to ask you a question about accounting for a small business she started at the beginning of the year. She said that her accounting software had a "closing entry" option. She was uncertain what this meant, when she should select it, and what impact it would have on her company's accounting records.

Required:
Prepare a response to your friend's questions.

UP3-3 (Importance of the chart of accounts)

You have been asked to give a brief presentation to members of your local chamber of commerce regarding the importance of the chart of accounts in relation to managing their business.

Required:
Prepare an overview of the key points you plan to address in your presentation.

UP3-4 (Normal balances)

One of your friends, who is also a classmate, came to you in the library and asked if you can explain the concept of normal balances to her. She was busy on social media during part of the class in which this topic was discussed.

Required:
Prepare your response.

Reading and Interpreting Published Financial Statements

RI3-1 (Closing entries, unearned revenue and prepaid expenses)

Le Château Inc. is a leading Canadian specialty retailer offering contemporary fashion apparel, accessories, and footwear to women and men. Exhibits 3-21 and 3-22 contain excerpts from the company's consolidated financial statements dated January 25, 2014.

EXHIBIT 3-21 EXCERPT FROM LE CHÂTEAU'S CONSOLIDATED STATEMENTS OF CHANGES IN SHAREHOLDERS' EQUITY

(in thousands of Canadian dollars)

RETAINED EARNINGS	2014	2013
Balance, beginning of year	94,239	102,956
Net Loss	(15,986)	(8,717)
Dividends Declared	-	-
Balance, end of year	**78,253**	**94,239**

EXHIBIT 3-22 **EXCERPT FROM NOTE 3**

"Gift cards or gift certificates [collectively referred to as "gift cards"] sold are recorded as deferred revenue and revenue is recognized at the time of redemption or in accordance with the Company's accounting policy or breakage. Breakage income represents estimated value of gift cards that is not expected to be redeemed by customers and is estimated based on historical redemption patterns."

Required:

a. Prepare the closing entries that would have been required to close the Income Summary and Dividends Declared accounts. Refer to Exhibit 3-21.
b. The company has deferred revenues of $3,712 thousand as at January 25, 2014. Refer to Exhibit 3-22 and explain the note in your own words.
c. The company has prepaid expenses of $2,292 thousand as at January 25, 2014. Identify two of Le Château's likely prepaid expenses and when they would be expensed.

RI3-2 (Retained earnings, depreciation and prepaid expenses)

High Liner Foods Inc. operates in the North American packaged foods industry and primarily processes and markets frozen seafood and distributes products to retail and food service customers. Exhibit 3-23 contains selected financial information for 2013.

EXHIBIT 3-23 **SELECTED 2013 FINANCIAL INFORMATION FOR HIGH LINER FOODS**

(in thousands of U.S. dollars)

Net Income	34,724
Retained Earnings, opening balance	66,373
Dividends Declared	10,305

Required:

a. Determine the company's ending Retained Earnings balance. Refer to Exhibit 3-23.
b. Identify three things that we know about the company because it has an opening balance in Retained Earnings.
c. During the year ended December 28, 2013, High Liner Foods had depreciation expense of $6,006 thousand on its production equipment, $213 thousand on its building structures, and $816 thousand on its computer hardware and peripherals. Prepare the adjusting entry that would have been required if the company recorded all of its depreciation in a single entry.
d. The company had prepaid expenses of $2,952 thousand as at December 28, 2013. Identify two types of likely prepaid expenses and explain when they would be expensed.

RI3-3 (Retained earnings, accrued liabilities and carrying value)

North West Company Inc. is a leading retailer to underserved rural communities and urban markets in northern and Western Canada and internationally. Its stores offer a broad range of products and services with an emphasis on food. Exhibit 3-24 contains an excerpt from the company's consolidated financial statements for the year ended January 31, 2014.

EXHIBIT 3-24 **EXCERPT FROM NORTH WEST COMPANY'S 2014 FINANCIAL STATEMENTS**

(in thousands of dollars)

Net Income	71,767
Retained Earnings, opening balance	128,224
Dividends Declared	54,229

Required:

a. Determine the company's ending retained earnings balance. Refer to Exhibit 3-24.
b. Identify three things that we know about the company because it has an opening balance in Retained Earnings.
c. The company had accounts payable and accrued liabilities of $128,999 thousand at January 31, 2014. Identify two possible liabilities the company may have had as part of this balance.
d. Based on the information below (given in thousands of dollars), determine the carrying value of the North West Company's building and computer equipment. Comment on how old or new these capital assets are and how you determined this.

	Cost	Accumulated Depreciation
Building	350,921	191,439
Fixtures & equipment	245,863	171,321

RI3-4 (Retained earnings, prepaid expenses and dividends)

Big Rock Brewery Inc. is a regional producer of premium craft beers and cider, which are sold across Canada. Exhibit 3-25 contains an excerpt from the company's consolidated financial statements for the year ended December 31, 2013.

EXHIBIT 3-25 EXCERPT FROM BIG ROCK'S 2013 FINANCIAL STATEMENTS

(in thousands of Canadian dollars)

Net Income	2,551
Deficit, Opening Balance	(68,739)
Dividends Declared	4,855

Required:

a. Determine the company's Retained Earnings (Deficit) balance using the information from Exhibit 3-25.
b. Identify three things that we know about the company because it has an opening deficit balance.
c. The company had $84,000 in prepaid insurance premiums at December 31, 2013. Which financial statement would this be presented on? When would the premiums be expensed?
d. On December 18, 2013, Big Rock's directors declared dividends of $0.20 per share on the company's 6,070,000 common shares. The dividend was paid on January 15, 2014. Prepare the journal entries necessary to record the declaration and payment of these dividends.

RI3-5 (Examine financial statement disclosures)

Required:

Find the annual report of a Canadian company that is listed on a Canadian stock exchange, and answer the following questions about it:

a. Has the company prepared a classified statement of financial position (balance sheet)? If not, look for an explanation and state it briefly.
b. Referring to items in the statement of financial position, explain what liquidity is and how it is reflected in the statement of financial position.
c. Discuss how important inventory is compared with the other assets on the company's statement of financial position. Also address how important capital assets (property, plant, and equipment) are to the company.
d. Does the company rely more heavily on debt financing or equity financing?

RI3-6 (Find additional information about a company)

Required:

For the company you selected in RI3-5, find at least three articles in the financial media that discuss the nature of this company's markets, and that forecast what the future may be for this sector of the economy. Write a one-page summary of your findings.

Cases

C3-1 Al's Gourmet Fish

Leadfoot Al decided to retire from a successful career in stock car racing and invest all his winnings in a fish farm. He had majored in genetics in university, and he experimented with many different species of fish before coming up with a catfish that had the texture and taste of ocean trout. After incorporating Al's Gourmet Fish Company and operating for two years, he decided to explore expansion possibilities. He talked with his banker about getting a loan and presented a statement of income for the current year, based strictly on cash flows, as follows:

Cash collected from sale of fish		$520,000
Less: Feed purchases	$460,000	
Purchase of new fish tank	40,000	
Wages paid	80,000	
Other operating expenses paid	20,000	600,000
Operating loss		(80,000)
Plus: Proceeds from sale of land		130,000
Net income		$ 50,000

From discussions with Al, the banker learned the following:

1. Of the cash collected in the current period from sales of fish, $120,000 was for shipments delivered to customers last year. All the sales made this year were collected before the end of the year.
2. The fish feed can be stored indefinitely, and about 40% of this year's feed purchases were still on hand at year end.
3. Two fish tanks were purchased last year at a total cost of $80,000. These tanks, along with the one purchased at the beginning of this year, were used all year. Each tank is expected to last five years.
4. The amount for wages includes $60,000 paid to Al, as compensation for his time devoted to the business.
5. There was a total of $1,000 in bills for other operating expenses for the current year that had not been recorded or paid by year end.
6. The land that was sold for $130,000 had been purchased two years ago for $90,000.

Required:
Provide Al and his banker with answers to the following questions:

a. What amount of revenue from the sale of merchandise should be reported in this period?
b. What amount of expense for fish food should be reported in this period? How should the remainder of the food be reported?
c. Should some amount for the fish tanks be included in calculating the income for the current period? If so, how much?
d. Is it all right for Al's company to pay him wages? Why or why not?
e. What amount for "other operating expenses" should be included in calculating the earnings for the current period?
f. The land was sold for more than its original purchase price. The difference between the selling price and the purchase price of a capital asset is called a gain, and is included on the statement of income in the period of the sale. What amount should be included in the company's earnings as the gain on the sale of the land?
g. How much did Al earn from his business this year?
h. Comment on whether you think Al should stay in the fish business or go back to auto racing. In addition to financial factors, briefly describe several non-financial considerations that would be relevant to this decision.

C3-2 Sentry Security Services

Samir Sarkov incorporated Sentry Security Services and began operations on January 1, 2016. After a busy year, Samir thinks his business has done well, at least in terms of the volume of work done. However, he has asked for your help in determining the financial results.

The company's accounting records, such as they are, have been kept by Samir's son. Although he kept good records of all the cash received and spent by the business during the year, he has no formal training in accounting. At the end of the year, he prepared the following statement:

SENTRY SECURITY SERVICES Statement of Cash Receipts and Disbursements For the Year Ended December 31, 2016		
Cash Receipts:		
Invested in the business by the Sarkov family	$ 25,000	
Received from customers for services provided	75,000	
Borrowed from the Provincial Bank	15,000	
		$115,000
Cash Disbursements:		
Paid to the Provincial Bank	6,500	
Rent paid	6,500	
Security equipment purchased	18,000	
Wages paid	37,000	
Security services truck payments made	25,000	
Insurance premiums paid	2,000	
Security system parts and supplies purchased	15,000	110,000
Cash remaining (equals the bank balance)		$ 5,000

After reviewing the records, you confirm that the amounts are correct, and you also discover these additional facts:

1. The business does most of its work for cash, but at the end of the year customers owe $5,000 for security services that were provided on account.
2. The amount borrowed from the Provincial Bank is a three-year loan, with an interest rate of 10% per year.
3. The amount paid to the bank during the year includes $1,500 of interest on the loan and $5,000 of principal.
4. The rental contract for the company's space covers a two-year period and requires payments of $500 per month, paid at the beginning of each month. In addition, the last month's rent had to be paid in advance. All the required payments have been made as scheduled.
5. The security equipment was purchased at the beginning of the year and has an estimated five-year lifespan, after which it will be worthless.
6. In addition to the wages that were paid during 2016, $250 is owed to employees for overtime that was worked during the last few days of the year. This will be paid early in 2017.
7. The security services truck payments consist of $21,000 paid to purchase the truck at the beginning of the year plus $4,000 paid for gas, oil, and repairs during the year. Samir Sarkov expects to use the truck for four years, after which he thinks he should be able to get about $1,000 for it as a trade-in on a new truck.
8. The $2,000 for insurance resulted from paying premiums on two policies at the beginning of the year. One policy cost $700 for one year of insurance coverage; the other policy cost $1,300 for two years of coverage.
9. In addition to the $15,000 of parts and supplies that were purchased and paid for during the year, creditors have billed the business $500 for parts and supplies that were purchased and delivered but not paid for.
10. A count at the end of the year shows that $1,750 of unused parts and supplies were still on hand.

Required:

a. Prepare an accrual-basis statement of income for the year ended December 31, 2016, and a classified statement of financial position for Sentry Security Services at the end of the year.
b. Comment on the company's performance during its first year of operations, and its financial position at the end of the year.

C3-3 Shirley's Snack Shop

Shirley Sze incorporated Shirley's Snack Shop on April 30, 2016, by investing $5,000 in cash. The following is a summary of the other events affecting the business during its first eight months of operations:

1. On May 1, Shirley acquired a licence from the municipality at a cost of $150. The licence allows her to operate the snack shop for a period of one year.
2. On May 2, she borrowed $10,000 from the bank and used most of it to buy equipment costing $9,600. The interest rate on the loan is 10%, and the interest is to be paid annually (each May). The entire principal

amount is repayable at the end of three years. Shirley estimates that the equipment will last 10 years, after which it will be scrapped. On December 31, 2016, she estimated that the equipment could have been sold for $9,200.

3. At the beginning of September, Shirley realized that she should have liability insurance and purchased a one-year policy effective immediately. The premium paid was $750.
4. Her business is located in a small shop near the university campus. The rental cost is $900 per month and she has paid nine months of rent thus far.
5. Shirley paid herself a salary of $1,000 a month, and a part-time assistant earned wages of $350 each month. However, she has not yet paid her assistant his wages for December.
6. Shirley's purchases of food supplies, on account, cost a total of $22,500. All but $4,500 of this has been used, and she still owes the supplier $4,000. Of the food supplies that have been used, most went into snacks that were sold to customers; however, Shirley ate some of them herself, as on-the-job meals. She estimates that the snacks she consumed were purchased from the supplier at a cost of approximately $200, and were priced to sell to her customers for approximately $400.
7. According to her bank records, Shirley received $42,300 from her customers and deposited this in the bank during the period. However, a customer still owes her $500 for snacks provided for a company party held shortly before the end of the year. The balance in her bank account on December 31 is $9,750.
8. Shirley thinks that she has had fairly successful operations since opening the business. However, she has no idea how to calculate its net income or determine its financial position.

Required:

a. Provide Shirley with a statement of income for the eight-month period ended December 31, 2016, and a statement of financial position as at that date.
b. Comment on the snack shop's performance during its first eight months of operations, and its financial standing as at December 31, 2016.

C3-4 Mbeke's Hardware Store

In the middle of January 2017, Mark Mbeke, the owner of Mbeke's Hardware Store, decided to expand the business by buying out a local lumberyard. To finance the purchase, Mark had to obtain financing from a local bank. The bank asked Mark to provide financial statements for the year ended December 31, 2016, as support for the loan application.

Over the last year, Mark was so busy managing the store that he had no time to review the financial aspects of its operations. However, when the company's bookkeeper provided him with a set of hastily prepared financial statements for 2016, Mark was pleasantly surprised to see that the hardware store's net income had increased from $60,000 in 2015 to $90,000 in 2016. He commented, "With financial results like these—a 50% increase in income during the past year—we should have no trouble getting the loan." However, further investigation revealed the following:

1. On January 2, 2017, the company repaid a $140,000 loan in full, including interest. The loan was a one-year, 10% term loan. No interest expense was recorded in 2016.
2. On January 3, 2017, wages of $10,000 were paid. A review of the time cards shows that these wages relate to work done in the last week of 2016.
3. Goods that originally cost $11,000 and were sold in December 2016 for $15,000 were returned by the customer on January 4, 2017. Accompanying the goods was a letter that stated, "As we agreed on December 30, 2016, these goods are not what we had ordered and are therefore being returned for full credit."
4. Mbeke's Hardware received bills totalling $2,000 in the first week of January 2017 for utilities and other operating costs incurred in 2016. They were immediately recorded as accounts payable when they were received.

Mark is concerned that some of these transactions may affect the company's financial statements for the year 2016, and therefore its ability to obtain the necessary bank financing.

Required:

a. Calculate the effect of each of these items on the store's net income for 2016.
b. By what percentage did the store's net income increase (or decrease) over the last year?
c. In light of this information, how should Mark proceed?
d. What should the bank do to ensure that it is receiving accurate financial information?

C3-5 Downunder Company

You have been retained by Downunder Company to straighten out its accounting records. The company's trusted accountant for the past 25 years suddenly retired to a tropical island in the South Pacific and, in his rush to get away, he seems to have misplaced the company's accounting records. Now the bank has asked for the latest financial statements, so it can determine whether to renew the company's loan. Luckily, you managed to find the following listing of accounts and their balances, in alphabetical order, written on the back of one of the accountant's travel brochures.

Accumulated Depreciation, Equipment	$ 4,000	Equipment (original cost)	51,500
Common Shares	20,000	Interest Expense	500
Accounts Receivable	20,200	Bank Loan Payable	15,000
Accounts Payable	13,000	Miscellaneous Expenses	8,000
Cash (in bank account and in cash box)	1,100	Sales to Customers	93,600
Cost of Goods Sold	41,000	Wages Expense	27,500
Inventory	7,900	Wages Payable	1,200
Depreciation Expense	2,000		

Required:

a. Based on the information available, prepare a statement of income for the year 2016 and a statement of financial position as at December 31, 2016. Note that there is no amount available for Retained Earnings, so you will have to enter whatever amount is required to make the statement of financial position balance.
b. Identify several additional pieces of information that would be needed for preparing more complete and accurate financial statements. (Hint: Think in terms of the types of adjustments that would normally be made.)

ENDNOTES

1. Gary P. Spraakman, "Management Accounting at the Historical Hudson's Bay Company: A Comparison to 20th Century Practices," *Accounting Historians Journal*, Vol. 26, No. 2, December 1999; Arthur J. Ray, *Give Us Good Measure*, University of Toronto Press, 1978; HBC 2013 annual report; HBC Heritage website, www.hbcheritage.ca/.
2. Yan Barcelo, "Devil in the Details," *CA Magazine*, January/February 2013.
3. CPA Standards and Guidance Collection; Part 1 – International Financial Reporting Standards; The Conceptual Framework.

CHAPTER 5 The Statement of Cash Flows

CORE QUESTIONS

If you are able to answer the following questions, then you have achieved the related learning objectives.

LEARNING OBJECTIVES

After studying this chapter, you should be able to:

INTRODUCTION

- Why is the statement of cash flows of significance to users?

1. Understand and explain why the statement of cash flows is of significance to users.

DISCUSS THE DIFFERENCES BETWEEN THE STATEMENTS OF CASH FLOWS AND INCOME

- How does the statement of cash flows differ from the statement of income?

2. Explain how the statement of cash flows and the statement of income differ.

UNDERSTANDING THE STATEMENT OF CASH FLOWS

- What are the categories of cash flows presented in the statement of cash flows and what are typical transactions included in each category?
- Why is so much significance placed on cash flows from operating activities?

3. Identify the three major types of activities that are presented in a statement of cash flows and describe some of the typical transactions included in each category of activity.

PREPARING THE STATEMENT OF CASH FLOWS

- How is "cash" defined?
- How is a statement of cash flows prepared?
- What is the difference between the direct and indirect methods of preparing cash flows from operating activities?
- Are there investing and financing activities that do not appear on the statement of cash flows?

4. Prepare a statement of cash flows using a comparative statement of financial position, a statement of income, and some additional information.

INTERPRETING CASH FLOW INFORMATION

- How can the information presented in a statement of cash flows be used to manage a company?
- What can cash flow patterns tell us?

5. Interpret a statement of cash flows and develop potential solutions to any cash flow challenges identified.

FINANCIAL STATEMENT ANALYSIS

- How do we determine what portion of a company's liabilities could be met with cash flows from operating activities?
- How do we determine how much net free cash flow a company generates?

6. Calculate and interpret a company's cash flows to total liabilities ratio and determine the amount of net free cash flow being generated.

The Dash for Cash

When Joseph-Armand Bombardier created a gas-powered "snow vehicle" in 1937, he probably could never have imagined the company he founded would one day be the third-largest civil aviation manufacturer in the world. It's also unique because it manufactures trains in addition to planes.

Montreal-based Bombardier, maker of such products as the iconic Dash 8 turboprop, had $18.2 billion in revenues in its year ended December 31, 2013. But as you would expect from a company that develops and manufactures aircraft and rail equipment that cost millions of dollars each, Bombardier requires a lot of cash to finance its operations. The company's CSeries smaller passenger jets are an example of where significant research and development costs are incurred long before the products are sold. When significant costs are incurred before collecting sales receipts or deposits from customers, companies like Bombardier can have cash flow problems.

In the first quarter of 2014, Bombardier had an outflow of $915 million in cash, meaning it paid out nearly $1 billion more than it brought in during that period. After these results were announced, the company's stock price dropped 6%. Investors must consider the risks related to businesses with high costs and long cash-to-cash cycles: the time it takes from when raw materials are purchased until the customer pays for the manufactured item. Companies try to shorten their cash-to-cash cycles, but it's difficult for Bombardier because planes and trains have multi-year development and manufacturing cycles.

Part of Bombardier's 2014 cash flow problem was a delay in the rollout of its CSeries planes, originally expected for late 2013 but pushed back to 2015, delaying the inflow of cash from operating activities (sales). Meanwhile, the planes' development costs increased from a planned $3.4 billion to $4.4 billion.

One of the ways companies like Bombardier address their long cash-to-cash cycles is to borrow the required funds, such as by issuing bonds. For example, Bombardier issued $2.0 billion in bonds during 2013 and another $1.8 billion in April 2014.

When assessing a company's liquidity—its ability to meet its short-term obligations—investors and creditors look at the company's cash balances. In spite of a $915-million outflow of cash, Bombardier assured investors that its liquidity was fine. It said its cash outflow would decrease in the rest of 2014 and pointed to its backlog of $69.7 million in unfilled product orders as at the end of 2013 as a future source of cash inflow. The company stated it would not need to issue more bonds in the near future to increase cash inflows. "We don't anticipate to go back to any sources to increase our liquidity. We have ample liquidity to meet our plans," said Chief Financial Officer Pierre Alary.[1]

INTRODUCTION

LEARNING OBJECTIVE 1
Understand and explain why the statement of cash flows is of significance to users.

Many users consider the **statement of cash flows** to be the most important financial statement in determining a company's future prospects. As we saw in the feature story on **Bombardier Inc.**, investors keep a close eye on whether cash is flowing into and out of a company. This information is presented in the the statement of cash flows, which categorizes the inflows and outflows of cash into operating, investing, and financing activities.

Why is the statement of cash flows of significance to users?

In Chapter 4, the basic revenue recognition criteria and the measurement of income were discussed. Although this is a very important perspective on a company's performance, other aspects that affect the company's overall health are not adequately captured by the statement of income. For example, creditors want to be able to assess a company's ability to generate sufficient cash to service its debts (to pay interest and repay the principal as it comes due). The use of accrual accounting means that the revenues and expenses on the statement of income do not correspond to the company's **cash flows**—inflows and outflows of cash—and therefore do not provide all of the information that creditors need. Aside from assessing profitability, creditors and other outside users of financial information need some way to assess an organization's cash flows and predict its future cash position. The statement of cash flows provides this perspective on an organization's performance, by summarizing its cash inflows and outflows and highlighting the activities that resulted in the net change in its cash position during the period.

Having an understanding of how cash flows into and out of a company is critical for users. The information presented in this statement enables users to:

- Assess the company's ability to generate cash flows from its core operations.
- Evaluate the cash flows the company has been able to obtain from investors (through the issuance of new shares) and creditors (through new borrowings).
- Assess the extent to which the company has invested cash to replace or add revenue-generating assets such as property, plant, and equipment.
- Determine the amount of cash that the company has used to repay debt.
- Evaluate the amount of cash dividends distributed to shareholders, together with the sources of that cash.

All of the uses noted above provide financial statement users with an historical perspective—how the company performed in prior periods. It is important to note that the information in the statement of cash flows is also used on a predictive basis—what a user can expect in the future. Specifically, information on a company's cash flows is used to:

- Estimate the value of the company, because a number of commonly used business valuation techniques are based on estimated future cash flows.
- Assess the company's ability to repay debt in the future.
- Evaluate the potential for the company to be able to pay dividends in the future.
- Estimate the company's future cash requirements and assess these needs relative to the company's existing cash and short-term investment balances, together with the company's access to funding that has already been secured (that is, existing operating lines of credit).

The statement of cash flows also serves as a key tool for financial statement users because it illustrates the relationships between the other statements. For example, while the statement of financial position shows the net change in property, plant, and equipment, and the statement of income shows the amount of any gain or loss on the sale of property, plant, and equipment, only the statement of cash flows will explain these amounts by presenting the amount of property, plant, and equipment purchased during the period along with the proceeds received from any disposals of these assets.

The statement of cash flows also explains the changes in key account balances. For example, while the statement of financial position may indicate the net change in a company's long-term debt (an increase or decrease), the statement of cash flows will explain the change. It will indicate how much the company has borrowed and how much principal it repaid during the year.

In Chapters 1 and 2, we discussed how the statement of cash flows summarizes a company's cash inflows and outflows by the three categories of business activities: operating activities, investing activities, and financing activities. Understanding what is included in each of these categories assists financial statement users in assessing the significance of the cash flows reported for each.

The primary focus of most financial statement users will be on the company's **operating activities**. These are the lifeblood of any company and should generate a positive cash flow (an inflow of cash). After all, the operating activities include all of the inflows and outflows related to the sale of goods and services—the activities that the company provides in its normal operations. A positive cash flow from operating activities indicates that a company's core business operations are generating more cash than it is using. This net inflow of cash may then be used for other activities, such as purchasing new capital assets, repaying debts, or paying dividends to shareholders. A negative cash flow from operations indicates that a company's regular operating activities required more cash than they generated. This may suggest that investments or capital assets may have to be sold and/or external sources of financing have to be found in order to offset this cash outflow and enable the company to continue to operate.

Assessing a company's cash flows from **investing activities** enables users to examine a company's decisions regarding the purchase or sale of property, plant, and equipment. If the company has made any long-term investments in other companies or disposed of ones made previously, the cash flows related to these transactions will also be reflected in this cash flow category. This information enables users to assess the company's strategy when it comes to replacing the property, plant, and equipment required to continue operations or whether additional assets are being acquired to provide the capacity to grow the company's operations.

Users will also examine a company's **financing activities** to assess the decisions made by management and/or the board of directors in relation to the company's debt and equity. They will determine whether the company incurred more debt or repaid principal during the period. They will also assess whether new shares were issued and whether any dividends were declared and paid. This information enables users to evaluate the company's financial strength and strategy, as well as to estimate its reliance on debt versus equity financing in the future.

Even those users who consider the statement of income to be the most important statement will examine it together with the statement of cash flows and statement of financial position to more fully understand and analyze a company. As a future user of financial information, it is important that you know what to look for on the statement of cash flows and understand what the amounts in its various categories mean. For this reason, we are going to show you how the statement is developed and how you can analyze it.

For Example

Canadian Tire Corporation, Limited began its 2013 fiscal year with $1,015.5 million in cash and cash equivalents and ended the year with $643.2 million. Users of the Company's financial statements would want to determine the reasons behind this $372.3-million decrease in cash and cash equivalents. Did it result from challenges with the company's retail operations? Is it because the company repaid debt? Is it because the company purchased significant amounts of property, plant, and equipment during the year? Being able to determine the answers to questions like these is critical for users, and the statement of cash flows provides them with the answers.[2]

DISCUSS THE DIFFERENCES BETWEEN THE STATEMENT OF CASH FLOWS AND THE STATEMENT OF INCOME

How does the statement of cash flows differ from the statement of income?

■ **LEARNING OBJECTIVE 2**
Explain how the statement of cash flows and the statement of income differ.

In each of the preceding chapters, we have discussed how financial statements, including the statement of income, are prepared using the accrual basis of accounting rather than the cash basis of accounting. As such, revenues are recognized on the statement of income when they have been earned rather than when cash is received from customers. In fact, as we saw in Chapter 4, determining when revenue has been earned has nothing to do with the receipt of cash. In terms of expenses, we have learned that these are recognized when they have been incurred under the accrual basis of accounting. Again, there are often differences between when an expense is incurred and when it is paid in cash.

As a result, the statement of income measures a company's performance for a period (usually a month, quarter, or year) on an accrual basis. While the revenue, expense, and net income amounts presented on this statement are very important, they do not represent cash flowing into and out of the business during that same period. If management is only paying attention to the statement of income and not to cash flows, they may think that all is well with the company, in spite of a looming cash shortfall. For example, if a significant portion of a company's sales are on account and customers are not paying these accounts on a timely basis, the company may be running short of cash in spite of an increase in sales. Alternatively, if a company's suppliers require it to pay for goods in advance or to make upfront deposits, the company may be paying out cash well in advance of these items becoming expenses; the payments would be accounted for as inventory or prepaid expenses. In this case, in spite of a statement of income that portrays the company as profitable, the company could also be running short of cash due to these payments. In other cases, companies can have significant non-cash expenses, such as depreciation and amortization. While these reduce net income, they have no impact on the amount of cash a company is able to generate from its operations.

KEY POINTS

The statement of cash flows differs from the statement of income because it:

- reflects the cash basis rather than the accrual basis of accounting, and
- focuses on more than just operating activities (it includes investing and financing activities).

Another key difference between the two statements has to do with the fact that the statement of income focuses only on the operating activities of a company. It reflects the profit or earnings generated from the company's sales to its customers less the expenses the company incurred to generate them. The statement of income does not reflect many of the transactions a company has with its creditors (such as borrowing funds or repaying principal) or shareholders (such as the proceeds of issuing shares or the payment of dividends). As such, even if there was little difference in the timing of revenues and expenses being recorded and their receipt and payment in cash, the statement of income would tell users only part of the story.

Information related to a company's cash payments for the purchase of property, plant, and equipment or the cash receipts from their sale is also not included on a company's statement of income. These cash flows related to a company's investing activities can be very significant and would not be apparent to financial statement users relying solely on the statement of income.

For Example

One of Canada's leading retailers of women's fashion, **Reitmans (Canada) Limited**, had net earnings of $10.8 million during the year ended February 1, 2014, yet it purchased more than $34.5 million in property, equipment, and intangible assets, and paid $41.9 million in dividends during the year. It did all of this without borrowing any money. A quick review of the company's statement of cash flows, specifically the company's cash flows from operating activities, illustrates how this was possible. It turns out that Reitmans had depreciation and amortization expenses and impairment losses of $63.7 million. While these expenses and losses reduced net income, they were non-cash charges. In fact, the company's cash flow from operating activities was an inflow of $84.716 million—an amount significantly different from net earnings. This example illustrates why it is important for financial statement users to consider both the statement of income and the statement of cash flows when assessing corporate performance.[3]

As its name implies, the statement of cash flows reports all transactions involving the receipt or payment of cash. This is not restricted to those resulting from a company's operating activities, but includes those related to its investing activities (from the purchase and sale of capital assets) and its financing activities (the transactions a company has with its creditors and investors).

UNDERSTANDING THE STATEMENT OF CASH FLOWS

LEARNING OBJECTIVE 3
Identify the three major types of activities that are presented in a statement of cash flows and describe some of the typical transactions included in each category of activity.

What are the categories of cash flows presented in the statement of cash flows and what are typical transactions included in each category?

In Chapter 1, we discussed how all of the activities that companies engage in can be grouped in to three categories: operating activities, investing activities, and financing activities. We also discussed how these categories provided the structure for the statement of cash flows. As such, we will not repeat that discussion here. It is beneficial, however, to review examples of the typical transactions included in each category of cash flows. This information is presented in Exhibit 5-1.

Exhibit 5-1 Typical Transactions for Each Category of Cash Flows

Typical Operating Activities	Inflows:	• Cash sales to customers • Collections of amounts owed by customers
	Outflows:	• Purchases of inventory • Payments of amounts owed to suppliers • Payments of expenses such as wages, rent, and interest • Payments of taxes owed to the government
Typical Investing Activities	Inflows:	• Proceeds from the sale of property, plant, and equipment • Proceeds from the sale of shares of other companies
	Outflows:	• Purchases of property, plant, and equipment • Purchases of shares of other companies
Typical Financing Activities	Inflows:	• Borrowing money • Issuing shares
	Outflows:	• Repaying loan principal • Paying dividends

KEY POINTS
Cash flows from operating activities are key because they:
- result from what the company is in the business of doing,
- are the source for future debt repayments,
- are the source for future dividends payments.

In terms of the order in which the three categories of cash flows are presented on the statement of cash flows, all companies present cash flows from operating activities first. Some companies then present cash flows from investing activities, while others present cash flows from financing activities. This is something to watch for when reviewing statements of cash flows. In this chapter, cash flows from investing activities will be presented after cash flows from operating activities, followed by cash flows from financing activities.

Why is so much significance placed on cash flows from operating activities?

As previously noted, cash flows from operating activities normally receive the greatest scrutiny from financial statement users. The cash flows in this category result from the company's normal activities: the sale of goods and services to customers. In other words, these cash flows are generated from what the company is in the business of doing. As such, it is natural that users focus on how successful the company has been at doing so. Since these cash flows are generated by the company's operations, they are considered to be internally generated, as opposed to cash flows that come from sources outside the company, such as from investors or creditors. It will be these operating cash flows that can be reinvested to grow the company, to repay debt, or to fund dividends.

HELPFUL HINT
If a company is able to generate positive cash flows from operating activities, you know that it will likely succeed and will continue to operate in the future. An inability to generate operating cash flows means that the company will face significant challenges in continuing to operate.

The Conceptual Framework
FAITHFUL REPRESENTATION AND THE STATEMENT OF CASH FLOWS

The conceptual framework notes that "information about cash flows helps users understand a (company's) operations, evaluate its financing and investing activities, assess its liquidity or solvency and interpret other information about its performance." Given the emphasis placed on the various cash flow categories, it is essential that management faithfully represent these by presenting them in the appropriate category. For example, prior to adopting IFRS, **Sino-Forest Corporation**, which traded on the TSX, treated timber sales as cash flows from operating activities but timber purchases as investing activities. This resulted in the company having positive operating cash flows and negative investing cash flows, the normal pattern for a successful, growing company. When it restated its results under IFRS for the first quarter of 2010, timber sales and timber purchases were both included in cash flows from operating activities. This changed cash flows from operating activities from a positive U.S. $51.4 million to a negative U.S. $122 million. This significant change would have given the users of the company's financial statements a very different perspective on the company's operations and future prospects.[4]

Without operating cash flows, the company's ability to continue would depend upon it being able to attract new capital by issuing additional shares or securing new loans. Neither of these is a likely possibility if investors or creditors are not confident in the company's ability to generate the operating cash flows that could be used to pay dividends, grow the company, make interest payments, or repay loan principal. Without operating cash flows or financing cash flows, the only cash inflows available would come from the company selling some of its property, plant, and equipment. They would, in effect, be "cannibalizing the company" by selling its cash-generating assets. Obviously, this would not be a sustainable strategy.

PREPARING THE STATEMENT OF CASH FLOWS

How is "cash" defined?

LEARNING OBJECTIVE 4
Prepare a statement of cash flows using a comparative statement of financial position, a statement of income, and some additional information.

The statement of cash flows explains the net change in a company's cash position during an accounting period. While it may sound simple, having an understanding about how "cash" is defined for purposes of this statement is important. Cash normally includes both **cash** and **cash equivalents**. As you would expect, cash includes amounts the company has on hand, together with balances in **demand deposits** (chequing and savings accounts) with banks and other financial institutions. Cash equivalents include short-term, highly liquid investments. They must be convertible into known amounts of cash and be maturing within the next three months, meaning that there is little risk of a change in their value, due to changes in interest rates or other economic factors. Investments in money market funds, short-term deposits, and Government of Canada treasury bills are examples of cash equivalents.

KEY POINTS

"Cash" includes:

- cash on hand,
- bank deposits, and
- cash equivalents.

Bank borrowings and repayments are normally considered to be cash inflows and outflows from financing activities. However, it is possible for certain borrowings to be considered as cash equivalents. For example, if a company has used a **bank overdraft facility** or has drawn on a **line of credit** from its bank, then the amount of the borrowing can be considered "negative cash" and included in the determination of the company's cash and cash equivalents. This is normally done when the overdraft facility or line of credit is used as part of the company's normal cash management strategy. In other words, the company regularly draws on these, but then repays these borrowings as cash is collected from customers.

For Example

FINANCIAL STATEMENTS

Reitmans (Canada) Limited reported the following cash and cash equivalents at February 1, 2014, and February 2, 2013:[5]

(amounts in thousands of dollars)

5. CASH AND CASH EQUIVALENTS

	February 1, 2014	February 2, 2013
Cash on hand and with banks	$ 19,224	$ 9,248
Short-term deposits, bearing interest at 0.9% (February 2, 2013 – 0.6%)	103,131	88,378
	$122,355	$97,626

How is a statement of cash flows prepared?

As was discussed in Chapter 1, the statement of cash flows is the final financial statement prepared. This is because information from the statement of income, the statement of financial position, and the statement of changes in equity is required in order to complete the statement of cash flows. As such, these other statements, together with some additional information, will be provided as the basis for preparing the statement of cash flows. Additional information is often provided related to the company's purchases and sales of property, plant, and equipment or the extent of bank borrowings or principal repayments during the period.

KEY POINTS

- The direct and indirect methods differ in *how* the cash flows from operating activities are determined.
- Total operating cash flows are the same under both methods.
- The choice of methods has no effect on cash flows from investing or financing activities.

Prior to preparing the statement of cash flows, companies have to make a decision regarding which method they will use for determining cash flows from operating activities. Accounting standard setters have identified two acceptable methods: the **direct method** and the **indirect method**. It is important to note that the total cash flows from operating activities are exactly the same regardless of the method; the only difference is in how the amount is determined. The choice of method has no impact on the other two categories of cash flow activities.

While standard setters have encouraged companies to use the direct method, the vast majority of public companies use the indirect method. This is because it is considered simpler to prepare and it uses information that is easily obtained within most accounting systems. Given the prevalence of the indirect method, we will use this method as we discuss the preparation of the statement of cash flows. We will review the direct method later in the chapter, so you can understand how it differs from the indirect method.

KEY POINTS

Advantages of the indirect method are:

- It is simpler to prepare.
- It uses information available in most accounting systems.
- It provides a linkage between net income and cash flows from operating activities.

The indirect method is also known as the *reconciliation method*. This is because when using the indirect method to determine cash flows from operating activities, the starting point is net income. Since net income is determined using the accrual basis of accounting, a reconciliation is required to adjust it to a cash basis. This reconciliation is a strength of the indirect method, in that it makes the linkage between net income and cash flows from operating activities very clear.

There are a number of different methods that can be used to prepare the statement of cash flows. These include the T account and worksheet methods. Both of these are very mechanical and do not promote a deeper understanding of the concepts underlying the statement of cash flows. We will illustrate the preparation of the statement of cash flows using a hybrid approach, which is based on a structured framework involving some T account analysis, but that also involves analyzing the information in the financial statements to logically determine the related cash flows. An overview of this methodical approach to preparing the statement of cash flows is presented in Exhibit 5-2.

Next, we will discuss how to apply this framework to the financial statements of a hypothetical company. The statement of financial position and statement of income for Matchett Manufacturing Ltd.

(MML) are presented in Exhibits 5-3 and 5-4. Additional information on the company's investing and financing activities is presented in Exhibit 5-5. The information provided, while typical of many small companies, has been simplified for illustrative purposes.

Exhibit 5-2 Steps for the Preparation of the Statement of Cash Flows

General

1. Determine the net change in cash during the period.
2. Read any additional information provided and cross-reference it to the related statement of financial position accounts.

Cash Flows from Operating Activities

3. Using the statement of income, record net income and adjust it for any non-cash items included on the statement (such as depreciation and amortization expense) and/or items that do not involve operating activities (such as gains and losses from the sale of property, plant, and equipment or investments).
4. Determine the net change in each current asset and current liability account (except for the Cash and the Dividends Payable accounts) and record the impact that these changes had on cash.

Cash Flows from Investing Activities

5. Determine and record the cash proceeds received from selling property, plant, and equipment and the cost of property, plant, and equipment purchased with cash during the period.
6. Determine and record the cash proceeds from the sale of shares of other companies (from the sale of investments) and the cost of any investments in other companies purchased with cash during the period.

Cash Flows from Financing Activities

7. Determine the amount of cash dividends paid during the period.
8. Determine and record the amount of cash received from borrowings made during the year (new loans or increases to existing loans) and the amount of cash principal repaid on loans during the period.
9. Determine the cash received from shares issued during the period.

General

10. Calculate the sum of the cash flows from operating, investing, and financing activities and agree it to the net change in cash for the period as determined in Step 1.

Exhibit 5-3 Matchett Manufacturing Ltd. Statement of Financial Position

MATCHETT MANUFACTURING LTD.
Statement of Financial Position
As at October 31, 2016

	2016	2015
ASSETS		
Current assets		
Cash	$ 19,050	$ 11,250
Accounts receivable	45,200	57,700
Inventories	76,500	49,000
Total current assets	140,750	117,950
Equipment	127,000	62,000
Accumulated depreciation, equipment	(25,200)	(35,000)
	$242,550	$144,950
LIABILITIES AND SHAREHOLDERS' EQUITY		
Current liabilities		
Accounts payable	$ 38,600	$ 36,200
Income taxes payable	1,200	3,800
Dividends payable	3,200	5,200
Total current liabilities	43,000	45,200
Loans payable	43,000	36,000
Common shares	50,000	40,000
Retained earnings	106,550	23,750
	$242,550	$144,950

Exhibit 5-4 Matchett Manufacturing Ltd. Statement of Income

MATCHETT MANUFACTURING LTD.
Statement of Income
For the Year Ending October 31, 2016

Sales revenue	$480,000
Cost of goods sold	305,000
Gross profit	175,000
Expenses	
Wage expense	53,900
Rent expense	13,250
Utilities expense	7,600
Depreciation expense	10,200
Interest expense	2,970
Income tax expense	4,980
Income from operations	82,100
Gain on sale of equipment	3,900
Net income	$ 86,000

Exhibit 5-5 Matchett Manufacturing Ltd. Additional Information

The following additional information was gathered in relation to the company's investing and financing activities:

a. Equipment that had originally cost $25,000 and had a net carrying amount of $5,000 was sold for $8,900 during the year.
b. No principal repayments were made on the loan during the year.

The completed statement of cash flows for MML Manufacturing Ltd. is presented in Exhibit 5-6, with each line item referenced to the related step from the suggested framework.

Exhibit 5-6 Matchett Manufacturing Ltd. Statement of Cash Flows

MATCHETT MANUFACTURING LTD.
Statement of Cash Flows
For the year ended October 31, 2016

Cash flows from operating activities		
Net income	$86,000	Step 3
Add: Depreciation expense	10,200	Step 3
Less: Gain on sale of equipment	(3,900)	Step 3
Add: Decrease in accounts receivable	12,500	Step 4
Less: Increase in inventory	(27,500)	Step 4
Add: Increase in accounts payable	2,400	Step 4
Less: Decrease in income taxes payable	(2,600)	Step 4
Net cash provided by operating activities	77,100	

continued

Exhibit 5-6 Matchett Manufacturing Ltd. Statement of Cash Flows (continued)

Cash flows from investing activities		
Add: Proceeds from the sale of equipment	8,900	Step 5
Less: Purchase of equipment	(90,000)	Step 5
Net cash used in investing activities	(81,100)	
Cash flows from financing activities		
Less: Payment of dividends	(5,200)	Step 7
Add: Proceeds of borrowing—loan payable	7,000	Step 8
Add: Proceeds from issuing common shares	10,000	Step 9
Net cash provided by financing activities	11,800	
Ending cash	19,050	Step 1
Opening cash	11,250	Step 1
Net change in cash	$7,800	Steps 1 and 10
Supplementary disclosures:		
Cash paid for interest	$2,970	
Cash paid for income tax	$7,580	

We will now review each line item from MML's statement of cash flows in greater detail.

The first two steps are general steps, which are required to set up the statement of cash flows.

Step 1 – Determine the net change in cash during the period.

This can be determined by subtracting the balance of cash and cash equivalents at the beginning of the accounting period from the balance of cash and cash equivalents at the end of the accounting period. MML began the year with $11,250 in cash and cash equivalents and ended the year with $19,050. We can quickly see that the company's cash balance increased by $7,800 during the year. The statement of cash flows will explain how the company's various activities resulted in this increased cash balance.

Step 2 – Read any additional information provided and cross-reference it to the related statement of financial position accounts.

This step, which may seem overly simplistic, will help to ensure that you remember to take the additional information into account when you are analyzing the related account(s). Without this step, many students forget to use these pieces of additional information, so give it a try and see if it helps you. In this case, item "a" from Exhibit 5-5, which relates to the sale of equipment, should be cross-referenced to the equipment account on the statement of financial position. Cross-referencing just means that the letter "a" should be added beside "Equipment" on the statement of financial position. Item "b" relates to the company's loans, so the letter "b" should be added next to "Loans payable."

As previously noted, the first section of the statement of cash flows to be prepared is the cash flows from operating activities. This section determines what the company's net income would have been if the cash basis of accounting had been used rather than the accrual basis. The calculation starts with net income, with two types of adjustments made to this amount. The first type of adjustment removes the effects of non-cash items that appear on most statements of income. The most common non-cash item is depreciation and amortization expense. The adjustments also adjust for items on the statement of income that are not operating activities. The most common adjustment involves gains and losses from the sale of property, plant, and equipment. The second type of adjustment removes the income effects of accrual accounting. Net income is reduced by the amount of accrued revenues (as no cash has been collected in relation to them) and increased by the amount of accrued expenses (as no cash has been paid in relation to them). This is done by calculating the changes in the company's current asset and current liability accounts. These two types of adjustments are the next two steps in the process.

HELPFUL HINT
It can be helpful to cross out the statement of income once you have determined net income, the amount of any non-cash items, and the amount of any gains or losses from investing activities. This ensures that you will not be tempted to go back and try to use any additional information from the statement of income.

Step 3 – Using the statement of income, record net income and adjust it for any non-cash items included on the statement (such as depreciation and amortization expense) and/or items that do not involve operating activities (such as gains and losses from the sale of property, plant, and equipment or investments).

From MML's statement of earnings, we can see that the company's net income for the year was $86,000. We can also see that the company reported $10,200 in depreciation expense. As an expense, it reduced net income for the period, but because it did not involve cash, we add it back in order to determine what net income would have been without this amount. Amortization expense is treated the same way.

MML also reported a gain of $3,900 from the sale of equipment during the year. Since this transaction involved the sale of property, plant, and equipment, it is considered to be an investing activity and does not belong in the operating activities section. Because the gain increased net income, it has to be subtracted in order to eliminate it; that is, to determine what net income would have been without it. If there had been a loss on the sale, the opposite would have been done. Because losses reduce net income, they are added back to net income in order to eliminate them. Gains and losses from the sale of investments in other companies are treated the same way, as they are also investing rather than operating activities.

Step 4 – Determine the net change in each current asset and current liability account (except for the Cash and the Dividends Payable accounts) and record the impact that these changes had on cash.

In this step, net income is adjusted to remove the effects of accrual accounting. This is done by calculating the change in each of the company's current asset and current liability accounts, with the exception of the Cash account (because this was done in Step 1) and the Dividends Payable account (because the payment of dividends is a financing activity rather than an operating activity). Once the amount of the change has been determined, it is analyzed to determine whether it resulted in cash flowing into or out of the company. For example, a net increase in the Inventory account would indicate that goods had been purchased, resulting in an outflow of cash. Alternatively, a decrease in Accounts Receivable would indicate that customers paid their accounts, resulting in an inflow of cash.

From MML's statement of financial position, we can see that:

- Accounts Receivable decreased by $12,500; the company began the year with receivables of $57,700 and ended with $45,200. This means that the company's customers paid their accounts, resulting in a cash inflow (an increase in cash flows from operating activities).
- Inventory increased by $27,500; the company began the year with $49,000 in inventory and ended with $76,500. This means that the company purchased goods, resulting in a cash outflow (a decrease in cash flows from operating activities).
- Accounts Payable increased by $2,400; the company owed its suppliers $36,200 at the start of the year and ended owing them $38,600. This tells us that some of the expenses on the statement of income have not yet been paid, so we need to add them back to determine what net income would have been without them. Sometimes it can help to think about what the cash flow impact would have been if the opposite had happened. In this case, if Accounts Payable had decreased, it would be clear that the company paid some of its accounts, resulting in a cash outflow. Since the Accounts Payable increased, we do the opposite and treat it as a cash inflow by adding the amount back to net income.
- Income Taxes payable decreased by $2,600; the company owed the government $3,800 at the beginning of the year, but only $1,200 at the end of the year. This means that the company paid the government, resulting in a cash outflow (a decrease in cash flows from operating activities).

From the above, you can see that when determining cash flow from operations, *increases* in current assets have to be *subtracted* from net income on the statement of cash flows, while *decreases* in current assets have to be *added*. We do the opposite for current liabilities: increases have to be *added* to net income on the statement of cash flows, while decreases in current liabilities have to be *subtracted*. Exhibit 5-7 presents this in a tabular format. It can be useful to use this to support your analysis.

Exhibit 5-7 Cash Flow Impact of Changes in Current Assets and Current Liabilities

	Increase	Decrease
Current Asset	–	+
Current Liability	+	–

Once we have completed Step 4, we can determine the cash flows from operating activities for the period. From Exhibit 5-6, we can see that MML's cash flows from operating activities totalled $77,100. As previously discussed, we would normally expect cash flows from operating activities to be positive, meaning that the company generated a net inflow of cash from its operations.

Once cash flows from operating activities have been determined, we will then calculate cash flows from investing activities. The process for doing this is outlined in steps 5 and 6. In Step 5, the extent of the company's cash investments in long-term revenue-generating assets is calculated, together with the cash proceeds received from the sale of these assets. Step 6 involves determining the cash outflows related to long-term investments in other companies. This includes outflows related to purchasing shares of other companies, together with the proceeds from disposing of these investments. It is important to note that some companies may not make investments in the shares of other companies. As this is the case with MML, Step 6 would not be required. This is discussed further below.

HELPFUL HINT

It can be helpful to check off or cross out each account on the statement of financial position once you have determined and recorded the cash flows related to it. This ensures that you do not forget any accounts. It also allows you to quickly see which accounts have yet to be dealt with as you begin each section of the statement of cash flows.

Step 5 – Determine and record the cash proceeds received from selling property, plant, and equipment and the cost of property, plant, and equipment purchased with cash during the period.

When beginning our analysis of the Equipment account, the note we added in Step 2 would remind us that we were provided with the following additional information:

a. Equipment that had originally cost $25,000 and had a net carrying amount of $5,000 was sold for $8,900 during the year.

TAKE5

The sale of this equipment would be the first investing activity reported in MML's cash flows from investing activities. Since cash was received, this would increase the company's cash flows from investing activities.

Notice that the equipment that was sold had an original cost of $25,000 and a net carrying amount of $5,000. Since the term *net carrying amount* is equal to the original cost minus the accumulated depreciation, this is an indirect way of telling us that the accumulated depreciation on the equipment was $20,000 ($25,000 − $5,000).

Considerable detail is often provided about disposals of property, plant, and equipment such as this. However, you should bear in mind that, for purposes of the statement of cash flows, what really matters is the amount of cash that was received from the sale. In this case, the amount of cash is given, $8,900, so it can be entered directly into the statement of cash flows.

MML's Equipment account had a balance of $62,000 at the beginning of the period (from Exhibit 5-3). Remember that this amount reflects the original *cost* of the equipment purchased by the company. We also know, from the preceding step, that equipment with a cost of $25,000 was sold during the year. When the disposal was recorded, the cost of the equipment sold would have been removed from the Equipment account, bringing its balance down to $37,000. Since the balance at the end of the period was $127,000 (from Exhibit 5-3), we can deduce that additional equipment costing $90,000 must have been purchased during the period. The purchase, which would have resulted in an outflow of cash, would be recorded as a negative amount under cash flows from investing activities.

Our analysis of the Equipment account is sufficient to identify all of MML's investing activities related to equipment and there is no need to analyze the company's Accumulated Depreciation account. It represents the cumulative depreciation expense related to all of the company's equipment, but as we have discussed, depreciation is a non-cash transaction. As such, changes in this account balance do not impact cash flows. In more advanced accounting courses, it is possible that you will need to analyze this account if the selling price of any dispositions of property, plant, and equipment is not provided, but this is beyond the scope of an introductory accounting course.

When an account such as Equipment is affected by more than one transaction during the period, you may find it helpful to use a T account to organize the known data and determine any missing amount. For example, here is how a T account could be used to determine how much equipment MML purchased in 2015:

Equipment			
Beginning balance (from Exhibit 5-3)	62,000		
		25,000	Cost of equipment sold (given)
Balance after sale of equipment	37,000		
Cost of equipment purchased	**90,000**	←	**This is the missing amount, which will produce the ending balance.**
Ending balance (from Exhibit 5-3)	127,000		

HELPFUL HINT
Remember that, although most current liabilities relate to operating activities, some relate to *financing* activities. Examples are short-term bank loans or notes payable that have been used to obtain financing through borrowing, and dividends payable.

Step 6 – Determine and record the cash proceeds from the sale of shares of other companies (the sale of investments) and the cost of any investments in other companies purchased with cash during the period.

From the assets section of MML's statement of financial position, we can see that the company had no investments in the shares of other companies at either the beginning or end of the year. As such, no further analysis is required to complete this step. When preparing the statement of cash flows for companies that have invested in other companies, any proceeds received from the sale of these shares during the period are treated as cash inflows from investing activities, while the cost of any shares purchased during the period is treated as an outflow of cash from investing activities.

Once a company's long-term asset accounts have been analyzed, the cash flows from investing activities are complete. We can then move on to determine the company's cash flows from financing activities. Steps 7, 8, and 9 outline how this is done. Financing activities generally involve changes to long-term liabilities and shareholders' equity accounts. However, they can also involve a few *current* liabilities. For example, in Step 4 of this analysis, we found that MML had one current liability, Dividends Payable, which was related to financing activities. Accordingly, the changes in this current liability account, as well as the changes in each long-term liability and shareholders' equity account, will be analyzed to determine the cash flows from financing activities.

Step 7 – Determine the amount of cash dividends paid during the period.

TAKE5

From Exhibit 5-3, we can see that MML began the year with dividends payable of $5,200 and ended the year with a balance of $3,200. Recall that in Chapter 1, we learned that dividends were a distribution of a company's retained earnings to its shareholders. As such, our analysis of the changes in the Dividends Payable account must be done in conjunction with an analysis of the Retained Earnings account. From Exhibit 5-3, we see that MML's Retained Earnings account had a balance of $23,750 at the beginning of the period and an ending balance of $106,550. The key to analyzing this $82,800 increase in Retained Earnings is to remember what affects this account. Each period, it is increased by net income (or decreased by a net loss) and decreased by any dividends declared. Because MML had net income of $86,000 in 2015, we would have expected the company's Retained Earnings balance to increase by this amount. Since it only increased by $82,800, we can deduce that dividends of $3,200 must have been *declared* during the year. However, the payment of dividends can take place weeks after they have been declared. As such, it is possible that dividends that have been declared near the end of an accounting period remain unpaid. An analysis of the Dividends Payable account will enable us to determine the amount of dividends that have been paid. If MML began the year with dividends payable of $5,200 and dividends of $3,200 were *declared* during the year, the company would have had a dividends payable balance of $8,400. As the company's ending balance in its Dividends Payable account was $3,200, we know that dividends of $5,200 were *paid* during the year. The payment of these dividends would be an outflow of cash and reported as a negative cash flow from financing activities.

Here is another example of how a T account can help you organize the known data and determine a missing amount. It shows how the Dividends Payable and Retained Earnings accounts can be used to determine the amount of dividends that MML declared and paid during the year:

Retained Earnings

		23,750	Beginning balance (from Exhibit 5-3)
		86,000	Net earnings for 2016 (given)
		109,750	Balance after earnings added
Dividends declared during year	3,200	←	**This is the missing amount, which will produce the ending balance**
		106,550	Ending balance (from Exhibit 5-3)

Dividends Payable

		5,200	Beginning balance (from Exhibit 5-3)
		3,200	Dividends declared (determined above)
		8,400	Balance
Dividends paid during year	5,200	←	**This is the missing amount, which will produce the ending balance**
		3,200	Ending balance (from Exhibit 5-3)

Step 8 – Determine and record the amount of cash received from borrowings (new loans or increases to existing loans) made during the year and the amount of cash principal repaid on loans during the period.

When beginning our analysis of the Loans Payable account, the note we added in Step 2 would remind us that we were provided with the following additional information:

b. No principal repayments were made on the loan during the period.

From this note, we know that MML had no cash outflows related to the repayment of principal on its loan payable during the year.

By looking at the Loans Payable account on MML's statement of financial position (Exhibit 5-3), we can see that the account increased by $7,000 during the year. The Loans Payable account had a balance of $36,000 at the beginning of the period and an ending balance of $43,000. From this, we know that the company must have borrowed at least $7,000 during the period. Since we know that the company repaid no principal on its loans during the year, we can deduce that this increase represents all of the company's borrowings. That is, there are no principal repayments netted against it. These new borrowings would have resulted in an inflow of cash and would be recorded as a positive amount under cash flows from financing activities.

Here is another example of how a T account can help you organize the known data and determine a missing amount. It shows how the Loans Payable account can be used to determine the principal repayments that MML made during 2015:

Loans Payable			
Loan principal repaid during year (given)	–	36,000	Beginning balance (from Exhibit 5-3)
		36,000	Balance after principal repayments
This is the missing amount, which will produce the ending balance.	→	**7,000**	**New borrowings**
		43,000	Ending balance (from Exhibit 5-3)

Step 9 – Determine the cash received from shares issued during the period.

From Exhibit 5-3, we can see that MML's Common Shares account increased by $10,000 during the year. The account balance was $40,000 at the beginning of the year and $50,000 at the end. This tells us that that company must have issued new common shares during the year and received proceeds of $10,000. The issuance of shares is a financing activity and the proceeds would be recorded as a cash inflow.

Step 10 – Calculate the sum of the cash flows from operating, investing, and financing activities and agree it to the net change in cash for the period as determined in Step 1.

We can now complete MML's statement of cash flows by simply entering a subtotal for each of the three sections, and then combining these into an overall net change in cash for the period. This has been done in Exhibit 5-6. We then check that the total of the cash flows determined for the three categories add up to the overall change in cash for the period that was determined in Step 1. In Step 1, we determined that MML's cash balance had increased by $7,800 during the period. This is equal to the total of cash flows from operating activities (an inflow of $77,100), cash flows from investing activities (an outflow of $71,100), and cash flows from financing activities (an inflow of $1,800).

Finally, to assist users in their analysis of cash flows, standard setters require a few additional pieces of cash flow-related information to be disclosed. Specifically, companies are required to disclose the amount of:

- interest paid and received during the period,
- dividends paid and received during the period, and
- income taxes paid during the period.

These disclosures can be presented at the end of the statement of cash flows or in the notes to the financial statements. MML has included the amount of dividends paid in its cash flows from financing activities, so no additional disclosure is required. The company's interest expense for the period was $2,970 (per Exhibit 5-4) and the company had no Interest Payable account. As such, this amount represents the interest paid by the company during the year. The company's income tax expense for the period was $4,980 (per Exhibit 5-4), but, as we saw in Step 4, the company also paid $2,600 in taxes owing at the beginning of the period. As such, the company's total payments related to income taxes were $7,580 and this is disclosed at the bottom of the statement of cash flows (Exhibit 5-6). No information is provided regarding any interest or dividends received by MML, so we will assume that there were none during the period.

As an alternative to presenting the supplementary disclosures (about the amount of cash used for interest and income tax) on the statement of cash flows, this information may be provided in the notes accompanying the financial statements.

What is the difference between the direct and indirect methods of preparing cash flows from operating activities?

The direct method of preparing cash flows from operating activities only differs from the indirect method in how the operating cash flows are determined and presented, but total cash flows from operating activities are the same under either method.

Rather than reconciling net income from the accrual basis of accounting to the cash basis, the direct method directly presents a company's operating cash flows by major category of cash receipts and payments. These categories commonly include:

- Receipts from customers
- Payments to suppliers
- Payments to employees
- Payments of interest
- Payments of income taxes

Essentially, the company is adjusting each line of the statement of income (sales revenue, cost of goods sold, wage expense, and so on) from the accrual basis to the cash basis, rather than just the bottom line (net income). For example, to determine its receipts from customers, a company will start with the sales revenue reported on the statement of income and then adjust it to remove the amount of sales made on account that have yet to be collected and increase it by collections on customer receivables outstanding from prior periods. Similar steps will be taken to adjust the expenses presented on the statement of income. For example, to determine its payments to employees, a company will start with the wage expense reported on the statement of income and then adjust it to remove the wages that remain unpaid and increase it for any payments made to employees of wages owing from prior periods.

Exhibit 5-8 illustrates how each of the common categories of cash receipts and payments can be determined.

Exhibit 5-8 Direct Method – Determining Cash Receipts/Payments from Common Categories

Category	Starting Point (from Statement of Income)	Adjustments (from Statement of Financial Position)
Receipts from Customers	Sales Revenue	+/– Change in Accounts Receivable
Payments to Suppliers	Expenses other than:	+/– Change in Inventory
	• Wage Expense	+/– Change in Prepaid Expenses
	• Interest Expense	+/– Change in Accounts Payable
	• Income Tax Expense	
	• Depreciation and Amortization Expense	
Payments to Employees	Wage Expense	+/– Change in Wages Payable
Payment of Interest	Interest Expense	+/– Change in Interest Payable
Payment of Income Taxes	Income Tax Expense	+/– Change in Income Taxes Payable

We can apply these steps to the information from Exhibits 5-3 and 5-4 to determine the cash flows from operating activities for Matchett Manufacturing Ltd. using the direct method, as shown in Exhibit 5-9.

Exhibit 5-9 Cash Flow from Operating Activities: Direct Method

Category	Starting Point (from Statement of Income)	A	Adjustments (from Statement of Financial Position)	B	Total = A + B
Receipts from Customers	Sales Revenue	480,000	Change in Accounts Receivable	12,500	492,500
Payments to Suppliers	Cost of Goods Sold	(305,000)	Change in Inventory	(27,500)	
	Rent Expense	(13,250)	Change in Prepaid Expenses	N/A	
	Utilities Expense	(7,600)	Change in Accounts Payable	2,400	(350,950)
Payments to Employees	Wage Expense	(53,900)	Change in Wages Payable	N/A	(53,900)
Payment of Interest	Interest Expense	(2,970)	Change in Interest Payable	N/A	(2,970)
Payment of Income Taxes	Income Tax Expense	(4,980)	Change in Income Taxes Payable	(2,600)	(7,580)
			CASH FLOWS FROM OPERATING ACTIVITIES		77,100

Notice that the total cash flows from operating activities is $77,100, the same amount that was determined using the indirect method. Also notice that Column B reflects the exact same analysis that was required in Step 4 of the indirect method. Finally, note that it is not necessary to have an adjustment for depreciation and amortization expenses (because these are non-cash transactions), nor for any gains and losses (because these are related to investing activities), as we are not starting our analysis with net income.

Other categories can be used under the direct method. Some companies separate payments to suppliers and payment of other operating expenses. Also, if a company has earned interest income, it would have a category presenting the receipts of interest.

For Example

Pacific Safety Products Inc. is headquartered in Arnprior, Ontario, and its shares trade on the TSX Venture Exchange. The company manufactures and sells a line of protective products for the defence and security markets. The company prepares its statement of cash flows using the direct method for determining cash flows from operating activities. The company's statements of cash flows for the years ended June 30, 2013 and 2012, were as follows:[6]

FINANCIAL STATEMENTS

PACIFIC SAFETY PRODUCTS INC.
CONSOLIDATED STATEMENTS OF CASH FLOWS
FOR THE YEARS ENDED JUNE 30,

	2013	2012
CASH FLOW FROM OPERATING ACTIVITIES		
Cash receipts from customers	**$ 13,758,593**	$ 15,813,155
Cash paid to suppliers and employees	**(13,342,225)**	(16,370,981)
Interest paid	**(116, 635)**	(92,119)
Interest received	**8,774**	12,493
Investment tax credits recovered	**16,036**	–
Income taxes recovered	**–**	6,319
Income taxes paid	**–**	(102,509)
CASH FLOW FROM (USED IN) OPERATING ACTIVITIES	**324,543**	(733,642)

(continued)

For Example (continued)

	2013	2012
CASH FLOW FROM INVESTING ACTIVITIES		
Purchase of property and equipment	**(44,019)**	(64,037)
Investment in intangible assets	**—**	(133,999)
CASH FLOW USED IN INVESTING ACTIVITIES	**(44,019)**	(198,036)
CASH FLOW FROM FINANCING ACTIVITIES		
Repayment of long-term debt	**(214,320)**	(214,320)
CASH FLOW USED IN FINANCING ACTIVITIES	**(214,320)**	(214,320)
INCREASE (DECREASE) IN CASH AND CASH EQUIVALENTS	**66,204**	(1,146,002)*
CASH AND CASH EQUIVALENTS, NET OF BANK INDEBTEDNESS, BEGINNING OF YEAR	**1,087,219**	2,204,709
Effect of exchange rate fluctuations on cash held	**27,486**	28,508
CASH AND CASH EQUIVALENTS, NET OF BANK INDEBTEDNESS, END OF YEAR (note 7)	**$ 1,180,909**	$ 1,087,219

**There was a $4 rounding difference in the company's published financial statements.*

Are there investing and financing activities that do not appear on the statement of cash flows?

Yes, it is possible for a company to have investing and financing activities that do not appear on the statement of cash flows. This would be the case if any of the following occurred:

- The company purchased property, plant, and equipment, by assuming debt or issuing shares rather than paying cash.
- The company acquired the shares of another company by assuming debt or issuing shares rather than paying cash.
- The company repaid debt by issuing shares rather than paying cash.

As these transactions did not involve the inflow or outflow of cash, they would not be presented on the statement of cash flows. Instead, they would be disclosed in the notes to the company's financial statements so that financial statement users were made aware of them.

INTERPRETING CASH FLOW INFORMATION

How can the information presented in a statement of cash flows be used to manage a company?

LEARNING OBJECTIVE 5
Interpret a statement of cash flows and develop potential solutions to any cash flow challenges identified.

Managing cash flows is a key challenge for most companies. It is essential that management have information on the cash flows from the company's operating, investing, and financing activities. This information can then be analyzed to determine whether there may be opportunities to enhance cash inflows and/or minimize cash outflows. The causes of cash flow challenges can be found in the statement of cash flows and management can then develop strategies to address them. Common cash flow challenges include:

- significant increases in sales volumes,
- lengthy cash-to-cash cycles, and
- undercapitalization (or inadequate financing).

We will look at each of these challenges in more detail.

While significant increases in sales volumes are a positive sign for a company, this can lead to cash flow challenges. These increased sales require companies to purchase or produce more and more inventory, as well as to expand their storage and operating capacity. Purchasing additional inventory and/or expanding production and storage capacity requires cash. This challenge is very common among start-up companies, which can often experience rapid growth of sales. Without adequate cash flow, these companies can "grow" themselves out of business.

Compounding the growth problem is the presence of a lengthy **cash-to-cash cycle**. As illustrated in Exhibit 5-10, this cycle is the time between when a company pays out cash to purchase goods or raw materials for manufacturing products until those goods are ultimately paid for by the customer. The longer the cash-to-cash cycle, the greater the company's cash requirements, and this issue is magnified in periods of high sales growth. Again, start-up companies often face challenges in this area because suppliers require them to pay for goods and raw materials up front, but it may take weeks or months before the start-up is able to sell the product and collect from customers. As we saw in our feature story on Bombardier Inc., lengthy cash-to-cash cycles for manufacturing multi-million-dollar items like planes and trains can also place pressure on cash flow.

KEY POINT
The longer a company's cash-to-cash cycle, the more pressure is placed on cash flow.

Exhibit 5-10 The Cash-to-Cash Cycle

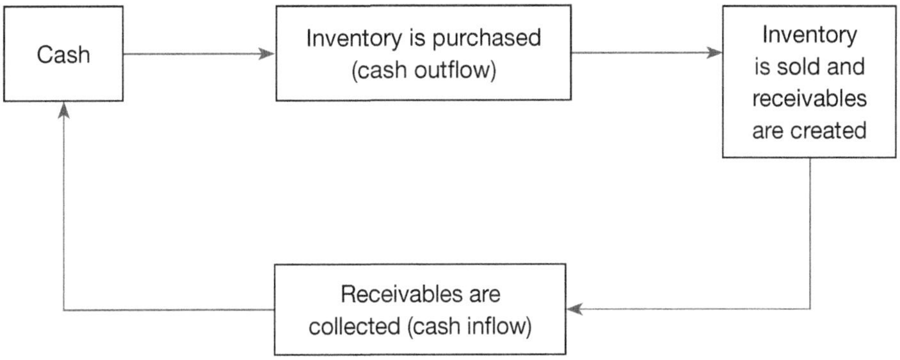

Finally, companies, especially start-ups, can be undercapitalized; that is, they are not sufficiently financed. It is common for companies to begin operations without a large enough pool of cash. This may be due to borrowing limitations or an inability to raise cash through the issuance of shares. When the company faces the need for a large amount of cash due to rapid growth, a lengthy cash-to-cash cycle, or the need to purchase capital assets, it may not have sufficient cash reserves to get through prolonged periods of net cash outflows.

Each of these challenges would be evident on the company's statement of cash flows. For example, significant cash outflows to purchase inventory, payments to suppliers and employees, or increases in accounts receivable would be reported in the company's cash flows from operating activities. Significant cash payments for property, plant, and equipment would be reflected in the company's cash flows from investing activities, while a lack of cash inflows from financing activities could also be observed.

Companies can resolve the common cash flow challenges by taking the following measures.

1. *Alleviate cash flow problems by reducing the rate of growth.*
   One way to solve cash flow challenges is to slow down the sales growth rate. However, reducing the growth rate may not be the best response because it will reduce net income and may hurt the company in the long run, as it attempts to develop a strong customer base. Limiting the growth in sales may divert customers to competing companies and, if these customers develop loyalties to the competitors, a company's long-term potential may be reduced. Regardless of these concerns, it may be a necessary step for companies facing cash flow challenges related to growth.

2. *Alleviate cash flow problems by shortening the cash-to-cash cycle.*
   Shortening the company's cash-to-cash cycle is another way to improve cash flow. There are many ways to do this. For example, increasing the amount of cash sales, accepting credit cards, or reducing the credit period for customers who buy on account would all reduce the cash-to-cash cycle. Alternatively, negotiating with suppliers to be able to purchase on credit would also reduce the cash-to-cash cycle; however, this generally requires the company to have established its creditworthiness to suppliers, which takes time.

   Companies have to carefully consider the sales terms they provide their customers. Customers may not be happy with having to pay cash or with reduced credit periods and may be able to

get better terms from competitors. While accepting credit cards would enable the company to collect its receivables more quickly, credit card companies charge fees and these additional costs will affect overall profitability.

3. *Alleviate cash flow problems by increasing the amount of capitalization.*
   Another way to solve the cash flow concerns is to address any undercapitalization problem; that is, to raise additional cash through financing activities. Two typical ways of doing this are to issue additional shares (equity financing) or to borrow the cash (debt financing). If additional shares are issued, it may dilute the ownership interest of existing shareholders, so this may be an unpopular decision. If the company enters into new borrowing arrangements, the company will have to service this debt by paying interest and repaying principal in future periods. Therefore, this may only be a short-term solution to the company's cash flow problems.

It should now be clear to you that (1) cash flow considerations are extremely important, and (2) the statement of cash flows provides additional information that is not captured by either the statement of income or the statement of financial position. For managers or other financial statement users, it is important to understand the relationship between the company's net income, its cash-to-cash cycle, and its statement of cash flows. It is also extremely important when evaluating a company's performance and cash position to understand how its receivables, payables, and inventory policies affect its cash flows.

Management and other financial statement users can also use three basic questions as a starting point for analyzing the statement of cash flows:

1. Is the cash from operating activities sufficient to sustain the company over the long term?
   A company can be healthy in the long run only when it produces sufficient cash from its operations. Although cash can be obtained from financing activities (issuance of new debt or shares) and from investing activities (the sale of investments or capital assets), there is a limit to the cash inflows that can be achieved from financing and investing activities. Financing inflows are limited by the willingness of lenders and shareholders to invest their money in the company. As the level of debt rises, so does the risk; consequently, the interest rate that must be paid will also increase. At some level of debt, the company becomes so risky that lenders will simply not lend more. Investing inflows are limited by amount of property, plant, and equipment that the company can dispose of and still remain in operation or the extent of any investments it has in the shares of other companies that can be sold. When the inflows from financing and investing are limited, if a company is to remain in business, it must generate sufficient cash inflows from operating activities to make the principal, interest, and dividend payments associated with the financing activities, and to continue investing at appropriate levels in property, plant, and equipment and other long-term assets.
2. Do any of the items on the statement of cash flows suggest that the business may be having problems?
   For example, a large increase in accounts receivable may indicate that the company is having difficulties collecting its receivables. A large increase in inventories may indicate that it is having trouble selling its products. A large increase in accounts payable may indicate that the company is having difficulty paying its bills. Large disposals of property, plant, and equipment may indicate that it is contracting, rather than expanding.
3. Of the sources and uses of cash, which ones are related to items or activities that will continue from period to period, and which are sporadic or non-continuing?
   A large source or use of cash in one period may not have long-term implications if it will not continue in the future. To address this question, the historical trend in the cash flow data must be considered. While some users will be interested in what has happened to cash in the current period, most are likely to be more interested in predicting the company's future cash flows. For example, a bank loan officer wants assurance that, if money is loaned to the company, the company will be able to pay it back. A stock analyst, on the

other hand, will want to know what cash flows can be expected over a long period of time, to ensure an adequate return on an investment in the company's shares. Users interested in the company's future will analyze this statement to try to decide which cash flows will continue in the future and which will not.

Ethics in Accounting

There are a number of actions that management can take that improve a company's cash flow from operating activities in the short term, but that may be detrimental to the company over the long term. For example, delaying payments to suppliers and employees would improve operating cash flows, but may jeopardize relationships with suppliers and upset employees. Delaying inventory purchases would also improve operating cash flows, but could result in lost sales due to stockouts.

What can cash flow patterns tell us?

A company's **cash flow pattern** is the direction (positive or negative) of its cash flows in the three categories: operating, investing, and financing. Given the three categories and that each could be positive (a net inflow of cash) or negative (a net outflow of cash), there are eight possible cash flow patterns. These are presented in Exhibit 5-11. Reviewing a company's cash flow pattern can provide financial statement users with quick means of initially assessing its financial condition. Of course, the dollar amount of each category is also critical, but the pattern helps users to quickly identify situations where more in-depth analysis would be required.

While it is possible to find companies that fit into each of the patterns, the majority of public companies fit into pattern 3 (+ / − / +) or 4 (+ / − / −). These companies are generating positive cash flows from their operating activities and are continuing to grow and replace property, plant, and equipment, which means negative cash flows from investing activities. They are either able to attract new debt or investors to finance part of this growth, which means positive cash flows from financing activities, or are repaying debt and paying dividends, which means negative cash flows from financing activities.

KEY POINT

The most common cash flow patterns are: (Operating / Investing / Financing)

+ / − / +
+ / − / −

For Example

Groupe Bikini Village Inc. is a public company, headquartered in Sainte-Julie, Quebec, which operates 53 stores across Eastern Canada selling swimwear, travel clothing, and accessories. The company's cash flow patterns for the years ended February 1, 2014, and February 2, 2013, were as follows:

	Operating	Investing	Financing
2014	+	−	−
2013	−	−	−

These basic patterns can quickly tell you a lot about the company. We can see that the company has struggled to generate cash flow from its operations, has repaid more capital than it has attracted, yet has continued to expand its operations. Of course, it would be important to analyze the cash flow results in more detail as well as to consider the dollar amounts of each cash flow, but this analysis would confirm the initial understanding provided by the cash flow pattern.[7]

Exhibit 5-11 outlines the profile of the company that would fit within each cash flow pattern. Being able to link the profile with the cash flow patterns enables financial statement users to develop expectations in terms of cash flows for companies they are analyzing. Cases in which the actual pattern differs from the expected pattern highlight the need for additional analysis.

Exhibit 5-11 Cash Flow Patterns[8]

Cash Flow from Operating Activities	Cash Flow from Investing Activities	Cash Flow from Financing Activities	Pattern Number and Company Profile
+	+	+	1. Successful, but actively repositioning or relocating using financing from operations together with cash from creditors and shareholders
+	+	–	2. Successful, mature company that is downsizing and returning capital to shareholders or repaying debt
+	–	+	3. Successful and growing, with growth partially financed by creditors and shareholders
+	–	–	4. Successful, with operating activities providing sufficient cash to finance growth and repay debt or pay dividends
–	+	+	5. Struggling, but using cash inflows from the sale of property, plant, and equipment and new borrowings to remain in operation
–	+	–	6. Struggling and using cash from the sale of property, plant, and equipment to repay creditors
–	–	+	7. A start-up or a struggling company that is able to attract financing for growth or reorganization
–	–	–	8. Struggling, but using existing cash balances to cover losses, purchase property, plant, and equipment, and repay creditors

FINANCIAL STATEMENT ANALYSIS

LEARNING OBJECTIVE 6
Calculate and interpret a company's cash flows to total liabilities ratio and determine the amount of net free cash flow being generated.

How do we determine what portion of a company's liabilities could be met with cash flows from operating activities?

Companies must be able to generate cash from their operating activities that is sufficient to repay their current and long-term liabilities. There are a number of cash flow ratios that are used to assess a company's ability to meet its liabilities through its operating cash flows. We will focus on one of these ratios, the **cash flows to total liabilities ratio**. This ratio is determined as follows:

$$\text{Cash flows to total liabilities} = \frac{\text{Cash flows from operating activities}}{\text{Total liabilities}}$$

This ratio measures the percentage of a company's total liabilities that could be met with one year's operating cash flows. It is important to note that total liabilities include both current and non-current liabilities and that only the current liabilities are due within the next year. In addition, some of the liabilities will not be paid in cash. For example, unearned revenues are often settled by providing services to customers. Also, the company may have other assets that could be used to settle liabilities, such as investments in the shares of other companies. As such, this ratio can be safely less than 1. Rather than using total liabilities, some analysts will calculate this ratio using long-term debt (including the current portion). This enables them to assess the company's ability to repay its debt using its operating cash flows. We will use the cash flows to total liabilities ratio as it is simple and the information necessary to calculate it is readily available for all financial statements.

The cash flows to total liabilities ratio for **Danier Leather Inc.** for the years ended June 28, 2014, and June 29, 2013, would be as follows:

	($ in thousands) 2014	2013
Cash flows to total liabilities	$= \frac{(\$4{,}907)}{\$12{,}222} = (0.40)$	$= \frac{\$6{,}752}{\$13{,}140} = 0.51$

From this, we can see that because Danier's cash flows from operating activities were negative in 2014, they could not cover any of the company's liabilities. This was a significant change from 2013, when it was able to cover 51% of its liabilities with its operating cash flows. While this trend is not positive, the company had cash reserves of more than $13.5 million at June 28, 2014, which would be more than enough to settle all of the company's liabilities if necessary.

How do we determine how much net free cash flow a company generates?

Free cash flow is a commonly used measure in the **management discussion and analysis (MD&A)** section of annual reports. The concept of free cash flow is to measure the amount of cash that a company generates from its operations that is in excess of the cash required to maintain the company's productive capacity. The term *free cash flow* is not a measure that has been defined by accounting standard setters. As such, it is often referred to as a **non-IFRS financial measure**. The implications of this are that there is no standardized definition for determining the measure. In practice, a variety of different definitions are used for this measure, making it a challenge for users to understand and interpret it.

Canadian accounting standard setters have attempted to address this by introducing **net free cash flow** as a standardized measure with a consistent definition. They have defined net free cash flow as follows:

$$\text{Net free cash flow} = \begin{array}{c}\text{Cash flows from}\\ \text{operating activities}\end{array} - \begin{array}{c}\text{Net capital}\\ \text{expenditures}^{1}\end{array} - \begin{array}{c}\text{Dividends on}\\ \text{preferred shares}\end{array}$$

[1]Net capital expenditures are equal to the total purchases of property, plant, and equipment less the proceeds from the sale of property, plant, and equipment.

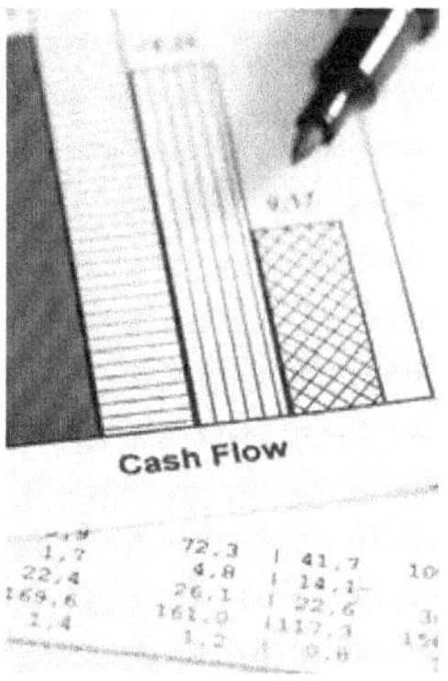

Net free cash flow is considered to be the cash flow generated from a company's operating activities that would be available to the company's common shareholders. While management has discretion with respect to the use of these cash flows, it is unlikely that the entire amount would be distributed to common shareholders. Instead, portions of these cash flows are likely to be used to repay debt, finance expansion plans, repurchase company shares, or make investments in other companies.

While a positive net free cash flow is considered to be a good thing, it is also important to consider why a company may have a negative free cash flow amount. It may be due to the company having made significant capital expenditures, such as buying property, plant, and equipment, during the period. If this is the case, then this is also positive, because these assets will be available to generate revenues for the company in future periods.

The net free cash flow for Danier Leather Inc. for the years ended June 28, 2014, and June 29, 2013, would be as follows:

($ in thousands)

$$\text{Net free cash flow} = \begin{array}{c}\text{Cash flows from}\\ \text{operating activities}\end{array} - \begin{array}{c}\text{Net capital}\\ \text{expenditures}\end{array} - \begin{array}{c}\text{Dividends on}\\ \text{preferred shares}\end{array}$$

$$\begin{aligned} 2014 &= (\$4{,}907) - \$6{,}079 - \$0 \\ &= (\$10{,}986) \\ 2013 &= \$6{,}752 - \$5{,}327 - \$0 \\ &= \$1{,}425 \end{aligned}$$

From this we can see that there was a significant decrease in the net free cash flow the company was able to generate from 2013 to 2014. We can see that the company went from having a free cash flow of $1.4 million to having a negative free cash flow of $11 million. This means that the company would need cash from its cash reserves or from other sources to continue operating. While this trend is not positive, Danier had a cash balance of $13.5 million at June 28, 2014, so the company had significant cash reserves available to support its operations.

Now that you know how a statement of cash flows is created, in the next chapter we'll take a closer look at cash and at another significant liquid asset: accounts receivable.

SUMMARY

1. **Understand and explain why the statement of cash flows is of significance to users.**
   - The statement of cash flows enables users to assess the cash generated from core operations, the cash that has been obtained from investors and creditors, the extent of new investment in capital assets, the cash available to repay debt, and the amount of cash distributed to shareholders as dividends.
   - The statement of cash flows also provides a basis for estimating the value of a company and predicting its ability to service its debt and pay dividends.
2. **Explain how the statement of cash flows and the statement of income differ.**
   - The statement of cash flows uses the cash basis of accounting, whereas the statement of income is prepared using the accrual basis.
   - The statement of income focuses only on a company's operating activities (its revenues and expenses). The statement of cash flows includes cash flows from operating activities, but it also includes cash flows related to investing and financing activities.
3. **Identify the three major types of activities that are presented in a statement of cash flows and describe some of the typical transactions included in each category of activity.**
   - The statement of cash flows categorizes a company's cash-related transactions into three categories: operating activities, investing activities, and financing activities.
   - Typical operating activities include cash sales to customers, collections of customer receivables, purchases of inventory, payments to suppliers, payments of wages, and payments of taxes.
   - Typical investing activities include cash purchases of property, plant, and equipment; purchases of shares of other companies; sales of property, plant, and equipment; and sales of shares in other companies.
   - Typical financing activities include the proceeds from issuing shares, the proceeds received from new loans, repayments of loan principal, and payments of cash dividends.
   - Cash flows from operating activities normally receive the greatest scrutiny as these are the cash flows that result from what the company is in the business of doing and are a key source for financing future growth. They are also the source for future debt repayments and/or dividend payments.
4. **Prepare a statement of cash flows using a comparative statement of financial position, a statement of income, and some additional information.**
   - Cash includes cash on hand, bank deposits, and cash equivalents (which are short-term, highly liquid investments with little risk of a change in their value).
   - There are two methods of preparing the statement of cash flows: the direct method and indirect method. The only difference between the two methods is how cash flows from operating activities is determined. Total operating cash flows are the same under both methods and the choice of method has no effect on cash flows from investing or financing activities.
   - The indirect method is simpler to prepare, uses information available in most accounting systems, and provides a linkage between net income and cash flows from operating activities.
   - To determine cash flows from operating activities under the indirect method, net income is adjusted for any non-cash expenses (depreciation and amortization), any gains or losses from investing activities, and changes in current asset and liability accounts (except for the Cash and Dividends Payable accounts).
   - To determine cash flows from operating activities under the direct method, cash flows are aggregated into categories that commonly include receipts from customers, payments to suppliers, payments to employees, payments of interest, and payments of income taxes. Each category is calculated using the relevant revenue or expense account(s) and adjusted for changes in the related current asset or current liability account.
   - Cash flows from investing activities are equal to the cash payments to purchase property, plant, and equipment less any cash receipts from sales of property, plant, and equipment. The amount of cash payments to purchase the shares of other companies and any proceeds from the sale of such shares are also included.
   - Cash flows from financing activities are equal to the cash received from issuing shares or the proceeds from any new loans less any principal repayments or dividends paid during the period.
   - The sum of the three cash flows should be equal to the net change in cash and cash equivalents for the period.
   - Companies are also required to disclose the amount of interest paid and received, the amount of dividends paid and received, and the amount of income taxes paid.
   - Any non-cash investing and financing activities should also be disclosed.
5. **Interpret a statement of cash flows and develop potential solutions to any cash flow challenges identified.**
   - Information from the statement of cash flows can help to identify challenges related to significant increases in sales volumes, lengthy cash-to-cash cycles, and undercapitalization.
   - The cash-to-cash cycle is the time between a company paying out cash to purchase goods and when those goods are ultimately paid for by customers. The longer the cycle, the more pressure is placed on cash flow.
   - When assessing a company's cash flows, users will consider whether the cash flows from operating activities are sufficient to sustain the company over time. They will also look for indications of concern related to the collection of receivables; excess inventories; an inability to settle payables; or significant sales of property, plant, and equipment.
   - A company's cash flow pattern is the direction (positive or negative) of its cash flows from operating, investing, and financing activities. Reviewing a company's cash flow pattern can provide users with a quick means of initially assessing its financial condition. The most common cash flow patterns are positive operating cash flows, negative investing cash flows, and either positive or negative financing cash flows.
6. **Calculate and interpret a company's cash flows to total liabilities ratio and determine the amount of net free cash flow being generated.**
   - The *cash flows to total liabilities ratio* can be determined by dividing cash flows from operating activities by total liabilities.
   - It measures the percentage of a company's total liabilities that could be met with one year's operating cash flows. When interpreting this ratio, it is important to remember that only a company's current liabilities must be settled within the next year.

- *Net free cash flow* is equal to cash flows from operating activities less net capital expenditures and any dividends on preferred shares. Net capital expenditures equal the total purchases of property, plant, and equipment less the proceeds from the sale of property, plant, and equipment.
- It is considered to be the cash flow generated from operations that would be available to the company's common shareholders. It would be reinvested in the company to grow the business, while a portion may be distributed to shareholders as dividends.

KEY TERMS

Bank overdraft facility (214)
Cash (213)
Cash equivalents (213)
Cash flow (209)
Cash flow pattern (227)
Cash flows to total liabilities ratio (228)
Cash-to-cash cycle (225)
Demand deposits (213)
Direct method (214)
Financing activities (210)
Free cash flow (229)
Indirect method (214)
Investing activities (210)
Line of credit (214)
Management discussion and analysis (MD&A) (229)
Net free cash flow (229)
Non-IFRS financial measure (229)
Operating activities (210)
Statement of cash flows (209)

ABBREVIATIONS USED

IFRS International Financial Reporting Standards
MD&A Management discussion and analysis

SYNONYMS

Indirect method | Reconciliation method

CHAPTER END REVIEW PROBLEM 1

The 2016 statement of financial position and statement of income of Beaman Industries Ltd. are presented in Exhibit 5-12. Beaman manufactures and distributes a broad range of electrical equipment to contractors and home renovation stores.

STRATEGIES FOR SUCCESS

- Start by setting up the outline of the statement of cash flows, with three sections labelled Operating Activities, Investing Activities, and Financing Activities. Leave a lot of space for the Operating Activities, as this is usually the biggest section.
- Follow the 10 steps from Exhibit 5-2.

EXHIBIT 5-12 SELECTED FINANCIAL STATEMENTS FOR BEAMAN INDUSTRIES LTD.

BEAMAN INDUSTRIES LTD.
Statement of Financial Position
As at March 31

	2016	2015
Assets		
Current assets:		
Cash	$ 32,970	$ 45,900
Accounts receivable	62,000	105,000
Inventory	91,000	55,200
Total current assets	185,970	206,100
Equipment	307,800	297,000
Accumulated depreciation, equipment	(128,520)	(111,420)
	$365,250	$391,680
Liabilities and Shareholders' Equity		
Current liabilities:		
Accounts payable	$ 74,900	$122,680
Total current liabilities	74,900	122,680
Bank loan payable	95,050	80,000
Common shares	180,000	180,000
Retained earnings	15,300	9,000
	$365,250	$391,680

BEAMAN INDUSTRIES LTD.
Statement of Income
For the year ended March 31, 2016

Sales revenue		$333,900
Cost of goods sold		157,500
Gross profit		176,400
Expenses		
Wages expense	$86,400	
Interest expense	14,400	
Depreciation expense	25,000	
Loss on sale of equipment	9,000	
Income tax expense	17,300	152,100
Net income		$ 24,300

Additional information:

1. During the year, equipment costing $63,000 was sold for $46,100.
2. The company made no principal repayments on its loans during the year.

Required:

Prepare the statement of cash flows for Beaman for the year ended March 31, 2016. Use the indirect method for determining cash flows from operating activities.

CHAPTER END REVIEW PROBLEM 2

The statement of cash flows for Pomeroy Distributors Ltd. for 2014 to 2016 is presented in Exhibit 5-13.

EXHIBIT 5-13 POMEROY DISTRIBUTORS LTD. STATEMENT OF CASH FLOWS

POMEROY DISTRIBUTORS LTD.
Statement of Cash Flows
(in thousands)
For the year ended May 31

	2016	2015	2014
Operating Activities:			
Net income	$10,575	$19,202	$19,786
Adjustments to convert net income to net cash from operating activities:			
Depreciation expense	7,805	7,040	6,457
(Gain) loss on sale of property, plant, and equipment	1,070	488	(212)
(Increase) decrease in:			
Receivables	(8,797)	(7,072)	(935)
Inventories	(23,513)	(11,872)	(18,687)
Prepaid expenses	660	(652)	(2,363)
(Decrease) increase in:			
Accounts payable	9,308	10,120	(3,734)
Accrued interest	(1,058)	1,458	646
Other accrued expenses	(2,332)	970	432
Income tax payable	(620)	–	(402)
Net cash provided (used) by operating activities	(6,902)	19,682	988
Investing Activities:			
Paid for purchase of property, plant, and equipment	(18,130)	(9,395)	(8,550)
Proceeds from sale of property, plant, and equipment	2,722	415	2,324
Net cash used by investing activities	(15,408)	(8,980)	(6,226)
Financing Activities:			
Additions to short-term borrowings	4,000	1,000	18,500
Repayments of long-term debt	–	(4,913)	(14,734)
Additions to long-term debt	22,000	–	5,000
Paid to purchase and retire shares		(1,885)	(2,448)
Received from the issuance of shares	678	–	–
Paid for dividends	(6,470)	(5,956)	(5,486)
Net cash provided (used) by financing activities	20,208	(11,754)	832
Net change in cash during period	(2,102)	(1,052)	(4,406)
Cash at beginning of period	3,226	4,278	8,684
Cash at end of period	$ 1,124	$ 3,226	$ 4,278

Required:

a. Consider Pomeroy's cash flow patterns from 2014 to 2016. What profile do these provide of the company?
b. Explain why so much cash was consumed by the company's operations in fiscal 2016.
c. dentify the two most significant recurring non-operating cash outflows over the last three years and comment on how the company has met these needs. Does this analysis support your initial assessment from part "a"?

Suggested Solution to Chapter End Review Problem 1

The completed statement of cash flows for Beaman Industries Ltd. for the year ended March 31, 2016, is shown below. Explanations for certain items follow the statement.

BEAMAN INDUSTRIES LTD.
Statement of Cash Flows
For the year ended March 31, 2016

Cash flows from operating activities:	
Net income	$24,300
add: Depreciation expense	25,000
add: Loss on sale of equipment	9,000
add: Decrease in accounts receivable	43,000
less: Increase in inventory	(35,800)
less: Decrease in accounts payable	(47,780)
Cash provided by operating activities	17,720
Cash flows from investing activities:	
add: Proceeds from sale of equipment	46,100
less: Purchase of equipment	(73,800)
Cash used for investing activities	(27,700)
Cash flows from financing activities:	
less: Payment of dividends	(18,000)
add: Proceeds of borrowing—loan payable	15,050
Cash used for financing activities	(2,950)
	(12,930)
Ending cash	32,970
Opening cash	45,900
Net change in cash	($12,930)

a. Because both depreciation expense and the loss on sale of equipment reduced net income, they are added back in order to eliminate the effect they had on net income. Depreciation is a non-cash expense and the loss on sale is related to an investing activity.
b. The following T accounts illustrate how the amount of equipment purchased and the dividends paid during the year were determined.

Equipment

Debit	Credit
297,000	
	63,000
73,800	
307,800	

Retained Earnings

Debit	Credit
	9,000
	24,300
18,000	
	15,300

Dividends Payable	
	—
	18,000
18,000	
	—

Suggested Solution to Chapter End Review Problem 2

a. Pomeroy's cash flow patterns over the past three years were as follows:

2014:	+ / − / +	The company was successful and growing, with growth financed by operations and also from financing provided by creditors and shareholders.
2015:	+ / − / −	The company was successful, with operating activities providing sufficient cash to finance growth and repay debt or pay dividends.
2016:	− / − / +	The company struggled operationally, but was able to attract financing to fund the acquisition of capital assets and the cash deficiency resulting from its operating activities.

A quick analysis of Pomeroy's cash flow patterns illustrates that the company began to struggle operationally in 2016. In 2014 and 2015, the company was able to generate cash from its operating activities, with almost $20 million generated from operations in 2015. The company has continued to increase its property, plant, and equipment each year, though some of these acquisitions were asset replacements (that is, replacements of the property, plant, and equipment sold during the period). In 2016, Pomeroy paid just over $18 million to acquire property, plant, and equipment, while receiving just under $3 million from the sale of property, plant, and equipment the company had finished using. In spite of its operational challenges in 2016, the company was able to attract new financing, receiving $22 million from new long-term borrowings and another $4 million from additional short-term borrowings. We would want to assess the company's operational challenges in greater depth to get a sense of where the difficulties were. For example, were they a result of declining sales, growth in inventory or receivables, or a reduction in the payment periods offered by suppliers?

b. In analyzing the company's cash flows from operating activities for 2016, it is clear that the biggest outflow was related to the increase in inventory. This resulted in cash outflows of more than $23 million during the year. This was a continuation of a trend that has seen the company's inventory levels increase significantly over the past three years, resulting in cash outflows of $54 million over the period. It would be important to know why the levels of inventories have increased so much. These changes in inventory level should also be compared with changes in sales revenues over the same period.

Accounts receivable have also been steadily increasing over the three-year period, with significant increases in 2015 and 2016. Again, this growth in receivables should be compared with the change in the sales revenues to determine if it is the growth in sales that is driving the increase in receivables. We should also determine if the company lengthened its credit terms. If increased sales and changes in credit terms do not explain the increase in receivables, it would indicate that Pomeroy is having trouble collecting from its customers.

A portion of the increased inventory levels was offset by financing provided by the company's suppliers through increased accounts payable. This covered all of the inventory increase in 2015, but only 40% of the increase in 2016. While the increase in accounts payable helps the company's cash flow situation, it may also indicate that Pomeroy is having trouble paying its bills and is therefore slowing down its payments to suppliers.

The fact that the company's net income fell by 45% in 2016 had a significant impact on its cash flow from operating activities for that year. In 2014 and 2015, Pomeroy was able to generate a net income of approximately $19 million and the company had positive cash flows from operations in both years. The significant decrease in net income in 2016 was one of the reasons the company's operating cash flows were negative in that year.

Overall, the biggest concern is likely the increase in inventory levels. The reason for the very large growth in inventories, particularly in 2016, should definitely be investigated.

c. Pomeroy's two most significant recurring cash outflows in the three years between 2014 and 2016 were related to the purchase of property, plant, and equipment, and the payment of dividends. Pomeroy's cash outflows to acquire property, plant, and equipment, net of the proceeds received from the sale of property, plant, and equipment, were over $30 million. Dividend payments during the three-year period resulted in cash outflows of almost $18 million.

The company met these cash needs though increased borrowings (short-term and long-term debt), cash flows from operations (in 2014 and 2015), and a drawdown of its existing cash balances. Pomeroy increased its debt by almost $31 million, net of repayments, during the three-year period. This was the largest source of cash inflows for the company, surpassing the net inflows of $14 million generated by the company's operating activities. The company's cash balances also decreased by more than $7 million between 2014 and 2016.

Pomeroy's operating activities produced a net inflow of cash in both 2014 and 2015, while there was a negative cash flow from operations in 2016. Between 2015 and 2016, cash flow from operations swung from close to a $20-million inflow to a $7-million outflow. This is consistent with the + / + / – pattern we observed for operating activities in part "a."

The net increase in property, plant, and equipment is consistent with the – / – / – pattern we observed in part "a" for investing activities. This, coupled with the increase in inventory levels noted in part "b," would be indicative of the company expanding its current operation (that is, increasing its warehouse and increasing the quantity and range of goods carried in inventory) or opening new locations and acquiring the inventory to stock them. We would want to investigate to determine which, if either, of these is the case. If one of these scenarios reflects the company's actions, it could be that cash is being spent up front to expand its current operation or establish the new locations, while these new products or new locations have yet to generate the expected cash flows through sales revenues.

This detailed analysis supports the assessment from part "a" that was based on an initial analysis of the company's cash flow patterns. This illustrates the usefulness of cash flow pattern analysis.

ASSIGNMENT MATERIAL

Discussion Questions

DQ5-1 Discuss why, in addition to preparing a statement of income, it is important for companies to also prepare a statement of cash flows.

DQ5-2 Discuss how a company's policies regarding receivables, inventory, and payables affect its cash flows relative to the income generated in a given period.

DQ5-3 In terms of cash flows, what is meant by the cash-to-cash cycle?

DQ5-4 For a company with a cash flow problem related to the length of its cash-to-cash cycle, list at least three potential reasons for the problem and suggest a possible solution for each.

DQ5-5 Describe the three major categories of activities that are shown on the statement of cash flows.

DQ5-6 Discuss the major difference between the direct method and the indirect method for presenting the operating section of a statement of cash flows.

DQ5-7 Explain why the indirect method of preparing cash flows from operating activities is also known as the *reconciliation method*.

DQ5-8 Explain why it is important to a company's financial health to have a positive cash flow from operations.

DQ5-9 Explain why, under the indirect method, depreciation is added to the net income to calculate the cash flow from operations. Is depreciation a source of cash, as this treatment seems to suggest?

DQ5-10 Explain what the outcome will be if a company increases its depreciation charges in an attempt to increase its cash flow from operations.

DQ5-11 Explain why the net cash flow from investing activities is usually a negative amount.

DQ5-12 Explain how the net cash flow from financing activities could be a negative amount.

DQ5-13 Explain how a gain on the sale of equipment would be treated in the operating activities section of a statement of cash flows prepared using the indirect method.

DQ5-14 Explain what it means if the net cash flow from investing activities is a positive amount.

DQ5-15 Explain how the net cash flow from financing activities could be a positive amount.

DQ5-16 Explain why a high sales growth rate can create significant cash flow problems for a company.

DQ5-17 Explain how the timing of cash flows relates to the purchase, use, and ultimate disposal of property, plant, and equipment.

DQ5-18 Explain why it is common for companies to have positive cash flows from operating activities and negative cash flows from investing activities.

DQ5-19 Explain how net free cash flow is determined and what it represents.

DQ5-20 When analyzing the statement of cash flows, explain why it is important to compare the current year's amounts with those of prior years.

Application Problems

AP5-1 (Classification of activities)

Required:
In what section of the statement of cash flows (operating, financing, or investing) would each of the following items appear?

a. Issuance of common shares to investors
b. Payment of dividends to shareholders
c. Purchase of new property, plant, and equipment
d. Proceeds from the sale of old property, plant, and equipment
e. Gain or loss on the sale of property, plant, and equipment
f. Net income
g. Proceeds from a bank loan
h. Retirement of debt
i. Proceeds from the sale of a long-term investment in another company
j. Net change in inventory

AP5-2 (Classification of activities)

Required:
Indicate whether each of the following items should be classified as an operating, investing, or financing activity on the statement of cash flows. If an item does not belong on the statement, indicate why.

a. Declaration of dividends on common shares, to be paid later
b. Payment of dividends on common shares
c. Purchase of equipment
d. Receipt of cash from the sale of a warehouse
e. Receipt of cash through a long-term bank loan
f. Interest payments on a long-term bank loan
g. Acquisition of land for cash
h. Investment in another company by purchasing some of its shares
i. Net decrease in accounts payable

AP5-3 (Effect of transactions on cash flows)

Required:
Classify each of the following transactions as increasing, decreasing, or having no effect on cash flows:

a. Purchasing inventory from a supplier on account
b. Purchasing office supplies and writing a cheque to cover the amount
c. Selling inventory to a customer on account
d. Buying a building by making a down payment and taking out a mortgage for the balance of the amount owed
e. Depreciating capital assets
f. Making a payment on a bank loan, where the amount paid includes interest and a portion of the principal
g. Issuing common shares
h. Declaring and paying dividends to shareholders
i. Paying wages owed to employees
j. Receiving interest owed from a customer

AP5-4 (Effect of transactions on cash flows)

Required:
Classify each of the following transactions as increasing, decreasing, or having no effect on cash flows:

a. Prepaying rent for the month
b. Accruing the wages owed to employees at the end of the month, to be paid on the first payday of the next month
c. Selling bonds to investors
d. Buying the company's own shares on the stock market
e. Selling merchandise to a customer who uses a debit card to pay for the purchase
f. Paying for inventory purchased earlier on account
g. Buying new equipment for cash
h. Selling surplus equipment at a loss
i. Paying the interest owed on a bank loan
j. Paying the income taxes owed for the year

AP5-5 (Effect of transactions on cash flows)

The following transactions occurred for Dussault Ltd.

1. Annual interest of 6% is paid on $500,000 of bonds payable that were issued last year.
2. A truck was purchased for $50,000 at the beginning of this year. The truck is being depreciated over five years at a rate of $10,000 per year.
3. Old equipment is sold for $40,000. The asset originally cost $160,000 and has accumulated depreciation of $125,000.
4. New equipment is purchased for $200,000. A cash payment of $50,000 is made and a long-term note payable for $150,000 is issued for the remainder.
5. A deposit of $2,000 is received in advance from a customer for goods to be delivered at a later date.
6. Income tax expense for the year is $85,000; $70,000 of this amount was paid during the year and the remainder will be paid next year.

Required:

For each of the above items:

a. Identify the accounts affected and give the amounts by which they would be increased or decreased.
b. State the amount of any cash flow and whether cash is increased or decreased.
c. Identify how each item would be reported in Dussault's statement of cash flows.

AP5-6 (Effect of transactions on cash flows)

The following transactions occurred for Mouawad Inc.

1. Inventory costing $300,000 was purchased on account.
2. A new vehicle costing $30,000 was purchased. Mouawad paid $5,000 as a down payment and the remaining $25,000 was financed through a bank loan.
3. Surplus land was sold for $80,000, which was $20,000 more than its original cost.
4. During the year, the company made a payment of $20,000 on its mortgage payable; $2,500 of this amount was for the interest on the debt.
5. Wages of $45,000 were charged to expense as they were incurred. No wages were owing to the employees at the end of the year.
6. The company declared and paid dividends of $30,000.

Required:

For each of the above items:

a. Identify the accounts affected and give the amounts by which they would be increased or decreased.
b. State the amount of any cash flow and whether cash is increased or decreased.
c. Identify how each item would be reported in Mouawad's statement of cash flows.

AP5-7 (Cash flow from operations)

Required:

For each of the following companies, calculate the cash flow from operations:

	NuVu Ltd.	ABC Inc.	Akhtar Ltd.
Sales revenue	$380,000	$575,000	$936,000
Cost of goods sold	210,000	330,000	620,000
Selling and administrative expenses	65,000	95,000	105,000
Depreciation expense	7,000	18,000	28,000
Interest expense	3,000	1,000	2,000
Income tax expense	18,000	35,000	45,000
Dividends paid	7,000	5,000	25,000
Increase/(Decrease) in			
Accounts receivable	(2,500) cash↑	5,000	(8,500)
Inventory	4,000	(8,000)	14,000
Property, plant, and equipment	50,000	(10,000)	60,000
Accounts payable	3,500	(6,500)	4,200
Interest payable	(1,500)	1,200	(500)
Income tax payable	2,500	(1,500)	6,500
Mortgage payable	20,000	(40,000)	10,000
Common shares	30,000	(5,000)	(80,000)

AP5-8 (Cash flow from operations)

Required:
For each of the following companies, calculate the cash flow from operations using the indirect method:

	Kotei & Sons Ltd.	SaskCo.	Movilla Ltd.
Sales revenue	$453,000	$790,000	$960,000
Cost of goods sold	235,000	420,000	550,000
Depreciation expense	40,000	70,000	80,000
Other operating expenses	50,000	60,000	70,000
Interest expense	15,000	20,000	35,000
Gain (loss) on sale of equipment	9,000	(15,000)	(14,000)
Dividends paid	6,000	10,000	12,000
Increase/(Decrease) in			
Accounts receivable	14,000	(16,000)	15,000
Inventory	(20,000)	25,000	(30,000)
Prepaid expenses	1,000	(2,400)	(2,600)
Property, plant, and equipment	220,000	(70,000)	150,000
Accounts payable	(8,000)	12,000	(8,000)
Interest payable	3,000	(8,000)	5,000
Bonds payable	(20,000)	50,000	60,000
Common shares	70,000	(10,000)	120,000

AP5-9 (Prepare statement of cash flows)

Organic Developments Ltd. (ODL) is an importer of organic produce from California. The company has been experiencing significant growth and is preparing to approach the bank for a loan to acquire additional capital assets. As CFO, you are tasked with preparing the statement of cash flows that is required as part of the loan application. You have the statement of financial position and the statement of income to help you prepare the statement of cash flows. In addition you also have the following information:

1. During the year, the company borrowed $14,000 by increasing its bank loan payable.
2. In September, ODL sold equipment for $6,000 cash. The equipment had originally cost $134,000 and had a net carrying amount of $14,000 at the time of sale.
3. In June, ODL acquired land with a value of $120,000 by issuing common shares with an equivalent value. The land is to be used as a site for a warehouse it hopes to construct in the next year.

ORGANIC DEVELOPMENTS LTD.
Statement of Financial Position
As at October 31

	2016	2015
Assets		
Current assets:		
Cash	$ 48,000	$ 36,000
Accounts receivable	58,000	68,000
Inventory	180,000	160,000
Total current assets	286,000	264,000
Equipment	620,000	540,000
Accumulated depreciation, equipment	(300,000)	(360,000)
Land	120,000	—
	$ 726,000	$ 444,000
Liabilities and Shareholders' Equity		
Current liabilities		
Accounts payable	$ 82,000	$ 40,000
Dividends payable	30,000	36,000
Total current liabilities	112,000	76,000
Bank loan payable	74,000	120,000
Common shares	300,000	180,000
Retained earnings	240,000	68,000
	$726,000	$444,000

ORGANIC DEVELOPMENTS LTD.
Statement of Income
For the year ended October 31, 2016

Sales revenue		$1,040,000
Cost of goods sold		520,000
Gross margin		520,000
Expenses		
Advertising expense	$ 30,000	
Wage expense	144,000	
Utilities expense	12,000	
Depreciation expense	60,000	
Rent expense	26,000	272,000
Net income from operations		248,000
Loss on sale of equipment		8,000
Net income		$240,000

Required:

a. Using the information, prepare the statement of cash flows for Organic Developments Ltd. for the year ended October 31, 2016.
b. Determine the cash flows from operating activities using the direct method.

AP5-10 (Prepare statement of cash flows)

Whiskey Industries Ltd., a Nanaimo, British Columbia–based company, has a December 31 year end. The company's comparative statement of financial position and its statement of income for the most recent fiscal year are presented here along with some additional information:

1. During the year, Whiskey Industries sold, for $500 cash, equipment that had an original cost of $1,000 and a net carrying amount of $200.
2. Whiskey Industries borrowed an additional $8,000 by issuing notes payable in 2016.
3. During the year, the company purchased a piece of land for a future manufacturing site for $200,000. The land was purchased with no money down and the company entered into a mortgage payable for the full amount.

WHISKEY INDUSTRIES LTD.
Statement of Financial Position
As at December 31, 2016

	2016	2015
Assets		
Current assets		
Cash	$ 6,050	$ 19,500
Accounts receivable	10,000	20,000
Prepaid rent	600	500
Inventory	40,000	30,000
Total current assets	56,650	70,000
Manufacturing equipment	159,000	100,000
Accumulated depreciation, manufacturing equipment	(69,200)	(50,000)
Land	200,000	0
Total Assets	$346,450	$120,000
Liabilities and Shareholders' Equity		
Current liabilities		
Accounts payable	$ 11,000	$ 6,000
Wages payable	600	400
Dividends payable	470	300
Total current liabilities	12,070	6,700
Mortgage payable	200,000	0
Notes payable	46,000	40,000
Common shares	29,000	25,000
Retained earnings	59,380	48,300
Total Liabilities and Shareholders' Equity	$346,450	$120,000

WHISKEY INDUSTRIES LTD.
Statement of Income
For the Year Ending December 31, 2016

Sales	$130,000
Cost of goods sold	80,000
Gross margin	50,000
Expenses	
Rent expense	7,100
Wage expense	9,600
Depreciation expense	20,000
Interest expense	600
Income tax expense	520
Income from operations	12,180
Gain on sale of equipment	300
Net income	$ 12,480

Required:

a. Using the information above, prepare the statement of cash flows for Whiskey Industries Ltd. for the year ended December 31, 2016, using the indirect method.
b. Determine the cash flows from operating activities using the direct method.

AP5-11 (Prepare statement of cash flows)

Required:
Using the following information, prepare the statement of cash flows for Harley Holdings Ltd. for the year ended January 31, 2016, using either method.

HARLEY HOLDINGS LTD.
Statement of Financial Position
As at January 31

	2016	2015
Assets		
Current assets:		
Cash	$ 50,000	$ 36,500
Accounts receivable	86,800	55,000
Inventory	95,600	101,700
Total current assets	232,400	193,200
Equipment	175,000	145,000
Accumulated depreciation, equipment	(43,500)	(39,000)
Land	120,000	170,000
	$ 483,900	$469,200
Liabilities and Shareholders' Equity		
Current liabilities:		
Accounts payable	$ 45,300	$ 62,200
Dividends payable	13,000	5,000
Total current liabilities	58,300	67,200
Bank loan payable	100,000	140,000
Common shares	150,000	130,000
Retained earnings	175,600	132,000
	$ 483,900	$469,200

HARLEY HOLDINGS LTD.
Statement of Income
For the year ended January 31, 2016

Sales revenue		$435,000
Cost of goods sold		295,000
Gross profit		140,000
Expenses		
Wages expense	$15,200	
Depreciation expense	26,500	
Rent expense	15,100	
Income tax expense	14,700	71,500
Operation income		68,500
Gain on sale of equipment		1,000
Net income		$ 69,500

Additional information:
1. Equipment costing $35,000 was sold for $14,000.
2. Land was sold at cost and none was purchased during the year.

AP5-12 (Prepare statement of cash flows)

Financial statement data for Metro Moving Company for 2016 follow.

METRO MOVING COMPANY
Comparative Statement of Financial Position

	Dec. 31, 2016	Dec. 31, 2015
Assets		
Cash	$ 68,600	$ 49,100
Accounts receivable	95,000	59,400
Prepaid insurance	30,000	20,000
Total current assets	193,600	128,500
Property, equipment, and vehicles	400,000	345,000
Accumulated depreciation	(110,400)	(105,900)
Total non-current assets	289,600	239,100
Total assets	$ 483,200	$ 367,600
Liabilities and shareholders' equity		
Accounts payable	$ 21,500	$ 18,600
Wages payable	3,000	4,000
Total current liabilities	24,500	22,600
Bank loan	50,000	60,000
Total liabilities	74,500	82,600
Common shares	200,000	200,000
Retained earnings	208,700	85,000
Total shareholders' equity	408,700	285,000
Total liabilities and shareholders' equity	$ 483,200	$ 367,600

METRO MOVING COMPANY
Statement of Income
For the year ended December 31, 2016

Moving revenue		$450,000
Gain on sale of vehicles		4,000
		454,000
Expenses		
Vehicle operating expenses	$102,400	
Wages expense	134,000	
Depreciation expense	59,500	
Interest expense	5,400	
Total expenses		301,300
Net income		$152,700

Additional information:

1. Vehicles that cost $65,000 and had a net carrying amount of $10,000 were sold for $14,000.
2. A cash payment was made to reduce the bank loan.
3. Dividends were declared and paid during the year.

Required:

a. Prepare a statement of cash flows for Metro Moving Company for the year ended December 31, 2016, using the indirect method.
b. Determine the cash flows from operating activities using the direct method.

AP5-13 (Prepare statement of cash flows)

Financial statement data for Gibbons Electronics Company for 2016 follow.

GIBBONS ELECTRONICS COMPANY
Comparative Statement of Financial Position

	Dec. 31, 2016	Dec. 31, 2015
Assets		
Cash	$ 285,000	$ 295,000
Accounts receivable	334,000	384,000
Inventory	311,000	266,000
Prepaid insurance	50,000	35,000
Total current assets	980,000	980,000
Property, plant, and equipment	650,000	590,000
Accumulated depreciation	(165,000)	(130,000)
Net capital assets	485,000	460,000
Total assets	$1,465,000	$1,440,000
Liabilities and shareholders' equity		
Accounts payable	$ 60,000	$ 50,000
Wages payable	15,000	10,000
Unearned revenue	50,000	35,000
Income taxes payable	55,000	45,000
Total current liabilities	180,000	140,000
Bonds payable	490,000	575,000
Total liabilities	670,000	715,000
Common shares	350,000	285,000
Retained earnings	445,000	440,000
Total shareholders' equity	795,000	725,000
Total liabilities and shareholders' equity	$1,465,000	$1,440,000

GIBBONS ELECTRONICS COMPANY
Statement of Income
For the year ended December 31, 2016

Sales revenue		$ 3,855,000
Gain on sale of equipment		10,000
		3,865,000
Expenses		
Cost of goods sold	$ 2,105,000	
Wages expense	353,000	
Depreciation expense	95,000	
Other operating expenses	555,000	
Interest expense	60,000	
Income taxes	345,000	
Total expenses		3,513,000
Net income		$ 352,000

Additional information:

1. Equipment that cost $100,000 and had a net carrying amount of $40,000 was sold for $50,000.
2. Dividends were declared and paid during the year.

Required:

a. Prepare a statement of cash flows for Gibbons Electronic Company for the year ended December 31, 2016. Include supplementary information to disclose the amounts paid for interest and income taxes using the indirect method.
b. Determine the cash flows from operating activities using the direct method.

AP5-14 (Prepare statement of cash flows)

Marchant Ltd. reported the following abbreviated statement of financial position and statement of earnings for 2016.

MARCHANT LTD.
Comparative Statement of Financial Position

	Dec. 31, 2016	Dec. 31, 2015
Cash	$ 60,000	$ 70,000
Accounts receivable	120,000	140,000
Inventory	320,000	280,000
Property, plant, and equipment	700,000	650,000
Less: Accumulated depreciation	(260,000)	(230,000)
Total assets	$ 940,000	$ 910,000
Accounts payable	$ 82,000	$ 85,000
Wages payable	8,000	10,000
Loan payable	350,000	400,000
Common shares	200,000	150,000
Retained earnings	300,000	265,000
Total liabilities and shareholders' equity	$ 940,000	$ 910,000

MARCHANT LTD.
Statement of Income
For the year ended December 31, 2016

Sales		$450,000
Cost of goods sold		240,000
Gross profit		210,000
Other expenses:		
Supplies expense	$ 15,000	
Depreciation expense	30,000	
Wages expense	100,000	
Other operating expenses	5,000	
Interest expense	24,000	174,000
		36,000
Other income		8,000
Net income		$ 44,000

Required:

a. Prepare a statement of cash flows for Marchant Ltd. for the year ended December 31, 2016, using the indirect method.
b. Determine the cash flows from operating activities using the direct method.
c. Was the cash flow generated by the company's operating activities during the year larger or smaller than the net income? Should these two amounts be the same? Explain.
d. Was the change in the amount of working capital during the year the same amount as cash from operating activities? Should these two amounts be the same? Explain. (Hint: Working capital = current assets − current liabilities.)

AP5-15 (Prepare statement of cash flows)

The comparative statement of financial position and statement of income for NextWave Company follow.

NEXTWAVE COMPANY
Comparative Statement of Financial Position

	Dec. 31, 2016	Dec. 31, 2015
Assets		
Cash	$ 66,700	$ 47,250
Accounts receivable	76,800	57,000
Inventory	121,900	92,650
Long-term investments	84,500	97,000
Property, plant, and equipment	280,000	235,000
Accumulated depreciation	(79,500)	(70,000)
	$550,400	$458,900
Liabilities and shareholders' equity		
Accounts payable	$ 52,700	$ 49,200
Income taxes payable	12,000	18,000
Bonds payable	100,000	70,000
Common shares	230,000	200,000
Retained earnings	155,700	121,700
	$550,400	$458,900

NEXTWAVE COMPANY
Statement of Income
For the year ended December 31, 2016

Sales revenue		$437,500
Gain on sale of equipment		3,700
		441,200
Expenses		
Cost of goods sold	$200,500	
Operating expenses (excluding depreciation)	63,800	
Depreciation expense	49,700	
Income tax expense	40,000	354,000
Net income		$ 87,200

Additional information:

1. Some of the long-term investments were sold at their carrying value. As a result, there was no gain or loss on this transaction.
2. Equipment costing $47,000 was sold for $10,500, which was $3,700 more than its net carrying amount at the time of disposal.

Required:

a. Prepare the company's statement of cash flows for 2016 using the indirect method.
b. Calculate the amount of cash that was paid for income taxes during 2016.
c. Determine the cash flows from operating activities using the direct method.

AP5-16 (Prepare statement of cash flows)

A comparative statement of financial position and a statement of earnings for Standard Card Company follow.

STANDARD CARD COMPANY
Statement of Financial Position

	Dec. 31, 2016	Dec. 31, 2015
Assets		
Current assets		
Cash	$134,000	$ 111,000
Accounts receivable	83,000	78,000
Inventory	200,000	110,000
Prepaid insurance	10,000	20,000
Total current assets	427,000	319,000
Non-current assets		
Equipment	305,000	350,000
Accumulated depreciation	(67,000)	(75,000)
Total non-current assets	238,000	275,000
Total assets	$665,000	$594,000
Liabilities		
Current liabilities		
Accounts payable	$ 88,000	$ 83,000
Interest payable	3,000	4,000
Unearned revenue	13,000	18,000
Total current liabilities	104,000	105,000
Long-term debt	100,000	150,000
Total liabilities	204,000	255,000
Shareholders' equity		
Common shares	200,000	115,000
Retained earnings	261,000	224,000
Total shareholders' equity	461,000	339,000
Total liabilities and shareholders' equity	$665,000	$594,000

STANDARD CARD COMPANY
Statement of Income
For the year ended December 31, 2016

Sales		$207,000
Expenses		
Cost of goods sold	$97,000	
Depreciation expense	12,000	
Insurance expense	10,000	
Interest expense	8,000	
Loss on sale of equipment	13,000	
Income tax	23,000	
Total expenses		163,000
Net income		$ 44,000

Additional information:
The loss on the sale of equipment occurred when a relatively new machine with a cost of $100,000 and accumulated depreciation of $20,000 was sold because a technological change had made it obsolete.

Required:

a. Prepare a statement of cash flows for the year ended December 31, 2016, using the indirect method.
b. Determine the cash flows from operating activities using the direct method.

AP5-17 (Prepare statement of cash flows)

Digiread Technologies Ltd. (DTL) is a privately held distributor of e-readers and tablets. The Calgary-based company is well established and is currently managed by its founder, Erin Jacobs. The company's financial statements are presented below, together with some additional information.

DIGIREAD TECHNOLOGIES LTD.
Statement of Income
As at December 31, 2016

Sales	$ 50,500,000
Cost of goods sold	34,400,000
Gross profit	16,100,000
Wage expense	4,000,000
Depreciation expense	1,200,000
Interest expense	1,900,000
Income tax expense	1,600,000
Net income from operations	7,400,000
Gain on sale of equipment	600,000
Net income	$ 8,000,000

DIGIREAD TECHNOLOGIES LTD.
Statement of Financial Position
As at December 31

	2016	2015
Assets		
Current assets:		
Cash	$15,500,000	$ 8,500,000
Accounts receivable (net)	11,500,000	15,500,000
Inventory	16,900,000	19,000,000
Total current assets	43,900,000	43,000,000
Equipment	39,400,000	30,000,000
Accumulated depreciation, equipment	(6,600,000)	(6,400,000)
Total Assets	$76,700,000	$66,600,000
Liabilities and Shareholders' Equity		
Current liabilities:		
Accounts payable	$11,900,000	$ 7,000,000
Wages payable	1,200,000	1,000,000
Total current liabilities	13,100,000	8,000,000
Bonds payable	21,000,000	26,000,000
Common shares	14,000,000	9,000,000
Retained earnings	28,600,000	23,600,000
Total Liabilities and Shareholders' Equity	$76,700,000	$66,600,000

DIGIREAD TECHNOLOGIES LTD.
Other Selected Financial Information for the Year Ended December 31, 2016

1. Total sales in 2016 were consistent with the prior year's and the company's dividend policy has remained consistent for the past five years.
2. During 2016, DTL sold a piece of equipment for $2.1 million. The equipment had originally cost $2.5 million and had a net carrying amount of $1.5 million at the time of sale.
3. On August 1, 2016, DTL's board of directors approved the retirement of bonds with a face value of $5 million through the issuance of common shares.

Required:
DTL's management shareholders have asked you to prepare the statement of cash flows for DTL using either the direct or indirect method for determining cash flows from operating activities. Prepare the statement for them.

AP5-18 (Prepare statement of cash flows)

Tangent Controls Ltd. is a manufacturer of crash-protected event recorders that are used in railway systems around the world to record event data. These data can be retrieved and analyzed to monitor and improve operations, but also to provide diagnostic data in the event of rail crashes. The small Ottawa-based company has customers across the world, but its largest market is North America. The company has been hurt by the U.S. economy, seeing a 12% decline in sales over the prior year. The company is hoping that the latest industry developments, which call for a significant increase in the shipment of oil by railcar, will mean an increase in sales. In the meantime, the company has been seeking new investors and has approached a leading Canadian venture capital firm to see if it might be interested in investing. As part of its approach, Tangent has provided the following financial information for the most recent fiscal year.

TANGENT CONTROLS LTD.
Statement of Financial Position
As at September 30

	2016	2015
Assets		
Current assets:		
Cash	$ -	$ 72,000
Accounts receivable (net)	601,000	378,000
Inventory	760,000	594,000
Total current assets	1,361,000	1,044,000
Equipment	1,608,000	1,908,000
Accumulated depreciation, equipment	(1,425,000)	(1,440,000)
Total Assets	$1,544,000	$1,512,000
Liabilities and Shareholders' Equity		
Current liabilities:		
Bank indebtedness	$ 22,000	$ -
Accounts payable	260,000	252,000
Total current liabilities	282,000	252,000
Bank loan payable	152,000	144,000
Common shares	900,000	900,000
Retained earnings	210,000	216,000
Total Liabilities and Shareholders' Equity	$1,544,000	$1,512,000

TANGENT CONTROLS LTD. Statement of Income For the year ended September 30, 2016	
Sales revenue	$6,070,000
Cost of goods sold	3,875,000
Gross profit	2,195,000
Wages expense	1,580,000
Utilities expense	290,000
Depreciation expense	225,000
Rent expense	79,000
Interest expense	47,000
Loss from operations	(26,000)
Gain on sale of equipment	40,000
Earnings before income tax	14,000
Income tax expense	3,000
Net income	$ 11,000

Additional information:

1. During the year, the company repaid principal of $30,000 on its loan payable.
2. During the year, equipment with a net carrying amount of $60,000 was sold.
3. No equipment was purchased during the year.

Required:

a. You work for the venture capital firm and have been tasked with preparing the statement of cash flows for Tangent using either the direct or indirect method for determining cash flows from operating activities. Prepare the statement.
b. Discuss significant observations from the statement of cash flows that your firm would want to consider.

AP5-19 (Determine cash collected from customers and paid to suppliers)

Southbend Company had sales of $734,000 for the year. The company reported accounts receivable of $54,000 at the end of last year and $60,000 at the end of this year. Southbend's cost of goods sold this year was $440,000. In last year's statement of financial position, the company reported inventory of $62,000 and accounts payable of $32,000. In this year's statement of financial position, Southbend reported inventory of $66,000 and accounts payable of $38,000.

Required:

i. Calculate the amount of cash that Southbend Company collected from its customers during the year.
ii. Calculate the amount of cash that Southbend paid to its suppliers for inventory during the year.

AP5-20 (Determine cash collected from customers and paid to suppliers)

Practical Company had sales of $315,000 for the year. The company reported accounts receivable of $30,000 at the end of last year and $34,000 at the end of this year. Practical's cost of goods sold this year was $246,000. In last year's statement of financial position, the company reported inventory of $49,000 and accounts payable of $33,000. In this year's statement of financial position, Practical reported inventory of $43,000 and accounts payable of $37,000.

Required:

i. Calculate the amount of cash that Practical Company collected from customers during the year.
ii. Calculate the amount of cash that Practical paid to suppliers for inventory during the year.

AP5-21 (Interpret statement of cash flows)

The following are the comparative statements of cash flows for Yellow Spruce Incorporated.

YELLOW SPRUCE INCORPORATED
Statements of Cash Flows
(in millions)

	2016	2015	2014
Operating activities			
Net income	$ 57	$ 86	$ 98
Add back:			
Depreciation expense	82	75	65
Loss (gain) on sale of investments	2	-	(11)
Effect of changes in working capital items:			
Accounts receivable	(38)	30	(39)
Inventory	(21)	(17)	(21)
Prepaid expenses	4	13	(9)
Accounts payable	27	(12)	35
Net cash inflow from operations	113	175	118
Investing activities			
Acquisition of property, plant, and equipment	(154)	(161)	(152)
Acquisition of investments	(23)	(51)	(72)
Proceeds from sale of property, plant, and equipment	16	11	27
Net cash outflow for investing activities	(161)	(201)	(197)
Financing activities			
Issuance of long-term debt	213	156	332
Repayment of long-term debt	(131)	(72)	(93)
Issuance of shares	12	-	-
Repurchase of shares	-	(38)	(84)
Dividends paid	(16)	(14)	(15)
Net cash inflow from financing activities	78	32	140
Overall increase in cash	30	6	61
Cash position at beginning of year	100	94	33
Cash position at end of year	$ 130	$ 100	$ 94

Required:

a. Discuss the company's ability to meet its non-operating needs for cash over these three years, and comment on the continuing nature of the major items that have appeared over this time period.
b. Comment on the changes in Yellow Spruce's accounts receivable, accounts payable, and inventory levels over these three years.
c. How did Yellow Spruce finance its repayment of long-term debt and its acquisition of property, plant, and equipment and investments in 2016?
d. Describe how the company's mix of long-term financing has changed during this three-year period, in terms of the proportion of debt versus equity. (Hint: Start by calculating the total amount of the increase or decrease in long-term debt, and comparing it with the total amount of the increase or decrease in shareholders' equity.)

AP5-22 (Cash flow patterns)

Urban Eats Ltd. (UEL) has been successfully operating upscale supermarkets in the Lower Mainland of British Columbia as well as a profitable on-line market through which customers place orders for home delivery by UEL. In the current year, UEL sold one of its warehouses while no new stores were acquired or opened. However, UEL's management team completed a successful bond issuance in order to position the company to be able to make a bid to acquire one of its competitors early in the next fiscal year.

Required:

Determine the cash flow pattern that you expect UEL to have and explain your rationale.

AP5-23 (Cash flow patterns)

Crafty Resources Ltd. is a new creator and publisher of children's craft kit books. It has created kits for dolls, twirled paper crafts, paper doll clothes, and so on. The publishing industry is characterized by lengthy credit periods for bookstores and a lack of credit granting on the part of paper suppliers and commercial grade copy and binding machine manufacturers.

Required:
Determine the cash flow pattern that you expect Crafty Resources to have in its first year of operation and explain your rationale.

User Perspective Problems

UP5-1 (Cash flows from operations)

In this chapter, we have emphasized the importance of carefully analyzing the operating section of the statement of cash flows. In fact, the operating activities section is always the first one listed on the statement.

Required:
From a user perspective, explain why this section is so important for understanding a company's financial health.

UP5-2 (Cash flow and compensation plans)

Required:
If you were the owner of a company and wanted to establish a management compensation plan to motivate your top managers, would you want to base your performance targets on cash flows from operations or on income from operations? Discuss the pros and cons of using these two measures of performance.

UP5-3 (Format of the statement of cash flows from a lender's perspective)

Required:
As a lender, discuss whether you would be satisfied with the current method of classifying cash flows into only three categories. In addition, discuss the normal treatment of interest expense within the statement of cash flows relative to the treatment of dividends and whether you think there are any problems with this.

UP5-4 (Statement of cash flows and lending decisions)

Required:
From the perspective of a bank loan officer, discuss why the statement of cash flows may or may not be more important than the statement of income when you are analyzing a company that is applying for a loan.

UP5-5 (Accrual accounting and cash flows)

Loan officer Han Blackford once commented that cash flow analysis has risen in importance due to a "trend over the past 20 years toward capitalizing costs and deferring more and more expenses. Although the practice may be better in terms of reporting expenses in the same period as the revenues they generated, it has also made it harder to find the available cash in a company, and easier for lenders to wind up with a loss." He further noted that recessions, and the bankruptcies that often result, draw attention to the need for better warning signals of the sort that cash flow analysis could provide.

Required:

a. Why would the process of capitalizing costs (recording them as assets to be depreciated over future periods) be better in terms of reporting expenses in the same period as the revenues they generated, yet make it harder to find the cash available in a company?
b. Explain why unexpected bankruptcies would draw attention to cash flow analysis. Your response should include a discussion of why the statements of income and financial position might not adequately alert users to impending bankruptcies.

UP5-6 (Statement of cash flows and investing decisions)

Required:
From the perspective of a stock analyst, discuss why the statement of cash flows may or may not be more important than the statement of income when analyzing a company to make a recommendation about investing in its shares.

UP5-7 (Analyze investment decision)

Jacques Rousseau is considering investing in Health Life Ltd., a pharmaceutical company. He read in the paper that this company is doing cancer research and is close to a breakthrough in developing a new drug that will be effective against bone cancer. The author of the article said that this was a good time to buy because, once the breakthrough happens, the share price is going to rise very rapidly. Jacques therefore decided to look at the company's most recent financial statements.

On the statement of financial position, he saw that the company had a significant amount of cash and short-term investments. It had some assets listed as "buildings and equipment under capital lease," which he interpreted to mean that the company was leasing its buildings and equipment rather than owning them. When he looked at the statement of income, he saw that there was no revenue. By far the largest expense was for research and development. The company had a loss during the current year, and the company reported a deficit on the statement of financial position. He thought that this made sense, because the company had yet to make its first medical breakthrough. The company had little debt, and its shares were recorded at approximately $35 million. When he looked at the notes, he saw that there were about 7 million shares issued. In fact, 1 million of those shares had been issued during the current year.

Required:

Help Jacques with his decision by answering the following questions:

a. Do you think that investing in this company would be risky? Explain.
b. Does the fact that Health Life is holding a large amount of cash and short-term investments mean that management is doing a good job? Explain in detail.
c. Is it possible for Jacques to make a rough estimate of how much longer the cash and short-term investments will last, assuming that the company does not get its breakthrough? What information would help him make this estimate?
d. Based on the number of shares that have been issued and the amount that is recorded in the share capital account, it is obvious that many investors have concluded that this is a good investment. Think carefully about this, and then list three or four advantages and disadvantages of buying shares in Health Life at this time.

UP5-8 (Interpret statement of cash flows data)

The 2016 financial statements of Green Company include the following statement of cash flows:

GREEN COMPANY
Statement of Cash Flows
For the year ended December 31, 2016

Operating:		
Net income	$ 644,000	
Adjustments to convert to cash:		
Depreciation expense	230,000	
Gain on sale of operating assets	(14,000)	
Change in current assets other than cash	(120,000)	
Change in current liabilities	80,000	
Cash provided by operations		$820,000
Investing:		
Purchase of property, plant, and equipment	(1,200,000)	
Proceeds from the sale of property, plant, and equipment	400,000	
Cash used for investing		(800,000)
Financing:		
Issuance of shares	1,000,000	
Retirement of bonds	(1,300,000)	
Dividends paid	(250,000)	
Cash used for financing		(550,000)
Decrease in cash		$(530,000)

Required:

a. Did Green Company increase or decrease its current assets, other than cash, during 2016? Is this change consistent with an increase in sales, or a decrease in sales, during the period? Explain.
b. From an investor's point of view, has Green Company become more risky or less risky in 2016? Explain.
c. Does Green Company appear to be expanding or contracting its operations? How can you tell? What other financial statement information might you examine to determine whether the company is expanding or contracting its operations?
d. Does Green appear to be able to maintain its productive capacity without additional financing? Explain.

UP5-9 (Interpret operating section)

The operating activities section of Johann Manufacturing Ltd.'s statement of cash flows is shown below. In answering the questions after the statement, assume that the net cash flows from Johann's investing and financing activities were zero; that is, that the cash inflows within the investing and financing sections were offset by the cash outflows.

JOHANN MANUFACTURING LTD.
Statement of Cash Flows
For the year ended December 31, 2016

Cash flows from operations:		
Net income		$ 632,000
Adjustments to convert earnings to cash flows:		
Depreciation expense	$110,000	
Loss on sale of investments	50,000	160,000
Change in current items other than cash:		
Accounts receivable	$ (80,000)	
Inventory	20,000	
Prepaid expenses	(45,000)	
Accounts payable	75,000	
Income tax payable	(14,000)	(44,000)
Cash provided by operations		748,000
Cash balance, January 1		566,000
Cash balance, December 31		$1,314,000

Required:

Use the preceding information to answer the following questions. If a question cannot be answered based on the information given, indicate why.

a. Have the accounts receivable increased or decreased this year? Explain briefly.
b. Has the inventory increased or decreased this year? Explain how this affects cash.
c. Did the amount of expenses prepaid by the company increase or decrease during the year? Does this help or hurt its cash position? Explain briefly.
d. Compared with last year, does the company seem to be relying more heavily, or less heavily, on trade credit to finance its activities? Explain briefly.
e. If you were a potential creditor, would you see any warning signs in the statement of cash flows that you would want to investigate before lending money to Johann Manufacturing? Explain briefly.
f. Johann Manufacturing has $2 million of bonds maturing in January 2017. Do you think the company will be able to meet its obligation to pay off the bonds, without obtaining additional long-term financing? Explain briefly.

UP5-10 (Net free cash flow)

Required:

As a lender, discuss why you might be interested in knowing a company's net free cash flow. How might it be factored into a lending decision?

UP5-11 (Net free cash flow)

Required:

As a shareholder or potential investor, discuss why you might be interested in knowing a company's net free cash flow. Comment on whether this measure is of more use than cash flows from operating activities.

Reading and Interpreting Published Financial Statements

RI5-1 (Analyze a company's statement of cash flows)

Exhibits 5-14A and B contain the consolidated statements of cash flows and related note disclosure for The Second Cup Ltd.

EXHIBIT 5-14A THE SECOND CUP LTD.'S 2013 STATEMENTS OF CASH FLOWS

STATEMENTS OF CASH FLOWS
For the periods ended December 28, 2013 and December 29, 2012
(Expressed in thousands of Canadian dollars)

	2013	2012
CASH PROVIDED BY (USED IN)		
Operating activities		
Loss for the period	$ (7,369)	$ (9,404)
Items not involving cash		
Depreciation of property and equipment	749	716
Amortization of intangible assets	502	451
Impairment charges	13,552	15,656
Amortization of deferred financing charges	38	82
Amortization of provisions	(116)	(89)
Amortization of leasehold inducements	69	26
Deferred income taxes	(1,772)	(993)
(Gain) Loss on disposal of capital related items	(197)	70
Movement in fair value of interest rate swap	44	(206)
Changes in non-cash working capital (note 21)	2,178	(1,159)
Cash provided by operating activities	7,678	5,150
Investing activities		
Proceeds from disposal of capital related items	1,240	350
Cash payments for capital expenditures (note 21)	(2,904)	(1,938)
Proceeds from repayment of leases receivable	–	36
Proceeds from repayment of notes receivable	13	185
Investment in notes receivable	(10)	–
Cash used by investing activities	(1,661)	(1,367)
Financing activities		
Dividends paid to shareholders	(3,367)	(5,298)
Repayment of note payable	–	(18)
Deferred financing charges	(29)	(50)
Payments on long-term lease	–	(2)
Cash used by financing activities	(3,396)	(5,368)
Increase (decrease) in cash and cash equivalents during the period	2,621	(1,585)
Cash and cash equivalents – Beginning of the period	3,880	5,465
Cash and cash equivalents – End of the period	$ 6,501	$ 3,880

Supplemental cash flow information is provided in note 21
See accompanying notes to the financial statements.

EXHIBIT 5-14B **EXCERPT FROM THE SECOND CUP LTD.'S 2013 ANNUAL REPORT**

21. SUPPLEMENTAL CASH FLOW INFORMATION

	2013	2012
Changes in non-cash working capital (inflow (outflow)):		
Trade and other receivables	$ 248	$ 722
Notes and leases receivable	248	(400)
Inventories	14	(58)
Prepaid expenses and other assets	505	(501)
Accounts payable and accrued liabilities	1,463	(780)
Provisions	1,212	349
Other liabilities	(65)	46
Gift card liability	(665)	207
Deposits from franchise partners	(602)	447
Income taxes	(180)	(1,191)
	$ 2,178	$(1,159)
Cash payments for capital expenditures		
Purchase of property and equipment	$(2,117)	$(1,758)
Purchase of intangible assets	(787)	(180)
	$(2,904)	$(1,938)
Supplementary information		
Interest paid	$ 522	$ 689
Income taxes paid	$ 1,687	$ 2,835

Required:

a. In total, how much did Second Cup's cash and cash equivalents change during 2013? Was this an increase or a decrease? How did this compare with the previous year?
b. Did Second Cup have net income or a net loss in 2013? How did this compare with the cash flows from operating activities? What was the largest difference between these two amounts?
c. What effect did the change in the company's accounts payable and accrued liabilities have on cash flows from operating activities in 2013? What does this tell you about the balance owed to these creditors?
d. Did the balance of outstanding gift cards increase or decrease during 2013? Was this considered to be an inflow or an outflow of cash?
e. Did Second Cup purchase property, plant, and equipment during 2013? Did the company receive any proceeds from the sale of property, plant, and equipment during the period?
f. Calculate Second Cup's net free cash flow for 2013 and 2012. Is the trend positive or negative?
g. Second Cup's total liabilities were $31,376 at December 28, 2013, and $31,980 at December 29, 2012. Determine the company's cash flows to total liabilities ratio. Comment on the change year over year.
h. If you were a user of Second Cup's financial statements—a banker or an investor—how would you interpret the company's cash flow pattern? How would you assess the risk of a loan to or an investment in Second Cup? Do you think the company is growing rapidly?

RI5-2 (Analyze a company's statement of cash flows)

Exhibits 5-15A and B show the consolidated statement of cash flows of Dollarama Inc. for the years ended February 2, 2014, and February 3, 2013, along with related note disclosure.

EXHIBIT 5-15A **DOLLARAMA INC.'S 2014 CONSOLIDATED STATEMENT OF CASH FLOWS**

	Note	52-weeks February 2, 2014 $	53-weeks February 3, 2013 $
Cash flows			
Operating activities			
Net earnings for the year		250,094	220,985
Adjustments for:			
Depreciation and amortization	18	47,898	39,284
Interest accrual long-term debt	10	3,017	(216)
Amortization of debt issue costs		592	1,133
Excess of receipts over amount recognized on derivative financial instruments	15	6,319	1,272
Recognition of deferred leasing costs		465	295
Recognition of deferred tenant allowances	12	(3,543)	(2,871)
Deferred lease inducements	12	3,750	5,328
Deferred tenant allowances	12	6,058	6,832
Share-based compensation	13	4,053	1,558
Deferred income taxes	14	4,469	6,921
Loss on disposal of assets		1,017	716
		324,189	281,237
Changes in non-cash working capital components	19	(15,811)	(24,198)
Net cash generated from operating activities		308,378	257,039
Investing activities			
Additions to property and equipment	7	(96,303)	(69,577)
Additions to intangible assets	8	(11,095)	(8,210)
Proceeds on disposal of property and equipment		552	256
Net cash used by investing activities		(106,846)	(77,531)
Financing activities			
Proceeds from senior unsecured notes	10	400,000	–
Disbursements on long-term debt		(264,420)	(10,361)
Proceeds from bank indebtedness		166,000	–
Repayment of bank indebtedness		(166,000)	–
Payment of debt issue costs		(2,797)	(837)
Repayment of finance leases		(985)	(695)
Dividends paid		(38,418)	(30,972)
Repurchase and cancellation of shares	13	(277,438)	(155,942)
Issuance of common shares		1,430	1,594
Net cash used by financing activities		(182,628)	(197,213)
Increase (decrease) in cash and cash equivalents		18,904	(17,705)
Cash and cash equivalents – Beginning of year		52,566	70,271
Cash and cash equivalents – End of year		71,470	52,566
Cash payment of interest		6,025	7,639
Cash payment of income taxes		89,801	75,090

EXHIBIT 5-15B **EXCERPT FROM DOLLARAMA INC.'S 2014 ANNUAL REPORT**

19. CONSOLIDATED STATEMENT OF CASH FLOWS INFORMATION

The changes in non-cash working capital components are as follows:

	February 2, 2014	February 3, 2013
	$	$
Accounts receivable	(165)	(3,954)
Deposits and prepaid expenses	374	(1,320)
Merchandise inventories	(26,295)	(22,512)
Accounts payable and accrued liabilities	11,809	587
Income taxes payable	(1,534)	3,001
	(15,811)	(24,198)

Required:

a. How did Dollarama's net income in 2014 compare with the cash flows from operating activities? What was the largest difference between these two amounts?
b. Did Dollarama increase or decrease the amount of inventory in its stores between 2013 and 2014? Is this consistent with the nature of the changes reflected in the company's cash flows from investing activities?
c. What effect did the change in the company's accounts payable and accrued liabilities have on cash flows from operating activities in 2014? What does this tell you about the balance owed to these creditors?
d. Examine the financing activities section of Dollarama's statement of cash flows and comment on the main differences between 2014 and 2013.
e. Dollarama's total liabilities were $702,614 at February 2, 2014, and $522,202 at February 3, 2013. Calculate the company's cash flows to total liabilities ratio and comment on whether this has improved or worsened from 2013 to 2014.
f. Calculate Dollarama's net free cash flow and discuss the company's ability to generate the cash required to continue to grow the company's operations and repay its debt.

RI5-3 (Analyze a company's statement of cash flows)

The consolidated statements of cash flows and related note disclosure for **Sirius XM Canada Holdings Inc.** are in Exhibits 5-16A and B. Sirius broadcasts satellite radio channels to subscribers.

EXHIBIT 5-16A **SIRIUS XM CANADA HOLDINGS INC.'S 2013 CONSOLIDATED STATEMENTS OF CASH FLOWS**

CONSOLIDATED STATEMENTS OF CASH FLOWS

For the year ended August 31 *(Canadian dollars)*	**Notes**	**2013**	2012
Cash provided by (used in)			
OPERATING ACTIVITIES			
Net income (loss) for the year		**12,190,542**	(4,178,816)
Add (deduct) items not involving cash			
Amortization of intangible assets	6	**33,167,880**	36,899,668
Depreciation of property and equipment	5	**2,407,716**	2,789,385
Loss on disposal of property and equipment	5	**11,109**	–
Deferred tax recovery	7	**5,374,778**	(8,312,710)
Stock-based compensation	13	**2,257,295**	1,493,400
Accrued interest		**–**	(5,088)
Interest accretion	10	**954,375**	950,583
Revaluation of derivatives	10	**(2,291,378)**	(1,213,473)
Foreign exchange losses		**769,540**	3,010
Net change in non-cash working capital and deferred revenue related to operations	18	**5,409,419**	12,649,125
Cash provided by operating activities		**60,251,276**	41,075,084

continued

EXHIBIT 5-16A **SIRIUS XM CANADA HOLDINGS INC.'S 2013 CONSOLIDATED STATEMENTS OF CASH FLOWS (continued)**

For the year ended August 31 *(Canadian dollars)*	**Notes**	**2013**	2012
INVESTING ACTIVITIES			
Purchase of property and equipment	5	**(753,788)**	(728,425)
Purchase of intangible assets	6	**(7,624,829)**	(3,700,491)
Prepayment of property and equipment		**(2,240,000)**	–
Purchase of short-term investments	14	**(5,306,295)**	–
Interest received on short-term investments	14	**176,649**	–
Cash (used in) investing activities		**(15,748,263)**	(4,428,916)
FINANCING ACTIVITIES			
Payment of dividends	12	**(53,706,925)**	–
Proceeds from exercise of stock options	13	**2,247,747**	464,132
Repayments of debt	10	**–**	(917,700)
Payment of related party promissory notes	9	**–**	(11,173,290)
Cash (used in) financing activities		**(51,459,178)**	(11,626,858)
Net (decrease) increase in cash and cash equivalents during the year		**(6,956,165)**	25,019,310
Cash and cash equivalents, beginning of year		**51,034,749**	26,015,439
Cash and cash equivalents, end of year		**44,078,584**	51,034,749

EXHIBIT 5-16B **EXCERPT FROM SIRIUS XM CANADA HOLDINGS INC.'S 2013 ANNUAL REPORT**

18. SUPPLEMENTAL CASH FLOW DISCLOSURE

The net change in non-cash working capital balances related to operations consists of the following:

For the year ended August 31	**2013**	2012
Decrease (increase) in assets		
Accounts receivable	**(1,226,308)**	(1,414,462)
Prepaid expenses	**(1,226,187)**	48,441
Inventory	**89,967**	1,941,122
Increase (decrease) in liabilities		
Trade, other payables and provisions	**5,582,248**	2,334,378
Due to related parties	**4,027,425**	745,399
Deferred revenue	**3,416,582**	11,493,635
Long-term liabilities	**(5,254,308)**	(2,499,388)
Net change in non-cash working capital related to operations	**5,409,419**	12,649,125

Operating activities include the following payments and receipts:

For the year ended August 31	**2013**	2012
Interest income received	**646,678**	360,906
Interest paid	**14,350,173**	14,429,138
Taxes paid	**–**	–

Required:

a. In total, how much did Sirius's cash and cash equivalents change during 2013? Was this an increase or a decrease? How did this compare with the previous year?
b. Did Sirius have net income or a net loss in 2013? How did this compare with the cash flows from operating activities? What was the largest difference between these two amounts?
c. What effect did the change in the company's trade, other payables, and provisions have on cash flows from operating activities in 2013? What does this tell you about the balance owed to these creditors?
d. Did the balance of deferred revenue increase or decrease during 2013? Was this considered to be an inflow or an outflow of cash? What does this tell you about the trend in the amount of the customers' prepaid subscription fees?
e. Calculate Sirius's net free cash flow for 2013 and 2012. Is the trend positive or negative?
f. Sirius's total liabilities were $370,878,874 at August 31, 2013, and $361,872,956 at August 31, 2012. Determine the company's cash flows to total liabilities ratio. Comment on the change year over year. Would your perspective on the results of this ratio calculation change if you were advised that approximately 40% of Sirius's liabilities were related to deferred revenue?
g. How did the dividends paid by Sirius to its shareholders compare with the company's net income and cash flows from operating activities?

RI5-4 (Analyze a company's statement of cash flows)

The consolidated statements of cash flows and related note disclosure for Big Rock Brewery Inc. are in Exhibits 5-17A and B.

EXHIBIT 5-17A **BIG ROCK BREWERY INC.'S 2013 CONSOLIDATED STATEMENTS OF CASH FLOWS**

BIG ROCK BREWERY INC.
Consolidated Statements of Cash Flows
(In thousands of Canadian dollars)

	Year ended	
	December 30, 2013	**December 30, 2012**
OPERATING ACTIVITIES		
Net income for the period	$ 2,551	$ 4,135
Items not affecting cash:		
Depreciation and amortization	3,157	3,228
Gain on sale of assets	(13)	(19)
Stock-based compensation	640	446
Deferred income tax expense (recovery)	(1,586)	1,168
Net change in non-cash working capital related to operations (note 25)	3,148	1,496
Cash provided by operating activities	7,897	10,454
FINANCING ACTIVITIES		
Dividend payments	(4,855)	(4,850)
Principal repayments of long-term debt	(2,042)	(641)
Cash received on exercise of options	—	131
Cash used in financing activities	(6,897)	(5,360)

continued

EXHIBIT 5-17A **BIG ROCK BREWERY INC.'S 2013 CONSOLIDATED STATEMENTS OF CASH FLOWS (continued)**

	December 30, 2013	December 30, 2012
INVESTING ACTIVITIES		
Purchase of property, plant and equipment	(2,992)	(1,487)
Purchase of intangibles	(6)	—
Proceeds from sale of equipment	34	19
Cash used in investing activities	(2,964)	(1,468)
Net increase (decrease) in cash	(1,964)	3,626
Cash, beginning of year	4,281	655
Cash, end of year	$ 2,317	$ 4,281
Supplemental cash-flow information		
Cash interest paid	$ 52	$ 103
Cash taxes paid	958	—

EXHIBIT 5-17B **EXCERPT FROM BIG ROCK BREWERY INC.'S 2013 ANNUAL REPORT**

25. CHANGE IN NON-CASH WORKING CAPITAL

	Year ended	
	December 30, 2013	December 30, 2012
Accounts payable and accrued liabilities	$ 1,649	$ 741
Inventory	884	472
Accounts receivable	1,005	430
Prepaid expenses	(390)	(147)
Total change in non-cash working capital	$ 3,148	$ 1,496

Required:

a. In total, how much did Big Rock's cash and cash equivalents change during 2013? Was this an increase or a decrease? How did this compare with the previous year?

b. How did Big Rock's net income in 2013 compare with the cash flows from operating activities? What was the largest difference between these two amounts?

c. What effect did the change in the company's accounts receivable have on cash flows from operating activities in 2013? What does this tell you about the balance owed by the company's customers?

d. What effect did the change in the company's accounts payable and accrued liabilities have on cash flows from operating activities in 2013? What does this tell you about the balance owed to these creditors?

e. Calculate Big Rock's net free cash flow for 2013 and 2012. Is the trend positive or negative?

f. How did the dividends paid by Big Rock to its shareholders compare with the company's net income and cash flows from operating activities?

g. If you were a user of Big Rock's financial statements—a banker or an investor—how would you interpret the company's cash flow pattern? How would you assess the risk of a loan to or an investment in Big Rock? Do you think the company is growing rapidly?

RI5-5 (Analyze a company's statement of cash flows)

The consolidated statements of cash flows and related note disclosure for Le Château Inc. are in Exhibits 5-18A and B.

EXHIBIT 5-18A **LE CHATEAU INC.'S 2014 CONSOLIDATED STATEMENTS OF CASH FLOWS**

Le Château Inc.

CONSOLIDATED STATEMENTS OF CASH FLOWS

Years ended January 25, 2014 and January 26, 2013
(In thousands of Canadian dollars)

	2014 $	2013 $
OPERATING ACTIVITIES		
Net loss	**(15,986)**	(8,717)
Adjustments to determine net cash from operating activities		
Depreciation and amortization *[notes 8 and 9]*	**18,723**	19,574
Write-off and net impairment of property and equipment and intangible assets *[notes 8 and 9]*	**1,897**	2,142
Loss on disposal of property and equipment *[note 8]*	**–**	108
Amortization of deferred lease credits	**(2,539)**	(1,285)
Deferred lease credits	**39**	1,088
Stock-based compensation	**978**	336
Provisions	**(102)**	338
Finance costs	**2,714**	3,063
Finance income	**(13)**	(23)
Interest paid	**(2,436)**	(2,863)
Interest received	**13**	28
Income tax recovery	**(5,722)**	(3,469)
	(2,434)	10,320
Net change in non-cash working capital items related to operations *[note 21]*	**(3,030)**	(6,340)
	(5,464)	3,980
Income taxes refunded	**2,108**	2,056
Cash flows related to operating activities	**(3,356)**	6,036
FINANCING ACTIVITIES		
Increase in bank indebtedness	**17,482**	13,600
Repayment of long-term debt	**(8,304)**	(16,323)
Issue of share capital upon exercise of options	**159**	–
Cash flows related to financing activities	**9,337**	(2,723)
INVESTING ACTIVITIES		
Additions to property and equipment and intangible assets *[notes 8 and 9]*	**(6,318)**	(9,237)
Proceeds from disposal of property and equipment *[note 8]*	**–**	514
Cash flows related to investing activities	**(6,318)**	(8,723)
Decrease in cash	**(337)**	(5,410)
Cash, beginning of year	**1,783**	7,193
Cash, end of year	**1,446**	1,783

EXHIBIT 5-18B **EXCERPT FROM LE CHATEAU INC.'S 2013 ANNUAL REPORT**

21. CHANGES IN NON-CASH WORKING CAPITAL

The cash generated from (used for) non-cash working capital items is made up of changes related to operations in the following accounts:

	January 25, 2014 $	**January 26, 2013 $**
Accounts receivable	**430**	447
Income taxes refundable	**(360)**	(340)
Inventories	**(1,660)**	(3,893)
Prepaid expenses	**(402)**	(326)
Deferred finance costs	**—**	(755)
Trade and other payables	**(1,192)**	(1,113)
Deferred revenue	**154**	(360)
Net change in non-cash working capital items related to operations	**(3,030)**	(6,340)

Required:

a. Determine the cash flow patterns for Le Château. In total, how much did Le Château's cash and cash equivalents change during 2014? Was this an increase or a decrease? How did this compare with the previous year?
b. How did Le Château's net loss in 2014 compare with the cash flows from operating activities? What was the largest difference between these two amounts?
c. What effect did the change in the company's inventory balance have on cash flows from operating activities in 2014? What does this tell you about the company's inventory balances? Does this cause any particular concerns given the nature of the company's operations?
d. What effect did the change in the company's trade and other payables have on cash flows from operating activities in 2014? What does this tell you about the balance owed to these creditors?
e. Calculate Le Château's net free cash flow for 2014 and 2013. Is the trend positive or negative?
f. If you were a user of Le Château's financial statements—a banker or an investor—how would you interpret the company's cash flow pattern? How would you assess the risk of a loan to or an investment in Le Château?

RI5-6 (Analyze a statement of cash flows)

Required:

For a company of your own choosing, answer the following questions based on its statement of cash flows:

a. Summarize the results for cash from operating, investing, and financing activities over the last two years.
b. Explain any significant changes in the items listed in part "a," from last year to this year.
c. Treating operations as a single source, what were the three most significant (largest) sources of cash in the most recent year?
d. Within the investing and financing sections, what were the four most significant (largest) uses of cash in the most recent year?
e. How has the company been financing its investing activities—through operating activities, financing activities, or both? Support your answer with numbers from the statement of cash flows.

Cases

C5-1 Atlantic Service Company

Atlantic Service Company was established in Moncton, New Brunswick, five years ago to provide services to the home construction industry. It has been very successful, with assets, sales, and profits increasing each year. However, Atlantic is experiencing serious cash shortages and is in danger of going into bankruptcy, because it cannot pay its suppliers and already has a very substantial overdraft at its bank. The president has asked you to analyze the statement of cash flows for the years 2016 and 2015, which appears below.

ATLANTIC SERVICE COMPANY
Statement of Cash Flows
As of December 31

	2016	2015
Operating activities:		
Net income	$200,000	$185,000
Adjustments to convert earnings to cash flows:		
Depreciation expense	25,000	20,000
Gain on sale of investments	3,000	2,000
Changes in non-cash working capital:		
Increase in accounts receivable	(35,000)	(25,000)
Increase in inventory	(30,000)	(20,000)
Increase in prepaid expenses	(5,000)	(4,000)
Increase in accounts payable	52,000	43,000
Net cash provided by operating activities	210,000	201,000
Financing activities:		
Repayment of short-term bank loan	(100,000)	(60,000)
Renewal of short-term bank loan	180,000	100,000
Dividends paid	(15,000)	(10,000)
Net cash provided by financing activities	65,000	30,000
Investing activities:		
Purchase of equipment	(300,000)	(250,000)
Net cash used by investing activities	(300,000)	(250,000)
Net decrease in cash during year	(25,000)	(19,000)
Cash position (bank overdraft) at beginning of year	(29,000)	(10,000)
Cash position (bank overdraft) at end of year	$ (54,000)	$ (29,000)

Required:
Write a memo that:

a. explains what appears to be causing the cash shortage and
b. recommends a plan to save the company from bankruptcy.

C5-2 Robertson Furniture Ltd.

Kayla Martchenko has just received a small inheritance from her grandparents' estate. She would like to invest the money and is currently reviewing several opportunities. A friend has given her the financial statements of Robertson Furniture Ltd., a company she found on the Internet. Kayla has reviewed the financial statements and is ready to invest in Robertson Furniture.

Before she invests, Kayla comes to you for some financial advice, because she knows you are taking an accounting course and may be able to give her some insights into the financial statements. She is convinced that this company will be a profitable investment because the statement of financial position indicates that the company's cash balances have been increasing very rapidly, from only $8,000 two years ago to $354,000 now.

Kayla has copied Robertson's statement of cash flows for you, so that you can see how much cash the company has been able to generate each year.

ROBERTSON FURNITURE LTD.
Statement of Cash Flows
As of December 31

	2016	2015
Operating activities:		
Net income (loss)	$ (4,000)	$ 12,000
Add back items not representing cash flows:		
Depreciation expense	20,000	40,000
Loss on disposal of property, plant, and equipment	12,000	10,000
Loss on sale of investments	4,000	3,000

continued

	2016	2015
Adjustment for working capital items:		
Increase in accounts receivable	(40,000)	(36,000)
Increase in inventory	(54,000)	(42,000)
Decrease in prepaid insurance	8,000	2,000
Increase in accounts payable	45,000	28,000
Cash flow from operating activities	(9,000)	17,000
Financing activities:		
Issuance of bonds payable	100,000	20,000
Issuance of shares	50,000	30,000
Payment of dividends	(2,000)	(20,000)
Cash flow from financing activities	148,000	30,000
Investing activities		
Sale of property, plant, and equipment	70,000	22,000
Sale of investments	50,000	20,000
Cash flow from investing activities	120,000	42,000
Overall increase in cash during year	259,000	89,000
Cash—beginning of year	97,000	8,000
Cash—end of year	$356,000	$ 97,000

Required:

a. Comment on Robertson Furniture's statement of cash flows and address Kayla's opinion that, in light of the amount of cash it has generated, the company must be a good investment.
b. Based on the results of your analysis of Robertson's statement of cash flows, outline several points that Kayla should investigate about this company before investing her inheritance in it.

C5-3 Ridlow Shipping Ltd.

Jim Shea is an accountant at King and Associates, which is an accounting firm based in Halifax, Nova Scotia. The firm specializes in dealing with small business clients who generally are very successful business people but have limited accounting knowledge.

Owen Ridlow is a client and the sole owner of Ridlow Shipping Ltd. He recently called Jim with some questions about the financial statements prepared for the year ended December 31, 2016. During the conversation, Owen made the following comment: "Jim, I am wondering why I have to pay you guys to prepare a statement of cash flows. I understand the importance of the statement of financial position and the statement of income, but since I always know how much cash I have in the bank and I reconcile my bank accounts regularly, why do I need a statement of cash flows? It seems to me that paying to have this statement prepared is an unnecessary expense."

Required:

Do you think Owen is at all justified in making this comment? Outline several points that Jim should raise in his discussion with Owen to explain the importance of the statement of cash flows and justify the need for it. Support your answer by referring to Ridlow Shipping's most recent statement of cash flows, which follows.

RIDLOW SHIPPING LTD.
Statement of Cash Flows
As of December 31

	2016	2015
Operating activities:		
Net income	$206,250	$254,500
Add back items not representing cash flows:		
Depreciation	40,000	50,000
Loss on sale of investments	6,000	2,000

continued

Adjustment for working capital items:		
Decrease (increase) in accounts receivable	(40,000)	16,000
Increase in inventory	(5,000)	(2,000)
Decrease in prepaid rent	750	500
Increase (decrease) in accounts payable	45,000	(28,000)
Net cash provided by operating activities	253,000	293,000
Financing activities:		
Repayment of bonds	(100,000)	–
Issuance of shares	50,000	–
Payment of dividends	(75,000)	(75,000)
Net cash consumed by financing activities	(125,000)	(75,000)
Investing activities:		
Sale of investments	50,000	20,000
Purchase of capital assets	(215,000)	(197,000)
Net cash consumed by investing activities	(165,000)	(177,000)
Overall increase (decrease) in cash during year	(37,000)	41,000
Cash balance at beginning of year	50,000	9,000
Cash balance at end of year	$ 13,000	$ 50,000

C5-4 Jones Printing

Ben Jones would like to expand his small printing business to include a new computerized colour printing system. To finance the purchase of this equipment, Ben has applied for a loan from a government venture capital agency. The agency requires a complete set of financial statements before it can approve any loan application, and assigns an employee to each applicant to help prepare the necessary financial statements.

You have been assigned to assist Ben with his application, and he has provided you with a statement of income and a statement of financial position for his business. You explain to Ben that a complete set of financial statements includes a statement of cash flows, and that one will have to be prepared for his company before the loan application can be processed. Ben does not understand the purpose of the statement of cash flows and what types of information he will have to gather in order to have one prepared for his business.

Required:
Prepare a brief memo to Ben explaining the purpose and structure of the statement of cash flows and outlining any additional information, beyond the statement of income and statement of financial position, that he will have to provide to enable you to prepare a statement of cash flows for his business.

C5-5 Kralovec Company

As discussed in the chapter, there are two methods for presenting the information in the operating activities section of the statement of cash flows: the direct method and the indirect method. Accounting standards generally express a preference for the direct method but allow the indirect method. The vast majority of companies prepare their statements of cash flows using the indirect method of presentation.

Presented below are two statements of cash flows for Kralovec Company. In the first one, the operating activities section is presented using the direct method; in the second statement, the indirect method is used.

KRALOVEC COMPANY
Statement of Cash Flows
For the year ended December 31, 2016

1. Direct Method	
Cash flows from operating activities	
Cash collections from customers	$ 6,446,000
Cash payments for operating expenses	(4,883,000)
Cash payments for interest	(80,000)
Cash payments for income taxes	(313,000)
Net cash provided by operating activities	1,170,000

continued

Cash flows from investing activities		
Sale of machinery	$ 140,000	
Purchase of machinery	(750,000)	
Net cash used by investing activities		(610,000)
Cash flows from financing activities		
Retirement of bonds	(100,000)	
Payment of dividends	(200,000)	
Net cash used by financing activities		(300,000)
Net increase in cash during year		260,000
Cash at beginning of year		130,000
Cash at end of year		$ 390,000

2. Indirect Method

Cash flows from operating activities		
Net income		$ 705,000
Adjustments to convert net earnings to net cash provided by operating activities:		
Depreciation expense	$ 470,000	
Loss on sale of machinery	34,000	
Increase in accounts receivable	(100,000)	
Decrease in inventory	35,000	
Increase in accounts payable	21,000	
Decrease in interest payable	(5,000)	
Increase in taxes payable	10,000	465,000
Net cash provided by operating activities		1,170,000
Cash flows from investing activities		
Sale of machinery	140,000	
Purchase of machinery	(750,000)	
Net cash used by investing activities		(610,000)
Cash flows from financing activities		
Retirement of bonds	(100,000)	
Payment of dividends	(200,000)	
Net cash used by financing activities		(300,000)
Net increase in cash during year		260,000
Cash at beginning of year		130,000
Cash at end of year		$ 390,000

Required:

a. As discussed in Chapter 2, understandability is an important qualitative characteristic of financial statements. With this in mind, compare the two statements above and comment on the understandability of the direct versus the indirect method of presentation in the operating activities section. Which approach do you think most users of financial statements would prefer?

b. Looking only at the first statement (presented using the direct method), analyze the cash flow data for Kralovec Company and note any significant points that can be observed from it regarding the company's operations during the year. Then repeat this process, looking only at the second statement (presented using the indirect method).

c. Based on your experience in working through part "b," which method of presentation do you find more useful (i.e. more relevant) for analyzing the cash flow data, understanding the company's operations, and identifying points to be investigated further? Explain why.

ENDNOTES

1. Solarina Ho, "Bombardier Results Raise Cash Burn Concerns, Hurt Stock," Reuters, May 1, 2014; Bertrand Marotte, "Investor Concern over Bombardier Spending Pushes Shares Lower," *The Globe and Mail*, May 1, 2014; David Parkinson, "Bombardier Cash Flow Needs to Reverse Course Soon," *The Globe and Mail*, May 1, 2014; Frederic Tomesco, "Bombardier Tumbles as Cash Usage Pace Nearly Doubles," Bloomberg, May 1, 2014; Bombardier 2013 Annual Report; Bombardier corporate website, www.bombardier.com.
2. Canadian Tire Corporation, Limited's 2013 annual report.
3. Reitmans (Canada) Limited's 2014 annual report.
4. IFRS - Conceptual Framework, OB20; Jeff Gray and Andy Hoffman, "Report Alleges Possibility Sino-Forest 'An Accounting Fiction,'" *The Globe and Mail*, April 15, 2012; Al and Mark Rosen, "Don't Be Suckered by Cash Flow Statements," Advisor.ca, August 1, 2011.
5. Reitmans (Canada) Limited's 2014 annual report.
6. Pacific Safety Products Inc.'s 2013 annual report.
7. Groupe Bikini Village's 2013 annual report.
8. Dugan, M., Gup. B., and Samson, W. (1999, Vol. 9). "Teaching the Statement of Cash Flows," *Journal of Accounting Education*, pp. 33–52.

CHAPTER 6 Cash and Accounts Receivable

CORE QUESTIONS

If you are able to answer the following questions, then you have achieved the related learning objectives.

INTRODUCTION

- Why are cash and accounts receivable of significance to users?

CASH

- What is included in the definition of "cash"?
- At what amount is cash reflected on the statement of financial position?

INTERNAL CONTROL

- What are the main principles of internal control?

BANK RECONCILIATION

- What is the purpose of a bank reconciliation and why must it be prepared?
- How is a bank reconciliation prepared?

ACCOUNTS RECEIVABLE

- What are accounts receivable?
- Why do companies sell on account?
- Are there any additional costs from selling on account?

BAD DEBTS

- At what amount are accounts receivable reflected on the statement of financial position?
- What is the allowance method of accounting for bad debts?
- How are bad debts estimated under the allowance method?
- What is the direct writeoff method and when is it acceptable to use it?
- How do companies shorten their cash-to-cash cycle?

FINANCIAL STATEMENT ANALYSIS

- What is liquidity and how is it assessed?
- How effective has the company been at collecting its accounts receivable?

LEARNING OBJECTIVES

After studying this chapter, you should be able to:

1. Explain why cash and accounts receivable are of significance to users.
2. Describe the valuation methods for cash.
3. Explain the main principles of internal control.
4. Explain the purpose of bank reconciliations, including their preparation and the treatment of related adjustments.
5. Explain why companies sell on account and identify the additional costs that result from this decision.
6. Describe the valuation methods for accounts receivable.
7. Explain the allowance method of accounting for bad debts.
8. Identify the two methods of estimating bad debts under the allowance method and describe the circumstances for using each method.
9. Explain the direct writeoff method of accounting for bad debts and when it is acceptable to use it.
10. Explain alternative ways in which companies shorten their cash-to-cash cycle.
11. Explain the concept of liquidity. Calculate the current ratio, quick ratio, accounts receivable turnover ratio, and average collection period ratio and assess the results.

Will That Be Cash or Credit?

If you had a summer lawn-mowing business, would you want customers to pay you in cash every time or would you accept an IOU for them to pay you later? If you allowed them to pay later, how much time would you give them before you came to collect your money?

If you were a company in the wholesale apparel business, like Montreal-based Gildan Activewear Inc., your credit policy would have to follow certain industry practices but not be too restrictive, or you could lose out on sales, and not be too loose, or you could end up with bad debts.

Gildan, which makes and markets family apparel such as underwear, fleece, and blank T-shirts ready for screen printing, invoices most sales with payment terms of 30 to 60 days. The company notes that it is industry practice that sales to wholesale distributors of seasonal products, especially in the last six months of the year, to be given extended payment terms, usually up to four months.

Among the credit risks Gildan faces is that its sales are concentrated: its 10 largest customers accounted for 53% of trade receivables in 2013. Many of those customers are highly leveraged, such as having bank loans for which their inventory is pledged as collateral. If a customer can't pay off its loan or obtain additional financing, it could result in Gildan having an uncollectible account receivable from that customer. "Future credit losses relating to any one of our top ten customers could be material and could result in a material charge to earnings," the company's credit risk note in its 2013 annual report states. At its fiscal year end of September 29, 2013, Gildan had U.S. $255 million in trade receivables (outstanding invoices, also known as accounts receivable), while its sales that fiscal year were almost U.S. $2.2 billion.

Gildan tries to reduce its credit risk. "The Company's extension of credit to customers involves considerable judgment and is based on an evaluation of each customer's financial condition and payment history. The Company has established various internal controls designed to mitigate credit risk, including a dedicated credit function which recommends customer credit limits and payment terms that are reviewed and approved on a quarterly basis by senior management," its annual report states. "Where available, the Company's credit departments periodically review external ratings and customer financial statements, and in some cases obtain bank and other references. New customers are subject to a specific validation and pre-approval process." Sometimes, Gildan will require riskier customers to pay up front, just like a lawn-mowing business might do with a new neighbour.

In 2014, Gildan announced it was buying Montreal-based Doris Inc., which makes women's hosiery, giving it access to Canadian retailers such as Shoppers Drug Mart and Hudson's Bay. Gildan will certainly monitor its credit practices with these new customers.[1]

INTRODUCTION

Our opening story talks about an apparel company's efforts to control its accounts receivable and limit the number of uncollectible accounts, or bad debts. Determining the value of the accounts receivable and estimating the amount that will be collected in cash is important for both external financial reporting and sound internal financial management. This chapter discusses accounting and management control issues related to an organization's most liquid assets: its cash and its receivables.

Why are cash and accounts receivable of significance to users?

LEARNING OBJECTIVE 1
Explain why cash and accounts receivable are of significance to users.

Cash and **accounts receivable** are a company's most liquid assets. These items, together with inventory (which will be discussed in Chapter 7), give the company the resources necessary to meet its immediate, short-term financial obligations. Users therefore need to have a good understanding of these items. For example, while cash seems to be straightforward, in reality it constitutes a number of things, including money physically on hand, amounts in bank accounts, and cheques held for deposit. Accounts receivable (also known as trade receivables) are amounts due from customers as a result of sales of goods or services and are typically due within 30 days. In some industries, this credit period may extend up to 180 days. (As we saw in the opening story, **Gildan Activewear Inc.** grants credit up to four months, or 120 days.) As a user, you need to know how much credit a company has extended to its customers and be aware of the potential for **uncollectible accounts**, also known as doubtful accounts or bad debts, that will never be paid by customers. You should also be able to assess how well the company has done historically at collecting its receivables.

Presenting cash and accounts receivable separately on the financial statements helps users evaluate a company's **liquidity**, or its ability to meet its obligations in the short term. In other words, users can assess how well positioned the company is in terms of having sufficient cash or current assets that will become cash (when the receivables are collected) to pay the company's current liabilities (such as accounts payable and wages payable) as they come due.

CASH

What is included in the definition of "cash"?

LEARNING OBJECTIVE 2
Describe the valuation methods for cash.

As noted above, cash includes the cash physically on hand at a company, such as the cash in the cash register drawers or in the company's safe. Cash also includes the cash represented by the customers' cheques held by the company for deposit and the cash held on deposit in the company's accounts at financial institutions (banks, credit unions, and so on). Cash also includes amounts known as **cash equivalents**. These are amounts that can be easily converted into known amounts of cash; that is, there is no doubt about the amount of cash that will be received when they mature. Cash equivalents also have short maturity dates (within three months of the date of acquisition). An example of a cash equivalent is a government treasury bill.

It is also possible for a company to have a negative cash balance. This would be the case if the company has a line of credit or overdraft facility and has drawn on it. We will discuss this situation in Chapter 9 on current liabilities.

At what amount is cash reflected on the statement of financial position?

The amount of cash and cash equivalents is presented on the statement of financial position. Cash is measured at its face value at the reporting date—the date that the statement of financial position is being prepared at. Cash may also be held in foreign currencies, such as U.S. dollars or euros. If this is the case, then these amounts are translated or converted into Canadian dollars using the rate of exchange at the statement of financial position date.

Companies normally prepare their financial statements using the currency of the country in which they are headquartered. Canadian companies typically prepare their financial statements in Canadian dollars, U.S. companies prepare their financial statements in U.S. dollars, and so on. It is possible for Canadian companies that are also listed on U.S. stock exchanges and file their financial statements in the United States to prepare their financial statements in U.S. dollars rather than Canadian dollars. We will see excerpts in this textbook from the financial statements of several Canadian companies that report in U.S. dollars.

INTERNAL CONTROL

LEARNING OBJECTIVE 3
Explain the main principles of internal control.

What are the main principles of internal control?

One of management's key responsibilities is to safeguard the company's assets. This includes ensuring that the company's assets are used effectively within the business and are not lost or stolen. All assets, including cash, inventory, and equipment, are common targets of theft either internally (by management or employees) or externally (by customers, delivery companies, and so on). To fulfill their responsibility to safeguard assets, management establishes a system of internal controls that are then continually monitored. Generally, cash is the asset most susceptible to theft and we will use it as an example to explain the elements of an internal control system.

KEY POINT
An internal control system includes:
- physical controls
- assignment of responsibilities
- separation of duties
- independent verification
- documentation

The key elements of an effective **internal control system** include:

1. **Physical Controls**
   These controls are designed to protect assets from theft, diversion, damage, or destruction. Management protects assets by ensuring that premises and resources are secure through the use of such things as locks, alarms, and fencing. In the case of cash, regular bank deposits should be made and any cash on hand should be securely stored in cash registers and safes.
2. **Assignment of Responsibilities**
   An essential characteristic of internal control is the assignment of responsibility to specific individuals. Control is most effective when only one person is responsible for each task. To illustrate, assume that at the end of the day the cash in the cash register drawer is less than the amount of cash sales rung up on the cash register. If only one person has operated the register, responsibility for the shortage can be determined immediately. If more than one individual has worked the register, it may be impossible to determine who is responsible for the shortage, unless each person is assigned a separate cash drawer.

KEY POINT
Where possible, the following duties should be separated:
- transaction authorization
- recording of transactions
- asset custody

3. **Separation of Duties**
   Separation of duties involves ensuring that individual employees cannot authorize transactions, record them, and have custody of the related assets. If these responsibilities are assigned to separate employees, no single employee will have the opportunity to defraud a company and conceal

the theft while performing the duties associated with their position. If duties are effectively separated, the only way for a theft or fraud to occur is through **collusion**, where two or more employees work together to commit the theft and conceal it.

For cash, separation of duties means that one person receives cash, another is authorized to sign cheques, and a third records the receipts or payments of cash in the accounting records. Personnel who receive, disburse, or otherwise handle cash should not maintain, or even have access to, the cash records. Bear in mind that "cash" transactions can occur in many forms. In addition to currency and cheques, cash transactions include credit card and debit card transactions, and other direct payments such as **electronic funds transfers (EFTs)** to and from the company.

4. **Independent Verification**
These controls involve one person checking the work of another. The independent verification can be internal, such as one employee checking the work of another, or external, such as an external auditor verifying transactions. When one person is responsible for verifying the work of another, behaving dishonestly without being detected would also require collusion.

In small companies, achieving the appropriate level of separation of duties and independent verification is more difficult because there is a limited number of employees. In this case, the owners or senior management must sometimes perform some of the key tasks and periodically verify the work of employees. When dealing with cash, independent verification may involve having the store manager double check the cash counts made by the store cashiers.

5. **Documentation**
Documents provide evidence that transactions and events have occurred, as well as an **audit trail** by which transactions can be traced back to source documents, if necessary. For example, the cash register tape is documentation for the amount of revenue earned and cash received. Similarly, a shipping document indicates that the goods have been shipped, and a sales invoice indicates that the customer has been billed for the goods. By adding a signature (or initials) to the documents, the individual responsible for the transaction or event can be identified. Whenever possible, documents should be prenumbered and used sequentially. This allows the company to verify that all of the documents used have been accounted for.

The main issues with cash are the control of cash to ensure that it is not lost or stolen, and the management of cash balances. Proper control of cash includes policies such as ensuring that all cash is deposited into bank accounts daily (or even more frequently), using secure safes and cash registers to hold cash until it is deposited, writing cheques or using debit or credit cards instead of using cash to pay expenses, and keeping as little cash on hand as possible.

BANK RECONCILIATION

What is the purpose of a bank reconciliation and why must it be prepared?

LEARNING OBJECTIVE 4
Explain the purpose of bank reconciliations, including their preparation and the treatment of related adjustments.

An important internal control procedure that is used by almost every company is the **bank reconciliation**. This ensures that any differences between the accounting records for cash and the bank statement received from the bank are identified, explained, and recorded where necessary. By doing this, business owners and managers have assurance that:

1. Every transaction recorded by the bank has also been recorded by the company or the reason why not has been explained.
2. Every transaction recorded by the company in its cash account(s) has also been recorded by the bank or the reason why not has been explained.

There are many reasons why a transaction may have been reflected in the company's accounting records but not by the bank or vice versa. Some common differences include:

- A cheque has been written and mailed out by the company but has yet to be deposited by the recipient. Until it is deposited, there is no way that the company's bank could be aware of it.

- The bank has charged service fees to the company's account. The company will not be aware of the fees until it receives the bank statement at the end of the month.
- The company has made a deposit on the last day of the month after the bank closed for business, by using the night deposit slot. The bank will credit the company's account for this deposit on the first business day of the new month.
- A company has deposited a cheque from one of its customers that is not honoured by the customer's bank because there are insufficient funds in the account to cover the cheque. The company will not be aware of this until the cheque is returned with the bank statement at the end of the month.

Bank reconciliations should be prepared for each bank account maintained by a company and this should be done at least monthly. If a company's cash position is very tight, then reconciliations may need to be prepared even more frequently.

Ethics in Accounting

There are numerous unethical ways that accounting records can be manipulated. Many transactions ultimately impact the cash account, including cash sales, collection of receivables, payment of expenses, settlement of payables, asset purchases, and so on. Ensuring the accuracy of the cash account minimizes the risk of fraudulent cash transactions being reflected in a company's accounts. Cash is either in the bank account or it is not, and bank reconciliations are a key control to assess this.

How is a bank reconciliation prepared?

The process of preparing a bank reconciliation is quite straightforward, if you bear in mind that the objective is to determine what the cash balance would be if the same items were recorded in both sets of records (the company's and the bank's). Accordingly, when an item is identified as being recorded in one set of records but not in the other, or recorded differently in one set of records than in the other, that item has to be included in the reconciliation. Whether it is added or deducted depends on whatever needs to be done with it, logically, to determine what the correct cash balance would be if each item were recorded correctly in both sets of records.

When reconciling the bank balance and general ledger (G/L) balance for an account, one of the simplest ways of thinking about the reconciliation is to split it in two. One side will be the "bank side," while the other side will be the "G/L side." The reconciling items on the bank side will be all those items that the company knows about, but the bank does not. The reconciling items on the G/L side will be all those items that the bank knows about, but the company does not until it receives the bank statement for the account at the end of the month.

Exhibit 6-1 illustrates the format of a bank reconciliation and identifies common items that require reconciliation.

Exhibit 6-1 The Format of a Bank Reconciliation

TAKE5

Things we know, but the bank does not	Bank side	Things the bank knows, but we don't until bank statement received	G/L side
	Bank Balance		G/L Balance
	add:		add:
	Outstanding Deposits		Interest
			EFT Receipts
	less:		less:
	Outstanding Cheques		Bank Charges
			EFT Payments
			NSF Cheques
	Reconciled Balance	=	Reconciled Balance

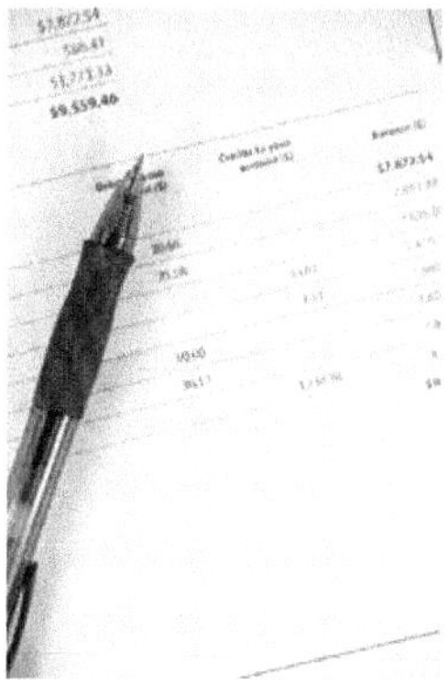

The following information about Gelardi Company will illustrate the process of preparing a bank reconciliation. As you consider each of the items that follow, refer to Exhibit 6-1 to see how the item is treated on the bank reconciliation.

- According to the bank statement received for the month of October 2016, the balance in Gelardi's bank account on October 31 was $8,916.39. This is the starting point for the bank portion of the reconciliation, labelled "Bank Balance."
- The balance in the company's Cash account in the general ledger on October 31, 2016, was $9,770.44. This is the starting point for the company portion of the bank reconciliation, labelled "G/L Balance."

Gelardi's accountant reviewed the bank statement, comparing the transactions recorded on it with the transactions recorded in the ledger account, and discovered the following differences:

Item	Which side of reconciliation?	How handled on bank reconciliation
1. The last deposit of the month, for $1,035.62, was made as a night deposit on October 31 and therefore was not recorded by the bank until the beginning of November. Consequently, it did not appear on the October bank statement.	Company knows, but bank does not. Therefore, adjust bank side.	Since this deposit has been added to Gelardi's ledger account but not to its bank account, it is listed as an addition in the bank portion of the reconciliation. The bank will record the addition to Gelardi's account on the first business day of November when it records the night deposits.
2. One of Gelardi's customers paid its account by making an electronic transfer from its bank into Gelardi's bank account. The amount appeared on the bank statement as an EFT deposit in the amount of $312.98. Until the bank statement was reviewed, Gelardi was not aware that this payment had been received.	Bank knows but company does not. Therefore, adjust company side.	Since this transaction has been recorded by the bank but not by Gelardi, an adjustment has to be made in the company portion of the reconciliation. As the item is a cash receipt, this amount has to be added to the G/L balance.
3. The bank subtracted a service charge of $25.75 from the company's bank account for October, but Gelardi's accountant had not yet recorded it in the company's books. Typically, a company only becomes aware of these charges when the bank statement is reviewed.	Bank knows but company does not. Therefore, adjust company side.	Since this charge has been deducted from the bank account but not from Gelardi's ledger, it is deducted on the company portion of the reconciliation, to reduce the G/L balance by the amount of the charge.
4. Cheque number 873 for $262.89, cheque number 891 for $200.00, and cheque number 892 for $65.78 were still outstanding at the end of October. That is, they had been mailed to suppliers, but had not yet cleared the bank. The cheques may still be in the mail or the recipients have yet to deposit them.	Company knows but bank does not. Therefore, adjust bank side.	Since these cheques have been deducted from Gelardi's ledger account but not from its bank account, they are deducted from the bank portion of the reconciliation to reflect the reduced cash balance that will be available when they eventually clear the bank.
5. The bank statement showed that $500.00 was deducted from Gelardi's account by the bank as payment of loan principal. The payment was not recorded in the company's ledger at the time of payment.	Bank knows but company does not. Therefore, adjust company side.	Since this payment has been deducted from the bank account but not recorded in Gelardi's ledger, it is deducted from the company portion of the reconciliation, reducing the G/L balance by the amount of the payment.

6. The bank returned a cheque from one of Gelardi's customers marked *NSF* (non-sufficient funds). This was a cheque for $186.80 that a customer used to pay off his account. Gelardi had deposited it and the bank had increased Gelardi's account balance to reflect this deposit. However, when Gelardi's bank sent the cheque to the customer's bank for payment, it was informed that the customer did not have enough money in his account to cover the cheque. Consequently, Gelardi's bank removed the amount from Gelardi's account and returned the cheque to Gelardi with the bank statement.	Bank knows but company does not. Therefore, adjust company side.	NSF cheques are also known as *bounced cheques*. Once the bank became aware of the NSF cheque, it adjusted Gelardi's account to reflect it. Gelardi was not aware of the NSF cheque until it was returned by the bank. Since Gelardi recorded an increase to cash when it originally received the cheque from the customer, it must now reduce cash in the G/L to reflect that the amount was never actually received and is still owing by the customer. It will be deducted from the company portion of the reconciliation. We will assume that there were no bank service charges related to the returned cheque.
7. The bank statement showed that cheque number 885 (which Gelardi had issued to pay for an advertising expense) was recorded by the bank as $246.81, while the company recorded this cheque as $426.81. A review of the cancelled cheques accompanying the bank statement showed that the amount recorded by the bank was correct.	Error! Made by company. Therefore, adjust company side.	As this was an error made by the company, an adjustment has to be made to the G/L balance. The amount of the error was $180 ($426.81 − $246.81). Since the company reduced its cash balance by $180.00 too much when it recorded this cheque, this amount needs to be added back to get the correct balance.
8. The bank deducted a cheque written by Gardeli Company (a different company) from Gelardi Company's account. The amount of the cheque was $127.53.	Error! Made by bank. Therefore, adjust bank side.	Since this was an error made by the bank, an adjustment has to be made to the bank balance. Since $127.53 was mistakenly taken out of Gelardi's bank account, this amount has to be added back to get the correct balance. Gelardi will need to inform the bank of the error.

Using the above information, the accountant would prepare the bank reconciliation as shown in Exhibit 6-2.

Exhibit 6-2 Gelardi Company Bank Reconciliation as at October 31, 2016

Bank Balance		$8,916.39	**G/L Balance**		$9,770.44
Add:	Outstanding deposit	1,035.62	Add:	EFT receipts	312.98
	Correction of error made by the bank	127.53		Correction of error made by the company	180.00
Deduct:	Outstanding cheques		Deduct:	Bank charges	(25.75)
	#873	(262.89)		Automatic deduction for loan payment	(500.00)
	#891	(200.00)		NSF cheque	(186.80)
	#892	(65.78)			
Reconciled Balance		$9,550.87	**Reconciled Balance**		$9,550.87

Once all of the differences between the bank's records and the company's records have been dealt with, the bank reconciliation is complete. The reconciliation shows that the actual amount of cash available at the end of October is $9,550.87, which is not the balance per the bank statement nor the balance in the general ledger prior to the reconciliation being completed. At this point, the company's records (the general ledger) still reflect a balance in the cash account of $9,770.44. To adjust this to the correct balance, the accountant needs to make journal entries for all of the adjustments on the G/L side of the bank reconciliation. These entries would be as shown in Exhibit 6-3.

HELPFUL HINT
The main objective of a bank reconciliation is to determine the correct cash balance. Therefore, items that the bank has not yet recorded must be added to, or deducted from, the balance shown on the bank statement, while items that the company has not yet recorded must be added to, or deducted from, the balance shown in the company's cash account.

Exhibit 6-3 Journal Entries from the Bank Reconciliation

Cash	312.98	
Accounts Receivable		312.98
Cash	180.00	
Advertising Expense		180.00
Bank Charges Expense	25.75	
Cash		25.75
Bank Loan Payable	500.00	
Cash		500.00
Accounts Receivable	186.80	
Cash		186.80

HELPFUL HINT
When correcting errors, the first thing to do is to determine who made the error (the bank or the company). This tells us which side of the bank reconciliation that the error will appear on. If the bank made the error, then it must be corrected on the bank side of the reconciliation and vice versa. The second thing to determine is whether the error resulted in the cash amount being too high or too low. If it is too high, then the error should be subtracted on the reconciliation. If it is too low, then the error should be added on the reconciliation.

Notice that the bank reconciliation gives you half of each journal entry before you start. All of the adjustments that were additions to the G/L balance are debits to cash, while all of the deductions are credits to the cash account.

Bank reconciliations are an important control procedure. They ensure that all transactions affecting the bank account have been properly recorded, providing the company with the correct balance of cash that it has available. They are normally made each month for every bank account, as soon as the bank statements are received. Practically, this means that bank reconciliations are always prepared effective the last day of the month, but are completed early in the subsequent month when the bank statement is received.

As previously stated, duties must be separated appropriately for effective internal control. In terms of the bank reconciliation, this means that the person who reconciles the bank account should not be the person who is responsible for either doing the banking or maintaining the accounting records. This will ensure that any errors or discrepancies will be found and properly corrected. This also ensures that no individual has an opportunity to misappropriate cash and then change the accounting records to cover the fraud.

The other issue associated with cash is cash management. Proper cash management involves maintaining sufficient cash in readily accessible bank accounts to be able to make payments when the need arises, while at the same time not keeping excessive amounts of cash. Because cash is an inactive asset—it does not earn a return except possibly a small amount of interest—companies usually try to keep as much of their cash invested in income-earning assets as they safely can. A company's cash management policies are critical for effectively managing its cash position and maximizing its total earnings. Advanced cash management techniques are not discussed in this book, but are a very important aspect of financial management for the company's shareholders and other stakeholders.

ACCOUNTS RECEIVABLE

What are accounts receivable?

■ **LEARNING OBJECTIVE 5**
Explain why companies sell on account and identify the additional costs that result from this decision.

Accounts receivable are amounts owed to a company by its customers. They arise as a result of normal business transactions, the sale of goods and services, that have been made on credit. Receivables may be supported by a written contract, but normally the arrangement is less formal, with only a sales invoice as supporting documentation. The outstanding amounts are normally non-interest-bearing for a 30-day period, though this may be longer depending upon the industry, customer relationship, and so on.

Why do companies sell on account?

KEY POINT
Companies sell on account to:
- increase total sales
- remain competitive
- generate additional forms of revenue (interest income)

Companies sell on account for a number of reasons. The most obvious reason is that selling on account increases overall sales. Most of us have purchased something on credit that we did not have the money for at the time of purchase. If companies required their customers to purchase with cash, many sales would never be made. Also, if a company's competitors sell on account, then the company must also do so if it wishes to remain competitive. While it may seem odd, selling on account can actually result in increased revenue. This can happen if the company's customers are unable to pay within the credit period. After this period, the receivable normally becomes interest-bearing and this interest can be a significant additional revenue stream for the company.

For Example

Canadian Tire Corporation is an excellent example of a company that has used its credit function to increase overall profits. In fact, the company even has its own federally regulated bank, the Canadian Tire Bank. In fiscal 2013, Canadian Tire's retail segment (the company's Canadian Tire, Mark's, SportChek, and other retail stores) had total revenues of $10,690.2 million, from which the company realized income before taxes of $463.4 million. In the same period, the company's financial services segment (such as the bank, Canadian Tire MasterCard, home and auto insurance sales, and in-store instant credit program) had total revenues of $1,025.9 million, from which the company realized income before taxes of $320.0 million. In other words, of the company's $784.6 million net income before taxes, approximately 40.8% of Canadian Tire's income before taxes comes from financial services rather than retail sales. The company financial statements also indicate that 72.1% of its financial services revenue is interest income. Clearly, this is a significant stream of additional revenues and profits for the company.[2]

Are there any additional costs from selling on account?

KEY POINT
When selling on account, companies incur costs such as:
- wages for the credit-granting function
- wages for the collections function
- bad debts expense

Yes! Companies incur a number of costs when they make the decision to sell on account. There are additional staff costs related to the credit-granting function. Companies will have to have employees who are responsible for authorizing customers to be able to purchase on account. They will need to take steps such as assessing the credit histories of customers seeking credit. There will also be staff costs related to the credit follow-up and collection functions. Employees will be needed who are responsible for sending statements to customers with outstanding accounts and for following up by mail or phone with those customers who do not pay their accounts by the due dates. The most significant cost from selling on account is likely to be the bad debts associated with those customers who fail to pay their accounts, known as **bad debts expense** (or doubtful accounts expense).

For Example

Winnipeg-based **New Flyer Industries Inc.**, which manufactures heavy-duty transit buses, has assessed that its risk of bad debts is mitigated, or lessened, by the fact that a "significant portion" of its customers are "well established transit authorities," which can usually pay their bills in full. "Historically, the Company has experienced nominal bad debts as a result of the customer base being principally comprised of municipal and other local transit authorities," New Flyer says in its 2013 annual report. Many of its customers are in the United States, where the U.S. federal government typically pays up to 80% of the capital costs of transit systems acquiring new buses, with the remaining 20% coming from state and municipal sources.[3]

The likelihood that a customer will default on payments depends on the customer's creditworthiness. A company can improve its chances of receiving payments by performing credit checks on its customers before granting them credit. Gildan Activewear in the opening story does this. However, a company must balance its desire to sell its products to the customer with the risk that the customer will not pay. Too strict a credit policy will mean that many customers will be denied credit and may therefore purchase their goods from other suppliers. Too loose a credit policy, and the company may lose more money from bad debts than it gains from additional sales. The company should do a cost-benefit analysis when determining its credit policies.

The company must also stay aware of changes in its industry and changes in the economy in general. Changes in interest rates, a downturn in the global economy, legislative changes, or adverse industry conditions can all impact a customer's credit status.

For Example

Canadian mining company **PotashCorp.** included this information about the company's credit-granting policies in its 2013 consolidated financial statements:

> The company seeks to manage the credit risk relating to its trade receivables through a credit management program. Credit approval policies and procedures are in place to guide the granting of credit to new customers as well as its continued expansion to existing customers. Existing customer accounts are reviewed every 12–18 months. Credit is extended to international customers based upon an evaluation of both customer and country risk. The company uses credit agency reports where available, and an assessment of other relevant information such as current financial statements and/or credit references before assigning credit limits to customers. Those that fail to meet specified benchmark creditworthiness may transact with the company on a prepayment basis or provide another form of credit support that it approves.

From this, we can see examples of the types of costs that are part of the company's credit management program and result from the company's decision to extend credit to its customers.[4]

FINANCIAL STATEMENTS

BAD DEBTS

At what amount are accounts receivable reflected on the statement of financial position?

LEARNING OBJECTIVE 6
Describe the valuation methods for accounts receivable.

Accounts receivable are reflected on the statement of financial position at their **carrying amount**, which is the full value of all the company's accounts receivable less the **allowance for doubtful accounts**. This is also known as the *allowance for credit losses*. Allowance for doubtful accounts is a contra-asset account. This means that it is associated with another asset account but its normal balance is contrary or opposite of what we would normally expect for an asset account. It represents management's best estimate of the total accounts receivable that it does not expect to be able to collect. The net amount is called the *carrying amount* and is what is normally presented on the statement of financial position.

When companies use the allowance for doubtful accounts, they are using the **allowance method**. Under this method, management estimates the amount of receivables that it expects it will be unable to collect and accounts for the related bad debts expense in the same period as the credit sales were reported. The company does not wait until some time in future, when some customers fail to pay, to record the bad debts expense.

KEY POINTS
- No entry can be made to the Accounts Receivable (A/R) account if an entry cannot be made to the A/R subledger. That is, you must know which customer's account is affected.
- Total A/R = Total in A/R subledger.

It is important to understand that Accounts Receivable is a **control account**. This means that a **subledger** (or **subsidiary**) **ledger** is used to manage all of the details in the account. In the case of accounts receivable (A/R), the A/R subledger is used to manage the individual account details of each of the company's customers. This detail is of critical importance and would be lost within the Accounts Receivable account. In simple terms, if a customer phones the company's A/R clerk to inquire about their outstanding balance, the clerk needs to have the customer's individual details readily at hand. This is the detail that would be found in the A/R subledger. If there were no subledger, then the A/R clerk would need to work through all of the detail in the Accounts Receivable account trying to pull out the information related to that particular customer. While this may not be a big deal for a company with only a few significant customers, for those with thousands of customers, it would not be practical.

Another critical thing to understand is that the total of all the accounts in the A/R subledger must equal the total of the Accounts Receivable account. In other words, the control account must always equal the total of the related subledger. This also means that an entry cannot be made to one if it cannot be made to the other. That is, we cannot record an entry in Accounts Receivable if we cannot make the same entry to one of the customer accounts in the A/R subledger. The A/R subledger should be regularly reconciled to the Accounts Receivable account to ensure the two remain in balance. This is normally done monthly.

Exhibit 6-4 shows how the Accounts Receivable account is related to the accounts receivable subledger and how the carrying amount of accounts receivable is determined.

Exhibit 6-4 Accounts Receivable and Allowance for Doubtful Accounts

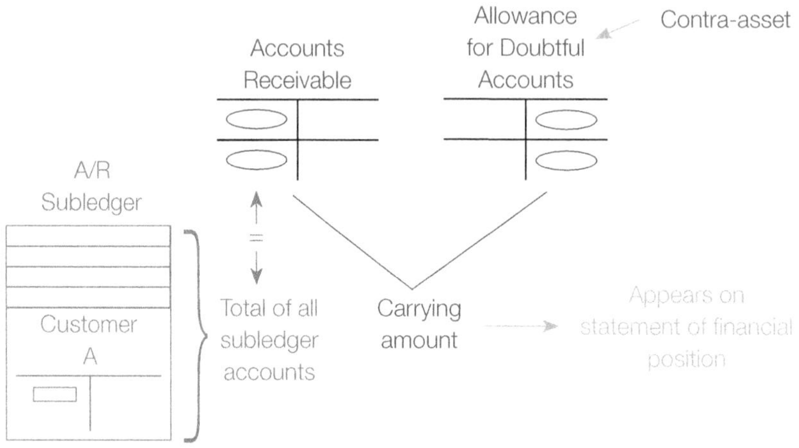

TAKE5

While all Canadian companies present trade receivables at their carrying amount (net of the allowance for doubtful accounts), the level of detail regarding the amount of the allowance for doubtful accounts varies. Bad debts expense is generally included as part of selling, general, and administrative expenses, rather than being separately disclosed. However, companies following IFRS must disclose changes in the allowance for doubtful accounts balance in the notes to the financial statements. The annual bad debts expense is presented as part of this note.

For Example

FINANCIAL STATEMENTS

RONA Inc.'s 2013 annual report included the following note disclosure related to the company's accounts receivable and allowance for doubtful accounts (amounts in thousands of Canadian dollars):

The aging of trade accounts receivable is as follows:

	As at December 29, 2013	As at December 30, 2012 Restated (Note 32)
Current	**$155,031**	$246,988
Past due 0–30 days	**38,650**	49,470
Past due 31–120 days	**22,473**	38,033
Past due over 121 days	**36,163**	34,675
Trade receivables	**252,317**	369,166
Less: allowance for doubtful accounts	**12,231**	14,748
Balance, end of year	**$240,086**	$354,418

(continued)

For Example (continued)

The allowance for doubtful accounts is mainly for customer accounts over 121 days past due.
The following table provides the change in allowance for doubtful accounts for trade receivables:

	2013	2012
		Restated (Note 32)
Balance, beginning of year	**$ 14,748**	$ 15,827
Doubtful accounts (recovery) expense	**(2,517)**	(1,079)
Balance, end of year	**$ 12,231**	$ 14,748

In the consolidated income statement, the doubtful accounts expense is recorded in selling, general and administrative expenses.

From this we can see that Rona expected that $12,231 or 4.85% of its receivables would be uncollectible as at December 31, 2013, which was a slight increase from the 3.99% expected at the end of the preceding year.[5]

What is the allowance method of accounting for bad debts?

■ LEARNING OBJECTIVE 7
Explain the allowance method of accounting for bad debts.

TAKE5

Each period, management estimates the amount of accounts receivable that it does not expect to be able to collect in the future. The company establishes an allowance for these doubtful accounts and records the bads debts expense in the same period in which the credit sales have been recorded. This is known as the allowance method. In this section, we will review the three key transactions that may occur under the allowance method. These are:

1. ***Establishing the allowance and recording the bad debts expense. This is called the allowance entry.*** At the end of each accounting period, management will use one of two methods (which are discussed later in the chapter) to estimate the amount of accounts receivable they do not expect to be able to collect. An allowance for doubtful accounts will be established to reduce the carrying amount accordingly. The journal entry for this transaction is:

Bad Debts Expense	XXX	
Allowance for Doubtful Accounts		XXX

It is important to understand that, at this point, management does not know which specific customers will not pay their accounts. Instead, they are simply using historical or industry averages to make an estimate. Since they do not know which specific customers will not be paying, they cannot make any entries in the A/R subledger and, therefore, they cannot make any entries in the Accounts Receivable control account. The contra-asset account, Allowance for Doubtful Accounts, is used instead.

This entry effects both the statement of income, by increasing expenses, and the statement of financial position, by reducing the carrying amount of accounts receivable.

2. ***Writing off a specific receivable. This is called the writeoff entry.*** Companies establish policies for when accounts are to be written off. A **writeoff** is the process of removing a specific customer's account receivable from a company's books when the account is deemed uncollectible. Some companies' writeoff policies may use timelines, such as writing off an account once it is more than 180 days overdue. Other companies may wait for specific indications, such as being notified of a customer's bankruptcy, before writing off an account. Once the specific customer account has been identified, entries can be made to both the A/R subledger and Accounts Receivable to reflect the writeoff. The journal entry for this transaction is:

Allowance for Doubtful Accounts	XXX	
Accounts Receivable		XXX

It may be helpful to view this entry as the company using up some of the allowance that had been previously established for accounts like this. It is also important to know that, even after a customer's account has been written off for accounting purposes, the company generally continues to try to collect the account. The company may do this itself or it may use a collection agency.

Note that this entry has no effect on the statement of income, nor does it change the carrying amount of receivables, because it has offsetting effects on the two accounts making up this amount.

3. ***Recovery of a specific receivable that has been previously written off. This is called a recovery entry.*** As previously mentioned, companies continue to pursue collection efforts even after accounts have been written off. If these efforts are successful and the customer makes full or partial payment on its account, this is considered a **recovery**. If an account receivable is recovered, the company's accounting records would show the customer as owing nothing because their account had previously been written off. As such, the company must first reverse the writeoff and then record the cash collection as it ordinarily does. The journal entries for this transaction are:

Accounts Receivable	XXX	
Allowance for Doubtful Accounts		XXX
Cash	XXX	
Accounts Receivable		XXX

It may be helpful to view this entry as the company re-establishing an allowance taken previously that it did not end up needing. It is important to note that by re-establishing the receivable and the allowance, the company has a complete history of its credit experience with that customer. In the A/R subledger, the company can see the sales to the customer, the account being written off, the reversal of the writeoff, and the eventual payment. This kind of detail will be important information for making future credit decisions regarding the customer.

This entry has no effect on the statement of income. However, it does affect the statement of financial position by increasing cash and decreasing the carrying amount of accounts receivable.

Let's review these entries using a numerical example in Exhibit 6-5.

Exhibit 6-5 The Allowance Method of Accounting for Bad Debts

Assume the following:

- The company began the year with $21,000 of accounts receivable and an allowance for doubtful accounts of $1,100.
- Total sales for the year were $140,000, of which 80% were on account.
- During the year, the company collected $101,000 of its accounts receivable.
- Historically, the company's bad debts have been approximately 4.5% of credit sales.
- The company's policy is to write off accounts that have been outstanding more than 180 days. The company uses a collection agency to try to collect accounts that have been written off. During the year, accounts with a value of $3,200 reached the 180-day mark and were written off. The collection agency was able to collect $1,800 from customers whose accounts have been written off.

Based on the above information, the journal entries related to bad debt and the allowance for doubtful accounts would be as follows:

1. Allowance entry:

Bad Debts Expense	5,040	
Allowance for Doubtful Accounts		5,040
($140,000 × 80%) × 4.5% = $5,040		

2. Writeoff entry:

Allowance for Doubtful Accounts	3,200	
Accounts Receivable		3,200

3. Recovery entries:

Accounts Receivable	1,800	
Allowance for Doubtful Accounts		1,800
Cash	1,800	
Accounts Receivable		1,800

Now, let's look at the impact of these entries on the related accounts. The T account information for the above scenario is shown in Exhibit 6-6.

Exhibit 6-6 The Allowance Method: T Accounts

STATEMENT OF FINANCIAL POSITION ACCOUNTS

Accounts Receivable

Beginning balance	21,000		
Credit sales	112,000		
		101,000	Collections
		3,200	Writeoff
Recovery	1,800		
		1,800	Recovery
Ending balance	28,800		

Allowance for Doubtful Accounts

		1,100	Beginning balance
		5,040	Allowance
Writeoff	3,200		
		1,800	Recovery
		4,740	Ending balance

STATEMENT OF INCOME ACCOUNTS

Sales Revenue

	140,000

Bad Debts Expense

5,040	

Based on the above transactions, accounts receivable would be presented as follows:

Accounts receivable (gross)	$28,800
Less: Allowance for doubtful accounts	4,740
Accounts receivable (net)	$24,060 → Carrying amount

The Conceptual Framework

ACCOUNTS RECEIVABLE AND FAITHFUL REPRESENTATION

Using the allowance for doubtful accounts ensures that accounts receivable are not overstated on the statement of financial position. The carrying amount of accounts receivable (that is, accounts receivable net of the allowance for doubtful accounts) represents management's best estimate of what it expects will be realized when these accounts are collected. As such, this treatment means that the asset, accounts receivable, is presented at the amount of cash flows expected to be realized from it.

HELPFUL HINT

The Allowance for Doubtful Accounts is a contra asset, and therefore it is a permanent account whose balance is cumulative and carried forward from one period to another. However, Bad Debts Expense (like all expenses) is a temporary account and therefore begins each period with a zero balance.

As noted previously, there are two methods used to estimate the amount of receivables that will not be collectible. These are the **percentage of credit sales method** and the **aging of accounts receivable method**. Each of these methods will be discussed in the following sections.

■ **LEARNING OBJECTIVE 8**
Identify the two methods of estimating bad debts under the allowance method and describe the circumstances for using each method.

How are bad debts estimated under the allowance method?

In order to use the allowance method of accounting for bad debts, companies must estimate the amount of bad debts expense at the end of each period. There are two methods that can be used to determine this amount:

1. **Percentage of credit sales method:** This method uses sales on account as the basis for the estimate. It is also known as the *statement of income method* because it is based on information from the statement of income.
2. **Aging of accounts receivable method:** This method uses an aging of the various receivables as the basis for the estimate. It is also known as the *statement of financial position method* because it is based on information from the statement of financial position.

Both are acceptable methods, so the choice is a management decision. It depends on whether management wishes to focus on income measurement (by matching expenses and revenues) or on asset valuation (by determining the net realizable value of the accounts receivable). It is also possible for companies to use a combination of the two methods. Some companies use the percentage of credit sales method when preparing their interim financial statements because it is quick and simple to apply and then use the aging method for their year-end financial statements because it involves a more thorough analysis of the company's accounts at year end.

Percentage of Credit Sales Method

The percentage of credit sales method of estimating bad debts is based on the assumption that the amount of bad debts expense is a function of the total sales made on credit. Bad debts expense is estimated by multiplying the credit sales for the period by the percentage that management estimates will be uncollectible. This percentage is normally based on the company's past collection experiences. In other words, historically, bad debts have averaged X% of credit sales. New businesses do not have this data and use industry data, such as data from Statistics Canada, or advice from an accounting firm to make their estimate.

Under this method:

$$\text{Bad Debts Expense} = \text{Sales on Account} \times \text{Historic \%}$$

As you can see, determining bad debts expense under this method is simple and quick, making it easy for companies to use. Exhibit 6-5 above illustrates this method, using a historical level of bad debts of 4.5% of credit sales.

Companies must adjust their percentage estimates to reflect the company's recent collection experience and changes in general economic conditions. If the company is experiencing more writeoffs than were estimated, the percentage should be increased for the next accounting period. Companies do not go back to prior periods to adjust the percentage or recalculate the bad debts expense. Therefore, an overestimate or underestimate in one period will be corrected by an adjustment to the percentage used in a subsequent period.

As mentioned at the beginning of this discussion, this basis of estimating bad debts emphasizes the matching of expenses with revenues. Accordingly, because the focus is on the amount of the expense rather than on the amount of the allowance, when the adjusting entry is made to record the bad debts expense and increase the allowance for doubtful accounts, *the existing balance in the allowance account is not considered.* The ending balance in the Allowance for Doubtful Accounts is therefore simply the net total of the various entries in that account. There is thus no predetermined percentage relationship between the ending balance in the allowance account and the related Accounts Receivable account, and it has nothing directly to do with the percentage that is used to estimate the bad debts expense.

Aging of Accounts Receivable Method

The aging of accounts receivable method uses a review of the length of time that the receivables have been outstanding as the basis for determining bad debts expense. As you might expect, the longer a receivable goes without being collected, generally the less likely it is to be collected. Just as companies have historic or industry data on the percentage of their credit sales that normally remain uncollected, they also have data on the collection experience for receivables of a certain age; that is, the percentage of customers who default on their accounts at each age threshold or grouping. These thresholds are determined by management, but the most common involve aging receivables into the following groupings (which are all based on the length of time that has transpired since the initial sale):

- Less than 30 days
- 31–60 days
- 61–90 days
- Greater than 90 days

Generally, the older the receivable, the higher the likelihood the company will be unable to collect it. Under this method, management looks at each customer's account balance and the individual sales that comprise each. The details of individual customer balances are found in the A/R subledger. Using this information, each customer's receivables balance is allocated to the various age groupings. For example, part of the balance may be from a recent sale, say, less than 30 days ago, while another portion of the balance may have been outstanding for 70 days.

Once all of the receivables in the A/R subledger have been allocated to the various age groupings, the total receivables balance for each age grouping is determined. The historical default rates for each age grouping are then applied to the related receivables balance. These amounts are added together, giving the company the total allowance for doubtful accounts, which should be established against the receivables balance. The bad debts expense for the period is then determined as the difference between the balance in the Allowance for Doubtful Accounts account before this analysis is prepared and the ending balance determined as a result of the analysis.

Let's look at an example of the aging of accounts receivable method, shown in Exhibit 6-7.

Exhibit 6-7 The Aging of Accounts Receivable Method

Assume that:

- The company has $12,000 in Accounts Receivable.
- The company's Allowance for Doubtful Accounts balance before the aging analysis is $800.

Step 1: Prepare aging analysis using information from the A/R subledger.

Step 2: Apply historic rates for each age grouping. (Note how rates increase with age of A/R.)

Customer's name	Total balance	Number of days the account receivable has been outstanding				
		1–30	31–60	61–90	91–120	121–180
T. E. Bansal	$2,700	$2,700				
R. C. Lortz	3,000	1,850	$1,150			
I. M. Owen	1,700		900	$800		
A. Rashad	1,100				$1,100	
O. L. Su	2,500	950	1,550			
T. Woznow	1,000					$1,000
	$12,000	$5,500	$3,600	$800	$1,100	$1,000
Estimated percentage uncollectible		**1%**	**5%**	**15%**	**35%**	**65%**
Total estimated writeoffs	**$1,390**	$55	$180	$120	$385	$650

Step 3: Total the amounts determined for each age grouping; the total is the required allowance for doubtful accounts.

Step 4: Determine the bad debts expense for the period. This is the amount that needs to be added to the balance in the Allowance for Doubtful Accounts account prior to the aging analysis to equal the amount determined in Step 3.

Allowance for Doubtful Accounts	
	800
	590 ← This amount = bad debts expense
	1,390

The allowance entry that would result from this example would be:

Bad Debts Expense	590	
Allowance for Doubtful Accounts		590

As it is a contra-asset account, Allowance for Doubtful Accounts would normally be expected to have a credit balance. However, it is possible for the account to have a debit balance during the year and it is important to be able to understand what could cause this and what it would tell us about the prior year's financial statements. Of the three key transactions discussed earlier in the chapter, only the writeoff entry results in a debit being recorded in Allowance for Doubtful Accounts. So, for there to be an overall debit balance in this account, a company would have had to write off more accounts than it had previously allowed for. In other words, writeoffs exceeded the amount of the allowance that had been established for doubtful accounts. If this was the case, then we know two things about the prior year's financial statements:

1. The bad debts expense for that year was understated (an insufficient allowance was established) and, therefore, net income was overstated.
2. The carrying amount of accounts receivable on the statement of financial position was overstated because an insufficient allowance was established.

HELPFUL HINT
Under the percentage of sales method, you adjust the allowance account *by* the amount calculated when you multiply the given percentage by the credit sales figure.
Under the aging of receivables method, you adjust the balance in the allowance account *to* the amount indicated by the aging analysis.

Because bad debts expense is an accounting estimate, changes to it are treated prospectively; that is, going forward. Changes are not treated retrospectively; that is, changes are not made to the prior year's financial statements. If there is a debit balance in Allowance for Doubtful Accounts prior to the aging analysis, then you have to add that amount to the required ending balance (which will always be a credit) in order to get the bad debts expense for the period. However, if the balance before the aging analysis is a credit, you have to subtract that amount from the required ending balance (also a credit) in order to determine the amount of bad debts expense for the period. In either case, the end result is the same: the final balance in the Allowance for Doubtful Accounts is adjusted to the amount that the aging schedule indicates as the amount of accounts receivable that are expected to be written off as bad debts in the future.

If it is based on a careful aging analysis, the aging of accounts receivable method will normally result in a better approximation of the net realizable value of the receivables than the percentage of credit sales method. However, the matching of expenses with revenues may not be as good if significant amounts of customers' accounts have been outstanding for more than a year. This is because, under these circumstances, the bad debts expense for the current year will include amounts applicable to the sales of prior years.

The following table summarizes the key differences between the methods:

Percentage of Credit Sales Method	Aging of Accounts Receivable Method
Focuses on income measurement by using credit sales revenue as the basis for calculating the bad debts expense.	**Focuses on asset valuation** by using accounts receivable as the basis for calculating the allowance for doubtful accounts.
Emphasizes statement of income relationships by ensuring that the amount of expense is logically related to the amount of revenue.	**Emphasizes statement of financial position relationships** by ensuring that the balance in the contra-asset account is logically related to the balance in the asset account.
Determines bad debts expense directly.	**Determines the ending Allowance for Doubtful Accounts balance; then bad debts expense can be determined.**
No analysis of Allowance for Doubtful Accounts required in order to determine bad debts expense.	**Analysis of Allowance for Doubtful Accounts required in order to determine bad debts expense.**

What is the direct writeoff method and when is it acceptable to use it?

▪ LEARNING OBJECTIVE 9
Explain the direct writeoff method of accounting for bad debts and when it is acceptable to use it.

As its name implies, the **direct writeoff method** involves companies recognizing bad debts expense only when they can directly write off a specific customer's account; that is, only when they know which customer is not going to pay. This means that companies must wait until an account has reached the age when the company's policy states that it should be written off (such as 180 days overdue) or when there is a specific indication (such as notification of a customer bankruptcy). Rather than recognizing an estimated amount for bad debts expense in the period of the sale and providing an allowance for future writeoffs, the direct writeoff method waits to recognize bad debts expense in the period in which the account is, in fact, uncollectible.

The direct writeoff method is often used by companies with an insignificant amount of bad debts. In this case, there would not be a significant or material (as discussed in Chapter 2) difference in the amount of bad debts expense regardless of which method is used.

Under the direct writeoff method, there is only a single journal entry. This is made when an account is written off and is as follows:

Bad Debts Expense	XXX	
Accounts Receivable		XXX

Note that *no allowance for doubtful accounts is used with the direct writeoff method*, and the debit to Bad Debts Expense reduces net income in the period in which the writeoff occurs.

The direct writeoff method is a simple way to account for bad debts. The company makes every reasonable effort to collect the account and, when it finally decides that an account is uncollectible, it records the entry to remove it from the accounting system. The problem with this method is that it results in the revenue being recognized in one accounting period and the associated bad debts expense being recorded in a later period. If bad debts are not significant, this mismatching will not be material and can be ignored. If bad debts are significant, however, this mismatching can distort the measurement of income enough for the direct writeoff method to be unacceptable. The appropriate method to use when bad debts are significant is the allowance method.

HELPFUL HINT
There are two main methods for dealing with bad debts: the allowance method and the direct writeoff method. If the allowance method is used, which it should be whenever bad debts are significant, there are two alternative approaches to estimating the amount of bad debts: the aging of accounts receivable method and the percentage of credit sales method.

Finally, note that bad debts expense is somewhat different from other expenses. It is more like a reduction in a revenue account, since it represents revenue the company will never receive. In recognition of this, a few companies report it as a direct reduction of the sales revenue amount on the statement of income. The majority of companies, however, show bad debts as an operating expense rather than as a reduction of revenues.

Ethics in Accounting

We have seen that bad debts expense is a function of management estimates. Management determines the percentages used to calculate bad debts expense under both the aging and percentage of credit sales methods. This provides management with an opportunity to manage earnings. They could minimize bad debts expense if they were motivated to maximize earnings or they could overstate the percentages used if they were motivated to minimize earnings. Bad debts expense is normally not significant relative to total revenues, so any manipulations would not have a large effect on net income. Nevertheless, it is an area of concern. The Canada Revenue Agency does not allow companies to deduct bad debts calculated using the allowance method. It essentially requires companies to follow the direct writeoff method for tax purposes. You will learn more about this in taxation courses you may take in the future.

LEARNING OBJECTIVE 10
Explain alternative ways in which companies shorten their cash-to-cash cycle.

How do companies shorten their cash-to-cash cycle?

As discussed in Chapter 5, companies are always looking for ways to shorten their cash-to-cash cycle. This cycle is the time between when companies pay out the cash to purchase goods or raw materials for manufacturing products until those goods are ultimately paid for by the customer. Selling to customers on account, as opposed to cash sales, actually lengthens this cycle because companies normally provide these customers with a 30-day credit period. During this time, the receivable is an inactive asset in that the company is not generating any return on it.

Exhibit 6-8 illustrates the cash-to-cash cycle.

Exhibit 6-8 The Cash-to-Cash Cycle

Companies look for ways to shorten the cash-to-cash cycle while still enjoying the benefits of selling on account, such as increasing sales and remaining competitive. One of the ways that they do this is to accept credit card purchases. By doing this, it is the credit card companies (financial institutions) that have to wait the 30 days to be paid, not the company making the sale. The sellers are usually paid within a day or two, depending upon their arrangements with the credit card company. These arrangements also result in the credit card company being responsible for many of the costs associated with credit sales, including credit granting, collections, and bad debts. In exchange for absorbing these costs, the credit card companies charge a fee to the merchants making the sales. This fee varies depending upon a number of factors, including transaction volume, but it is normally between 1% and 5%. The fee is known as the **credit card discount**. These fees are the reason why many smaller merchants have a minimum sales amount before they allow customers to use a credit card and why some smaller merchants don't accept credit cards at all.

Let's look at an example of how a company would record a credit card transaction, including the related fee. If a company made a $3,500 credit card sale and the credit card discount was 3%, the journal entry would be as follows:

Accounts Receivable—Credit Card Company	3,395	
Credit Card Expense	105	
Sales Revenue		3,500

Then, when the company receives payment from the credit card company a day or two later, the entry is the normal cash collection entry. If the company has an arrangement whereby the credit card sales are paid within the same day, then the debit to Accounts Receivable would be replaced with a debit to Cash.

Another way that companies try to shorten the cash-to-cash cycle is to motivate their customers to pay their accounts receivable before the end of the 30-day credit period. They often do this by offering a **sales discount**. While these vary across industries, a fairly typical one is illustrated in Exhibit 6-9, which uses the common shorthand for sales terms, including "n" for *net*.

Exhibit 6-9 Sales Discounts

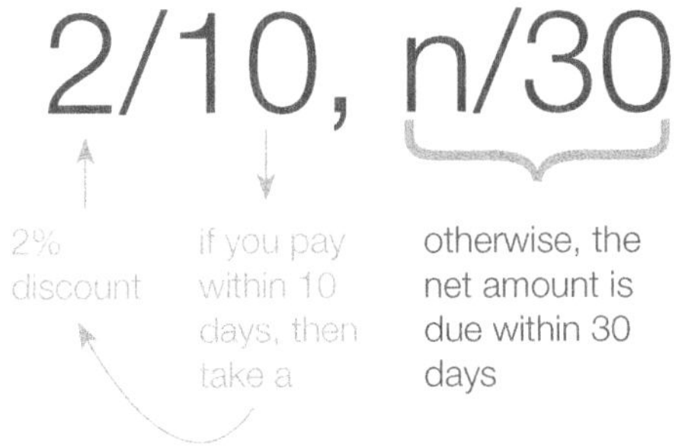

TAKE5

Companies looking to shorten their cash-to-cash cycle can also sell their accounts receivable to another company, typically a financial institution. This process is known as **factoring** and is becoming increasingly common in Canada. While the journal entries for factoring are beyond the scope of an introductory accounting course, it is important that you understand some of the terms related to factoring transactions. The company purchasing the accounts receivable is known as the **factor** and it may purchase the receivable **with recourse** or **without recourse**. If the receivables are purchased with recourse, then the factor is able to come back to the seller for payment if it is unable to collect the receivable. If the receivables are purchased without recourse, then the factor will bear the loss of any receivable it is unable to collect. Obviously, the factor will pay less than face value for the receivables, because the difference is how it makes its money on the transaction. The factor would also pay less if the transaction was on a without recourse basis than if it was on a with recourse basis.

For Example

According to its 2013 annual report, Canadian food processor **Maple Leaf Foods Inc.** uses "very limited recourse accounts receivable securitization programs as (an) additional source of financing." At December 31, 2013, the company had $166.4 million in trade receivables being serviced under these programs. "In return for the sale of its trade receivables, the company will receive cash of $50.9 million and notes receivable (non-interest bearing) in the amount of $115.5 million." These arrangements enabled the company to receive approximately 30% of the cash value of these receivables sooner than if it had waited to collect them.

FINANCIAL STATEMENT ANALYSIS

What is liquidity and how is it assessed?

LEARNING OBJECTIVE 11
Explain the concept of liquidity. Calculate the current ratio, quick ratio, accounts receivable turnover ratio, and average collection period ratio and assess the results.

As discussed in Chapter 1, and earlier in this chapter, liquidity refers to the company's ability to convert assets into cash so that liabilities can be paid. An important part of the analysis of short-term liquidity comes from considering the short-term assets on the statement of financial position. There are two very common ratios that provide quantitative measures of short-term liquidity: the current ratio and the quick ratio.

Current Ratio

The **current ratio**, which is also known as the **working capital ratio**, is measured by comparing the current assets with the current liabilities. It is calculated as follows:

$$\text{Current ratio} = \frac{\text{Current assets}}{\text{Current liabilities}}$$

Remember that current assets are those that are going to be converted into cash within the next year or operating cycle, and that current liabilities are going to require the use of cash within the next year or operating cycle. As such, if this ratio is greater than 1, then it means that the company has more than $1 in current assets for every $1 of current liabilities. As such, it indicates that the company should be able to meet its expected obligations over the coming year. This ratio can vary significantly, depending on the type of industry and the types of assets and liabilities that are considered current. As such, comparing current ratios across industries may not be relevant, whereas comparing the ratio year to year for the same company would be relevant. For effective analysis, it is important to be aware of industry norms and to analyze data across multiple periods.

We can calculate the current ratios for **Danier Leather** and **Le Château** as follows.

Danier's Current Ratio:

$$= \frac{39{,}970}{10{,}790} = 3.70$$

Le Château's Current Ratio:

$$= \frac{137{,}173}{62{,}284} = 2.20$$

This tells us that Danier had $3.70 in current assets for every $1 in current liabilities, while Le Château had $2.20 in current assets for every $1 of current liabilities. Both companies appear to be well positioned to meet their liabilities as they come due over the next year. In terms of which company is in better position, the answer is not as simple as looking at which company has the highest ratio. If the ratio is too high, then the company may not be managing its assets effectively: it may have too much cash on hand, significant receivables, or overly high levels of inventory. Answering this question requires an analysis of the company's specific current assets.

Quick Ratio

One problem with using the current ratio as a measure of short-term liquidity is that some current assets may be much less liquid than others. In other words, they may take considerable time to become cash. An example is inventory, some of which may be on hand for a number of months before it can be sold and then it may take another month or more before the related receivable is collected. Some current assets may never become cash, such as prepaid expenses. In the case of manufacturing companies, the inventory may be even less liquid as it will often include raw materials or partially manufactured goods. As a result, if a company has significant levels of inventory requiring lengthy sales periods, then the current ratio will not adequately measure the company's short-term liquidity.

Another ratio, the **quick ratio** (also known as the **acid test ratio**), can be used to assess short-term liquidity. It differs from the current ratio because the numerator only includes the **quick assets**, which are the company's current assets less inventory and prepaid expenses. The quick ratio takes into account the shortcomings of the current ratio. The quick ratio is calculated as follows:

$$\text{Quick ratio} = \frac{\text{Current assets} - \text{Inventory} - \text{Prepaid expenses}}{\text{Current liabilities}}$$

As with the current ratio, the quick ratio gives the user the number of dollars of quick assets that the company has with which to pay each dollar of its current liabilities. Again, this ratio can vary significantly depending on the type of industry. Just as with the current ratio, the quick ratio can vary significantly across industries. Also, analyzing the ratio across multiple periods provides the most meaningful context for interpreting changes.

Let's again compare the results of Danier Leather with Le Château; this time, to get a better understanding of the quick ratio.

Danier's Quick Ratio:

$$= \frac{39{,}970 - 21{,}721 - 643}{10{,}790} = 1.63$$

Le Château's Quick Ratio:

$$= \frac{137{,}173 - 124{,}878 - 2{,}292}{62{,}284} = 0.16$$

This tells us that Danier had $1.63 in quick assets for every $1 in current liabilities, while Le Château had only $0.16 in quick assets for every $1 of current liabilties. As such, Danier is well positioned to meet its liabilities as they come due over the next year, whereas Le Château would only be able to meet just over a quarter of its liabilities over the next year based on its quick assets. This would mean that it is critical that Le Château be able to sell through its inventory and collect these sales in a timely manner (which would normally not be an issue in a retail environment). If this is the case, there are no issues, as we have seen from the current ratio that the company would be able to meet its short-term obligations.

Again, it may be that Danier's solid quick ratio is the result of the company having too much cash on hand or too high a level of receivables. An analysis of the company's specific quick assets would be needed to determine if there were any issues related to company's asset management.

The current and quick ratios are two of the ratios that are often analyzed by the company's lenders, such as banks. Lenders are understandably concerned with the borrower's ability to service their debt, including repaying the portion of the loan due within the next year. The current and quick ratios allow lenders to assess debt-servicing ability. Lenders will often build current ratio and quick ratio-related **covenants** into their lending agreements. Covenants will be discussed in greater detail in Chapter 10, but they are essentially minimum conditions set by the lender which, if not met, can trigger immediate repayment of the loan. Lenders may set minimum current and quick ratios that must be met and it is important for financial statement users to be aware of this.

Ethics in Accounting

Because ratios can be critical, especially if related covenants are in place in lending agreements, there is the potential for them to be manipulated by management. For example, it is possible for a company to manipulate the current ratio at year end.

For example, consider a company that has $10,000 in current assets (consisting of $3,000 in cash and $7,000 in inventory) and $5,000 in current liabilities just before the end of the year. Its current ratio would be 2 ($10,000 ÷ $5,000). Suppose that the company uses all its $3,000 in cash to pay off $3,000 worth of current liabilities at year end. This greatly improves the current ratio, increasing it to 3.5 ($7,000 ÷ $2,000), and the company looks more liquid. Notice, however, that the company is actually less liquid. In fact, it is very illiquid in the short term because it has no cash, and must sell its inventory and wait until it collects on those sales before it will have any cash to pay its bills. In this case, the current ratio is deceptive. This shows how important it is to analyze multiple ratios. In this case, looking at a second short-term liquidity ratio, the quick ratio, would provide more insight into the company's liquidity.

How effective has the company been at collecting its accounts receivable?

Accounts Receivable Turnover Ratio

As previously mentioned, accounts receivable are generally non-interest-bearing for at least 30 days. During this period, the asset is essentially inactive: it is not generating any return for the company. As discussed, to lessen the impacts of this inactivity, companies take various steps to shorten their cash-to-cash cycle; that is, reducing the length of time it takes until cash returns to the company in the form of customer payments. The sooner a company can collect its receivables, the sooner the cash can be used in the business to settle payables, purchase inventory, and so on. The effectiveness with which these collection efforts are taking place can be assessed using the **accounts receivable turnover ratio**. This ratio is calculated by dividing the credit sales (because cash sales do not give rise to receivables) for the period by the average accounts receivable, as follows:

$$\text{Accounts receivable turnover ratio} = \frac{\text{Credit sales}}{\text{Average accounts receivable*}}$$

$$\text{*Average accounts receivable} = (\text{Accounts receivable at the beginning of the year} + \text{Accounts receivable at the end of the year})/2$$

In this context, *turnover* means how often the accounts receivable are turned over, or how often they are collected in full and replaced by new accounts. This is the first of the asset turnover ratios we will explore in the text. A good rule of thumb when thinking about asset turnover is that a higher number is better than a lower number. In other words, we would consider a company that collects its receivables more frequently than another to be doing a better job.

Calculating this ratio from financial statement data usually requires you to assume that all the sales are credit sales. If the analyst has more detailed information about the composition of sales, then some adjustment can be made in the numerator to include only the sales on account. In addition, information in the financial statements may indicate that not all receivables are from customers. Therefore, a more sophisticated calculation would include only customer receivables in the denominator, as only these relate to the credit sales figure in the numerator.

Average Collection Period

Once you have determined the accounts receivable turnover ratio for a company, it is a simple step to calculate the average length of time, in days, that it takes the company to collect its receivables. This is known as the **average collection period** and is determined as follows:

$$\text{Average collection period} = \frac{365 \text{ days}}{\text{Accounts receivable turnover}}$$

Retailers like Danier Leather and Le Château typically have very low levels of receivables because they accept credit card payments rather than granting credit to their customers directly. As such, we will look at the results of **Ten Peaks Coffee Company Inc.**, a British Columbia-based specialty coffee company, to get a better understanding of the accounts receivable turnover and average collection period ratios. Ten Peaks is a premium green coffee decaffeinator and also provides a range of green coffee handling and storage services. The company sells its products to retail coffee houses. Like Gildan Activewear, Ten Peaks is therefore a wholesaler, not a retailer, so its accounts receivable are with businesses, not consumers. Let's look at Ten Peaks' A/R turnover ratio and average collection period ratio.

2013 A/R Turnover Ratio:

$$= \frac{53{,}873}{(3{,}962 + 4{,}972)/2} = 12.1$$

2012 A/R Turnover Ratio:

$$= \frac{59{,}301}{(4{,}198 + 3{,}962)/2} = 14.5$$

2013 Average Collection Period Ratio:

$= 365/12.1 = 30.2$ days

2012 Average Collection Period Ratio:

$= 365/14.6 = 25.2$ days

From this we can see that Ten Peaks' receivables turn over just about monthly, which tells us that the company's receivables are not outstanding for long. In fact, the company's average collection period in 2013 was 30.2 days. On a comparative basis, we can see that the time taken to collect its receivables has increased by 5 days from 2012, thereby extending the company's cash-to-cash cycle.

Another way to analyze the performance of accounts receivable collection is to compare a company's average collection period with the company's normal credit terms. If the company's normal credit terms are 30 days, then you would expect that the average collection period would be 30 days or fewer. This analysis is only possible if the details of a company's normal credit terms are known. This is not something that is generally disclosed in the financial statements or annual report.

SUMMARY

1. **Explain why cash and accounts receivable are of significance to users.**
   - As a company's most liquid assets, cash and accounts receivable provide the resources necessary to meet immediate, short-term financial obligations.
   - Knowing a company's cash and receivables balances enables users to assess a company's liquidity (its ability to meet its obligations in the short term).
2. **Describe the valuation methods for cash.**
   - Cash includes the cash physically on hand, on deposit at financial institutions, and any cash equivalents.
   - Cash equivalents are amounts that can be converted into known amounts of cash and must be maturing within three months of the acquisition date.
   - Cash is measured at its face value at the reporting date, with any foreign currency translated into Canadian dollars using the rate of exchange at the statement of financial position date.
3. **Explain the main principles of internal control.**
   - An internal control system includes (1) physical controls (locks, alarms, cash registers); (2) assignment of responsibilities (making one person responsible for each task); (3) separation of duties (separation of transaction authorization, recording, and asset

custody); (4) independent verification (either internal or external); and (5) documentation (receipts, invoices, and so on).

4. **Explain the purpose of bank reconciliations, including their preparation and the treatment of related adjustments.**
   - A bank reconciliation ensures that any differences between the accounting records for cash and the bank statement are identified and explained.
   - The reconciliation adjusts the bank balance for items that the company is aware of but the bank is not (outstanding cheques and outstanding deposits). It also adjusts the company's cash balance for items that appear on the bank statement that have not yet been reflected in the company's records (such as bank charges, interest, and cheque returns due to non-sufficient funds).
   - Journal entries must be made for each adjustment required to the company's cash balance in order to adjust the cash balance in the general ledger.

5. **Explain why companies sell on account and identify the additional costs that result from this decision.**
   - Companies sell on account to increase total sales, remain competitive, and generate additional revenue (interest).
   - When selling on account, companies incur additional costs, including wages for the credit-granting function, wages for the collections function, and bad debts expense.

6. **Describe the valuation methods for accounts receivable.**
   - Accounts receivable are reflected on the statement of financial position at their carrying amount, which is equal to the full amount of all receivables less the allowance for doubtful accounts.
   - The allowance for doubtful accounts represents management's best estimate of the total accounts receivable that it expects it will be unable to collect.

7. **Explain the allowance method of accounting for bad debts.**
   - The allowance method involves management estimating the amount of receivables that they expect they will be unable to collect. The estimated bad debts expense is recorded in the same period in which the credit sales were reported rather than waiting to record the bad debt until the customers fail to pay.
   - Since the specific customers who will not pay are unknown at the time the bad debts expense is estimated, no adjustment can be made to the Accounts Receivable account. Instead, the amount is recorded in Allowance for Doubtful Accounts, a contra-asset account.
   - Under the allowance method, journal entries are required to initially record the bad debts expense, to record the writeoff of specific receivables once they are known, and to record the recovery of any receivables that have previously been written off.

8. **Identify the two methods of estimating bad debts under the allowance method and describe the circumstances for using each method.**
   - The two methods of estimating bad debts under the allowance method are: the percentage of credit sales method and the aging of accounts receivable method.
   - With the percentage of credit sales, the estimated bad debts expense is determined using a percentage (historic or industry average) of credit sales revenue. No analysis of the allowance for doubtful accounts is required to determine bad debts expense.
   - With the aging of accounts receivable method, an estimate of uncollectible accounts is made using a percentage (historic or industry average), with bad debts expense equal to the amount required to adjust the Allowance for Doubtful Accounts balance to this estimated total. An analysis of allowance for doubtful accounts is required to determine bad debts expense.

9. **Explain the direct writeoff method of accounting for bad debts and when it is acceptable to use it.**
   - Under the direct writeoff method, there is no accounting for bad debts expense until a specific customer's account is written off. As such, an allowance for doubtful accounts is not needed.
   - This method is not acceptable under accounting standards in Canada, but it is sometimes used by companies with an insignificant amount of bad debts because the difference between it and the allowance method would not result in material differences.

10. **Explain alternative ways in which companies shorten their cash-to-cash cycle.**
    - One way that companies shorten their cash-to-cash cycle is to accept credit cards rather than offering their customers credit directly. The company is able to collect much more quickly from the credit card companies than it would from customers.
    - Another way that companies shorten the cash-to-cash cycle is to offer sales discounts to encourage customers who have purchased on account to pay their accounts early. A common sales discount is "2/10, n/30," which entitles customers to a 2% discount if they pay they account within 10 days; otherwise, the net amount is due within 30 days.
    - Some companies also factor (sell) their accounts receivable to a financial institution (known as a *factor*) in order to shorten their cash-to-cash cycle. The receivables may be sold with recourse (the company remains responsible for their ultimate collection) or without recourse (the factor assumes collection responsibility).

11. **Explain the concept of liquidity. Calculate the current ratio, quick ratio, accounts receivable turnover ratio, and average collection period ratio and assess the results.**
    - Liquidity refers to a company's ability to convert assets into cash so that liabilities can be paid.
    - The current ratio is equal to current assets divided by current liabilities and is a measure of the amount of current assets the company has relative to each dollar of current liabilities.
    - The quick ratio is a stricter measure of liquidity than the current ratio. This is because it is determined without including inventory and prepaid expenses. Specifically, the ratio is equal to current assets less inventory and prepaids divided by current liabilities.
    - The accounts receivable turnover ratio is equal to credit sales divided by average accounts receivable. It measures how often accounts receivable are collected in full during the period.
    - The average collection period is the average length of time, in days, that it takes a company to collect its receivables. It is calculated by dividing 365 by the accounts receivable turnover ratio.

KEY TERMS

Accounts receivable (269)
Accounts receivable turnover ratio (289)
Acid test ratio (288)
Aging of accounts receivable method (281)
Allowance for doubtful accounts (277)
Allowance method (277)
Audit trail (271)
Average collection period (290)
Bad debts expense (276)
Bank reconciliation (271)
Carrying amount (277)
Cash (269)
Cash equivalent (270)
Collusion (271)
Control account (277)
Covenant (289)
Credit card discount (286)
Current ratio (287)
Direct writeoff method (285)
Electronic funds transfer (EFT) (271)
Factor (287)
Factoring (287)
Internal control system (270)
Liquidity (269)
Percentage of credit sales method (281)
Quick assets (288)
Quick ratio (288)
Recovery (280)
Sales discount (286)
Subledger (277)
Uncollectible accounts (269)
With recourse (287)
Without recourse (287)
Working capital ratio (287)
Writeoff (279)

ABBREVIATIONS USED

A/R	Accounts Receivable
EFT	Electronic funds transfer
G/L	General ledger

SYNONYMS

Accounts receivable | Trade receivables
Aging of accounts receivable method | Statement of financial position method
Bad debts expense | Doubtful accounts expense
Current ratio | Working capital ratio
Percentage of credit sales method | Statement of income method
Quick ratio | Acid test ratio
Subledger | Subsidiary ledger
Uncollectible accounts | Doubtful accounts | Bad debts

CHAPTER END REVIEW PROBLEM 1

During 2016, Kumar Company sold $150,000 of goods on credit and collected $135,000 from its customers on account. The company started the period with a balance of $15,000 in Accounts Receivable and a balance in the Allowance for Doubtful Accounts of $450. During 2016, Kumar wrote off $2,725 of accounts receivable. Kumar estimates that 2% of its credit sales will ultimately be uncollectible.

Required:

a. Show the journal entries that would be made during the year that affect Accounts Receivable and the Allowance for Doubtful Accounts. Then, calculate the amount of bad debts expense for 2016 and make the journal entry to record it.
b. What amount(s) would be reported on the statement of financial position at the end of 2016 regarding accounts receivable?
c. Now assume that, instead of using the percentage of credit sales method to estimate its bad debts expense, Kumar Company performed an aging analysis of its accounts receivable at the end of 2016 and determined that it should have an allowance for doubtful accounts of $1,000. How would this affect your answers to parts "a" and "b" above?

STRATEGIES FOR SUCCESS

- Bear in mind that the allowance method recognizes bad debts expense at the end of each period, when adjusting entries are made, and provides an allowance for accounts that will be written off. Therefore, when writeoffs occur, they are debited to the allowance account rather than to the expense account.
- Remember that the percentage of credit sales approach applies the estimated percentage to the credit sales to determine the appropriate amount of bad debts expense. When the adjusting journal entry is made to record this, the existing balance in Allowance for Doubtful Accounts is ignored.
- In the aging of accounts receivable approach, the aging analysis indicates the appropriate amount of allowance for doubtful accounts. The existing balance in Allowance for Doubtful Accounts must be considered to determine the correct amount for the adjusting journal entry.

CHAPTER END REVIEW PROBLEM 2

Big Rock Brewery Inc. is a Calgary-based producer of all-natural craft beers and cider that are sold in nine provinces and three territories in Canada. Exhibits 6-10A and 6-10B contain excerpts from the company's 2013 financial statements.

Required:

Using the information in the exhibits, calculate the following ratios for 2013 and 2012 and briefly comment on whether these ratios have improved or worsened:

a. Current ratio
b. Quick ratio
c. Accounts receivable turnover ratio (Note: Assume all sales were on account. Also, at December 30, 2011, the company's accounts receivable were $2,788 thousand.)
d. Average collection period

EXHIBIT 6-10A

BIG ROCK BREWERY INC.'S 2013 CONSOLIDATED STATEMENTS OF COMPREHENSIVE INCOME

FINANCIAL STATEMENTS

BIG ROCK BREWERY INC.
Consolidated Statements of Comprehensive Income
(In thousands of Canadian dollars, except per share amounts)

	Year ended	
	December 30, 2013	December 30, 2013
Net revenue (Notes 3.2 and 4)	$41,587	$46,057
Cost of sales (Notes 5 and 24)	20,260	21,149
Gross profit	21,327	24,908
Expenses		
Selling expenses (Notes 6 and 23)	12,910	13,987
General and administrative (Notes 7 and 24)	4,821	4,945
Depreciation and amortization	314	358
Operating expenses	18,045	19,290
Operating profit	3,282	5,618
Finance costs (Note 8)	9	93
Other income	286	351
Other expenses	109	147
Income before income taxes	3,450	5,729
Current income tax expense (Note 9)	2,485	426
Deferred income tax expense (recovery) (Note 9)	(1,586)	1,168
Net income and comprehensive income for the period	$ 2,551	$ 4,135

EXHIBIT 6-10B

BIG ROCK BREWERY INC.'S 2013 CONSOLIDATED STATEMENTS OF FINANCIAL POSITION

FINANCIAL STATEMENTS

BIG ROCK BREWERY INC.
Consolidated Statements of Financial Position
(In thousands of Canadian dollars)

	December 30, 2013	December 30, 2012
ASSETS		
Non-current assets		
Property, plant and equipment (Note 11)	$ 35,142	$ 35,277
Intangible assets (Note 12)	108	128
	35,250	35,405
Current		
Inventories (Note 13)	2,983	3,892
Accounts receivable (Notes 14 and 22)	1,353	2,358
Prepaid expenses and other (Note 15)	754	364
Cash	2,317	4,281
	7,407	10,895
Total assets	$ 42,657	$ 46,300
LIABILITIES AND SHAREHOLDERS' EQUITY		
EQUITY		
Shareholders' capital (Note 16)	$100,109	$ 100,109
Contributed surplus (Notes 16 and 17)	892	701
Accumulated deficit	(71,043)	(68,739)
	29,958	32,071

continued

FINANCIAL STATEMENTS

EXHIBIT 6-10B **BIG ROCK BREWERY INC.'S 2013 CONSOLIDATED STATEMENTS OF FINANCIAL POSITION (continued)**

BIG ROCK BREWERY INC.
Consolidated Statements of Financial Position
(In thousands of Canadian dollars)

	December 30, 2013	December 30, 2012
LIABILITIES		
Non-current		
Long term debt (Notes 18 and 22)	—	1,342
Share-based payments (Note 17)	687	238
Deferred income taxes (Note 9)	4,745	6,331
	5,432	7,911
Current		
Accounts payable and accrued liabilities (Notes 19 and 22)	4,100	3,978
Dividends payable (Notes 20 and 22)	1,214	1,214
Current portion of long-term debt (Notes 18 and 22)	—	700
Current taxes payable (Note 9)	1,953	426
	7,267	6,318
Commitments (Note 26)		
Total liabilities and shareholders' equity	$ 42,657	$ 46,300

Suggested Solution to Chapter End Review Problem 1

a. The following journal entries would be made during the year by Kumar Company:

Accounts Receivable	150,000	
Sales Revenue		150,000
Cash	135,000	
Accounts Receivable		135,000
Allowance for Doubtful Accounts	2,725	
Accounts Receivable		2,725
Bad Debts Expense	3,000	
Allowance for Doubtful Accounts		3,000
(150,000 × 2% = 3,000)		

b. The statement of financial position at the end of 2016 would show the following:

Accounts receivable	$27,275*
Less: Allowance for doubtful accounts	725**
Net carrying value of accounts receivable	$26,550
Or	
Accounts receivable (net)	$26,550

*Beginning balance $15,000 + Credit sales $150,000 − Cash collections $135,000 − Writeoffs $2,725

**Beginning balance $450 − Writeoffs $2,725 + Adjustment $3,000

c. The first three journal entries would not be affected; they would be exactly the same as shown above. The calculation of the bad debts expense would differ, though, and requires that you first determine the balance in Allowance for Doubtful Accounts before adjustment, as follows:

Beginning balance $450 (credit) − Write-offs $2,725 (debit) =
Balance before adjustment $2,275 (debit)

This must then be compared with the required allowance, as estimated by the aging analysis of the accounts receivable outstanding at year end. As stated in the problem, this indicated that an allowance of $1,000 was required. In order to adjust the existing balance in the allowance account (a debit of $2,275) to the required balance (a credit of $1,000), an adjustment must be made that credits the allowance account by $3,275 and debits Bad Debts Expense by the same amount. The year-end adjustment would therefore be as follows:

Bad Debts Expense	3,275	
Allowance for Doubtful Accounts		3,275

The statement of financial position at the end of 2016 would show the following:

Accounts receivable	$27,275
Less: Allowance for doubtful accounts	1,000
Net carrying value of accounts receivable	$26,275
Or	
Accounts receivable (net)	$26,275

Suggested Solution to Chapter End Review Problem 2

Current ratio:

2013: $\frac{7{,}407}{7{,}267} = 1.02$

2012: $\frac{10{,}895}{6{,}318} = 1.72$

Big Rock's current ratio has decreased significantly in 2013, as the company has $1.02 in current assets for every $1 in current liabilities, which is down from $1.72 in the prior year. Based on this, the company can meet its current liabilities as they come due.

Quick ratio:

2013: $\frac{7{,}407 - 2{,}983 - 754}{7{,}267} = 0.51$

2012: $\frac{10{,}895 - 3{,}892 - 364}{6{,}318} = 1.05$

Big Rock's quick ratio has decreased significantly in 2013, as the company has $0.51 in quick assets for every $1 in current liabilities, which is down from $1.05 in the prior year. Based on this information, it is critical for the company to sell its inventory and collect its receivables to meet current liabilities.

Accounts receivable turnover ratio:

2013: $\frac{41{,}587}{(2{,}358 + 1{,}353)/2} = 22.4$

2012: $\frac{46{,}057}{(2{,}788 + 2{,}358)/2} = 17.9$

Big Rock's A/R turnover ratio improved in 2013, as the company turned over its receivables 22.4 times during the year, which is up from 17.9 in 2012. This means that cash is being collected quicker than in the prior year.

Average collection period for accounts receivable:

2013: $\frac{365}{22.4} = 16.3$ days

2012: $\frac{365}{17.9} = 20.4$ days

Big Rock's average collection period was 20.4 days in 2013, which is four days quicker than in the prior year, so this was an improvement. From this, we can see that the company's customers normally pay their accounts just over two weeks from the date of sale.

STRATEGIES FOR SUCCESS

- Remember that the quick ratio includes only the most liquid current assets. Inventories and prepaid expenses should be excluded.
- In any ratio that involves a comparison between amounts from the statement of income and amounts from the statement of financial position (such as the accounts receivable turnover ratio), the statement of financial position amounts should, if possible, be averages.

ASSIGNMENT MATERIAL

Discussion Questions

DQ6-1 Explain why internal control is so important, especially for cash. Describe three types of internal control measures that organizations can put in place.

DQ6-2 Identify the special challenge that small organizations face when implementing effective internal control systems.

DQ6-3 Identify three of the common principles of internal control discussed in the chapter. Using a pharmacy as an example, give one example of how a pharmacy applies each of the three principles you have identified.

DQ6-4 Using a movie theatre as an example, identify three of the five principles of internal control. For each internal control principle you identify, give one example of a control that a movie theatre uses.

DQ6-5 Identify three of the common principles of internal control discussed in the chapter. Using your campus bookstore as an example, give one example of how it applies each of the three principles you have identified.

DQ6-6 Explain the purpose of a bank reconciliation and how it relates to internal control.

DQ6-7 Explain, in your own words, why there might be a difference between the cash balance per a company's general ledger and the closing balance on its monthly bank statement for the same account.

DQ6-8 When a company is thinking about making sales on account, what are some of the additional costs it needs to consider?

DQ6-9 Explain, in your own words, why a company may decide to accept credit cards rather than extend credit directly to its customers.

DQ6-10 Explain, in your own words, why a company needs to use the Allowance for Doubtful Accounts account when recording its bad debts expense each period.

DQ6-11 What is an "allowance for doubtful accounts"? Your explanation should include what type of account it is, why it is created, and how it is used.

DQ6-12 Identify two methods for estimating uncollectible accounts under the allowance method of accounting for bad debts. Outline how to implement each of these methods.

DQ6-13 Describe and compare the allowance method and the direct writeoff method for determining bad debts expense.

DQ6-14 Why is the allowance method of accounting for bad debts more consistent with accounting standards than the direct writeoff method? Under what circumstances is the direct writeoff method acceptable?

DQ6-15 Explain what it means if Allowance for Doubtful Accounts has a debit balance prior to the year-end bad debts entry.

DQ6-16 Identify and explain two ways that companies can shorten their cash-to-cash cycle related to accounts receivable.

DQ6-17 Describe two ratios that measure current liquidity, and compare the information they provide. Which measure is more likely to produce the lowest result for most companies? Why is this the case?

DQ6-18 Describe a ratio that can be used to assess the management of accounts receivable, and explain what information it provides.

DQ6-19 When calculating the accounts receivable turnover ratio, is a higher number generally better than a lower number? Explain your rationale.

Application Problems

AP6-1 (Preparation of bank reconciliation)

On May 31, 2016, JB Games Ltd. received its bank statement from the East Coast Savings Bank showing that JB had a balance of $12,200. The company's general ledger showed a cash balance of $8,600 at that date. A comparison of the bank statement and the accounting records revealed the following information:

1. A cheque from one of JB's customers in the amount of $1,120 that had been deposited during the last week of May was returned with the bank statement as NSF.
2. Bank service charges for the month were $55.
3. The company had written and mailed out cheques with a value of $4,235 that had not yet cleared the bank.
4. Cheque #791, which was a payment for advertising expenses of $230, was incorrectly recorded in the general ledger as $320.
5. During the month, the bank collected a $2,000 note receivable plus the outstanding interest on behalf of JB. The note was interest-bearing at 5% per annum and had been outstanding for one year.
6. The cash receipts for May 31 amounted to $1,650 and had been deposited in the night drop slot at the bank on the evening of May 31. These were not reflected on the bank statement for May.

Required:

a. Prepare the bank reconciliation for JB at May 31, 2016.
b. Prepare any journal entries necessary as a result of the bank reconciliation prepared in part "a."

AP6-2 (Preparation of bank reconciliation)

Infinity Emporium Company received the monthly statement for its bank account, showing a balance of $66,744 on August 31. The balance in the Cash account in the company's accounting system at that date was $71,952. The company's accountant reviewed the statement and the company's accounting records and noted the following.

1. After comparing the cheques written by the company and those deducted from the bank account in August, the accountant determined that all six cheques (totalling $6,180) that had been outstanding at the end of July were processed by the bank in August. However, five cheques written in August, totalling $4,560, were outstanding on August 31.
2. A review of the deposits showed that a deposit made by the company on July 31 for $11,532 was recorded by the bank on August 1, and an August 31 deposit of $12,240 was recorded in the company's accounting system but had not yet been recorded by the bank.
3. The August bank statement also showed:
   - a service fee of $24,
   - a customer's cheque in the amount of $204 that had been returned NSF,

- a bank loan payment of $900, which included interest of $130, that the bank had deducted automatically, and
- a customer's note for $3,500 plus $100 interest on the note that the bank had collected for Infinity Emporium and deposited in its account.

Required:

a. Prepare a bank reconciliation as at August 31. (Hint: Items that were outstanding last month but have been processed this month should no longer affect the bank reconciliation, since both the company and the bank now have them recorded.)
b. How much cash does Infinity Emporium actually have available as at August 31?
c. Explain how the adjusted (corrected) balance of cash, as determined by the bank reconciliation, could be higher than both the balance shown on the bank statement and the balance shown in the company's Cash account.
d. Prepare adjusting journal entries to record all the necessary adjustments to bring the Cash account to its correct balance.

AP6-3 (Placement of items on bank reconciliation)

Henri Heinzl is preparing a bank reconciliation for his business, Heinzl Company.

Required:

Indicate whether each of the following items would be added to the bank balance, deducted from the bank balance, added to the cash account balance in the general ledger (G/L), or deducted from the cash account balance in the general ledger (G/L). If any of the items do not have to be included in the bank reconciliation, explain why.

a. A deposit of $2,310 at the end of the previous month was processed by the bank on the first day of this month.
b. A $683 cheque written by Heinzl Company was erroneously processed through its account as $638 by the bookkeeper.
c. The bank statement showed a service charge of $15 for the month. Heinzl Company has not yet recorded this charge in its cash account.
d. A customer deposited an amount owed to Heinzl Company directly into its bank account. Henri had not recorded it yet.
e. Three cheques written by Heinzl Company totalling $6,842 have not yet been processed by the bank.
f. The bank lists a customer cheque that was received by Heinzl and deposited in the company's bank account as NSF.
g. A deposit of $1,280 made by Heinzl Company was recorded by the bank as $1,290. Heinzl Company had made an error in counting the money before making the deposit.
h. Three cheques that were outstanding at the end of the previous month are shown on the bank statement as having been processed by the bank this month.
i. Cash received by Heinzl Company on the last day of the month and deposited that evening is not shown on the bank statement.
j. An automatic payment for the company's electricity bill was processed by the bank. Heinzl Company had received notification from the electrical company, and recorded the amount as a payment earlier in the month.
k. A loan to Heinzl Company from the bank became due on the 21st of the month and the bank deducted the payment from the company's account. Henri had forgotten about the loan coming due.

AP6-4 (Placement of items on bank reconciliation)

You are preparing the bank reconciliation for your company, Hanneson Holdings Ltd., as at October 31.

Required:

Indicate whether each of the following items would be added to the bank balance, deducted from the bank balance, added to the cash account balance in the general ledger (G/L), or deducted from the cash account balance in the general ledger (G/L). If any of the items do not have to be included in the bank reconciliation, explain why.

a. Service charges of $35 were charged by the credit union during the month.
b. Cheques that Hanneson Holdings had written and mailed out that had not yet cleared the credit union amounted to $1,600.
c. One of your customers made an electronic payment to your account at the credit union in the amount of $1,050.
d. The cash receipts for October 31 amounted to $2,750 and had been deposited in the night drop slot at the credit union on the evening of October 31. These were not reflected on the bank statement for October.
e. A cheque from one of your customers in the amount of $270 that had been deposited during the last week of October was returned with the bank statement as NSF.
f. One deposit, for a receipt from a customer paying off its account, was incorrectly recorded by your bookkeeper. The correct amount of the receipt was $230, but the bookkeeper had recorded it as $320.

AP6-5 (Preparation of bank reconciliation)

Kinte Products Limited had a balance in its cash account of $38,755 on October 31, 2016. This included $2,650 of cash receipts from October 31, which had not yet been deposited in the bank. On the same date, its bank account had a balance of $42,301. Comparing the bank statement with the company's records indicated that the following cheques were outstanding on October 31:

#1224	$1,991
#1230	1,336
#1232	2,286
	$5,613

The following were shown on the bank statement and not yet recorded by the company:

- $376 deducted for a customer's cheque that was returned to Kinte Products marked NSF
- $420 added as a result of the direct deposit of an income tax refund from the Canada Revenue Agency
- $1,200 added as a result of a note collected by the bank and deposited in the company's account, representing $1,000 of principal and $200 of interest
- $34 deducted for service charges for the month

While preparing the data for its bank reconciliation, the company discovered that it had made an error in recording one of its deposits for cash sales during the month. The actual amount deposited was $2,282, but Kinte Products had recorded it as $2,882. The bank had also made an error in recording one of the company's cheques that was a payment to a supplier on account. The cheque had been issued in the amount of $336, but the bank processed it as $363.

Required:

a. Prepare a bank reconciliation for Kinte Products Limited as at October 31, 2016.
b. Prepare any journal entries required to adjust the cash account as at October 31, 2016.

AP6-6 (Preparation of bank reconciliation)

The April 30, 2016, bank statement for Comet Company showed a cash balance of $7,582. The cash account in the company's general ledger (G/L), according to the company's records on April 30, had a balance of $4,643. The following additional data were revealed during the reconciliation process:

1. A deposit of $652 that had been made by the company on March 31 was processed by the bank in April, and a deposit of $1,531 made on April 30 had not yet been processed by the bank.
2. The bank statement listed a deposit for $360 that was mistakenly put in Comet Company's bank account; it should have gone to Comment Company's account.
3. Comet Company determined that there were three cheques that had not yet been processed by the bank: #466 for $1,250, #467 for $520, and #470 for $1,350.
4. The bank had collected a note receivable for $1,000 from one of Comet Company's customers. An additional $15 in interest had been added to its account.
5. The bank service charge for the month was $25.

Required:

a. Prepare a bank reconciliation for Comet Company as at April 30, 2016.
b. What cash balance should Comet Company report on its statement of financial position as at April 30, 2016?
c. Prepare the journal entries that are required to bring Comet Company's cash account to its correct balance.

AP6-7 (Preparation of bank reconciliation)

Catalina Holdings Ltd. (CHL), a Calgary-based property management company, is owned by Leslie Smeal. Leslie is trying to prepare a bank reconciliation for CHL's bank account for October 31, 2016. A review of CHL's bank statement and accounting records showed the following:

1. The cash balance per the bank statement was $26,936.89.
2. The accounting records showed a balance in the cash account of $21,260.16.
3. Two cheques that had been written and mailed by CHL had not been cashed. These were cheques #5109 for $10,505.10 and #5112 for $5,303.07.
4. CHL was paid $19.99 in interest by the bank during October.
5. A cheque for $1,125.58 that had been part of CHL's deposit on October 23 was not honoured by the bank because the client had insufficient funds.
6. Bank service charges for the month were $92.
7. Cheque #5101, which was for a utility payment, was incorrectly recorded by CHL's bookkeeper as $960 when the actual cheque was for $690 (which was the correct amount owing by CHL).
8. The bank had collected $3,110.25 on behalf of CHL related to a note receivable from one of CHL's clients. This included $110.25 in interest.
9. A deposit for $12,314.10 was made through the night deposit slot late on the evening of October 31.

Required:

a. Prepare a bank reconciliation at October 31, 2016.
b. Prepare the journal entries necessary as a result of the bank reconciliation

AP6-8 (Accounts receivable and uncollectible accounts—percentage of credit sales method)

Dundee Company started business on January 1 of the current year. The company made total sales of $900,000 during the year, of which $150,000 were cash sales. By the end of the year, Dundee had received payments of $675,000 from its customers on account. It also wrote off as uncollectible $10,000 of its receivables when it learned that the customer who owed this amount had filed for bankruptcy. That was Dundee Company's only entry related to bad debts for the period.

Dundee uses the allowance method of accounting for bad debts. Since Dundee is a new company and does not have past experience to base its own estimates on, it decides to use 3% of credit sales as an estimate for its bad debts expense, which is the average percentage for its industry.

Required:

a. What amount of Bad Debts Expense would Dundee Company report on its statement of income for the year?
b. Record the journal entry to write off the account of the customer who declared bankruptcy.
c. What Allowance for Doubtful Accounts balance would be reported on the statement of financial position at the end of the year?
d. What Accounts Receivable balance would be reported on the statement of financial position at the end of the year?
e. Evaluate the reasonableness of the balance in Allowance for Doubtful Accounts at the end of the year.

AP6-9 (Accounts receivable and uncollectible accounts—percentage of credit sales method)

Majestic Equipment Sales Company, which sells only on account, had a $120,000 balance in its Accounts Receivable and a $4,200 balance in its Allowance for Doubtful Accounts on December 31, 2015. During 2016, the company's sales of equipment were $820,000 and its total cash collections from customers were $780,000.

During the year, the company concluded that customers with accounts totalling $6,000 would be unable to pay, and wrote these receivables off. However, one of these customers subsequently made a payment of $850 (note that this amount is not included in the cash collections noted above). At the end of 2016, management decided that it would use an estimate for bad debts of 1% of its credit sales.

Required:

a. Prepare the journal entries to record all the 2016 transactions, including the adjustment for bad debts expense at year end.
b. Show how the accounts receivable section of the statement of financial position at December 31, 2016, would be presented.
c. What amount of bad debts expense would appear in the statement of income for the year ended December 31, 2016?

AP6-10 (Accounts receivable and uncollectible accounts—percentage of credit sales method)

The trial balance of M&D Inc. shows a $50,000 outstanding balance in Accounts Receivable at the end of the first year of operations, December 31, 2015. During the fiscal year, 75% of the total credit sales were collected and no accounts were written off as uncollectible. The company estimated that 1.5% of the credit sales would be uncollectible. During the following year, 2016, M&D had sales, all on account, totaling $250,000. It collected 80% of these sales, together with 95% of the outstanding receivables from 2015. During 2016, the accounts of seven customers who owed a total of $3,800, were judged uncollectible and were written off. During the year, the company recovered $1,500 from customers whose accounts had previously been written off (note that this amount was not included in the collection figures given above). The company estimated its bad debt expense to be 1% of its credit sales.

Required:

a. Prepare the necessary journal entries for recording all the preceding transactions in the accounting system of M&D Inc. for 2015 and 2016.
b. Show the accounts receivable section of the statement of financial position at December 31, 2016.

AP6-11 (Accounts receivable and uncollectible accounts—percentage of credit sales method)

A large corporation recently reported the following amounts on its year-end statements of financial position:

	2016	2015
Accounts receivable	$8,800,000	$8,400,000
Allowance for doubtful accounts	105,000	95,000

A footnote to these statements indicated that the company uses a percentage of its credit sales to determine its bad debts expense, that $60,000 of uncollectible accounts were written off during 2015 and $80,000 of uncollectible accounts were written off in 2016, and that there were no recoveries of accounts written off.

Required:

a. Determine the amount of bad debts expense that must have been recorded by the company for 2016.
b. How were the company's net receivables affected by the writeoff of the $80,000 of accounts in 2016?
c. How was the company's net earnings affected by the $80,000 writeoff of accounts in 2016?

AP6-12 (Accounts receivable and uncollectible accounts—aging of receivables method)

The following is an aging schedule for a company's accounts receivable as at December 31, 2016:

Customer's name	Total amount owed	Current (not yet due)	Number of days past due 1–30	31–60	61–90	Over 90
Aber	$ 20,000		$ 9,000	$11,000		
Bohr	30,000	$ 30,000				
Chow	35,000	15,000	5,000		$15,000	
Datz	18,000					$18,000
Others	158,000	95,000	15,000	13,000	15,000	20,000
	$261,000	$140,000	$29,000	$24,000	$30,000	$38,000
Estimated percentage that will be uncollectible		3%	6%	10%	25%	50%
Estimated value of uncollectibles	$ 34,840	$ 4,200	$ 1,740	$ 2,400	$ 7,500	$19,000

On December 31, 2016, the unadjusted balance in the Allowance for Doubtful Accounts (prior to the aging analysis) was a credit of $9,000.

Required:

a. Journalize the adjusting entry for bad debts on December 31, 2016.
b. Journalize the following selected events and transactions in 2017:
   i. On March 1, an $800 customer account that originated in 2017 is judged uncollectible.
   ii. On September 1, an $800 cheque is received from the customer whose account was written off as uncollectible on March 1.
c. Journalize the adjusting entry for bad debts on December 31, 2017, assuming that the unadjusted balance in Allowance for Doubtful Accounts at that time is a *debit* of $1,000 and an aging schedule indicates that the estimated value of uncollectibles is $33,500.

AP6-13 (Accounts receivable and uncollectible accounts—aging of receivables method)

Xanadu Ltd. has accounts receivable totalling $142,800 and a $3,640 credit balance in its Allowance for Doubtful Accounts prior to adjustment on December 31, 2016. The company uses an aging analysis of its receivables to estimate its uncollectible accounts.

The aging analysis shows the following:

Month of Sale	Accounts Receivable on December 31st
December	$ 91,000
November	26,040
September and October	16,800
July and August	8,960
	$142,800

The company's estimates of bad debts are as follows:

Age of Accounts	Estimated % Uncollectible
Current	2%
1–30 days past due	10%
31–90 days past due	25%
Over 90 days past due	40%

Required:

a. Determine the total estimated uncollectibles as at December 31, 2016.
b. Prepare the adjusting entry for the expected Bad Debts Expense as at December 31, 2016.

AP6-14 (Accounts receivable and uncollectible accounts—aging of receivables method)

On December 31, 2015, Ajacks Company reported the following information in its financial statements:

Accounts receivable	$1,193,400
Allowance for doubtful accounts	81,648
Bad debt expense	80,448

During 2016, the company had the following transactions related to receivables:

1. Sales were $10,560,000, of which $8,448,000 were on account.
2. Collections of accounts receivable were $7,284,000.
3. Writeoffs of accounts receivable were $78,000.
4. Recoveries of accounts previously written off as uncollectible were $8,100 (note that this amount is not included in the collections referred to in note 2 above).

Required:

a. Prepare the journal entries to record each of the four items above.
b. Set up T accounts for the Accounts Receivable and the Allowance for Doubtful Accounts and enter their January 1, 2016, balances. Then post the entries from part "a" and calculate the new balances in these accounts.
c. Prepare the journal entry to record the bad debts expense for 2016. Ajacks Company uses the aging of accounts receivable method and has prepared an aging schedule, which indicates that the estimated value of the uncollectible accounts as at the end of 2016 is $93,000.
d. Show what would be presented on the statement of financial position as at December 31, 2016, related to accounts receivable.

AP6-15 (Accounts receivable and uncollectible accounts—aging of receivables method)

The following information relates to Bedford Company's accounts receivable:

Accounts receivable balance on December 31, 2015	$ 900,000
Allowance for doubtful accounts balance on December 31, 2015	55,000
Credit sales made in 2016	5,800,000
Collections from customers on account in 2016	4,900,000
Accounts receivable written off in 2016	70,000
Accounts previously written off that were recovered in 2016 (not included in the collections above)	6,000

An aging analysis estimates the uncollectible receivables on December 31, 2016, to be $80,000. The allowance account is to be adjusted accordingly.

Required:

a. Calculate the ending balance in Accounts Receivable, as at December 31, 2016.
b. Calculate the Allowance for Doubtful Accounts balance, before adjustment, as at December 31, 2016.
c. Calculate the bad debts expense for the year 2016.

AP6-16 (Percentage of credit sales and aging of accounts receivable methods)

Clean Sweep Ltd. manufactures several different brands of vacuum cleaners, from hand-held models to built-in central vacuums. It sells its products to distributors on credit, giving customers 30 days to pay. During the year ending June 30, 2016, Clean Sweep recorded sales of $1,550,000. At June 30, the company prepared the following aging schedule:

Receivable Amount	Number of Days Outstanding	Estimated Percentage that Will Be Collected
$150,000	Less than 30	96%
50,000	31 to 45	93%
75,000	46 to 90	90%
100,000	More than 90	75%

The Allowance for Doubtful Accounts had a credit balance of $19,000 before the year-end adjustment was made.

Required:

a. Prepare the adjusting entry to bring Allowance for Doubtful Accounts to the desired level.
b. Clean Sweep's sales manager thinks the company would increase sales if it extended its normal collection cycle to 60 days from its current 30 days. Should the president accept or reject this recommendation? Why? What factors should be considered in making this decision?
c. What suggestions would you make regarding Clean Sweep's management of its accounts receivable?

AP6-17 (Comparison of all methods of accounting for uncollectible accounts)

DejaVu Company has been in business for several years and has the following information for its operations in the current year:

Total credit sales	$3,000,000
Bad debts written off in the year	60,000
Accounts receivable balance on December 31 (after writing off the bad debts above)	500,000

Required:

a. Assume that DejaVu Company decides to estimate its bad debts expense at 2% of credit sales.
    i. What amount of bad debts expense will the company record if it has a *credit* balance (before adjustment) of $5,000 in its Allowance for Doubtful Accounts on December 31?
    ii. What amount of bad debts expense will it record if there is a *debit* balance (before adjustment) of $5,000 in its Allowance for Doubtful Accounts on December 31?

b. Assume that DejaVu Company estimates its bad debts based on an aging analysis of its year-end accounts receivable, which indicates that a provision for uncollectible accounts of $40,000 is required.
    i. What amount of bad debts expense will the company record if it has a *credit* balance (before adjustment) of $5,000 in its Allowance for Doubtful Accounts on December 31?
    ii. What amount of bad debts expense will it record if there is a *debit* balance (before adjustment) of $5,000 in its Allowance for Doubtful Accounts on December 31?

c. What amount of bad debts expense will DejaVu report if it uses the direct writeoff method of accounting for bad debts?

d. State the two main reasons for using the allowance method to account for bad debts, rather than the direct writeoff method.

AP6-18 (Comparison of all methods of accounting for uncollectible accounts)

Crystal Lights Company manufactures and sells light fixtures for homes, businesses, and institutions. All of its sales are made on credit to wholesale distributors. Information for Crystal Lights for the current year follows:

Total credit sales	$3,500,000
Accounts receivable at December 31 (after writing off uncollectible accounts)	450,000

Required:

Assume that Crystal Lights estimates its bad debts based on an aging analysis of its year-end accounts receivable, which indicates that a provision for uncollectible accounts of $34,000 is required.

a. If there is a *debit* balance of $6,000 in its Allowance for Doubtful Accounts on December 31, before adjustment:
    i. What amount will the company report on its statement of income as bad debts expense?
    ii. What amount will it report on its statement of financial position as the net value of its accounts receivable?

b. If there is a $6,000 *credit* balance in the Allowance for Doubtful Accounts on December 31, before adjustment:
    i. What amount will the company report on its statement of income as bad debts expense?
    ii. What amount will it report on its statement of financial position as the net value of its accounts receivable?

Assume that Crystal Lights decides to estimate its bad debts expense at 1% of credit sales.

c. If there is a *debit* balance of $6,000 in its Allowance for Doubtful Accounts on December 31, before adjustment:
    i. What amount will the company report on its statement of income as bad debts expense?
    ii. What amount will it report on its statement of financial position as the net value of its accounts receivable?

d. If there is a $6,000 *credit* balance in the Allowance for Doubtful Accounts on December 31, before adjustment:
    i. What amount will the company report on its statement of income as bad debts expense?
    ii. What amount will it report on its statement of financial position as the net value of its accounts receivable?

Assume that Crystal Lights uses the direct writeoff method of accounting for bad debts and that the company wrote off accounts totalling $17,500 as uncollectible during the year.

e. What amount will the company report on its statement of income as bad debts expense?

f. What amount will it report on its statement of financial position as the net value of its accounts receivable?

Recall the discussion in the chapter on the allowance method.

g. Briefly outline the main advantages of the allowance method of accounting for bad debts.

AP6-19 (Current and quick ratios)

The following amounts were reported by Liquid Company in its most recent statement of financial position:

Cash	$ 40,000
Accounts receivable	130,000
Short-term investments	18,000
Inventory	390,000
Prepaid insurance	35,000
Capital assets (net)	960,000
Accounts payable	85,000
Wages and salaries payable	37,000
Income tax payable	45,000
Sales tax payable	10,000
Short-term notes payable	90,000
Five-year bank loan	50,000

Required:

a. Calculate the current ratio and quick ratio for Liquid Company.

b. Based on a review of other companies in its industry, the management of Liquid Company thinks it should maintain a current ratio of 2.2 or more, and a quick ratio of 0.9 or more. Its current and quick ratios at the end of the prior year were 2.1 and 0.8, respectively. How successful has the company been in achieving the desired results this year?

c. How could the company improve its current position? What risks, if any, may be associated with the strategy you have suggested?

AP6-20 (Current and quick ratios)

The following amounts were reported by Moksh Ltd. in its most recent statement of financial position:

	2016	2015
Cash and cash equivalents	$ 50,000	$ 79,000
Accounts receivable (net)	170,000	120,000
Inventory	480,000	280,000
Prepaid expenses	11,000	5,000
Property, plant, and equipment (net)	420,000	360,000
Accounts payable	230,000	135,000
Wages and salaries payable	46,000	32,000
Income tax payable	23,000	18,000
Long-term bank loan payable	380,000	260,000
Common shares	220,000	220,000
Retained earnings	232,000	179,000

The company had sales of $860,000 in 2016 and $740,000 in 2015. All sales were on account.

Required:

a. Calculate the current ratio and quick ratio for Moksh Ltd. for the current and preceding year. Comment on whether the ratios have improved or worsened.

b. If Moksh's bank loan includes covenants that the company must maintain a minimum current ratio of 1.5 and a minimum quick ratio of 1.0, what would you advise Moksh's management to do?

c. Calculate Moksh's accounts receivable turnover ratio and average collection period for the current and preceding years. For the accounts receivable turnover ratio, use the balance of accounts receivable at each year end for this calculation, rather than average balances. Comment on whether these ratios have improved or worsened.

d. If Moksh's normal credit terms are "n/30," assess the company's collection experience for the current and preceding years.

AP6-21 (Liquidity evaluation)

The following statement of financial position accounts and amounts were for Classic Ltd. on October 31:

	2016	2015
Equipment	$350,000	$343,000
Bank loan payable (long-term)	322,000	336,000
Prepaid expenses	2,800	4,200
Accumulated depreciation, equipment	123,200	117,600
Income taxes payable	19,600	16,800
Inventory	315,000	322,000
Wages payable	36,400	33,600
Accounts receivable	64,400	51,800
Unearned revenue	67,200	56,000
Retained earnings	84,000	72,800
Common shares	70,000	70,000
Cash	67,200	50,400
Accounts payable	77,000	68,600

Required:

a. Prepare a classified comparative statement of financial position for Classic Ltd. as at October 31, 2016.
b. Calculate the amount of Classic's working capital (current assets minus current liabilities) at the end of its fiscal years 2016 and 2015. Has the company's working capital position improved or deteriorated during this period?
c. Calculate Classic's current ratios at the end of its fiscal years 2016 and 2015. Has its current ratio improved or deteriorated during this period?
d. Calculate Classic's quick ratios at the end of its fiscal years 2016 and 2015. Has the company's quick ratio improved or deteriorated during this period?
e. Based on the results from parts "b," "c," and "d," do you think Classic's overall liquidity position improved or deteriorated during this period?
f. How might Classic evaluate whether its overall liquidity is adequate?

User Perspective Problems

UP6-1 (Bank reconciliation and cash management)

Your friend, who owns a small landscaping business, asks you the following questions:

> "Someone told me that I should be preparing bank reconciliations for my business account. Why do I need to do this? If I want to know how much cash I have in the business, can't I just look at my bank balance online?"

Required:
Respond to your friend's questions.

UP6-2 (Bank reconciliation and cash management)

Required:
As a manager of a company, explain why a bank reconciliation would be important to your cash management.

UP6-3 (Bank reconciliation)

You own a small plumbing company that has an in-house bookkeeper. Since you are busy at the various job sites, the bookkeeper's responsibilities include billing and collections. She sends out invoices and statements to customers and processes payments received in person and by mail. She also prepares the monthly bank reconciliations.

Required:

a. Why is it important that you review the bank reconciliation each month?
b. What kind of information should you be looking at when you do this?

UP6-4 (Estimation of uncollectible accounts receivable)

There is a management compensation plan at See Saw Company that includes bonuses for managers when the company achieves a certain level of reported net income.

Required:
What incentives might this create for management to influence the estimate of the uncollectible portion of the accounts receivable?

UP6-5 (Accounts receivable and uncollectible accounts)

Ontario Company manufactures and sells high-quality racing and mountain bicycles. At the end of 2015, Ontario's statement of financial position reported total Accounts Receivable of $250,000 and an Allowance for Doubtful Accounts of $18,000. During 2016, the following events occurred:

1. Credit sales in the amount of $2,300,000 were made.
2. Collections of $2,250,000 were received on account.
3. Customers with total debts to Ontario Company of $38,000 were declared bankrupt and those accounts receivable were written off.
4. Bad debts expense for 2016 was recorded as 2% of credit sales.

Required:
As the chief financial officer for Ontario Company, you have been asked by a member of the executive committee to do the following things.

a. Explain the effects of each of the above transactions on the company's financial statements.
b. Show how the accounts receivable will be reported on Ontario's statement of financial position as at December 31, 2016.
c. Evaluate the adequacy of the amount in the company's Allowance for Doubtful Accounts account as at December 31, 2016.

Fulfill the executive committee member's request.

UP6-6 (Accounts receivable and uncollectible accounts)

Lowrate Communications is in the cellular telephone industry. The following selected information has been compiled for the company (in thousands of dollars):

	2016	2015	2014
Accounts receivable (net)	$ 1,469.8	$ 1,230.6	$ 1,044.8
Allowance for doubtful accounts	128.9	121.9	118.0
Accounts written off	305.4	267.6	296.8
Bad debts expense	312.4	271.5	267.0
Sales revenue (all on account)	12,661.8	11,367.8	10,420.0

Required:

a. In each of the three years presented, what percentage of the company's total accounts receivable is estimated to be uncollectible?
b. In each of the three years presented, what percentage of the sales revenue is the bad debts expense?
c. Did Lowrate's collection of accounts receivable improve or deteriorate over this three-year period?
d. What was Lowrate's average collection period for 2016? Has this improved over the prior year?

Reading and Interpreting Published Financial Statements

RI6-1 (Accounts receivable and credit risk)

Big Rock Brewery Inc., which is based in Calgary, Alberta, is a publicly listed company. The company's products are sold across the country in nine provinces and three territories as well as being exported to Korea.

One of the reporting requirements for financial instruments is that a company must disclose if it has a high concentration of receivables from certain customers or categories of customers, because this may increase the company's level of credit risk as it depends greatly on the ability of those customers to pay their accounts. In accordance with this requirement, in its 2013 annual report, Big Rock disclosed the following:

> Big Rock has a concentration of credit risk because a majority of its accounts receivable are from provincial liquor boards, under provincially regulated industry sale and payment terms. The Corporation is not exposed to significant credit risk as payment in full is typically collected by provincial liquor boards at the time of sale and receivables are with government agencies. While substantially all of Big Rock's accounts receivable are from provincial government liquor authorities, the timing of receipts of large balances may vary significantly from period to period. The majority of product sold outside of Canada, which is included in GST and other receivables, is done so on a 'Cash on Delivery' basis with no credit risk.

Required:
How would this disclosure affect your assessment of Big Rock's level of credit risk?

RI6-2 (Analysis of accounts receivable)

According to its 2013 annual report, RONA Inc. is the largest Canadian distributor and retailer of hardware, home renovation, and gardening products. RONA's 2013 financial statements contained the following information, in thousands of Canadian dollars:

	2013	2012
Sales	$4,192,192	$4,444,175
Trade receivables (net)	$240,086	$354,482
Allowance for doubtful accounts	$12,231	$14,748

Required:

a. What percentages of RONA Inc.'s accounts receivable were considered uncollectible in each of 2013 and 2012? Is the trend favourable or unfavourable?
b. Calculate RONA's accounts receivable turnover rates for 2013 and 2012 using the ending balances of the receivables for each year rather than the average receivables. Is the trend favourable or unfavourable?
c. What was the average number of days taken by RONA to collect its accounts receivable in 2013? In 2012? Do these figures provide insights beyond what the results in part "b" showed? Explain.

RI6-3 (Analysis of accounts receivable)

According to the company's 2013 annual review, Finning International Inc. is "the world's largest Caterpillar equipment dealer." The company is headquartered in Vancouver, but has operations in Western Canada, South America, and the United Kingdom and Ireland. The following information is taken from Note 4 of the financial statements in Finning's 2013 financial report:

December 31 ($ thousands)	2013 Gross	2013 Allowance	2012 Gross	2012 Allowance
Not past due	**$619,839**	**$ 2**	$548,989	$ —
Past due 1–30 days	**156,644**	**1**	160,844	—
Past due 31–90 days	**80,998**	**299**	73,470	872
Past due 91–120 days	**8,956**	**883**	15,264	820
Past due greater than 120 days	**55,822**	**24,161**	50,464	28,005
Total	**$922,259**	**$25,346**	$ 849,031	$29,697

The movement in the allowance for doubtful accounts in respect of trade receivables during the period was as follows:

For years ended December 31 ($ thousands)	2013	2012
Balance, beginning of year	**$29,697**	$20,737
Additional allowance	**5,849**	19,994
Receivables written off	**(10,540)**	(11,134)
Foreign exchange translation adjustment	**340**	100
Balance, end of year	**$25,346**	$29,697

The allowance amounts in respect of trade receivables are used to record possible impairment losses unless the Company is satisfied that no recovery of the amount owing is possible; at that point the amount is considered not recoverable and the financial asset is written off.

Required:

a. Based on the above information, what is the trend of the collectibility of the company's receivables? Did the amount of accounts being written off increase in 2013?
b. Calculate the percentage the allowance represents of each of the age groupings in 2013. Have these percentages changed from 2012? What do these percentages tell you about Finning's receivables after they are more than 120 days overdue?
c. Based on the above information, what was Finning's bad debts expense for 2013?

RI6-4 (Current ratio, quick ratio, and accounts receivable turnover)

High Liner Foods Incorporated processes and markets prepared frozen seafood throughout Canada, the United States, and Mexico under the High Liner and Fisher Boy brands. It also produces private label products, and supplies restaurants and institutions.

Exhibit 6-11 contains financial statements that were included in the company's 2013 annual report:

EXHIBIT 6-11A **HIGH LINER FOODS INCORPORATED'S 2013 CONSOLIDATED STATEMENT OF INCOME**

CONSOLIDATED STATEMENT OF INCOME

(in thousands of U.S. dollars, except per share amounts)	Notes	Fifty-two weeks ended December 28, 2013	December 29, 2012
Revenues		**$ 947,301**	$ 942,631
Cost of sales		**731,884**	735,970
Gross profit		**215,417**	206,661
Distribution expenses		**53,368**	44,511
Selling, general and administrative expenses		**98,902**	100,862
Impairment of property, plant and equipment		**—**	13,230
Business acquisition, integration and other expenses		**3,256**	10,741
Results from operating activities		**59,891**	37,317
Finance costs		**16,329**	36,585
(Income) loss from equity accounted investee, net of income tax		**(86)**	196
Income before income taxes		**43,648**	536
Income taxes			
Current	20	**12,378**	5,442
Deferred	20	**(86)**	(7,109)
Total income tax expense (recovery)		**12,292**	(1,667)
Net income		**$ 31,356**	$ 2,203

EXHIBIT 6-11B **HIGH LINER FOODS INCORPORATED'S 2013 CONSOLIDATED STATEMENT OF FINANCIAL POSITION**

CONSOLIDATED STATEMENT OF FINANCIAL POSITION

(in thousands of U.S. dollars)	Notes	December 28, 2013	December 29, 2012
ASSETS			
Current:			
Cash		**$ 1,206**	$ 65
Accounts receivable	9	**91,334**	73,947
Income taxes receivable		**3,509**	5,145
Other financial assets	22	**1,524**	533
Inventories	8	**254,072**	222,313
Prepaid expenses		**2,952**	2,991
Total current assets		**354,597**	304,994
Non-current:			
Property, plant and equipment	6	**97,503**	89,268
Deferred income taxes	20	**4,656**	7,207
Other receivables and miscellaneous assets		**1,906**	2,035
Intangible assets	5	**105,253**	110,631
Goodwill	5	**111,999**	112,873
Total non-current assets		**321,317**	322,014
Assets classified as held for sale	7	**542**	4,819
Total assets		**$ 676,456**	$ 631,827

continued

EXHIBIT 6-11B

HIGH LINER FOODS INCORPORATED'S 2013 CONSOLIDATED STATEMENT OF FINANCIAL POSITION (continued)

(in thousands of U.S. dollars)	Notes	**December 28, 2013**	December 29, 2012
LIABILITIES AND SHAREHOLDERS' EQUITY			
Current:			
Bank loans	12	**$ 97,227**	$ 59,704
Accounts payable and accrued liabilities	10	**103,215**	101,441
Provisions	11	**240**	1,614
Other current financial liabilities	22	**459**	550
Income taxes payable		**2,543**	1,165
Current portion of long-term debt	13	**—**	34,237
Current portion of finance lease obligations	13	**979**	1,039
Total current liabilities		**204,663**	199,750
Non-current:			
Long-term debt	13	**226,929**	213,359
Other long-term financial liabilities	22	**5,597**	1,130
Other long-term liabilities		**1,044**	1,532
Long-term finance lease obligations	13	**1,647**	2,181
Deferred income taxes	20	**43,998**	45,126
Future employee benefits	14	**7,929**	13,791
Total non-current liabilities		**287,144**	277,119
Liabilities directly associated with the assets held for sale	7	**—**	1,604
Total liabilities		**491,807**	478,473
Shareholders' equity:			
Common shares	16	**80,260**	75,169
Contributed surplus		**13,781**	7,719
Retained earnings		**90,792**	66,373
Accumulated other comprehensive (loss) income		**(184)**	4,093
Total shareholders' equity		**184,649**	153,354
Total liabilities and shareholders' equity		**$ 676,456**	$ 631,827

Required:

a. Calculate High Liner's following ratios for both 2013 and 2012:
   i. Current ratio
   ii. Quick ratio
   iii. Accounts receivable turnover (use the balance of accounts receivable at each year end for this calculation, rather than average balances)
   iv. Average collection period

b. Comment on the results of the above ratio calculations and any significant trends they reveal.

RI6-5 (Current ratio, quick ratio, and accounts receivable turnover)

Saputo Inc. is a Montreal-based producer and distributor of dairy products, including cheese and yogurt products. According to the company's website, it is "one of the top ten dairy processors in the world."

Exhibit 6-12 shows the company's statement of financial position for the year ended March 31, 2014.

EXHIBIT 6-12A SAPUTO INC.'S 2014 CONSOLIDATED BALANCE SHEETS

CONSOLIDATED BALANCE SHEETS

(in thousands of CDN dollars)

As at	March 31, 2014	March 31, 2013
ASSETS		
Current assets		
Cash and cash equivalents	$ 39,346	$ 43,177
Receivables	807,409	624,553
Inventories (Note 4)	933,232	770,158
Income taxes (Note 14)	30,867	2,786
Prepaid expenses and other assets	84,992	71,882
	1,895,846	1,512,556
Property, plant and equipment (Note 6)	1,928,761	1,617,195
Goodwill (Note 7)	1,954,691	1,569,592
Trademarks and other intangibles (Note 7)	484,830	454,876
Other assets (Note 8)	79,968	29,962
Deferred income taxes (Note 14)	12,796	9,459
Total assets	$ 6,356,892	$ 5,193,640
LIABILITIES		
Current liabilities		
Bank loans (Note 9)	$ 310,066	$ 181,865
Accounts payable and accrued liabilities	897,222	748,318
Income taxes (Note 14)	124,206	144,064
Current portion of long-term debt (Note 10)	393,600	152,400
	1,725,094	1,226,647
Long-term debt (Note 10)	1,395,694	1,395,900
Other liabilities (Note 11)	48,396	74,101
Deferred income taxes (Note 14)	348,548	191,320
Total liabilities	$ 3,517,732	$ 2,887,968
EQUITY		
Share capital	703,111	663,275
Reserves	242,282	38,049
Retained earnings	1,830,911	1,604,348
Equity attributable to shareholders of Saputo Inc.	2,776,304	2,305,672
Non-controlling interest (Note 16)	62,856	–
Total equity	$ 2,839,160	$ 2,305,672
Total liabilities and equity	$ 6,356,892	$ 5,193,640

The company's revenues for the year ended March 31, 2014, were as shown in Exhibit 6-12B.

EXHIBIT 6-12B EXTRACT FROM SAPUTO INC.'S 2014 CONSOLIDATED STATEMENTS OF EARNINGS

CONSOLIDATED STATEMENTS OF **EARNINGS**

(in thousands of CDN dollars, except per share amounts)

Years ended March 31	2014	2013
Revenues	$ 9,232,889	$ 7,297,677

Required:

a. Calculate Saputo's following ratios for both 2014 and 2013:
   i. Current ratio
   ii. Quick ratio
   iii. Accounts receivable turnover (use the balance of accounts receivable at each year end for this calculation, rather than average balances)
   iv. Average collection period

b. Comment on the results of the above ratio calculations and any significant trends they reveal.

RI6-6 (Current ratio, quick ratio, and accounts receivable turnover)

Exhibit 6-13 is from the Vancouver Fraser Port Authority's 2013 financial report.

EXHIBIT 6-13A **VANCOUVER FRASER PORT AUTHORITY'S 2013 CONSOLIDATED STATEMENT OF FINANCIAL POSITION**

(Expressed in thousands of dollars)
As at December 31

	2013	2012
Assets		
Current		
Cash and cash equivalents (notes 8 and 11)	**$ 121,783**	$ 160,042
Short-term investments (note 9)	**501**	600
Accounts receivable and other assets (notes 8 and 10)	**79,102**	40,932
Total current assets	**201,386**	201,574
Investments in securities (note 9)	**2,523**	1,997
Investment in joint venture (note 7)	**7**	—
Long-term receivables (note 10)	**6,399**	5,237
Deferred charges	**1,541**	1,247
Intangible assets (note 15)	**2,771**	2,521
Property and equipment (note 6)	**1,146,996**	1,023,199
	$1,361,623	$1,235,775
Liabilities and Equity of Canada		
Current		
Accounts payable and accrued liabilities (note 12)	**$ 76,394**	$ 40,270
Provisions (note 19)	**12,932**	13,006
Provision for investments in joint venture held for sale (note 7)	**—**	69
Short-term borrowing (note 13)	**1,600**	1,700
Payments in lieu of taxes	**400**	2,422
Deferred revenue	**13,468**	11,876
Current portion of long-term obligations (note 13)	**45**	43
Total current liabilities	**104,839**	69,386
Other employee benefits	**1,280**	1,483
Accrued benefit liability (note 14)	**11,754**	13,205
Deferred revenue	**27,598**	28,312
Provisions (note 19)	**3,836**	4,020
Other deferred amounts	**3,267**	3,214
Long-term obligations (note 13)	**99,699**	99,667
Total liabilities	**252,273**	219,287
Commitments and contingent liabilities (notes 17 and 18)		
Equity of Canada		
Contributed capital	**150,259**	150,259
Retained earnings	**959,091**	866,229
Total equity of Canada	**1,109,350**	1,016,488
	$1,361,623	$1,235,775

EXHIBIT 6-13B

NOTE 10 TO VANCOUVER FRASER PORT AUTHORITY'S 2013 CONSOLIDATED FINANCIAL STATEMENTS

10. ACCOUNTS RECEIVABLE AND OTHER ASSETS

(a) Accounts receivable and other assets

	2013	2012
Trade receivables	$ 12,995	$ 5,734
Provision for impairment	(3,326)	(3,113)
Restricted funds	7,698	3,125
Federal Government accrued grants	24,795	6,713
Other project partners accrued recoveries	9,270	2,615
Property rent related accrued revenues	12,906	11,861
Port related accrued revenues	6,279	7,090
Other	8,485	6,907
	$ 79,102	$ 40,932

At December 31, 2013, accounts receivable and other assets includes $7,697,585 in restricted funds (2012 – $3,124,409). Restricted funds are project related deposits, provincial share of lease revenue, and foreshore property owner deposits. Once information has been submitted to the VFPA's satisfaction, project related deposits are refunded in full plus interest. Provincial share of lease revenue is paid semi-annually. The foreshore property owner deposits are held to guarantee that the dykes on such properties will be maintained by the owners.

The single largest amount of the restricted funds is $3,724,766 of government funding to promote best practices for marine transportation of liquid bulk commodities (2012 – $757,498 was held for the replacement of a pile wall and a protection system at a terminal).

As of December 31, 2013, accounts receivables of $7,901,639 (2012 – $1,073,631) were past due but not impaired. These relate to a number of customers for whom there is no recent history of default. The ageing analysis of these trade receivables is as follows:

	2013	2012
Up to 90 days	$ 7,461	$ 691
91 to 120 days	88	68
Over 120 days	353	315
	$ 7,902	$ 1,074

As of December 31, 2013, trade receivables of $3,656,190 (2012 – $3,533,837) were provided for. The amount of the provision was $3,325,932 as of December 31, 2013 (2012 – $3,112,631). The individually impaired receivables mainly relate to customers disputing lease terms and conditions. The ageing of these receivables is as follows:

	2013	2012
Up to 90 days	$ 171	$ 227
91 to 120 days	2	52
Over 120 days	3,483	3,255
	$3,656	$3,534

Movements on the provision for impairment of accounts receivables are as follows:

	2013	2012
Balance, January 1	$ 3,113	$ 3,358
Provision for receivables impairment	232	238
Receivable written off during the year as uncollectable	(19)	(36)
Unused amounts reversed	–	(447)
Balance, December 31	$ 3,326	$ 3,113

Required:

a. Calculate the following ratios for both the current and preceding year:
   i. Current ratio
   ii. Quick ratio

   How do they compare with each other? Why is this the case?

b. Calculate the Port's allowance for doubtful accounts as a percentage of its accounts receivable for the current and preceding years. Also calculate the percentage of the Port's accounts receivable that were past due for both years. Comment on the trend.

c. What would the Port's allowance and writeoff entries have been for 2013?

RI6-7 (Accounts receivable and doubtful accounts)

BlackBerry Limited (formerly Research In Motion Ltd.) is known for its BlackBerry hand-held devices and the Playbook tablet. Based in Waterloo, Ontario, its shares trade on the Toronto Stock Exchange and the NASDAQ. The following information was taken from the 2014 annual report (in U.S. $ millions):

	2014	2013
Revenues	$ 6,813	$11,073
Accounts receivable, net of allowance for doubtful accounts of $17 in 2014 and $17 in 2013	$ 972	$ 2,352

Required:

a. Is the balance in BlackBerry's accounts receivable at the end of 2014 significantly higher or lower than it was at the end of 2013? Quantify your answer and ensure that you consider the company's sales trends.
b. Has the company's accounts receivable turnover and average collection periods changed significantly over the prior year? Use the balance of accounts receivable at each year end for the account receivable turnover calculation, rather than average balances.
c. What possible explanations can you suggest for the change in accounts receivable turnover?

RI6-8 (Examine and analyze company's financial statements)

Required:
Follow your instructor's guidelines for choosing a company and do the following:

a. Prepare an analysis of the company's cash (and cash equivalents, if applicable), gross accounts receivable, and allowance for doubtful accounts, by doing the following:
   i. List the beginning and ending balances in these accounts.
   ii. Calculate the net change, in both dollar and percentage terms, for the most recent year.
b. If any of the accounts in part "a" has changed more than 10%, suggest an explanation for this change.
c. Calculate the following ratios for the most recent two years and then comment on both their reasonableness and any significant changes in them:
   i. Current ratio
   ii. Quick ratio
   iii. Allowance for doubtful accounts divided by gross accounts receivable
   iv. Accounts receivable turnover rate and average collection period (in days)

Cases

C6-1 Versa Tools Inc.

Versa Tools Inc. is a small tool and die manufacturing shop located in southwestern Ontario. The company's main shareholder, Arthur Eshelman, is becoming increasingly concerned about the safety and security of the company assets and, in particular, its cash. In the past, Arthur handled all the cash transactions. However, with increasing production levels and plans to expand into a plastics division, he has been too busy to continue with this hands-on approach.

Currently, there is only one person in the accounting department, a clerk who is responsible for recording all the cash receipts and disbursements and for depositing all the cash. Because she is so busy, cash is usually deposited in the bank only once a week. Until it is deposited, all cash collected is locked in a desk drawer in the main office.

The accounting clerk has no formal accounting education. In fact, she is a graduate of a local art school and is working at Versa only to earn enough money to move to Toronto and begin a career as a graphic artist. She often notes the cash receipts on slips of paper until she has time to enter them into the computer system several days later.

Finally, Arthur has not been preparing bank reconciliations. When asked about the bank reconciliations, he replied, "I'm so busy running the business that I don't have time to check every item on the bank statement each month. Besides, with the high fees that it charges us each month, shouldn't I be able to rely on the bank to keep an accurate record of the balance in our account?"

Required:
Prepare a memo to Arthur outlining the basic cash controls that should be put into place at Versa Tools Inc. to ensure the proper management and protection of its cash.

C6-2 Slackur Company

Slackur Company is a very profitable small business. However, it has not given much consideration to internal controls. For example, in an attempt to keep its clerical and office expenses to a minimum, the company has combined the jobs of cashier and bookkeeper. As a result, Rob Rowe handles all the cash receipts, keeps the accounting records, and prepares the monthly bank reconciliations.

On November 30, 2016, the balance on the company's bank statement was $18,380.00. The outstanding cheques on that date were #143 for $241.75, #284 for $258.25, #862 for $190.71, #863 for $226.80, and #864 for $165.28. Included with the statement was a bank credit memorandum in the amount of $300.00, indicating the bank's collection of a note receivable for Slackur on November 25, and a debit memorandum in the amount of $50.00 for the bank's service charges for the month. Neither of these transactions had been recorded by Slackur Company.

The company's Cash account had a balance of $21,892.72 on November 30, 2016, which included a substantial amount of undeposited cash on hand. Because he needed cash for holiday shopping and knew that the company's internal controls were weak, Rob decided to take some of the undeposited cash for his personal use and report undeposited cash of only $3,845.51. In an effort to conceal his theft, he then prepared the following bank reconciliation:

Balance per bank statement, November 30		$18,380.00
Add: Undeposited receipts		3,845.51
Less: Outstanding cheques		
No. 862	$190.71	
No. 863	226.80	
No. 864	165.28	(582.79)
Add: Note collected by bank		300.00
Less: Bank service charges		(50.00)
Corrected bank balance, November 30		$21,892.72
Cash balance per books, November 30		$21,892.72

When he presented this to the general manager, she called the bank to determine whether the undeposited receipts on November 30 had since been deposited, and was happy to hear the bank confirm that Rob Rowe had made a cash deposit of $3,845.51 on the morning of December 1. She then reviewed the bank reconciliation to satisfy herself that the items on it seemed reasonable, and that it was balanced. Assuming that everything must be in order, she then thanked Rob for his good work and made a mental note to herself that he should be given a $500 year-end bonus.

Required:

a. Determine the amount of cash stolen by Rob Rowe. (Hint: Prepare a corrected bank reconciliation, treating the true amount of undeposited cash as an unknown. Then solve for this unknown, and compare the reported amount of undeposited cash with the true amount.)
b. Explain what Rob Rowe did in the bank reconciliation that he prepared to try to conceal his theft. (Hint: You should be able to identify items whose combined effects match the amount of the discrepancy that you calculated in part "a.")
c. What should Slackur Company do differently to prevent this type of occurrence?

C6-3 Sanjay Supplies Limited

Sanjay Supplies Limited is concerned about its ability to pay its debts. Selected financial information follows.

Sanjay Supplies Limited
Selected Financial Information (in thousands)

Years ended October 31	2016	2015	2014
Sales on credit	$17,100	$16,300	$12,700
Cash	20	60	210
Short-term investments (cashable on demand)	—	—	40
Accounts receivable	2,130	1,510	1,180
Inventories	1,730	1,250	940
Short-term bank loans (payable on demand)	560	140	—
Accounts payable	340	490	610
Other short-term liabilities	80	80	80

Required:
Analyze the information and explain why Sanjay is experiencing problems with its cash balance. What could Sanjay do to reduce these problems?

C6-4 Heritage Mill Works

Heritage Mill Works sells finished lumber and mouldings to a variety of housing contractors. Given the nature of the business, most of its sales are on credit, and careful management of credit and bad debts is critical for success. The normal credit period is 60 days.

The company's owners significantly emphasize the operating results as they appear on the statement of income. They believe that accurate net earnings are the best indicator of any business's success. The owners are currently looking at revising their credit-granting policies in light of a number of large writeoffs that were made in the past year. They are also wondering whether interest-bearing notes receivable with longer credit terms should be used in the future for certain types of customers and for very large sales.

The controller has asked you to estimate bad debts expense for the company, to be used in preparing the annual financial statements. The company had sales of $3,450,000 during the year, of which 90% were on credit. Historically, the percentage of bad debts has varied from 2% to 4% of credit sales. Bad debts are usually higher in times of economic downturns. Business has been strong this year for the entire industry, since interest rate reductions have led to a boom in new housing starts.

The balance in the Accounts Receivable account on December 31 is $330,000. During the year, the company had written off $73,400 of accounts receivable as uncollectible.

Required:

a. Provide the controller with an estimate of the bad debts expense for the current period. Be prepared to justify your recommendation to the controller. Be sure to comment on the magnitude of the accounts receivable that were written off as uncollectible during the year.
b. Discuss the trade-offs that must be considered when deciding credit-granting policies.
c. Explain why it might be appropriate to use notes receivable for certain types of customers or very large sales.
d. What other steps could this company take to reduce the risk of not collecting its receivables in the future?

C6-5 MegaMax Theatre

The MegaMax Theatre is located in the MetroMall and employs six cashiers. Two of them work from 12:30 to 6:00 p.m., and the other four from 6:00 to 11:30 p.m. The cashiers receive payments from customers and operate machines that eject serially numbered tickets. Some customers use debit or credit cards, but most payments are cash. The rolls of admission tickets are inserted and locked into the machines by the theatre manager at the beginning of each cashier's shift.

The cashiers' booths are located just inside the entrance to the lobby of the theatre. After purchasing their tickets, customers take them to a doorperson stationed at the entrance to the theatre, about 10 metres from the cashiers' booths. The doorperson tears each ticket in half and drops the ticket stub into a locked box. The other half of the ticket is returned to the customer.

At the end of each cashier's shift, the theatre manager removes the ticket rolls from each cashier's machine, counts the cash, and then totals it with the debit card and credit card transactions. Each cash count sheet is initialled by the cashier involved. The cash receipts from the first shift are stored in a safe located in the manager's office until the end of the day.

At the end of the day, the manager deposits the cash receipts from both shifts in a bank night deposit vault located in the mall. In addition, the theatre manager sends copies of the cash count sheets and the deposit slip to the company controller to be verified, and to the accounting department to be recorded.

Finally, the manager compares the total amount received by each of the cashiers with the number of tickets they issued, and notes any discrepancies, which are then discussed with the cashiers before their next shift.

Required:

a. Outline the main internal control considerations for cash receipts generally, and briefly discuss how they apply to MegaMax Theatre's cash receipts procedures.
b. Discuss any weaknesses in the current internal control system that could enable a cashier and/or doorperson to misappropriate cash.

ENDNOTES

1. Nicolas Van Praet, "Gildan Activewear Inc Moves into Women's Intimate Apparel with $110-million Doris Inc Acquisition," *Financial Post*, June 19, 2014; Gildan Activewear Inc. 2013 annual report; Gildan corporate website, www.gildan.com.
2. Canadian Tire Corporation's 2013 annual report.
3. New Flyer Industries Inc. 2013 annual report.
4. PotashCorp. 2013 annual integrated report.
5. RONA Inc.'s 2013 annual report, Note 26.

CHAPTER 12 Financial Statement Analysis

CORE QUESTIONS

If you are able to answer the following questions, then you have achieved the related learning objectives.

LEARNING OBJECTIVES

After studying this chapter, you should be able to:

INTRODUCTION

- What is financial statement analysis?
- What is the process for analyzing financial statements?

1 Understand and explain the process of financial analysis.

THE CONTEXTS FOR FINANCIAL STATEMENT ANALYSIS

- What are the common contexts for financial statement analysis?
- Why is an understanding of context essential to the analysis?

2 Identify the common contexts for financial statement analysis and explain why an awareness of context is essential to the analysis.

BUSINESS INFORMATION

- Why is it essential to understand the business being analyzed?

3 Explain why knowledge of the business is important when analyzing a company's financial statements.

- What information is the financial statement analysis based on and where is it found?

4 Identify the types of information used when analyzing financial statements and where it is found.

FINANCIAL STATEMENT ANALYSIS PERSPECTIVES

- What is the difference between retrospective and prospective analysis?
- What is the difference between trend analysis and cross-sectional analysis?

5 Explain the various perspectives used in financial statement analysis, including retrospective, prospective, trend, and cross-sectional analysis.

FINANCIAL STATEMENT ANALYSIS TECHNIQUES

- What is common-size analysis?
- How is ratio analysis used to analyze financial statements?
- What are the common categories of ratios?

6 Identify the different metrics used in financial analysis, including common-size analysis and ratio analysis, and explain how they are used.

RATIO ANALYSIS

- What liquidity ratios are commonly used?
- What activity ratios are commonly used?
- What solvency ratios are commonly used?
- What profitability ratios are commonly used?
- What equity analysis ratios are commonly used?

7 Identify, calculate, and interpret specific ratios that are used to analyze the liquidity, activity, solvency, profitability, and equity of a company.

LIMITATIONS OF RATIO ANALYSIS

- What are the limitations of ratio analysis?

8 Identify and explain the limitations of ratio analysis.

Student Stock Analysts Try to "Beat the Street"

Every campus has a number of clubs—from sports teams to the student newspaper. But a growing number of Canadian universities have investment clubs in which students are investing and managing funds. While some clubs run simulations, a number of clubs invest real money, often cash that has been donated to their universities' endowment and scholarship funds.

The students, usually studying finance or business at the undergraduate or graduate level, apply what they've learned about analyzing the financial statements of public companies to try to pick winning stocks. Some investment clubs run simulations which do not involve actual cash. In these, students invest in certain stocks and see whether the stocks appreciate at a higher rate than various stock indexes, or see who among the club members "makes" the most money from trading the stocks.

There are a handful of investment clubs where students invest real money. Among them are Brock University, Concordia University, the University of British Columbia, the University of New Brunswick, Queen's University, and McGill University.

At Queen's University, some MBA and Master of Finance students participate in the Queen's University Alternative Asset Fund (QUAAF), a notional company with a corporate structure that is a fund of hedge funds, which are funds with investments in stocks and other vehicles that are not sold to the public. Started by eight MBA students who each put up $6,000 of their own money, QUAAF subsequently received an amount, reported to be in the six figures, from the university's endowment fund to manage.

In Montreal, all the students in the Honours Investment Management program at McGill University's Desautels Faculty of Management work for Desautels Capital Management Inc., Canada's first university-owned, student-run registered investment firm. It has two funds: an equity fund of stocks and a fixed income fund, which includes foreign currency and mortgage assets. Students with the equity fund can work as analysts, analyzing the financial statements of companies in a certain sector. Twelve teams each manage $250,000 in assets. Student analysts meet twice a week to discuss market conditions and, based on their analysis of the companies' financial performance, recommend which stocks to buy, sell, or hold. In early 2012, Desautels Capital Management owned stocks of companies as diverse as TELUS, Metro Inc., Canadian Tire Corporation, and Canadian National Railway.

"We look for undervalued stocks and bonds that the street overlooks. Our edge is that we are young and diverse, and often we find the 'next big thing' before [Bay] Street does," said Ivan Di, Bachelor of Commerce student and a Desautels equity strategist. Typically, stock analysts use data in companies' financial statements to calculate ratios measuring profitability, liquidity, activity, and other things that indicate performance.

How did Desautels student analysts do in analyzing financial statements and picking winners? When the firm was launched in 2008, it had $1 million in donations that had been made to the business school some 20 years earlier. By late 2012, it had grown to about $3 million in assets. The funds consistently match the performance of indexes—an excellent return for paying attention in class.[1]

INTRODUCTION

LEARNING OBJECTIVE 1
Understand and explain the process of financial analysis.

In each chapter of this book, we have sought to enhance your understanding of financial accounting information and you should now be able to read financial statements with understanding, just like the students in the campus investment clubs in our feature story. Now that you have this perspective, it is time to step back, put the pieces from each chapter together, and discuss how financial statements are analyzed as a whole.

What is financial statement analysis?

In Chapter 1, we discussed how the primary goal of this book was to help you become an intelligent user of accounting information by enhancing your ability to read and understand corporate financial statements. We also identified many circumstances and career paths in which these skills would be necessary.

Through the various chapters, you have been introduced to a number of ratios, each related to the topic(s) under discussion in that chapter. In this chapter, these will be organized cohesively, enabling you to think about analysis as a structured activity.

In this chapter, we will use the term *analyst* to describe the person doing the analysis. It is important to understand that this analysis could be undertaken from the perspective of any of the financial statement users we discussed in Chapter 1. These included existing shareholders, potential investors, creditors, securities analysts, and credit rating agencies. When necessary, we will identify the perspective(s) being used in the analysis.

Financial statement analysis is the process of evaluating a company's performance based on an analysis of their financial statements: the statement of financial position, statement of income, statement of changes in equity, statement of cash flows, and the notes to the financial statements. The analysis would include calculating ratios, looking at relationships within the financial statements, and comparing the results with historical or industry benchmarks.

Analysts use financial statement analysis to help them evaluate corporate performance and the risks related to investment or lending decisions involving the company. These decisions are supported by other information, including an industry analysis, site visits, interviews with management, or other steps the analysts believe will assist in their decision-making. Financial statement analysis does not provide all of the answers, but it does provide signals about financial health, cash flows, and operating efficiency. Equally importantly, financial statement analysis will generate additional questions and point to areas that require further analysis.

This chapter provides an overview of financial statement analysis and a discussion of the basic techniques involved. However, financial statement analysis is a large and complex area, so this is intended to serve only as an introduction to the topic. It is also important that you understand that each financial statement analysis is unique and the techniques used will often differ from analysis to analysis. Each needs to be tailored to fit the context, including the nature of the company and its industry.

In this chapter, we will use the financial statements of Saputo Inc. to illustrate the analysis process. Saputo is headquartered in Montreal and is Canada's largest dairy processor and one of the 10 largest in the world. The company's products are sold in 40 countries under brand names including Saputo, Neilson, Nutrilait, and Frigo Cheese Heads. Saputo sells its cheese and milk products, including yogourt and creams, to supermarket chains, retailers such as convenience stores and specialty cheese stores, restaurants, distributors, and mass merchandisers. The company also has a small grocery products division that produces and distributes snack cakes. The information presented in this chapter comes from Saputo's 2014 annual report, which covers the year that ended on March 31, 2014.

What is the process for analyzing financial statements?

While the context for performing a financial analysis can vary and different analysts will structure their analysis in different ways, it is possible to use a general framework when performing an analysis. The following five-step process, adapted from the Chartered Financial Analyst Institute's financial statement analysis framework, will help you approach financial statement analysis in a logical manner.

The steps in the process are as follows:

1. Determine the purpose and context of the analysis.
2. Collect the information needed for the analysis.
3. Prepare common-size analysis and calculate ratios or other metrics.
4. Analyze and interpret the metrics from Step 3.
5. Develop conclusions and recommendations.

Let's discuss each step in turn.

1. **Determine the purpose and context of the analysis.**
   From the outset, it is critical that you understand the purpose or context for the analysis. One way of doing this is to determine the questions that the analysis will assist in answering. For example, should we extend credit to this company? Should we invest in this company? Knowing the context for the analysis or the type of questions you are trying to answer will help you make decisions regarding the type(s) of information that you will need to gather and determine the tools or techniques that would best support this analysis.
2. **Collect the information needed for the analysis.**
   Having completed Step 1, the analyst can then focus on obtaining the necessary data. Sources of data will be discussed later in the chapter, but certainly include the company's annual report, which includes the annual financial statements and management's discussion and analysis (MD&A). Industry data (including industry ratios and trends) and other economic data (such as inflation rates and exchange rates) may also be gathered. It is important to understand that the analyst must move beyond the four financial statements and use information from the notes to the financial statements. The notes contain important information that is not available on the face of the financial statements. The analyst will also attend the quarterly conference call and webcast for analysts in which company officials review quarterly and annual results, and are available to answer questions.
3. **Prepare common-size analysis and calculate ratios or other metrics.**
   In this step, the analyst will prepare common-size financial statements and calculate the ratios or other metrics identified in Step 1. Caution must be exercised in this step. It is easy to program an Excel file to calculate dozens and dozens of ratios, not all of which will be

meaningful. The challenge is to ensure the right data are being used and the metrics being calculated make sense given the purpose of the analysis.

4. **Analyze and interpret the metrics from Step 3.**
   Using the ratios or metrics calculated in Step 3, combined with the knowledge of the company and other information gathered, the analyst analyzes the information and interprets the results. This might involve comparing the ratios with those from previous years, or with industry averages to help form opinions. This step is where the analyst adds the most value to the analysis. For example, instead of looking at individual ratio results in isolation, they can be assessed collectively, compared with common-size analysis for consistency, and so on.
5. **Develop conclusions and recommendations.**
   In this final step, conclusions and recommendations are made based on the analysis performed in Step 4. These are answers to the questions established in Step 1. When developing conclusions, it is important that the analysis differentiate between factual results and the analyst's opinion(s).

THE CONTEXTS FOR FINANCIAL STATEMENT ANALYSIS

What are the common contexts for financial statement analysis?

LEARNING OBJECTIVE 2
Identify the common contexts for financial statement analysis and explain why an awareness of context is essential to the analysis.

There are a wide variety of contexts that commonly require the analysis of financial statements. These include:

- An investment analyst or stockbroker may undertake an analysis in order to make a recommendation to clients to buy, sell, or continue to hold shares of a particular company.
- A commercial lender may undertake an analysis to assess the creditworthiness of a loan applicant or analyze the financial statements of an existing borrower to determine whether they have complied with any loan covenants.
- A company's credit department may analyze the financial statements of customers seeking credit terms.
- A company may analyze the financial statements of companies that may be potential acquisition targets.
- A pension fund may analyze the financial statements of companies it is considering as potential investments or of the companies it is currently invested in.

Why is an understanding of context essential to the analysis?

Understanding the context for the analysis is essential because it will determine the type of information and data that will be required. It will also drive decisions regarding the techniques that will be used to complete the analysis. Given the wide variety of available information and potential techniques, understanding the context provides focus to both areas.

Each analyst will tailor the analysis to the demands of the decision to be made. For example, a banker trying to decide whether to make a short-term loan will likely use the company's historic results, in addition to comparing these with other companies in the same or similar industries. The historic results are important because they will help the lender determine the company's ability to service the debt. A banker would also consider the client's financial projections, especially its cash flow projections, as part of this assessment. The lender must also be aware of industry trends in order to get an overall assessment of how well a particular company performs relative to its competitors.

An investment analyst, on the other hand, will analyze the company's results relative to other companies. Analysts must consider the return versus risk trade-off across many companies. They must, therefore, directly compare companies in different industries and, often, in different countries. While the investment analyst would also look at the company's historic results, they would focus on the potential for growth and returns to the shareholders.

In this chapter, we take a general approach to financial statement analysis. In order to provide a broad understanding of the possible techniques, we will discuss a wide variety of ratios, without focusing on a particular context. However, we will identify contexts where one particular ratio may be more helpful than others.

BUSINESS INFORMATION

■ **LEARNING OBJECTIVE 3**
Explain why knowledge of the business is important when analyzing a company's financial statements.

Why is it essential to understand the business being analyzed?

Understanding the business means more than understanding a company's financial statements. It means having a grasp of the operating activities of the business, the underlying economics, the risks involved, and the external economic factors that are crucial to the company's long-term and short-term health. It means having an understanding of the various types of businesses that the company is in.

For example, a major company such as **Canadian Tire Corporation, Limited** is involved in more than auto parts, tires, and auto service. The company is a major retailer of hardware and sporting goods, and is one of Canada's largest independent retailers of gasoline. In addition, the company owns FGL Sports, which is Canada's largest sporting goods retailer. The company's banners include Sport Chek, Sport Mart, Atmosphere, and Intersport. The company also operates Mark's, a leading Canadian clothing retailer, whose banners include Mark's, Mark's Work Wearhouse, and L'Équipeur. Finally, Canadian Tire also operates a significant financial services division. In fact, the company is a regulated financial institution (similar to a bank) and more than 4 million Canadians hold a Canadian Tire MasterCard. Given the range of the company's operations, it's essential for an analyst to understand the various businesses when performing analysis and assessing the risks related to the company.

When analyzing companies that have diverse business activities like Canadian Tire Corporation, analysts rely on segmented information. For example, while Canadian Tire's annual report presents the results of all of its operations summarized in a single set of consolidated financial statements, it also includes financial information broken down for its retail segment, its real estate segment, and its financial services segment. In accounting terms, we describe different business activities within a company, or different geographic regions in which it operates, as **operating segments**. If a company has more than one distinctive operating segment and meets certain quantitative thresholds, it is required to disclose information related to the segments in a note to the financial statements. Segments can differ significantly with regard to risk and are affected in different ways by such economic factors as commodity prices, inflation, exchange rates, and interest rates. Segmented information allows users to better assess the overall risks facing the company and the success of the different segments in which the company operates. An overall assessment of the company must take into consideration the relative significance of each segment.

Returning to Saputo, it reports two segments, which it refers to as sectors: the dairy products sector and the grocery products sector. When discussing the results of the operations, it further breaks the dairy products sector into two regions: Canada, Argentina, and Europe; and the United States.

Understanding a company's business also requires an analyst to understand the corporation's strategies because companies follow different strategies to achieve success. While a detailed discussion of corporate strategy is beyond the scope of this book, you should be familiar with a few basic strategies that companies follow. The two most common strategies are:

- being a low-cost producer, and
- following a product differentiation strategy.

A low-cost producer focuses on providing goods or services at the lowest possible cost and selling at low prices. To be successful, these companies need to sell a high volume of goods at the lower prices. This strategy works best when competing products are similar and price is the most important decision factor for customers. Discount grocery chains or discount retailers usually follow this strategy.

The product differentiation strategy is to sell products that are specialized or to provide superior service that customers are willing to pay a premium for. If the company can make a higher profit margin on the goods or services provided, it does not need to sell as many goods to make the same level of total profit as a company that sells more for less—it can succeed with a lower volume. Gourmet grocery or specialty stores and high-end retailers usually follow this strategy.

Understanding the company's strategy will help you interpret the financial results and explain differences if, for example, you are trying to compare a discount retailer with a specialty store and are wondering why the results are so different.

The products Saputo produces and sells are closer to commodity-type products. There is little to distinguish its cheeses or other products from competitors. Consumers often choose based on price. This means that Saputo needs to follow a strategy closer to low-cost producer than product differentiation. In the overview to its annual report, Saputo refers to the goals of improving overall efficiencies and it has been consolidating production and distribution facilities.

What information is the financial statement analysis based on and where is it found?

LEARNING OBJECTIVE 4
Identify the types of information used when analyzing financial statements and where it is found.

The primary source of information is the company's annual report. You will recall from Chapter 1 that the annual report contains several sections, including the **management discussion and analysis (MD&A)**, the auditors' report, the financial statements, and the notes to the financial statements. The financial statements have been discussed at length throughout this book, so we will not repeat those here. We will, however, discuss the MD&A and the auditors' report a bit more to enhance your understanding of these two important sections.

Management Discussion and Analysis

You can usually gain a basic understanding of the company's range of business activities, including its recent achievements and management's future expectations, by reading the first section of the company's annual report and the MD&A. The first section contains the description of the company, some general highlights of the year, and letters to the shareholders from the CEO and the chief financial officer. Annual reports may also contain data other than strictly financial data, such as numbers of employees or sales volumes expressed in physical units rather than dollars, which can be useful for the analyst.

The MD&A is a very important section for an analyst to read. In it, management discusses many aspects of the company's financial performance in greater detail. It includes a discussion of past results, but also of management's expectations for the future and the risks the company is facing. The objective of the MD&A is to allow the user to see the company through the eyes of management. Although this descriptive section of most annual reports does not explain everything you need to know about the company, it does provide some insight into what the company does and the types of risks it faces.

From Saputo's MD&A, we can learn that the company's strategy is to provide high-quality food products to customers and develop new platforms and new markets primarily through acquisition. As noted earlier, the company is also focused on improving operational efficiency. At the beginning of October 2013, Saputo made a bid to take over Warrnambool Cheese and Butter Factory Company Holdings Limited, a large Australian dairy processor. Warrnambool produces a line of dairy products similar to Saputo's and this acquisition provided the company with access to the Australian market as well as a base for exports to Asia and Oceania. By January 21, 2014, Saputo had acquired enough shares to have a controlling interest. By February 14, 2014, the date the takeover bid ended, the company was ultimately able to acquire 88% of the outstanding shares of Warrnambool. The Warrnambool acquisition cost approximately $450 million, of which $390 million was financed by new long-term debt. This explains the increase in total assets and debt that we will see in subsequent trend analysis. Because the acquisition occurred close to the year end, the effect on the statement of income was not significant because only the revenues and expenses for the period between January 21, 2014 (the date when control of the company was achieved) and the March 31, 2014, year end are included. The acquisition did have a significant impact on the company's statement of financial position because the assets and liabilities of Warrnambool are included in the year-end balances. We will see that the size and timing of the acquisition were significant enough to affect some of the ratios we calculate.

The Auditors' Report

Another item of interest to analysts is the auditors' report. It provides the opinion of the external auditor appointed by the company's board of directors, on behalf of the company's shareholders, regarding whether the company's financial results are fairly presented. Financial statement users, including analysts, value this opinion because the auditor is an independent third party.

TAKE5

KEY POINTS

- An unqualified audit opinion means that the company's external auditors are of the opinion that the company's financial statements are fairly presented.
- Canadian audit firms use standard wording for their audit opinions to make it easy for users to understand them.

It is important to understand that the auditor's report does not guarantee the accuracy of the information contained in the financial statements. Financial statements are prepared by management, and management has primary responsibility for them. Auditors express their opinion on whether the financial statements present the information fairly according to accounting standards, which are IFRS in the case of most Canadian public companies. The auditor's report does not indicate whether the information contained in the financial statements is positive or negative. It remains the reader's responsibility to interpret the information provided.

The vast majority of auditors' reports will be *unqualified* opinions. This means that the auditor is of the opinion that the financial statements are fairly presented. In other words, the auditor has no qualifications to make on the information. Canadian auditors use a standardized opinion, meaning they all use the same wording. This makes it easy for a user to understand the auditors' opinion. An unqualified (or "clean") audit opinion is one in which the auditors do not express any concerns, reservations, or qualifications regarding the financial statements. Deloitte LLP in their auditor's report provide a typical *unqualified* auditor's opinion for the 2014 financial statements of Saputo.

> In our opinion, the consolidated financial statements present fairly, in all material respects, the financial position of Saputo Inc. as at March 31, 2013 and 2012, and its financial performance and its cash flows for the years then ended in accordance with International Financial Reporting Standards.

The above paragraph states that without any exceptions, in their professional opinion, the financial statements fairly present the company's financial position and the results of its operations in accordance with the applicable accounting standards (IFRS in the case of Saputo). This is what the users of the financial statements want to see; any other type of audit opinion warrants very careful consideration. An unqualified audit report for Danier Leather is reproduced in Appendix A of this text.

FINANCIAL STATEMENT ANALYSIS PERSPECTIVES

LEARNING OBJECTIVE 5
Explain the various perspectives used in financial statement analysis, including retrospective, prospective, trend, and cross-sectional analysis.

What is the difference between retrospective and prospective analysis?

As discussed earlier, financial statement analysis is done to help decision-makers with investment or lending decisions. Normally those decisions have future consequences. For example, lenders try to forecast companies' future cash flows to ensure that the borrower will be able to service the loan; that is, pay interest and repay principal. When the analyst is trying to determine what the future results of the company may be, it is known as **prospective analysis**, which is forward-looking.

KEY POINTS

- Prospective analysis is forward-looking.
- Retrospective analysis is historical.

The challenge with prospective analysis is that the world is an uncertain place; no one can predict the future with complete accuracy. In trying to predict future outcomes, generally the most reliable source of data available is the company's historical results. To the extent that an analyst expects the future to follow past trends, they can use **retrospective analysis**, which is historical, as the basis for predicting future outcomes. For example, if the company had a 7% growth rate historically and we expect that to continue, then we can build prospective numbers based on these expectations. If the analyst is to rely on retrospective analysis, they must be confident that past results are a suitable predictor of future outcomes. This requires them to be aware of any significant changes in either the company's operations or in the industry in which it operates that would make it likely that future outcomes will differ from past results. When this is considered likely, the information being used as a basis for the analysis must be adjusted or an alternative source found.

In many cases, a company's historic results provide a solid foundation for predicting future outcomes. When this is the case, an analysis of the historic results is in order. There are two major types of retrospective analyses: trend analysis and cross-sectional analysis.

What is the difference between trend analysis and cross-sectional analysis?

With **trend analysis**, the analyst examines a company's information from multiple periods (normally years) to look for any patterns in the data over time. For example, examining the sales data over a five-year period would enable the analyst to determine whether sales are increasing, decreasing, or remaining stable. If no significant changes have occurred within the company or the industry in which it operates, the trend observed would provide a basis for predicting the company's future sales. If changes have taken place or are expected to that would negate this assumption, there is no reason to perform trend analysis.

Many companies recognize the importance of trend analysis and provide five-year or 10-year summaries to help users make this analysis. In the first part of its annual report, Saputo prepares a review covering a three-year period. Because this is not adequate for the purpose of a trend analysis, Exhibit 12-1 extracts some of the key accounts from Saputo's analysis and has extended the summary to five years using data obtained from earlier annual reports. From this, we can see that net revenues have increased significantly, though not exactly steadily, from 2010 to 2014. Net earnings increased from 2010 to 2011, and then fell in 2012 before recovering in 2013 and increasing in 2014. This should lead the analyst to question what occurred in 2012 and whether it is something that could occur again in future periods.

KEY POINTS

Trend analysis:

- compares results of the same company over a period of time (such as 3–10 years), and
- is useful for identifying patterns and changes.

Exhibit 12-1 Saputo Inc. Comparison of Key Figures

(in $ thousands)

	2014	2013	2012	2011	2010
Statement of earnings data					
Net revenues	9,232,889	7,297,677	6,930,370	6,002,932	5,810,582
Operating costs excluding depreciation, amortization, acquisition, and restructuring	8,212,544	6,436,905	6,099,439	5,214,651	5,118,511
EBITDAR	1,020,345	860,772	830,931	788,281	692,071
Depreciation and amortization	146,607	116,629	101,943	105,981	113,506
Acquisition, restructuring, impairment costs	45,663	42,277	125,000	13,600	
Interest costs and financial charges	69,085	34,099	24,650	23,874	35,062
Net earnings	533,966	481,921	380,840	450,051	382,714
Selected balance sheet (statement of financial position) data					
Total assets	6,356,892	5,193,640	3,599,120	3,578,331	3,253,451
Interest-bearing debt	2,099,360	1,730,165	546,506	549,069	442,362
Shareholders' equity	2,839,160	2,305,672	2,105,686	2,072,635	2,028,598
Statement of cash flows data					
Net cash generated from operations	656,310	645,792	522,987	588,520	583,615
Additions to property, plant, and equipment, net of proceeds on disposal	223,371	177,336	105,716	105,822	106,334

Note: The 2010 financial statements were prepared under the former Canadian "generally accepted accounting principles" standards while the 2011 to 2014 financial statements were prepared under IFRS. If 2010 were to be restated for comparative purposes, there would be small differences in some numbers. The effect of the adjustments is not considered material enough to change the discussion in this chapter.

FINANCIAL STATEMENTS

Saputo reports a figure for **EBITDAR** (earnings before interest, taxes, depreciation, acquisition, and restructuring) on its financial statements. It is the metric the company uses to evaluate recurring operating performance. EBITDAR grew steadily throughout the five-year period. Therefore, the drop in net earnings in 2012 must have come from other costs, such as acquisition and restructuring costs. Learning to spot figures or trends is a useful skill for an analyst. Between 2010 and 2104, EBITDAR has normally been between 11% and 12% of net revenues, but in 2011 it was 13.1%. A more detailed analysis of these costs could be prepared using additional data that Saputo discloses in the notes to its financial statements, including changes in raw materials costs and selling costs. Saputo has been growing through an aggressive acquisition program. Since 1997, it has acquired more than 20 other companies. We will discuss the effect of that strategy on other parts of the financial statements as we work through our analysis.

A review of the statement of financial position items presented shows that assets grew substantially between 2010 and 2014 (from $3,253,451 thousand to $6,356,892 thousand). You would expect assets

HELPFUL HINT

As you are performing your analysis, keep track of questions as they arise. You may find the answers to them later in your analysis, or they may help you refine your analysis and help you think of other ratios that should be calculated. In the end, if you are still not satisfied, you may want to ask further questions of management or research other sources.

to increase to support the increased sales as a result of the acquisitions. It appears that the acquisitions were financed primarily by interest-bearing debt because this grew from $442,362 thousand to $2,099,360 thousand, and to a lesser extent through equity. From the statement of cash flows, we can see that cash from operations has increased steadily (with the exception of 2012), which is useful for servicing the increase in long-term debt, including interest charges, which grew from $34,953 thousand in 2013 to $65,837 thousand in 2014.

Saputo's full financial statements upon which two of the five years of data in Exhibit 12-1 were based are in Exhibits 12-2A to C. These statements provide additional details in support of the key figure data presented above. The level of detail also illustrates why analysts pull out these key figures, making it easier to focus on them without getting lost in the detail of the financial statements. The information from these statements will be used to prepare a variety of analyses in the remainder of this chapter.

KEY POINTS

Cross-sectional analysis compares the results of two or more companies, normally operating in the same industry.

Cross-sectional analysis compares the data from one company with those of another company over the same time period. Normally, the companies should operate in the same industry, perhaps as competitors. Cross-sectional analysis may also compare one company with an average of the other companies in the same industry. For example, you might compare the growth in sales for **Groupe Danone**, the France-based producer of dairy and yogourt products, with Saputo. However, any cross-sectional comparisons must consider that different companies use different accounting methods; for example, different depreciation methods or different inventory cost formulas. In addition, different companies in different countries may use different accounting principles. Fortunately, both Saputo in Canada and Groupe Danone in France use IFRS. Comparing across countries has been greatly facilitated with the growing use of IFRS around the world, resulting in fewer accounting differences and, therefore, easier and more meaningful international comparisons.

Exhibit 12-2A Saputo Inc.'s 2014 Consolidated Balance Sheets

FINANCIAL STATEMENTS

CONSOLIDATED **BALANCE SHEETS**

(in thousands of CDN dollars)

As at	**March 31, 2014**	March 31, 2013
ASSETS		
Current assets		
Cash and cash equivalents	**$ 39,346**	$ 43,177
Receivables	**807,409**	624,553
Inventories (Note 4)	**933,232**	770,158
Income taxes (Note 14)	**30,867**	2,786
Prepaid expenses and other assets	**84,992**	71,882
	1,895,846	1,512,556
Property, plant and equipment (Note 6)	**1,928,761**	1,617,195
Goodwill (Note 7)	**1,954,691**	1,569,592
Trademarks and other intangibles (Note 7)	**484,830**	454,876
Other assets (Note 8)	**79,968**	29,962
Deferred income taxes (Note 14)	**12,796**	9,459
Total assets	**$6,356,892**	$5,193,640
LIABILITIES		
Current liabilities		
Bank loans (Note 9)	**$ 310,066**	$ 181,865
Accounts payable and accrued liabilities	**897,222**	748,318
Income taxes (Note 14)	**124,206**	144,064
Current portion of long-term debt (Note 10)	**393,600**	152,400
	1,725,094	1,226,647

continued

Exhibit 12-2A Saputo Inc.'s 2014 Consolidated Balance Sheets (continued)

As at	**March 31, 2014**	March 31, 2013
Long-term debt (Note 10)	**1,395,694**	1,395,900
Other liabilities (Note 11)	**48,396**	74,101
Deferred income taxes (Note 14)	**348,548**	191,320
Total liabilities	**$3,517,732**	$2,887,968
EQUITY		
Share capital	**703,111**	663,275
Reserves	**242,282**	38,049
Retained earnings	**1,830,911**	1,604,348
Equity attributable to shareholders of Saputo Inc.	**2,776,304**	2,305,672
Non-controlling interest (Note 16)	**62,856**	–
Total equity	**$2,839,160**	$2,305,672
Total liabilities and equity	**$6,356,892**	$5,193,640

Exhibit 12-2B Saputo Inc.'s 2014 Consolidated Statements of Earnings

CONSOLIDATED STATEMENTS OF **EARNINGS**

(in thousands of CDN dollars, except per share amounts)

FINANCIAL STATEMENTS

Years ended March 31	**2014**	**2013**
Revenues	**$9,232,889**	$7,297,677
Operating costs excluding depreciation, amortization, acquisition, restructuring and other costs (Note 5)	**8,212,544**	6,436,905
Earnings before interest, depreciation, amortization, acquisition, restructuring, other costs and income taxes	**1,020,345**	860,772
Depreciation and amortization (Notes 6 and 7)	**146,607**	116,629
Acquisition, restructuring and other costs (Note 22)	**45,663**	42,277
Interest on long-term debt	**53,239**	29,896
Other financial charges (Note 13)	**15,846**	4,203
Earnings before income taxes	**758,990**	667,767
Income taxes (Note 14)	**225,024**	185,846
Net earnings	**$ 533,966**	$ 481,921
Attributable to:		
Shareholders of Saputo Inc.	**533,097**	481,921
Non-controlling interest (Note 16)	**869**	–
	$ 533,966	$ 481,921
Earnings per share (Note 15)		
Net earnings		
Basic	**$ 2.73**	$ 2.44
Diluted	**$ 2.70**	$ 2.41

FINANCIAL STATEMENTS

HELPFUL HINT

A word of caution: Most companies, like Saputo, present their financial information with the most recent year closest to the account titles. But occasionally a company might present its information the other way, with the earliest year closest to the account titles. When you are reading financial statements, be careful to observe the format used or you may end up thinking sales are falling when they are, in fact, growing!

Exhibit 12-2C Saputo Inc.'s 2014 Consolidated Statements of Cash Flows

CONSOLIDATED **STATEMENTS OF CASH FLOWS**

(in thousands of CDN dollars)

Years ended March 31	**2014**	2013
Cash flows related to the following activities:		
Operating		
Net earnings	**$ 533,966**	$ 481,921
Adjustments for:		
Stock-based compensation	**22,084**	17,537
Interest and other financial charges	**69,085**	34,099
Income tax expense	**225,024**	185,846
Depreciation and amortization	**146,607**	116,629
Gain on disposal of property, plant and equipment	**(122)**	(53)
Restructuring charges related to plant closures	**22,096**	23,820
Share of joint venture earnings	**(1,406)**	–
Funding of employee plans in excess of costs	**(6,486)**	(12,485)
	1,010,848	847,314
Changes in non-cash operating working capital items	**(129,363)**	(4,425)
Cash generated from operating activities	**881,485**	842,889
Interest and other financial charges paid	**(65,837)**	(34,953)
Income taxes paid	**(159,338)**	(162,144)
Net cash generated from operating activities	**656,310**	645,792
Investing		
Business acquisition	**(449,578)**	(1,433,945)
Additions to property, plant and equipment	**(223,624)**	(178,237)
Proceeds on disposal of property, plant and equipment	**253**	901
Other	**803**	(13,719)
	(672,146)	(1,625,000)
Financing		
Bank loans	**77,810**	21,884
Proceeds from issuance of long-term debt	**390,000**	1,198,565
Repayment of long-term debt	**(175,045)**	(38,100)
Issuance of share capital	**41,861**	38,468
Repurchase of share capital	**(154,371)**	(190,404)
Dividends	**(175,321)**	(161,651)
	4,934	868,762
Decrease in cash and cash equivalents	**(10,902)**	(110,446)
Effect of exchange rate changes on cash and cash equivalents	**7,071**	9,486
Cash and cash equivalents, beginning of year	**43,177**	144,137
Cash and cash equivalents, end of year	**$ 39,346**	$ 43,177

FINANCIAL STATEMENT ANALYSIS TECHNIQUES

What is common-size analysis?

■ **LEARNING OBJECTIVE 6**
Identify the different metrics used in financial analysis, including common-size analysis and ratio analysis, and explain how they are used.

Although a company's financial data can reveal much about its performance, certain relationships are more easily understood when some elements of the data are compared with other elements. This is where **common-size analysis** comes in. It involves converting the dollar values in the financial statements into percentages of a specific base amount. For example, when preparing common-size analysis of a statement of financial position, the base used is normally total assets. When preparing common-size analysis of a statement of income, the base is normally total revenues. This means that each item on a **common-size statement of financial position** is determined as a percentage of total assets, while each item on a **common-size statement of income** is expressed as a percentage of total revenues. This presentation format makes it much easier for an analyst to quickly understand the degree of change.

KEY POINTS
- A common-size statement of financial position uses total assets as the base.
- A common-size statement of income uses total revenues as the base.

In Exhibit 12-3, we have applied common-size analysis to Saputo's statements of income for three years, expressing each item as a percentage of total revenues; that is, the amount of each item on the statement of income ÷ total revenues for that year.

Exhibit 12-3 Common-Size Statement of Income: Saputo Inc.

	2014	2013	2012
Revenues	100.0%	100.0%	100.0%
Operating costs excluding those below	88.9%	88.2%	88.0%
EBITDAR	11.1%	11.8%	12.0%
Depreciation and amortization	1.6%	1.6%	1.5%
Acquisition, restructuring, and impairment costs	0.5%	0.6%	1.8%
Interest on long-term debt and other financial charges	0.7%	0.5%	0.4%
Earnings before taxes	8.2%	9.2%	8.4%
Income tax expense	2.4%	2.5%	2.9%
Net earnings(1)	5.8%	6.6%	5.5%

(1) Note: Some numbers do not appear to add due to rounding differences.

TAKE5

FINANCIAL STATEMENTS

We observed from Exhibit 12-1 that revenues, operating profit (EBITDAR), and net earnings have been increasing for Saputo but in 2012 net earnings had experienced a decline. This common-size statement of earnings gives us a better understanding of those changes for the past three years, but you could also do a longer series using previous years' financial statements. It shows that Saputo's net earnings as a proportion of revenues have fallen from 6.6% in 2013 to 5.8% in 2014, but that this percentage is above the level achieved in 2012. Because operating costs are the largest expense on the statement, it makes sense to look more closely at these costs. Saputo's operating costs as a proportion of sales have been increasing over the three-year period, from 88.0% of sales in 2012 to 88.9% in 2014, a 0.9-percentage-point increase. It is costing Saputo more to produce the goods it sells. This has caused the operating profit (EBITDAR) to fall from 12.0% to 11.1% and signals to the user that, despite its goal to improve cost efficiencies, Saputo has not been able to keep its major operating costs in check.

Changes in operating profit (EBITDAR) could reflect a shift to selling more products that are more expensive to produce, or perhaps price cuts were required due to competitive or economic conditions, or perhaps cost control has just been ineffective. An analyst would want to try to find out more information about the cause of the change, either from management or by performing additional analysis. Most of Saputo's products require raw milk or cheese as inputs and its MD&A discusses the price fluctuations of those inputs and the effect on its results. An analyst will examine a company's financial statements carefully when sales are rising or falling. If sales are rising and the cost of those sales rises proportionately more than the sales themselves, the new sales are costing the company more and management should be looking for ways to control the costs. As a percentage of sales, when all other costs remain the same, an increase in the operating costs results in an identical decrease in net income. Imagine if you sell an item for $1.00 and it now costs you $0.03 more to make or acquire the item than it did last year. This means there will be $0.03 less to spend on other items or left over as net income. Let's try to look for more interesting relationships on the statement of income for Saputo:

- Net earnings as a percentage of sales actually increased by 0.3 percentage points from 2012 to 2014, from 5.5% of sales to 5.8%. As Saputo's major operating costs as a percentage of sales increased by 0.9 percentage points (from 88.0% to 88.9%), the company must have been able to control other costs well enough to prevent net earnings from declining by the amount of the increase in its operating costs. Many of the items between its operating profit (EBITDAR) and the net earnings are unusual or non-recurring costs such as the restructuring and goodwill impairment charges shown on its statement of earnings.
- Income tax as a proportion of sales decreased, which could explain why net earnings did not decrease as much as operating profit (EBITDAR), but income tax expense is generally not under management's control. A more useful margin might be the earnings before tax margin, which decreased by 0.2 percentage points, from 8.4% to 8.2%.
- It is difficult to draw strong conclusions in this case without additional information. For example, although Saputo discloses its cost of sales in the notes to the financial statements, it is combined with other operating costs on the statement of income. Consequently, our common-size statement does not break down this information for our analysis. The signals on this common-size statement of income are mixed: the major operating costs are increasing but overall, the effect on net earnings is smaller. The analyst would want to discuss unusual expenses such as goodwill impairment and restructuring with management to determine how much weight should be given to their impact.

Common-size statements could also be prepared for the statement of financial position and the statement of cash flows. The common-size data could then be used in a trend analysis, as we have done for the statement of income, or they could be used in a cross-sectional analysis of different companies. In fact, common-size statements are particularly useful in cross-sectional analysis because they allow you to compare companies of different sizes.

How is ratio analysis used to analyze financial statements?

As we have seen throughout the preceding chapters, ratio analysis can be used to compare a company's results from period to period, or to compare one company with others. It also enables users to compare companies of different sizes more easily.

The ratios compare the relationships between various elements in the financial statements, such as:

- an amount from one statement, such as the statement of income, and an amount from another, such as the statement of financial position (for example, cost of goods sold relative to inventory);
- amounts from the statement of financial position (such as current assets relative to current liabilities); or
- amounts from the statement of income (such as cost of goods sold relative to total sales revenue).

HELPFUL HINT

When commenting on ratios and trends, be sure to use evaluative or interpretive terms. Do not simply make superficial, mathematical observations; show that you understand what the figures *mean*.

For example, do not simply say that a ratio or percentage is higher/lower or increasing/decreasing. Instead, try to use terms such as *stronger/weaker, better/worse*, and *improving/deteriorating*, when you describe the numeric results.

Although ratios tell you about the relationship between two figures and changes in that relationship from year to year, or compared with another company, they do not tell you the reason for the changes. That is, ratios will tell you *what* happened but not *why*. For example, if inventory turnover slowed, is it a problem with not being able to sell existing inventory or has the company introduced new product lines that have a longer selling or manufacturing period? As such, interpreting the results of ratio analysis requires the user to apply judgement. Often ratios raise as many questions as they answer. They are more often attention-directing—highlighting areas that should be explored further—than conclusive. As such, interpreting the ratio results, rather than simply calculating them, is the most important job of an analyst.

When interpreting ratios, you should state more than whether the ratio simply increased or decreased. You should recall, from the ratios looked at earlier in the book, that some ratios are considered to have improved if they increase, while the opposite is true for others. It may also be possible for a small increase in a ratio to indicate improvement, but too large an increase to indicate a concern. For example, an increase in the current ratio may indicate improved liquidity, but if it is too high there may be problems with excessive inventory levels or with the collection of accounts receivable.

You will usually need to do further research and analysis to understand the reasons for the changes. Sometimes changes in ratios are referred to as **red flags**—they identify areas that the user needs to investigate further.

You should also be careful not to draw conclusions too readily from limited amounts of data. In this chapter, due to time and space constraints, we are limited to only three years of ratios for Saputo and no cross-sectional comparisons with other companies or the industry. Looking at longer time series and cross-sectional comparisons with other companies or industry data would greatly improve the analysis. In a complete analysis of our sample company, Saputo, an analyst would seek more information before making any decisions.

What are the common categories of ratios?

You have already been introduced to ratios that related to the specific content of each chapter in this book. In fact, 24 different ratios have been discussed throughout the book. While this may seem like a large number, it is important to note that there are many other ratios used in business. The 24 ratios we have focused on include many of the most commonly used ratios and will provide you with the tools to undertake meaningful ratio analysis of most companies.

The 24 ratios we have studied can be organized into common categories. Let's take a minute and think about the way golf clubs are organized in a golf bag. Are they just put into the bag randomly or are they organized in some way? Normally, most golfers try to organize them. For example, all the drivers are placed in a section of the bag, as are the irons and putters. That way, when the golfer needs to select a club, they can quickly find the one that best suits their need without having to look through them all. Analysts do a very similar thing with ratios, bundling them into common categories according to the broad measure they can be used to assess. That way, when an analyst needs a ratio to assess a certain measure, they can select one from the relevant category rather than having to consider all of them. We will use five common categories of ratios: **liquidity ratios, activity ratios, solvency ratios, profitability ratios,** and **equity analysis ratios**. Exhibit 12-4 presents the five common categories of ratios and identifies where the ratios that we have studied fit.

Exhibit 12-4 Common Categories of Ratios

Category and Description	Common Ratios in the Category	Chapter
1. Liquidity Ratios – used to assess a company's ability to meet its obligations in the near future	Current Ratio	6
	Quick Ratio	6
2. Activity Ratios – used to assess how efficiently a company manages its operations	Accounts Receivable Turnover	6
	Average Collection Period	6
	Inventory Turnover	7
	Days to Sell Inventory	7
	Accounts Payable Turnover	9
	Accounts Payable Payment Period	9
3. Solvency Ratios – used to assess a company's ability to meet its long-term obligations	Debt to Equity	10
	Net Debt as a Percentage of Total Capitalization	10
	Interest Coverage	10
	Cash Flows to Total Liabilities	5
4. Profitability Ratios – used to assess a company's ability to generate profits	Gross Profit Margin	7
	Net Profit Margin	2
	Return on Equity	2
	Return on Assets	2
5. Equity Analysis Ratios – used to assess shareholder returns	Basic Earnings per Share (EPS)	4
	Price/Earnings (P/E) Ratio	11
	Dividend Payout	11
	Dividend Yield	11
	Net Free Cash Flow	5

Note: Only 21 of the 24 ratios presented in the text are included in this table. The other three are unique to the analysis of property, plant, and equipment and do not fit within the five common categories. These are: Average Age, Average Age Percentage, and Fixed Asset Turnover, all from Chapter 8.

Before completing ratio analysis for Saputo, let's review the ratio formulas for the 21 ratios discussed above. These are presented in Exhibit 12-5.

Exhibit 12-5 Ratio Summary

	Ratio	Formula	Result
Liquidity	Current Ratio	Current Assets / Current Liabilities	Ability to meet current obligations with current assets
Liquidity	Quick Ratio	(Current Assets − Inventory − Prepaid Expenses) / Current Liabilities	Ability to meet current obligations with most liquid assets
Activity	Accounts Receivable Turnover	Credit Sales / Average Accounts Receivable	Efficiency of receivables collection
Activity	Average Collection Period	365 days / Accounts Receivable Turnover	Number of days to collect receivables
Activity	Inventory Turnover	Cost of Goods Sold / Average Inventory	How frequently inventory is turned over during period
Activity	Days to Sell Inventory	365 days / Inventory Turnover	Number of days to sell through inventory
Activity	Accounts Payable Turnover	Credit Purchases / Average Accounts Payable	How frequently creditors are paid
Activity	Accounts Payable Payment Period	365 days / Accounts Payable Turnover	Number of days to pay suppliers
Solvency	Debt to Equity	Net Debt / Shareholders' Equity	Amount of debt relative to shareholders' equity
Solvency	Net Debt as a Percentage of Total Capitalization	Net Debt / (Shareholders' Equity + Net Debt)	Portion of total financing represented by debt
Solvency	Interest Coverage	EBITDA (Earnings before Interest, Taxes, Depreciation, and Amortization) / Interest Expense	Ability to cover interest expense from earnings
Solvency	Cash Flows to Total Liabilities	Cash Flows from Operating Activities / Total Liabilities	Portion of total obligations that could be met with operating cash flows
Profitability	Gross Profit Margin	Gross Margin / Sales Revenue	Profit after product costs to cover other operating costs
Profitability	Net Profit Margin	Net Income / Sales Revenue	Net profit earned on each $1 of sales
Profitability	Return on Equity	Net Income / Average Total Shareholders' Equity	Rate of return on resources provided by investors
Profitability	Return on Assets	Net Income / Average Total Assets	Rate of return on assets used
Equity Analysis	Basic Earnings per Share	(Net Income − Preferred Dividends) / Weighted Average Number of Common Shares Outstanding	Profit earned on each common share
Equity Analysis	Price/Earnings	Market Price per Share / Earnings per Share	Multiple of EPS represented by current share price
Equity Analysis	Dividend Payout	Dividends per Share / Earnings per Share	Proportion of income paid out as dividends
Equity Analysis	Dividend Yield	Dividends per Share / Price per Share	Rate of return provided by dividends relative to current share price
Equity Analysis	Net Free Cash Flow	Cash Flows from Operating Activities − Net Capital Expenditures − Dividends on Preferred Shares	Cash flow generated from operating activities that would be available to common shareholders

RATIO ANALYSIS

What liquidity ratios are commonly used?

■ **LEARNING OBJECTIVE 7**
Identify, calculate, and interpret specific ratios that are used to analyze the liquidity, activity, solvency, profitability, and equity of a company.

As discussed in Chapters 1 and 6, when assessing a company's liquidity, we are focused on determining a company's ability to convert assets into cash so that liabilities can be paid. An important part of liquidity analysis considers the company's ability to meet its short-term obligations with its short-term assets. Two ratios that are commonly used are the **current ratio** and the **quick ratio**.

Current Ratio

Current Ratio	$\dfrac{\text{Current Assets}}{\text{Current Liabilities}}$	Ability to meet current obligations with current assets

$$2014 \quad \frac{\$1{,}895{,}846}{\$1{,}725{,}094} = 1.10$$

$$2013 \quad \frac{\$1{,}512{,}556}{\$1{,}226{,}647} = 1.23$$

$$2012 \quad \frac{\$1{,}399{,}464}{\$902{,}441} = 1.55$$

Note: All of the dollar amounts in the ratio calculations are in thousands of Canadian dollars.

Based on the above, Saputo had $1.10 of current assets for every $1 in current liabilities in 2014. While the company's current ratio declined during the year, it is still greater than 1.0, indicating that there are more than enough current assets with which to settle current liabilities. Upon reviewing the current assets, we can see that cash and cash equivalents decreased (the company used some cash in an acquisition), while accounts receivable, inventory, income taxes, and prepaids all increased, also likely due to the acquisition. While Saputo's total current assets increased, the growth in current liabilities, especially in the current portion of its long-term debt, was greater, which decreased liquidity and lowered the current ratio.

One rule of thumb for the current ratio is that for most industries, it should be 1.0 or more, but it is not uncommon to see companies with current ratios of less than 1.0. The size of this ratio depends on the type of business and the types of assets and liabilities that are considered current. For example, a company that sells primarily on a cash basis and does not have any accounts receivable, like a grocery store, normally has a low current ratio.

It is important to note that it is possible for a company to be *too liquid*—to have too much money invested in assets such as cash and accounts receivable that do not generate any returns for the company.

You should also realize that different users may have different perceptions about liquidity. A creditor or banker would prefer high levels of liquidity because that reduces the risk that the company may not be able to repay the debt. However, a shareholder or investor does not want a company to have too much money in cash or cash equivalents because there is an opportunity cost of having money tied up in low-earning assets.

Quick Ratio

Quick Ratio	$\dfrac{\text{Current Assets} - \text{Inventory} - \text{Prepaid Expenses}}{\text{Current Liabilities}}$	Ability to meet current obligations with most liquid assets

$$2014 \quad \frac{\$1{,}895{,}846 - \$933{,}232 - \$84{,}992}{\$1{,}725{,}094} = 0.51$$

$$2013 \quad \frac{\$1{,}512{,}556 - \$770{,}158 - \$71{,}882}{\$1{,}226{,}647} = 0.55$$

$$2012 \quad \frac{\$1{,}399{,}464 - \$712{,}885 - \$54{,}576}{\$902{,}441} = 0.70$$

Based on the above, the quick ratio of 0.51 in 2014 is lower than the quick ratio of 0.55 in 2013, which should not be surprising. Remember that when we discussed the current ratio we noted increases in Saputo's current liabilities and a decrease in its cash balance.

Like the current ratio, the desirable level for this ratio depends on the type of industry. The rule of thumb for this ratio is that it should be approximately 1.0 or more but industries without accounts receivable may have a very low quick ratio.

Taken together, the current ratio and quick ratio indicate that Saputo's liquidity position is solid and there are no working capital concerns. However, the company's liquidity has declined and additional information on the reasons for this would be useful. Developing meaningful analysis is a challenge when there is ratio information for only a few years, and especially when major acquisitions have occurred during that time period. This illustrates the importance of trend analyses, because having ratios beyond just two or three years would enable you to see broader patterns. Cross-sectional analyses should also be undertaken with other companies in the food-processing industry.

What activity ratios are commonly used?

The activity ratios provide additional insight into how efficiently the company manages its operations and are sometimes called **operating efficiency ratios**. We looked at a number of asset-related activity ratios in Chapters 6 and 7 involving accounts receivable and inventory. We also looked at two liability-related activity ratios in Chapter 9 involving accounts payable. These activity ratios help the analyst assess the company's management of its working capital.

Accounts Receivable Turnover and Average Collection Period

Accounts Receivable Turnover	$\frac{\text{Credit Sales}}{\text{Average Accounts Receivable}}$	Efficiency of receivables collection

$$2014 \quad \frac{\$9{,}232{,}889}{(\$624{,}553 + \$807{,}409)/2} = 12.9$$

$$2013 \quad \frac{\$7{,}297{,}677}{(\$487{,}502 + \$624{,}553)/2} = 13.1$$

$$2012 \quad \frac{\$6{,}930{,}370}{(\$460{,}807 + \$487{,}502)/2} = 14.6$$

When the **accounts receivable turnover** ratio is calculated based on information from the financial statements, the assumption is usually made that all sales revenues were on account. This is necessary because no information is normally provided indicating the percentage of credit sales (or sales on account) versus cash sales. If the turnover ratio were being prepared for internal use by management, this type of information would be available and only credit sales would be used when calculating it. In this case, it is probable that most of Saputo's sales are credit sales, since it sells its products to retailers and wholesale distributors. Companies that sell directly to the public, like grocery stores, tend to sell primarily on a cash basis and hence have few (if any) credit sales.

Note that average accounts receivable should only include receivables related to credit sales (trade receivables). It should not include other miscellaneous receivables (such as income tax receivable or advances to employees). We have assumed that the receivables on Saputo's balance sheet are all related to credit sales.

Finally, although we have included only two years of financial information in Exhibits 12-2A, B, and C, we have obtained additional information for the fiscal year ended March 31, 2011, and included it in the calculation of the average accounts receivable shown above, as well as in other ratios that use average rather than year-end figures. While we recommend you trace the amounts used in the calculations in these ratios back to Exhibits 12-2A, B, and C as appropriate, you will not be able to trace the figures shown for 2012 because they have not been included in the chapter. You could trace them if you obtained the company's 2012 financial statements from the company's website or through SEDAR (www.sedar.com).

Average Collection Period	$\frac{\text{365 days}}{\text{Accounts Receivable Turnover}}$	Number of days to collect receivables

2014	$\frac{365}{12.9} = 28.3$ days
2013	$\frac{365}{13.1} = 27.9$ days
2012	$\frac{365}{14.6} = 25.0$ days

The accounts receivable turnover can also be used to determine the **average collection period**. Users may find that average collection period is easier to interpret than accounts receivable turnover. Although companies probably do not sell goods or collect receivables every day of the year, the convention is to calculate it based on a 365-day period.

To determine how effectively a company is at collecting its receivables, its accounts receivable turnover must be compared with the company's credit terms. For example, companies that normally allow customers 30 days to pay, would be expected to have an accounts receivable turnover of 12 (365 days/30 days = 12). An accounts receivable turnover higher than 12 would mean that the company is collecting its receivables faster, speeding the flow of cash from the company's customers.

With an accounts receivable turnover of 12.9 times, it appears that Saputo is collecting its receivables, on average, in 28.3 days. Since we have no information on Saputo's credit terms, we will assume that the company's normal credit terms are 30 days. If you were working for a financial institution considering lending the company funds, you would be able to obtain this information from the company. Assuming the company provides 30-day credit terms, the company is collecting its receivables on a timely basis. Its customers are, on average, paying slightly faster than the terms given and Saputo is benefitting from the earlier cash inflows. The 2014 turnover is lower (worse) than in 2013 (13.1 times) and 2012 (14.6 times), indicating that the collection rate for its receivables has been slowing. This could be related to the acquisition of Warrnambool in 2014 and U.S.-based dairy producer Morningstar in 2013. Only two months of sales for Warrnambool are included in revenues, which understates the revenues (numerator) relative to the accounts receivable. However, overall collection of accounts seems strong for the company.

A decrease in the accounts receivable turnover or a higher average collection period can indicate that the company is having difficulty collecting its accounts receivable. Alternatively, the company may be selling to customers with higher credit risk or may have old accounts receivable requiring writeoff.

Inventory Turnover and Days to Sell Inventory Ratios

Inventory Turnover	$\frac{\text{Cost of Goods Sold}}{\text{Average Inventory}}$	How frequently inventory is turned over during period

2014	$\frac{\$7,419,529}{(\$770,158 + \$933,232)/2} = 8.7$
2013	$\frac{\$5,816,940}{(\$712,885 + \$770,158)/2} = 7.8$
2012	$\frac{\$5,523,298}{(\$662,194 + \$712,885)/2} = 8.0$

The **inventory turnover ratio**, introduced in Chapter 7, gives the analyst some idea of how fast inventory is sold or, alternatively, how long the inventory is held prior to sale.

All companies are required to disclose the amount of their cost of goods sold. Some companies include this information directly on the statement of income, while others disclose information about it in the notes to their financial statements, as was the case with Saputo. Exhibit 12-6 shows how cost of sales was disclosed in Note 4 to the company's financial statements.

Exhibit 12-6 Excerpt from Saputo Inc.'s 2014 Annual Report: Calculation of Cost of Sales

FINANCIAL STATEMENTS

NOTE 4 INVENTORIES

in 000s	**March 31, 2014**	March 31, 2013
Finished goods	**$ 651,660**	$ 551,733
Raw materials, work in progress and supplies	**281,572**	220,971
Inventory write-down	**–**	(2,546)
Total	**$ 933,232**	$ 770,158

The amount of inventories recognized as an expense in operating costs for the year ended March 31, 2014 is $7,419,529,000 ($5,816,940,000 for the year ended March 31, 2013).

For fiscal 2014, no write-down ($2,546,000 at March 31, 2013) was included as an expense in "Operating costs excluding depreciation, amortization, acquisition, restructuring and other costs" under the caption "Changes in inventories of finished goods and work in process" in Note 5.

Days to Sell Inventory $= \frac{365 \text{ days}}{\text{Inventory Turnover}}$ Number of days to sell through inventory

2014 $\frac{365}{8.7} = 41.9$ days

2013 $\frac{365}{7.8} = 46.8$ days

2012 $\frac{365}{8.0} = 45.6$ days

The **days to sell inventory ratio** tells us how many days, on average, that it took the company to sell through its average inventory.

The average number of days that inventory is held depends on the type of inventory produced, used, or sold. In Saputo's case, its major operations are the sale of food products to both retailers and wholesalers. The 41.9 days, therefore, is the average length of time that costs remain in inventory, from original processing to sale of the products to customers. Because the product is perishable, you would expect a reasonably quick turnover, but remember this is an average of all products: some dairy products (yogourt or cream) would require a quicker turnover than some cheeses that might be aged. You would want to review this turnover ratio over time and compare it with the inventory turnover ratios of other companies producing and selling similar products. Saputo's inventory turnover is the highest it has been in three years, which means it has done well at turning over its inventories and the ratio is fairly constant between the two years, which is also a positive sign. We can see that, on average, the company took just under 42 days to sell through its inventory, which is just about 5 days quicker than it did in 2013; this should improve or shorten the company's cash-to-cash cycle as the time it took the company to collect its receivables was consistent from 2013 to 2014 (about 28 days).

Saputo is a processing company, and the inventory turnover ratio that we calculated used all types of its inventory, including raw materials, work in process, finished goods, and supplies. A more appropriate inventory turnover measure could be to use only the finished goods amounts, which could be done as Saputo discloses the components of its inventory in Note 4 (Exhibit 12-6). To simplify the calculation, we have just used total ending inventory.

An inventory turnover ratio that has changed significantly from one period to the next or that is significantly different from that of others in the industry may be a warning sign. If the ratio is lower, it could indicate that the company is having trouble selling its inventory, or perhaps has obsolete inventory on hand that overstates the company's current ratio and levels of liquidity, similar to a low accounts receivable turnover. If the inventory turnover ratio is too high, there is a risk the company's inventory level might be too low—it might be losing sales if it does not have enough items on hand to meet orders.

Accounts Payable Turnover and Accounts Payable Payment Period Ratios

Accounts Payable Turnover	$\dfrac{\text{Credit Purchases}}{\text{Average Accounts Payable}}$	How frequently creditors are paid

$$2014 \quad \frac{\$7{,}582{,}603}{(\$748{,}318 + \$897{,}222)/2} = 9.2$$

$$2013 \quad \frac{\$5{,}874{,}213}{(\$571{,}814 + \$748{,}318)/2} = 8.9$$

$$2012 \quad \frac{\$5{,}573{,}989}{(\$573{,}779 + \$571{,}814)/2} = 9.7$$

The challenge with the **accounts payable turnover** ratio is that a company's credit purchases do not appear directly in the financial statements. An alternative is to use the cost of goods sold in place of credit purchases, because the cost of goods sold is more readily available either in the statement of income or in the accompanying notes. If the level of inventories did not change dramatically during the period, this would be a good approximation.

Recall that in Chapter 9, we learned how rearranging the elements in the cost of goods sold (COGS) model enabled us to determine the amount of credit purchases as follows:

COGS Model	Rearranged Model	2014	2013	2012
Beginning Inventory	Cost of Goods Sold	$7,419,529	$5,816,940	$5,523,298
+ Purchases	− Beginning Inventory	− 770,158	− 712,885	− 662,194
− Ending Inventory	+ Ending Inventory	+ 933,232	+ 770,158	+ 712,885
= Cost of Goods Sold	= Purchases	$7,582,603	$5,874,213	$5,573,989

Accounts Payable Payment Period	$\dfrac{\text{365 days}}{\text{Accounts Payable Turnover}}$	Number of days to pay suppliers

$$2014 \quad \frac{365}{9.2} = 39.7 \text{ days}$$

$$2013 \quad \frac{365}{8.9} = 41.0 \text{ days}$$

$$2012 \quad \frac{365}{9.7} = 37.6 \text{ days}$$

HELPFUL HINT
When you interpret the activity ratios, remember that the turnover ratios and the "days to" ratios move in opposite directions. For example, a higher accounts receivable or inventory turnover ratio is normally good, because it indicates that the company is collecting receivables or selling inventory more quickly. However, an increase in the average collection period or the days to sell inventory is normally a bad sign because it indicates a slowdown in those activities.

With an accounts payable turnover of 9.2, Saputo's **accounts payable payment period** was 39.7 days in 2014. This indicates, on average, how long it takes Saputo to pay its payables. Interpreting this ratio depends on the credit terms of the company's suppliers. If the terms are 30 days, Saputo appears to be exceeding them; if the terms are 60 days, Saputo appears to be paying too quickly. If a company is paying too quickly, it is not taking advantage of the fact that accounts payable normally do not charge interest and hence are "free" credit. However, if the company is paying too slowly, there may be interest charges for late payments. Additional information on the payment terms would enhance this analysis. In addition, cross-sectional and trend analysis should be undertaken.

What solvency ratios are commonly used?

Solvency is the company's ability to pay its obligations in the long term (more than one year into the future). Analysts use it as a key indicator of a company's level of risk. A trend analysis of the statement of cash flows and the company's cash flow patterns over time should provide much of the insight you need to assess a company's abilities to service its long-term debt. Two dimensions are used to assess solvency: (1) risk, based on the level of **leverage** in the company, and (2) **coverage**, based on the company's ability to meet its interest and debt payments. We will look at four ratios that are commonly used in the assessment of long-term solvency: the **debt to equity ratio, net debt as a percentage of total capitalization**, the **interest coverage ratio**, and the **cash flows to total liabilities ratio**. The first two are often referred to as **leverage ratios**, and the latter two as **coverage ratios**.

Leverage Ratios

Debt to Equity	$\frac{\text{Net Debt}}{\text{Shareholders' Equity}}$	Amount of debt relative to shareholders' equity

2014	$\frac{\$2,060,014}{\$2,839,160} = 0.73$
2013	$\frac{\$1,686,988}{\$2,305,672} = 0.73$
2012	$\frac{\$\ 402,369}{\$2,105,686} = 0.19$

In Chapter 10, we learned that net debt was equal to a company's interest-bearing debt less cash and cash equivalents. Saputo's net debt for 2014, 2013, and 2012 was as follows:

	Bank loans	$ 310,066
	+ Current portion of long-term debt	393,600
2014	+ Long-term debt	1,395,694
	− Cash and cash equivalents	(39,346)
	= Net debt	$2,060,014
	Bank loans	$ 181,865
	+ Current portion of long-term debt	152,400
2013	+ Long-term debt	1,395,900
	− Cash and cash equivalents	(43,177)
	= Net debt	$1,686,988
	Bank loans	$ 166,631
	+ Current portion of long-term debt	–
2012	+ Long-term debt	379,875
	− Cash and cash equivalents	(144,137)
	= Net debt	$ 402,369

The debt to equity ratio measures the amount of debt the company has relative to shareholders' equity. The result is the amount of debt the company has for each dollar in shareholders' equity. The higher a company's debt load, the higher (worse) its debt to equity ratio will be. In Chapter 10, we also discussed leverage and learned that leverage means the company uses debt to finance some of its assets. We also noted that the more leverage a company has, the riskier its position and the higher its fixed commitments to pay interest are. Comparing the amount of debt with the amount of equity, as is done with the debt to equity ratio, is one way of assessing this risk.

A variety of formulas are used to calculate the debt to equity ratio. Some use total liabilities rather than net debt, while others use interest-bearing short-term and long-term debt without taking a company's cash balance into account. Since the ratio results will differ depending upon the formula used, it is important that you be aware of how the various ratios have been calculated when analyzing them and especially when comparing them with those that have been determined by someone else for a comparable company.

The debt to equity ratio illustrates that the amount of debt Saputo uses in its financing has increased from \$0.19 for every dollar in shareholders' equity in 2012 to \$0.73 in 2013 and 2014. The ratio is almost four times higher in 2013 and 2014 and is a result of the company's two significant acquisitions (Warrnambool and Morningstar), which were largely financed using long-term debt.

Net Debt as a Percentage of Total Capitalization

$$\frac{\text{Net Debt}}{\text{Shareholders' Equity} + \text{Net Debt}}$$

Portion of total financing represented by debt

$$2014 \quad \frac{\$2,060,014}{\$2,839,160 + \$2,060,014} = 0.42 \text{ or } 42\%$$

$$2013 \quad \frac{\$1,686,988}{\$2,305,672 + \$1,686,988} = 0.42 \text{ or } 42\%$$

$$2012 \quad \frac{\$402,369}{\$2,105,686 + \$402,369} = 0.16 \text{ or } 16\%$$

From the net debt as a percentage of total capitalization ratio, we can see that debt represented 42% of total capitalization in 2014 and 2013, up from 17% in 2012. In other words, the mix of debt and equity used to finance the company's assets changed significantly in 2013. Saputo added debt to finance major acquisitions in 2013 (Morningstar) and again in 2014 (Warrnambool). In the MD&A, management stated that they wanted to increase the company's use of leverage, which is consistent with the results of these ratios.

The two leverage ratios have sent consistent messages to the user. Based on these results, the user would want to consider whether the level of debt is appropriate for Saputo. Again, a cross-sectional analysis could reveal whether the company has excessive debt compared with other companies. As a general guide, however, the average corporate debt on the books of non-financial companies in Canada was approximately 36% of total assets at the end of 2013.[2] With a ratio of 42% in 2014, Saputo is just above that average.

Coverage Ratios

Interest Coverage

$$\frac{\text{EBITDA}}{\text{Interest Expense}}$$

Ability to cover interest expense from earnings

$$2014 \quad \frac{\$1,020,345}{\$53,239} = 19.2$$

$$2013 \quad \frac{\$860,772}{\$29,896} = 28.8$$

$$2012 \quad \frac{\$830,931}{\$23,081} = 36.0$$

The interest coverage ratio calculates the number of times a company's earnings could pay its interest expense. The higher the number, the less risk there is of the company being unable to meet its interest obligations through earnings. We can see from the results of this ratio that Saputo appears to have no concerns with meeting its interest expense through earnings because earnings were 19.2 times interest charges in 2014. This is down from 28.8 times in 2013 and 36.0 times in 2012, but this decrease is consistent with our expectations from the company's increased debt load. Because the coverage is still high, it is not of concern.

Cash Flows to Total Liabilities	$\frac{\text{Cash Flows from Operating Activities}}{\text{Total Liabilities}}$	Portion of total obligations that could be met with operating cash flows

2014	$\frac{\$656,310}{\$3,517,732} = 0.19$	
2013	$\frac{\$645,792}{\$2,887,968} = 0.22$	
2012	$\frac{\$522,987}{\$1,493,434} = 0.35$	

In addition to determining the level of risk that a company is exposed to through its use of debt to finance its assets, users want to assess the company's ability to meet the interest and principal payments that arise from the debt obligations. We will assess this using the cash flows to total liabilities ratio. This ratio measures the percentage of a company's total liabilities that could be met with one year's operating cash flows. It is important to note that total liabilities include both current and non-current liabilities and that only the current liabilities are due within the next year. In addition, some of the liabilities will not be paid in cash. For example, unearned revenues are often settled by providing services to customers. The company may also have other assets that could be used to settle liabilities, such as investments in the shares of other companies. As such, this ratio can safely be less than 1.0.

Saputo's ratio has fallen from 35% in 2012 to 22% in 2013 and again to 19% in 2014. This means that in 2014 just under one fifth of Saputo's total liabilities could be paid off with the current levels of operating cash flow. Dividing this ratio into 1, we can determine how many years of operating cash flow would be required to pay off the company's liabilities. Based on the operating cash flows generated in 2014, it would take 5.3 years (1/0.19) to generate enough cash to pay off the liabilities that existed at year end in 2014.

What profitability ratios are commonly used?

Profitability measures help analysts assess the potential return. The profitability ratios such as **gross profit margin** and **net profit margin**, introduced in Chapters 7 and 2, can be combined with the return ratios, return on assets, and return on equity to assess a company's overall performance.

Gross Profit Margin

Gross Profit Margin	$\frac{\text{Gross Margin}}{\text{Sales Revenue}}$	Profit after product costs to cover other operating costs

2014	$\frac{\$1,813,360}{\$9,232,889} = 0.196 \text{ or } 19.6\%$	
2013	$\frac{\$1,480,737}{\$7,297,677} = 0.203 \text{ or } 20.3\%$	
2012	$\frac{\$1,407,072}{\$6,930,370} = 0.203 \text{ or } 20.3\%$	

For most companies, cost of goods sold is the largest single expense. Companies need to closely monitor their gross profit margin to ensure that gross profit will be sufficient to cover all other expenses. Changes in a company's gross profit margin would indicate a change in the product's profitability, indicating changes in the cost structure or pricing policy.

Using the sales revenue as reported on the statement of earnings and the cost of goods sold information from Note 4 to its financial statements, we can quantify the company's gross margin as follows:

Revenues − Cost of Sales = Gross Margin

2014: $9,232,889 − $7,419,529 = $1,813,360

2013: $7,297,677 − $5,816,940 = $1,480,737

2012: $6,930,370 − $5,523,298 = $1,407,072

We can see that Saputo's gross profit margin dropped slightly in 2014 to 19.6% after remaining unchanged from 2012 to 2013. In other words, in 2014, for each $1.00 in sales, the company had $0.196 remaining after product costs to cover its other costs (down from $0.203 in 2013 and 2012). The fact that the company gross profit margin stayed constant tells us that the company was able to control its costs or was able to pass these additional costs along to its customers in the form of higher prices. Either way, the company was able to hold its margins, which is a positive signal.

Net Profit Margin

Net Profit Margin	$\frac{\text{Net Income}}{\text{Sales Revenue}}$	Net profit earned on each $1 of sales

2014	$\frac{\$533{,}966}{\$9{,}232{,}889}$	= 0.058 or 5.8%
2013	$\frac{\$481{,}921}{\$7{,}297{,}677}$	= 0.066 or 6.6%
2012	$\frac{\$380{,}840}{\$6{,}930{,}370}$	= 0.055 or 5.5%

While net profit margin indicates the overall profitability of the company, it does not provide any information about how that profit was achieved. When it is analyzed together with the gross profit margin, a more complete picture comes to light. Earlier, we saw that Saputo's gross profit margin decreased by 0.7 percentage points from 20.3% in 2013 to 19.6% in 2014. When analyzing the company's net profit margin, we can see that it decreased 0.8 percentage points from 2013 to 2014. As such, we know that most of this was the result of a lower gross margin and not the result of increases in other costs (depreciation, acquisition costs, restructuring costs, impairment charges, interest, or income taxes).

In addition to the profitability of earnings relative to revenues, it is important to examine the earnings relative to the amount invested to earn them. If two companies generate the same amount of net earnings, but one company requires twice as many assets to do so, that company would clearly be a less desirable investment. In Chapter 2, we discussed two profitability ratios related to the amounts invested to generate earnings: **return on equity** and **return on assets**. Return on equity measures the return generated by a company on the equity invested by shareholders (return from the perspective of investors). Return on assets measures return from the perspective of management. Management obtains resources from both shareholders and creditors and invests them in assets. The return generated on this investment in assets is then used to repay creditors and provide returns to shareholders.

Return on Equity Ratio

Return on Equity	$\frac{\text{Net Income}}{\text{Average Total Shareholders' Equity}}$	Rate of return on resources provided by investors

2014	$\frac{\$533{,}966}{(\$2{,}305{,}672 + \$2{,}839{,}160)/2}$	= 0.208 or 20.8%
2013	$\frac{\$481{,}921}{(\$2{,}105{,}686 + \$2{,}305{,}672)/2}$	= 0.218 or 21.8%
2012	$\frac{\$380{,}840}{(\$2{,}072{,}635 + \$2{,}105{,}686)/2}$	= 0.182 or 18.2%

The return on equity (ROE) ratio shows that Saputo earned a 20.8% ROE in 2014. This is a 1.0 percentage point decrease from the previous year's ROE of 21.8%, but still 2.6 percentage points higher than in 2012. This ROE of 20.8% should be compared with the ROE of other similar companies or with the results of Saputo over time. Cross-sectional comparisons of ROE are difficult in that differences in the risks involved should result in differences in returns. Differences in the risks cannot, however, always explain large differences in returns, because there are many factors that affect ROE.

Return on Assets Ratio

Return on Assets	$\dfrac{\text{Net Income}}{\text{Average Total Assets}}$	Rate of return on assets used

2014	$\dfrac{\$533{,}966}{(\$5{,}193{,}640 + \$6{,}356{,}892)/2} = 0.092 \text{ or } 9.2\%$
2013	$\dfrac{\$481{,}921}{(\$3{,}599{,}120 + \$5{,}193{,}640)/2} = 0.110 \text{ or } 11.0\%$
2012	$\dfrac{\$380{,}840}{(\$3{,}578{,}331 + \$3{,}599{,}120)/2} = 0.106 \text{ or } 10.6\%$

We can see that Saputo's return on assets (ROA) decreased by 1.8 percentage points from 2013 to 2014. The return on assets ratio is useful in measuring the overall profitability of the funds invested in the company's assets. However, comparisons of ROAs across industries must be made with care. The level of ROA reflects, to some extent, the risk that is inherent in the type of assets that the company invests in. Investors trade off risk for return. The more risk investors take, the higher the return they demand. If the company invested its assets in a bank account, which is a very low-risk investment, it would expect a lower return than if it invested in oil exploration equipment, which is a high-risk business. Although this factor cannot explain all the variations in ROA between companies, it must be kept in mind. It may be useful to perform a trend analysis of this ratio and to look at the changes in the elements used to determine the ratio, such as the growth in net income relative to the change in net assets.

What equity analysis ratios are commonly used?

Equity analysts are interested in the long-term risk and return of the company, as measured by many of the ratios discussed so far. But equity analysts and investors are uniquely interested in the relative value of the company's shares. This is assessed using the equity analysis ratios.

Basic Earnings per Share

Basic Earnings per Share	$\dfrac{\text{Net Income} - \text{Preferred Dividends}}{\text{Weighted Average Number of Common Shares Outstanding}}$	Profit earned on each common share

In Chapter 4, we learned how to calculate **basic earnings per share (EPS)**, including how to determine the weighted average number of common shares outstanding. The weighted average calculation requires us to know the date when shares were either issued or repurchased. This information is not typically available to an analyst outside the company because it is not required to be disclosed in the annual report. Financial statement users are told the number of shares issued and repurchased, but not the specific dates. However, since accounting standards require EPS to be reported on the statement of income or in a note accompanying the financial statements, we can rely on the company to prepare the calculation for us.

In the case of Saputo, the company had only common shares outstanding, so we do not need to worry about any preferred dividends. The company had 195,068,912 common shares issued and outstanding at the end of 2014, down from 196,619,440 common shares that were issued and outstanding at the end of 2013. This net reduction resulted from the company issuing 1,701,272 common shares under its share option plan, but also repurchasing 3,251,800 common shares. Exhibit 12-7 presents the note from Saputo's financial statements related to EPS.

Exhibit 12-7 Excerpt from Saputo Inc.'s 2014 Annual Report: Earnings Per Share Note

FINANCIAL STATEMENTS

NOTE 15 EARNINGS PER SHARE

	2014	2013
Net earnings attributable to shareholders of Saputo Inc.	**$ 533,097**	$ 481,921
Weighted average number of common shares outstanding	**195,123,232**	197,589,714
Dilutive options	**2,551,443**	2,731,407
Weighted average diluted number of common shares outstanding	**197,674,675**	200,321,121
Basic earnings per share	**$ 2.73**	$ 2.44
Diluted earnings per share	**$ 2.70**	$ 2.41

From Exhibit 12-7, we can see that Saputo's basic EPS was $2.73 in 2014, up 11.9% from the EPS of $2.44 in 2013. This increase in EPS is considered a positive signal.

The major problem with using EPS as a measure of performance is that it ignores the level of investment. Companies with the same earnings per share might have very different rates of return, depending on their investment in net assets. Because of this, the best use of the EPS figure is in a trend analysis, determining how it has changed within the same company over time, rather than in a cross-sectional analysis, determining how one company's EPS compares with another's.

A detailed discussion of **diluted earnings per share** and how it is calculated is beyond the scope of this book. However, it is important that you understand the difference between basic EPS and diluted EPS. The reason the diluted EPS measure is presented is that companies may issue securities that are convertible into common shares. Examples of these types of securities are convertible debt, convertible preferred shares, and stock options. The key feature of these securities is that they are all convertible into common shares under certain conditions. If additional common shares are issued upon their conversion, the earnings per share number could decrease because of the larger number of shares that are outstanding. This is called the *potential dilution of earnings per share*. A diluted EPS figure is determined to reflect what EPS would have been if all of these securities had been converted into common shares. As you would expect, diluted EPS will be less than basic EPS whenever dilutive securities exist.

P/E Ratio

Price/Earnings	$\frac{\text{Market Price per Share}}{\text{Earnings per Share}}$	Multiple of EPS represented by current share price

2014 $$\frac{\$55.69^{3}}{\$2.73} = 20.4$$

2013 $$\frac{\$51.58}{\$2.44} = 21.1$$

2012 $$\frac{\$43.21}{\$1.89} = 22.9$$

Note: Market price per share data was the closing share price on the last trading day closest to year end. This information can be obtained from various financial websites.

The **price/earnings (P/E) ratio**, or **P/E multiple**, was introduced in Chapter 11 and relates the market price of a company's shares with its earnings per share. This ratio is thought of by many analysts as the amount investors are willing to pay for a dollar's worth of earnings. The interpretation of this ratio is somewhat difficult because stock market share prices are affected by many factors and are not well understood. It might help to think of the multiple in terms of its inverse. If a company is earning $1 per common share and its shares are selling for $20 on the stock market, this indicates that the current multiple is 20, meaning the current price of the stock is 20 times the current earnings per share. The inverse of this multiple is 1/20, or 5%. This indicates that the shares are returning 5% in the form of earnings per share when compared with the market price.

On March 31, 2014, the company's year end, Saputo's common shares were trading on the Toronto Stock Exchange (TSX) at approximately \$55.69 per share. Its P/E ratio on that date was 20.4 (\$55.69/\$2.73).

Remember that the earnings per share is the portion of the earnings that is attributable to an individual share: it is not the amount that the company normally pays out as a dividend to each shareholder. A shareholder earns a return both from receiving dividends and from the change in the price of the share. Therefore, the return calculated from the P/E ratio will differ from the actual return. Many factors affect the level of stock market prices, including the prevailing interest rates and the company's future prospects. It is sometimes useful to think that the market price reflects the present value of all of the company's future expected earnings. Companies with a low growth potential or higher levels of risk tend to have lower P/E ratios, because investors are not willing to pay as much per dollar of earnings if the earnings are not expected to grow much or are more risky. Conversely, companies with high growth potential or lower levels of risk tend to have higher P/E ratios. Many factors ultimately affect the P/E ratio, but the earnings per share figure serves as an important link between the accounting numbers in the financial statements and the stock market price of the company's shares.

Dividend Payout Ratio

Dividend Payout	$\frac{\text{Dividends per Share}}{\text{Earnings per Share}}$	Proportion of income paid out as dividends

$$2014 \quad \frac{\$0.92}{\$2.73} = 0.337 \text{ or } 33.7\%$$

$$2013 \quad \frac{\$0.84}{\$2.44} = 0.344 \text{ or } 34.4\%$$

$$2012 \quad \frac{\$0.76}{\$1.89} = 0.402 \text{ or } 40.2\%$$

In Chapter 11, we also learned about the **dividend payout ratio**. This ratio measures the portion of a company's earnings that is distributed as dividends.

From the calculations above, we can see that Saputo's dividend payout ratio was 33.7% in 2014, down from 34.4% in 2013. This percentage is consistent with the company's goal, which is stated in its MD&A, of returning approximately 30% of its net earnings to shareholders through the declaration and payment of dividends. In Note 24 on dividends in Exhibit 12-8, we can see that the total amount of dividends paid per share increased from \$0.84 per share in 2013 to \$0.92 per share in 2014, a 9.5% increase. So, while Saputo paid out a lower portion of its earnings as dividends, the total dividends paid to shareholders did increase. Trend analysis should be used to analyze the dividend payout ratio, in order to have a broad picture of the company's dividend practices.

Exhibit 12-8 Excerpt from Saputo Inc.'s 2014 Annual Report: Dividends Note

FINANCIAL STATEMENTS

NOTE 24 DIVIDENDS

During the year ended March 31, 2014, the Company paid dividends totalling \$175,321,820, or \$0.92 per share (\$161,651,170, or \$0.84 per share for the year ended March 31, 2013).

Dividend Yield Ratio

Dividend Yield	$\frac{\text{Dividends per Share}}{\text{Price per Share}}$	Rate of return provided by dividends relative to current share price

$$2014 \quad \frac{\$0.92}{\$55.69} = 0.0165 \text{ or } 1.65\%$$

$$2013 \quad \frac{\$0.84}{\$51.58} = 0.0163 \text{ or } 1.63\%$$

$$2012 \quad \frac{\$0.76}{\$43.21} = 0.0176 \text{ or } 1.76\%$$

The **dividend yield ratio** was also presented in Chapter 11. It measures the dividends an investor will receive relative to the price per share. The yield measures the return provided to shareholders as dividends, but does not factor in any returns resulting from capital appreciation (an increase in share price).

Throughout the text, we have discussed the two ways in which shareholders realize returns: through the receipt of dividends and through capital appreciation (growth in share price). The dividend yield ratio measures the return from the first of these. From the calculations above, we can see that Saputo's shareholders realized a dividend yield of 1.65% in 2014, up slightly from 1.63% in 2013. That being said, it is important to consider the variable on which the yield is based. Both the amount of dividends per share and the price per share increased in 2014. These increases are positive for investors who have continued to hold shares. New investors would need to consider the 1.65% yield relative to other possible investments. They would also need to factor in the potential for future increases in share price.

Net Free Cash Flow

Net Free Cash Flow	Cash Flows from Operating Activities	−	Net Capital Expenditures	−	Dividends on Preferred Shares	Cash flow generated from operating activities that would be available to common shareholders

2014	$656,310 −	$223,371 −	$0 =	$432,939
2013	$645,792 −	$177,336 −	$0 =	$468,456
2012	$522,987 −	$105,716 −	$0 =	$417,271

In Chapter 5, we learned that **net free cash flow** is considered to be the cash flow generated from a company's operating activities that would be available to the company's common shareholders. We also mentioned that it is unlikely that the entire amount would be distributed to shareholders. Instead, portions of it are used to repay debt, finance expansion plans, repurchase company shares, and so on.

The ratio analysis above illustrates that the net free cash flow generated by Saputo decreased by 7.6% in 2014, falling from $468,456 in 2013 to $432,939 in 2014. While the decrease is not a positive sign, we can see that the company continues to generate significant net free cash flow, which provides it with additional financial flexibility.

LIMITATIONS OF RATIO ANALYSIS

What are the limitations of ratio analysis?

LEARNING OBJECTIVE 8
Identify and explain the limitations of ratio analysis.

It is important to be aware of a number of limitations inherent in ratio analysis. These must be considered when performing ratio analysis or interpreting its results. These limitations include:

1. **Accounting policies**
   As we have discussed throughout the text, a company's accounting policies will affect its results. Public companies in Canada use IFRS, but some also use U.S. accounting standards. You must be aware of significant differences in accounting treatment if you are analyzing the results of companies using different accounting policies. This is also an issue even if the companies being compared both use IFRS, because it allows for some choices and requires assumptions and estimates. For example, some assets and liabilities are carried at historical cost values while others are at market values. Some companies may depreciate their capital assets using the straight-line method, while others may use an accelerated or production-based method. These choices will affect the financial statements and, in turn, the ratios determined based on them.

2. **Definitions of ratios**
   There are often several ways to calculate a given ratio or different names given to the same ratio. Therefore, if you are trying to interpret a ratio that has been calculated by the company and presented in its annual report or is from some other source, it is important that you understand how it was determined before you attempt to interpret it.
3. **Diversity of operations**
   The degree of diversity in a company's operations will affect your ability to interpret ratios related to it. For example, it will be easier to interpret the ratios of a company that operates in one industry, or in one country, than it will be for a multinational company with highly diverse operations. Data on a company's operating segments can help to reduce this concern. While diversity of operations can make it difficult to compare companies, it does not normally affect trend analysis for the same company unless the company's mix of operations has also changed over time, such as if it has acquired or divested of major segments.
4. **Seasonality**
   Companies normally choose to have their financial year end at the end of their business cycle. For example, fashion retailers **Reitmans (Canada) Limited** and **Le Château Inc.** have year ends of January 31, which is after the holiday sales period. Choosing such a year end means that there is less inventory on hand to count; it is easier to make estimates for things like sales returns, bad debts, and warranties; and staff is less busy. It follows that the balances on the statement of financial position may be lower than the average balances for the year and that ratios based on those values will be affected. The effects of seasonality can be somewhat mitigated by using the quarterly financial information that public companies are required to report.
5. **Potential for manipulation**
   Certain ratios, like the current and quick ratios, are based on figures at one point in time. This makes it possible for a company to manipulate them. This can be done by either undertaking or postponing transactions that affect the balances used to calculate the ratio in order to produce a more desirable number. This is sometimes referred to as **window dressing**. For example, a company could choose to delay inventory purchases to enhance its current and quick ratios.

Everything you learned in the previous chapters built up to this one, giving you the knowledge to use various tools, including common financial ratios, to analyze and interpret financial statements. You should now have a solid foundation in financial accounting knowledge that will help you use accounting information to make good decisions in a variety of circumstances.

SUMMARY

1. **Understand and explain the process of financial analysis.**
   - Financial analysis involves evaluating a company's performance based on the information in its financial statements, MD&A, and so on.
   - A basic five-step analysis process includes: (1) determining the purpose or context for the analysis, (2) collecting the required information, (3) preparing common-size analysis and calculating ratios, (4) analyzing and interpreting the common-size analysis and ratios, and (5) developing conclusions and recommendations.
2. **Identify the common contexts for financial statement analysis and explain why an awareness of context is essential to the analysis.**
   - Financial statement analysis is conducted in a variety of contexts, including share purchase/hold/sale decisions, lending decisions, credit application decisions, and corporate acquisitions analysis.
   - The context for the analysis is important in determining the most appropriate tools for the analysis, such as trend analysis (the same company's results over time) or cross-sectional analysis (one company's results relative to another's).
3. **Explain why knowledge of the business is important when analyzing a company's financial statements.**
   - Interpreting the results of ratios and other analysis requires the analyst to have an understanding of the business, including the various activities the company is engaged in and any significant changes to the company's operations during the period being analyzed.

- Companies present information on any distinct operating segments that meet certain thresholds. These segments can be based on different types of businesses the company is involved in or the different geographic regions it operates in, if applicable.
- Understanding a company's strategies is also essential to being able to interpret financial statement analysis correctly.

4. **Identify the types of information used when analyzing financial statements and where it is found.**
   - The primary source of the information used in the analysis is a company's annual report. It includes the company's comparative financial statements, management's discussion and analysis of the most recent results, and the auditors' report.

5. **Explain the various perspectives used in financial statement analysis, including retrospective, prospective, trend, and cross-sectional analysis.**
   - Retrospective analysis is historical analysis (assessing past results), while prospective analysis is forward-looking analysis (trying to determine what the future results may be).
   - There are two major types of retrospective analysis: trend analysis and cross-sectional analysis.
   - Trend analysis involves assessing results over a period of time, such as 3 to 10 years, and looking for patterns or changes over time.
   - Cross-sectional analysis normally involves comparing the results of one company with other companies in the same industry, including competitors. In certain contexts, cross-sectional analysis can also involve comparisons with companies in other industries.

6. **Identify the different metrics used in financial analysis, including common-size analysis and ratio analysis, and explain how they are used.**
   - Common-size analysis involves restating the various amounts in the financial statements into percentages of a specific base amount. For example, statements of income can be restated so that each amount is a percentage of total revenues or statements of financial position can be restated so that each amount is a percentage of total assets. Common-size statements make it easy to identify the degree of changes from period to period.
   - Ratio analysis is also commonly used to assess a company's results from one period to the next or to compare one company with others.
   - Ratios are useful for identifying issues that require further investigation, but do not provide the reason for the changes.
   - There are five common categories of ratios: liquidity, activity, solvency, profitability, and equity analysis ratios.
   - The formulas for the various ratios in each category are presented in Exhibit 12-5.

7. **Identify, calculate, and interpret specific ratios that are used to analyze the liquidity, activity, solvency, profitability, and equity of a company.**
   - The current and quick ratios are used to analyze liquidity.
   - The ratios commonly used to assess activity include accounts receivable turnover, average collection period, inventory turnover, days to sell inventory, accounts payable turnover, and accounts payable payment period ratio.
   - The debt to equity, net debt as a percentage of total capitalization, interest coverage, and cash flows to total liabilities ratios are used to analyze solvency.
   - Profitability is assessed using the gross profit margin, net profit margin, return on equity, and return on assets ratios.
   - Equity analysis uses the basic earnings per share, price/earnings, dividend payout, dividend yield, and net free cash flow ratios.

8. **Identify and explain the limitations of ratio analysis.**
   - The limitations of ratio analysis include companies using different accounting policies or estimates, the existence of different ratio definitions, the challenge of comparing diverse operations, the impacts of seasonality in terms of when ratio analysis is conducted, and the potential for manipulation by management.

KEY TERMS

Accounts payable payment period (560)
Accounts payable turnover (559)
Accounts receivable turnover (556)
Activity ratios (553)
Average collection period (557)
Basic earnings per share (EPS) (564)
Cash flows to total liabilities ratio (560)
Common-size analysis (551)
Common-size statement of financial position (551)
Common-size statement of income (551)
Coverage (560)
Coverage ratios (560)
Cross-sectional analysis (548)
Current ratio (555)
Days to sell inventory ratio (558)
Debt to equity ratio (560)
Diluted earnings per share (565)
Dividend payout ratio (566)
Dividend yield ratio (567)
EBITDAR (547)
Equity analysis ratios (553)
Gross profit margin (562)
Interest coverage ratio (560)
Inventory turnover ratio (558)
Leverage (560)
Leverage ratios (560)
Liquidity ratios (553)
Management discussion and analysis (MD&A) (545)
Net debt as a percentage of total capitalization (560)
Net free cash flow (567)
Net profit margin (562)
Operating efficiency ratios (556)
Operating segments (544)
P/E multiple (565)
Price/earnings (P/E) ratio (565)
Profitability ratios (553)
Prospective analysis (546)
Quick ratio (555)
Red flags (552)
Retrospective analysis (546)
Return on assets (ROA) (563)
Return on equity (ROE) (563)
Solvency ratios (553)
Trend analysis (546)
Window dressing (568)

ABBREVIATIONS USED

EBITDA	Earnings before interest, taxes, depreciation, and amortization
EBITDAR	Earnings before interest, taxes, depreciation, amortization, acquisition, and restructuring
EPS	Earnings per share
MD&A	Management discussion and analysis
P/E ratio	Price/earnings ratio
ROA	Return on assets
ROE	Return on equity

SYNONYMS

Activity ratios | Operating efficiency ratios
Price/earnings (P/E) ratio | P/E multiple

CHAPTER END REVIEW PROBLEM

The consolidated statements of financial position, net earnings and comprehensive income, and cash flows for Dollarama Inc. are presented in Exhibits 12-9A to C. Dollarama is Canada's largest operator of dollar stores. The company's headquarters are in Montreal, and it operates stores in every province.

EXHIBIT 12-9A **DOLLARAMA INC.'S 2014 CONSOLIDATED STATEMENT OF FINANCIAL POSITION**

Dollarama Inc.
Consolidated Statement of Financial Position as at
(Expressed in thousands of Canadian dollars)

	Note	February 2, 2014 $	February 3, 2013 $
Assets			
Current assets			
Cash and cash equivalents		71,470	52,566
Accounts receivable		5,963	5,798
Deposits and prepaid expenses		5,382	5,756
Merchandise inventories		364,680	338,385
Derivative financial instruments	15	11,455	3,710
		458,950	406,215
Non-current assets			
Property and equipment	7	250,612	197,494
Intangible assets	8	129,436	122,201
Goodwill	8	727,782	727,782
Total assets		1,566,780	1,453,692
Liabilities and shareholders' equity			
Current liabilities			
Accounts payable and accrued liabilities	9	128,857	101,286
Dividend payable		9,823	8,099
Income taxes payable		22,102	23,636
Derivative financial instruments	15	–	185
Current portion of finance lease obligations	11	1,022	604
Current portion of long-term debt	10	3,017	–
		164,821	133,810

continued

EXHIBIT 12-9A

DOLLARAMA INC.'S 2014 CONSOLIDATED STATEMENT OF FINANCIAL POSITION (continued)

	Note	February 2, 2014 $	February 3, 2013 $
Non-current liabilities			
Long-term debt	10	395,446	262,071
Finance lease obligations	11	1,484	–
Deferred rent and tenant inducements	12	51,592	45,327
Deferred income taxes	14	89,271	80,994
Total liabilities		702,614	522,202
Commitments	11		
Shareholders' equity			
Share capital	13	493,602	517,306
Contributed surplus		10,884	8,157
Retained earnings		346,478	403,266
Accumulated other comprehensive income	13	13,202	2,761
Total shareholders' equity		864,166	931,490
Total liabilities and shareholders' equity		1,566,780	1,453,692

EXHIBIT 12-9B

DOLLARAMA INC.'S 2014 CONSOLIDATED STATEMENT OF NET EARNINGS AND COMPREHENSIVE INCOME

Dollarama Inc.
Consolidated Statement of Net Earnings and Comprehensive Income for the years ended
(Expressed in thousands of Canadian dollars, except share and per share amounts)

	Note	52-weeks February 2, 2014 $	53-weeks February 3, 2013 $
Sales		2,064,676	1,858,818
Cost of sales		1,299,092	1,163,979
Gross profit		765,584	694,839
General, administrative and store operating expenses		363,182	339,662
Depreciation and amortization	18	47,898	39,284
Operating income		354,504	315,893
Net financing costs	18	11,673	10,839
Earnings before income taxes		342,831	305,054
Provision for income taxes	14	92,737	84,069
Net earnings for the year		250,094	220,985

continued

EXHIBIT 12-9B **DOLLARAMA INC.'S 2014 CONSOLIDATED STATEMENT OF NET EARNINGS AND COMPREHENSIVE INCOME (continued)**

	Note	52-weeks February 2, 2014 $	53-weeks February 3, 2013 $
Other comprehensive income			
Items to be reclassified subsequently to net earnings			
Unrealized gain on derivative financial instruments, net of reclassification adjustment		14,249	1,093
Income taxes relating to component of other comprehensive income		(3,808)	(308)
Total other comprehensive income, net of income taxes		10,441	785
Total comprehensive income for the year		260,535	221,770
Earnings per share			
Basic net earnings per common share	17	$3.48	$3.00
Diluted net earnings per common share	17	$3.47	$2.94
Weighted average number of common shares outstanding during the year (*thousands*)	17	71,838	73,660
Weighted average number of diluted common shares outstanding during the year (*thousands*)	17	72,046	75,190

EXHIBIT 12-9C **DOLLARAMA INC.'S 2014 CONSOLIDATED STATEMENT OF CASH FLOWS**

Dollarama Inc.
Consolidated Statements of Cash Flows for the years ended
(Expressed in thousands of Canadian dollars)

	Note	52-weeks February 2, 2014 $	53-weeks February 3, 2013 $
Cash flows			
Operating activities			
Net earnings for the year		250,094	220,985
Adjustments for:			
Depreciation and amortization	18	47,898	39,284
Interest accrual long-term debt	10	3,017	(216)
Amortization of debt issue costs		592	1,133
Excess of receipts over amount recognized on derivative financial instruments	15	6,319	1,272
Recognition of deferred leasing costs		465	295
Recognition of deferred tenant allowances	12	(3,543)	(2,871)
Deferred lease inducements	12	3,750	5,328
Deferred tenant allowances	12	6,058	6,832
Share-based compensation	13	4,053	1,558
Deferred income taxes	14	4,469	6,921
Loss on disposal of assets		1,017	716
		324,189	281,237

continued

EXHIBIT 12-9C **DOLLARAMA INC.'S 2014 CONSOLIDATED STATEMENT OF CASH FLOWS (continued)**

	Note	52-weeks February 2, 2014 $	53-weeks February 3, 2013 $
Changes in non-cash working capital components	19	(15,811)	(24,198)
Net cash generated from operating activities		308,378	257,039
Investing activities			
Additions to property and equipment	7	(96,303)	(69,577)
Additions to intangible assets	8	(11,095)	(8,210)
Proceeds on disposal of property and equipment		552	256
Net cash used by investing activities		(106,846)	(77,531)
Financing activities			
Proceeds from senior unsecured notes	10	400,000	–
Disbursements on long-term debt		(264,420)	(10,361)
Proceeds from bank indebtedness		166,000	–
Repayment of bank indebtedness		(166,000)	–
Payment of debt issue costs		(2,797)	(837)
Repayment of finance leases		(985)	(695)
Dividends paid		(38,418)	(30,972)
Repurchase and cancellation of shares	13	(277,438)	(155,942)
Issuance of common shares		1,430	1,594
Net cash used by financing activities		(182,628)	(197,213)
Increase (decrease) in cash and cash equivalents		18,904	(17,705)
Cash and cash equivalents – Beginning of year		52,566	70,271
Cash and cash equivalents – End of year		71,470	52,566
Cash payment of interest		6,025	7,639
Cash payment of income taxes		89,801	75,090

Required:
Calculate the following ratios for the year ending February 2, 2014, based on the data provided in Exhibits 12-9A to C. Comment on what the ratios tell you about the company, providing your comments for each of the five categories of ratios (liquidity, activity, solvency, performance, and equity). Also identify any further analysis that should be undertaken.

Short-Term Liquidity Ratios

a. Current ratio
b. Quick ratio

Activity Ratios

c. Accounts receivable turnover and average collection period: because Dollarama does not extend credit to its customers, these ratios are not applicable
d. Inventory turnover and days to sell inventory
e. Accounts payable turnover and accounts payable payment period (assume that trade payables were $58,937 in 2014 and $50,786 in 2013)

Solvency Ratios

f. Debt to equity ratio
g. Net debt as a percentage of total capitalization
h. Interest coverage (assume cash interest payments are equal to interest expense)
i. Cash flow to total liabilities

STRATEGIES FOR SUCCESS

- Print out a copy of Dollarama's financial statements and lay them out so that you can move easily between them without having to flip through the pages of the book. Next, open your textbook to the Ratio Summary (Exhibit 12-5) so that you can easily see the formulas for all of the ratios.
- Determine the information required to calculate each ratio from the financial statements. Calculate each ratio.
- The comments on the ratios are the hardest part, because one ratio by itself tells you only one piece of the story. Refer back to the discussion in your notes, or in the text, regarding what each ratio indicates, and then try to put into words what the amount you have calculated for each ratio means. Don't just comment on each specific ratio, try to keep the category in mind and provide an overall interpretation. Keep in mind the type of operation Dollarama operates. You may have even been in one of the company's stores at some point, so try to draw on this knowledge of its operations as well.

Performance Ratios

j. Gross profit margin
k. Net profit margin
l. Return on equity
m. Return on assets

Equity Analysis Ratios

n. Price/earnings ratio (assume a share price of $84, nearest closing price to year end)
o. Dividend payout ratio (assume that dividends of $0.56 per share were paid during the year)
p. Dividend yield
q. Net free cash flow (assume that there are no preferred shares outstanding)

Suggested Solution to Chapter End Review Problem

Ratios for Dollarama Inc. for the year ending February 2, 2014:

(Amounts used in the ratios are in thousands of dollars.)

Liquidity Ratios

a.	Current Ratio	Current Assets / Current Liabilities	
		$458,950 / $164,821	2.78
b.	Quick Ratio	(Current Assets − Inventory − Prepaid Expenses) / Current Liabilities	
		($458,950 − $364,680 − $5,382) / $164,821	0.54

Activity Ratios

c1.	Accounts Receivable Turnover	Credit Sales / Average Accounts Receivable	
		N/A – Dollarama does not extend credit	N/A
c2.	Average Collection Period	365 days / Accounts Receivable Turnover	
		N/A – Dollarama does not extend credit	N/A
d1.	Inventory Turnover	Cost of Goods Sold / Average Inventory	
		$1,299,092 / (($338,385 + $364,680)/2)	3.70
d2.	Days to Sell Inventory	365 days / Inventory Turnover	
		365 / 3.70	98.6 days
e1.	Accounts Payable Turnover	Credit Purchases / Average Accounts Payable	
		$1,325,387[1] / (($50,786 + $58,937)/2) [1]Credit Purchases = COGS − Beginning Inventory + Ending Inventory = $1,299,092 − $338,385 + $364,680	24.2
e2.	Accounts Payable Payment Period	365 days / Accounts Payable Turnover	
		365 / 24.2	15.1 days

Solvency Ratios

f.	Debt to Equity	$\frac{\text{Net Debt}}{\text{Shareholders' Equity}}$	
		$\frac{\$702,614 - \$71,470}{\$864,166}$	0.73
g.	Net Debt as a Percentage of Total Capitalization	$\frac{\text{Net Debt}}{\text{Shareholders' Equity + Net Debt}}$	
		$\frac{\$702,614 - \$71,470}{\$864,166 + \$702,614 + \$71,470}$	0.422
h.	Interest Coverage	$\frac{\text{EBITDA}}{\text{Interest Expense}}$	
		$\frac{\$342,831 + \$47,898}{\$6,025}$	64.8
i.	Cash Flows to Total Liabilities	$\frac{\text{Cash Flows from Operating Activities}}{\text{Total Liabilities}}$	
		$\frac{\$308,378}{\$702,614}$	0.439

Profitability Ratios

j.	Gross Profit Margin	$\frac{\text{Gross Margin}}{\text{Sales Revenue}}$	
		$\frac{\$765,584}{\$2,064,676}$	0.371
k.	Net Profit Margin	$\frac{\text{Net Income}}{\text{Sales Revenue}}$	
		$\frac{\$250,094}{\$2,064,676}$	0.121
l.	Return on Equity	$\frac{\text{Net Income}}{\text{Average Total Shareholders' Equity}}$	
		$\frac{\$250,094}{(\$931,490 + \$864,166)/2}$	0.279
m.	Return on Assets	$\frac{\text{Net Income}}{\text{Average Total Assets}}$	
		$\frac{\$250,094}{(\$1,453,692 + \$1,566,780)/2}$	0.166

Equity Analysis Ratios

n.	Price/Earnings	$\frac{\text{Market Price per Share}}{\text{Earnings per Share}}$	
		$\frac{\$84.00}{\$3.48}$	24.14
o.	Dividend Payout	$\frac{\text{Dividends per Share}}{\text{Earnings per Share}}$	
		$\frac{\$0.56}{\$3.48}$	0.161
p.	Dividend Yield	$\frac{\text{Dividends per Share}}{\text{Price per Share}}$	
		$\frac{\$0.56}{\$84.00}$	0.007
q.	Net Free Cash Flow	Cash Flows from Operating Activities − Net Capital Expenditures − Dividends on Preferred Shares	
		\$308,378 − \$107,398 − \$0	\$200,980

Liquidity Ratios

The current ratio of 2.78 is considered on the high side and indicates that Dollarama has $2.78 in current assets for each $1 in current liabilities. The much lower quick ratio (0.54) indicates that Dollarama has large amounts of current assets invested in inventories. (Almost 80% of current assets are composed of inventories.) From the statement of financial position, we can see that 78% of the company's current liabilities are related to accounts payable and accrued liabilities. Of these, about half represent trade payables. Assuming that the company can continue to sell its inventory, it should have no difficulty in meeting its current obligations. Overall there appear to be no liquidity concerns for Dollarama.

Activity Ratios

The inventory turnover of 3.7 times indicates that there is enough inventory on hand to cover 98.6 days of sales. This appears a bit slow given the nature of Dollarama's business, but trend analysis and cross-sectional analysis would be needed to substantiate whether there are concerns in this area.

The accounts payable turnover of 24.2 times indicates that the company pays its suppliers an average of 15.1 days after incurring the obligation. To interpret this correctly, you would need to know the terms that Dollarama's suppliers offer. If their terms are net/30 days, then the company is paying too quickly, but we would need to determine if the company receives purchase discounts for quick payment.

The activity ratios paint a picture that is consistent with what we saw from the liquidity analysis: Dollarama is a company that carries considerable inventory, yet pays its suppliers quickly.

Solvency Ratios

Dollarama's debt to equity ratio is 73%, which indicates that the company uses $0.73 in debt financing for every $1 in equity. The net debt to total capitalization ratio indicates that 42.2% of the company's financing is provided by debt. The company had total long-term debt of $398,463 ($3,017 + $395,446), with less than 1% of this due within the next 12 months. We would want to look at the notes to the financial statements to get a sense of when the rest of the long-term debt will be due.

The interest coverage ratio of 64.8 indicates that Dollarama has no issues generating sufficient earnings to cover the interest expense on its debt. The cash flows to total liabilities ratio of 0.439 indicates that the company could repay its entire debt in under two and a half years (1/0.439 = 2.28 years) from operating cash flows. Overall, Dollarama's solvency appears to be sufficient. Its debt levels are supported by strong cash flows.

Profitability Ratios

In analyzing the performance of any company, one of the first things to consider is the net earnings and its trend. Dollarama had net earnings of $250,094 in 2014, which is up 13.2% from 2013. This is a positive trend. The company's net profit margin was 12.1% in 2014, meaning that there was $0.12 in net profit for every $1 in sales. The company's gross profit margin was 37.1% in 2014. Some trend analysis and cross-sectional analysis on gross profit would be very useful in helping us to reach a meaningful conclusion regarding trends and comparative results on this key ratio.

Dollarama had a return of equity of 27.9%, demonstrating that the company did a good job of using leverage to generate returns for shareholders. The company's return on assets was 16.6%. Again, some trend analysis would help us reach conclusions in this area.

Equity Analysis Ratios

Dollarama's P/E ratio of 24.14 shows that its shares are relatively expensive and that the potential for significant capital appreciation may be limited. The company is paying 16.1% of its earnings out to shareholders as dividends, providing them with a limited yield of only 0.7%. The company is generating a significant amount of net free cash flow ($200,980 in 2014), meaning that it has significant internally generated capital to repay debt, pursue additional growth opportunities, or possibly increase its dividends to shareholders.

In conclusion, Dollarama's liquidity, activity, solvency, performance, and equity analysis ratios do not raise any significant concerns. Ratios for more than one year, which would allow for additional trend analysis, and cross-sectional analysis would better support this conclusion and could identify other potential concerns.

ASSIGNMENT MATERIAL

Discussion Questions

DQ12-1 Explain what is meant by the term *financial statement analysis*. What analysis or information might an analyst use in their decision-making process?

DQ12-2 Identify and explain some common contexts in which financial statement analysis is used.

DQ12-3 Briefly describe the steps followed in preparing a financial statement analysis.

DQ12-4 Explain the link between retrospective and prospective analysis. Describe two types of retrospective analysis.

DQ12-5 Explain how the analysis of a company might be different for an investor than a creditor.

DQ12-6 Explain why knowledge of a business is important when using ratio analysis. What aspects of the business should you learn more about?

DQ12-7 What information other than the financial statements would be of interest to an analyst in a company's annual report? Describe how an analyst would use it.

DQ12-8 Explain what an analyst might determine from preparing a common-size statement of income.

DQ12-9 Explain what an analyst might determine from preparing a common-size statement of financial position.

DQ12-10 Explain the difference between trend analysis and cross-sectional analysis and provide an example of when each might be used.

DQ12-11 Identify the five main types of ratios used in this chapter to analyze a company. What does each group of ratios attempt to measure?

DQ12-12 Briefly explain, in your own words, what each of the following ratios helps the analyst to assess and whether the analyst would generally perceive an increase in the ratio as a positive change.

a. Current ratio
b. Quick ratio
c. Accounts receivable turnover
d. Inventory turnover
e. Accounts payable turnover

DQ12-13 Briefly explain, in your own words, what each of the following ratios helps the analyst to assess and whether the analyst would generally perceive an increase in the ratio as a positive change.

a. Debt to equity ratio
b. Net debt as a percentage of total capitalization
c. Interest coverage
d. Cash flows to total liabilities
e. Gross profit margin
f. Net profit margin
g. Return on equity
h. Return on assets

DQ12-14 Briefly explain, in your own words, what each of the following ratios helps the analyst to assess and whether the analyst would generally perceive an increase in the ratio as a positive change.

a. Basic earnings per share
b. Price/earnings
c. Dividend payout
d. Dividend yield
e. Net free cash flow

DQ12-15 Contrast liquidity and solvency ratios in terms of what each category is used to assess.

DQ12-16 Briefly explain the difference between basic EPS and diluted EPS.

DQ12-17 Briefly explain why the dividend yield does not fully capture the return realized by a shareholder during the period.

DQ12-18 Explain how the accounts receivable and inventory turnover ratios can be useful in assessing a company's liquidity, especially when considered together with the current ratio.

DQ12-19 Why are ratios that use cash flows useful under accrual-based accounting?

DQ12-20 Explain how two companies in the same business (use retail clothing stores as an example) can earn the same profit (or net income), yet have very different operating strategies and different net profit margin ratios.

DQ12-21 Explain how the current ratio can be manipulated as a measure of liquidity.

DQ12-22 Explain the limitations of ratio analysis.

Application Problems

AP12-1 (Common-size analysis and differences in profitability)

Comparative financial statement data for First Ltd. and Foremost Ltd., two competitors, follow:

	First Ltd.		Foremost Ltd.	
	2016	2015	2016	2015
Net sales	$337,500		$1,950,000	
Cost of goods sold	202,500		1,092,000	
Operating expenses	68,250		468,000	
Interest expense	3,375		37,800	
Income tax expense	17,400		70,500	
Current assets	165,000	$142,500	1,020,000	$ 780,000
Capital assets (net)	420,000	367,500	1,530,000	1,425,000
Current liabilities	52,500	42,750	225,000	2,400,000
Long-term liabilities	67,500	95,250	630,000	540,000
Share capital	345,000	270,000	1,200,000	1,125,000
Retained earnings	120,000	102,000	495,000	300,000

Required:

a. Prepare a common-size analysis of the 2016 statement of income data for First Ltd. and Foremost Ltd.
b. Calculate the return on assets and the return on shareholders' equity for both companies.
c. Comment on the relative profitability of these companies.
d. Based on your calculations above, identify two main reasons for the difference in their profitability.

AP12-2 (Common-size analysis and differences in profitability and leverage)

Comparative financial statement data for Cool Brewery Ltd. and Northern Beer Ltd., two competitors, follow (amounts in thousands):

	Cool Brewery Ltd.		Northern Beer Ltd.	
	2016	2015	2016	2015
Net sales	$206,700		$40,500	
Cost of goods sold	100,500		15,300	
Operating expenses	85,400		17,190	
Interest expense	7,800		370	
Income tax expense	4,700		1,130	
Cash	12,000	$ 10,000	4,500	$ 2,500
Other current assets	86,000	80,500	8,200	7,400
Long-term assets (net)	210,000	209,600	29,100	30,700
Current liabilities	71,900	60,800	3,900	4,000
Long-term liabilities	103,900	117,500	8,000	7,400
Share capital	51,200	48,500	17,800	16,700
Retained earnings	81,000	73,300	12,100	12,500

Required:

a. Prepare a common-size analysis for 2016 for Cool Brewery Ltd. and Northern Beer Ltd.
b. Calculate the return on assets and the return on shareholders' equity for both companies.
c. Comment on the relative profitability of these companies.
d. Based on your calculations above, identify two main reasons for the difference in their profitability.

e. Calculate the debt to equity ratio for both companies at the end of 2016.
f. Calculate the net debt as a percentage of total capitalization for both companies.
g. Compare the use of leverage by these companies based on the ratios calculated in parts "e" and "f."

AP12-3 (Liquidity and profitability analysis)

Cathy's Cuisine Ltd. is a small restaurant and catering business started three years ago by Cathy Crosby. Initially the company's operations consisted of a small diner. In 2015, the company added the catering services as a way to expand sales without having to add space for seats. As the catering side of the business grew in 2016, the company purchased a used vehicle for deliveries. All sales in the diner are cash, debit, or credit card, but for catering jobs, customers are invoiced after the event. Most of the company's suppliers offer terms of 30 days. Selected financial information for Cathy's Cuisine Ltd. follows.

	2016	2015
Assets		
Cash	$ 8,600	$ 3,200
Accounts receivable	15,500	10,000
Inventory	10,900	6,000
Land	15,000	15,000
Building and equipment	30,000	25,000
Total assets	$ 80,000	$ 59,200
Liabilities and Equity		
Accounts payable	$ 9,500	$ 8,000
Short-term note payable	1,800	0
Mortgage payable current	2,500	2,500
Mortgage payable	22,500	25,000
Share capital	12,000	12,000
Retained earnings	31,700	11,700
Total liabilities and equity	$ 80,000	$ 59,200
Other information		
Sales	$180,000	$150,000
Cost of goods sold	80,000	75,000
Net income	20,000	5,500

Required:

a. Assume the growth in sales in 2016 is primarily from the catering business. Calculate the gross profit margins and the net profit margins and comment on whether you think the company should be focusing on the catering business or the diner.
b. Calculate the company's current ratio and quick ratio for both years and comment on the company's liquidity. Do you think the company is more liquid or less in 2016? What items on the statement of financial position support your position?
c. Calculate the company's accounts receivable turnover ratio for 2016. How quickly is the company collecting its receivables? Do you think it is doing a good job of managing its receivables?
d. Assume that 50% of the sales come from the catering business and recalculate the accounts receivable turnover for 2016. How does that affect your assessment of how receivables are being managed?
e. Calculate the company's inventory turnover ratio for 2016.
f. Calculate the company's accounts payable turnover ratio for 2016. Are suppliers being paid on time?
g. Using your analysis of the company's receivables and payables, what would you recommend be done to improve the management of those accounts?
h. Prepare a brief memo to Cathy outlining why it may be useful to break out the company's financial results by segment (diner and catering).

AP12-4 (Liquidity ratios)

The financial data for Alouette Resources Ltd. are as follows (amounts in thousands):

	2013	2014	2015	2016
Current assets				
Cash	$ 240	$ 160	$ 280	$ 320
Accounts receivable	800	1,040	960	860
Inventories	1,300	1,840	2,480	3,620
Prepaid expenses	200	200	300	200
	$2,540	$3,240	$4,020	$5,000
Current liabilities				
Accounts payable	$1,200	$1,320	$1,560	$1,640
Accrued salaries	140	200	240	300
Other current liabilities	200	300	320	600
	$1,540	$1,820	$2,120	$2,540

Required:

a. Calculate the current and quick ratios for 2013 through 2016.
b. Comment on the short-term liquidity position of Alouette.
c. Is your analysis is part "a" a trend analysis or a cross-sectional analysis? What is this type of analysis most useful for?
d. Which ratio do you think is the better measure of short-term liquidity for Alouette? Can you tell? Explain. What would your answer depend on?

AP12-5 (Basic strategies)

You are considering investing in the retail sector and have identified two companies for further analysis. Financial information for the two companies is as follows:

(in thousands)	Company A	Company B
Sales	$1,250,000	$1,400,000
Cost of goods sold	687,500	980,000
Net income	100,000	63,000
Average inventory	215,800	150,600
Average total assets	833,333	525,555

Required:

a. Calculate and compare the following ratios for the two companies:
   i. Return on assets
   ii. Gross margin
   iii. Net profit margin
   iv. Inventory turnover
   v. Days to sell inventory
b. Which company is likely following a low-cost producer strategy? Support your conclusion with reference to the ratios in part "a." What strategy might the other company be following?

AP12-6 (Accounts receivable turnover)

The financial data for Michaels' Foods Inc. and Sunshine Enterprises Ltd. for the current year are as follows (amounts in thousands):

	Annual Sales	Accounts Receivable Jan. 1	Accounts Receivable Dec. 31
Michaels' Foods	$60,600	$6,200	$8,100
Sunshine Enterprises	30,100	1,800	2,050

Required:

a. Calculate the accounts receivable turnover for each company assuming that all sales are on account.
b. Calculate the average number of days required by each company to collect its receivables.
c. Which company appears to be more efficient at handling its accounts receivable?
d. What additional information would be helpful in evaluating management's handling of the collection of accounts receivable?

AP12-7 (Inventory turnover)

Information on the activities of Novel-T Toys Ltd. is as follows:

	2012	2013	2014	2015	2016
Cost of goods sold	$893,100	$1,002,700	$1,174,500	$1,326,300	$1,391,780
Average inventory	128,450	157,100	206,310	323,420	442,990

Required:

a. Do a trend analysis of the inventory turnover for each year. Also calculate the days to sell inventory ratio for the respective years.
b. Is Novel-T Toy Ltd. managing its inventories efficiently? Do you have enough information to answer this question? If not, what else do you need to know?
c. Provide an example of a situation where management may deliberately reduce inventory turnover, but still be operating in the company's best long-term interests.

AP12-8 (Inventory turnover)

The financial data for Ken's Fresh Fruits Incorporated and Al's Supermarket Ltd. for the current year are as follows:

	Annual Cost of Goods Sold	Inventory Jan. 1	Inventory Dec. 31
Ken's Fresh Fruits	$ 9,875,600	$ 695,000	$ 695,600
Al's Supermarket	53,885,000	4,776,500	1,040,500

Required:

a. Calculate the inventory turnover for each company.
b. Calculate the days to sell inventory ratio for each company.
c. Knowing the type of inventory these companies sell, comment on the reasonableness of the inventory turnover. Which company manages its inventory more efficiently?
d. Which company would be a more profitable investment? Can we tell? Explain.
e. What are the potential problems with fast inventory turnovers? Would these be a concern for Ken's Fresh Fruits?

AP12-9 (Liquidity ratios and limitations)

Manitoba Manufacturing Inc. (MMI) has a loan from the Canadian National Bank to help finance its working capital. The terms of the loan are that the bank will lend MMI an amount up to 33% of its inventory balance and 50% of its accounts receivable. One of the loan covenants requires that MMI maintain a current ratio greater than 2.0. Information related to MMI's current assets and current liabilities is shown in the following table:

In thousands	2016	2015
Cash	$ 115	$ 160
Accounts receivable	875	870
Inventory	1,930	1,650
Other current assets	240	280
Bank loan, current	400	200
Accounts payable	995	950
Other current liabilities	40	80

Required:

a. Does MMI satisfy the loan covenant in both years?
b. Based on the loan size requirement only of the loan covenant, what is the maximum amount of loan MMI could borrow in each year?
c. Based on a review of the accounts receivable balances, do you think sales have grown for MMI in 2016 over 2015?
d. Identify three different ways management could have "managed" the statement of financial position to ensure that MMI met the loan covenant in 2016.

AP12-10 (Analysis using selected ratios)

The following ratios and other information are based on a company's comparative financial statements for a two-year period:

	2016	2015
Current ratio	1.84	2.20
Quick ratio	1.07	0.89
Net debt as a percentage of total capitalization ratio	0.43	0.58
Debt to equity ratio	0.75	1.38
Earnings per share	$ 0.24	$ 0.15
Gross profit margin	42.3%	45.6%
Total assets	$2,143,702	$3,574,825
Current assets	$ 965,118	$1,462,763

Required:

a. What is the amount of current liabilities at the end of 2016?
b. What is the amount of total debt at the end of 2016?
c. What is the total shareholders' equity at the end of 2016?
d. Do you think this company is a retail company, a financial institution, or a service organization? Explain.
e. If the company has 1,650,200 common shares outstanding during 2016 and has issued no other shares, what was its net income for 2016?
f. Based on the information available, what is your assessment of the company's liquidity? Explain.
g. Given the limited information, what is your assessment of the company's overall financial position? Explain, identifying what changes you see between 2015 and 2016 that appear particularly significant.
h. What changes do you see between 2015 and 2016 that appear particularly significant? What explanations might there be for the changes identified in "g"?

AP12-11 (Analysis using selected ratios)

HomeStar Ltd. is a chain of retail hardware stores with total assets of $2.5 billion. Selected financial ratios for HomeStar are as follows:

	2016	2015	2014
Current ratio	2.35	2.38	2.39
Quick ratio	0.56	0.51	0.58
Inventory turnover	5.57	5.33	5.27
Debt to equity ratio	0.68	0.87	0.86
Return on assets	7.3%	9.0%	9.8%
Gross profit margin	7.71%	8.36%	8.73%
Net profit margin	3.28%	3.87%	4.19%
Return on equity	11.4%	15.1%	16.8%

In 2014, HomeStar was affected by a decline in the demand for home hardware items and the entry of a major U.S. chain into the market.

Required:

a. Briefly discuss what these financial ratios indicate about how HomeStar was affected by the events of 2014.
b. Which measures have deteriorated during the subsequent periods?
c. Which ratios indicate positive action taken by HomeStar during the subsequent periods?

AP12-12 (Activity ratios)

The following financial information is for Ambroise Industries Inc.:

	2016	2015
Sales	$5,000,000	$4,500,000
Cost of goods sold	2,250,000	2,025,000
Accounts receivable	585,500	558,800
Inventory	770,800	707,400
Accounts payable	200,750	195,250
Total assets	1,875,200	1,690,500

Ambroise is a distributor of auto parts operating in eastern Ontario that offers 30-day terms and has all sales on credit. The company has a large inventory due to the number of parts it stocks for different makes and models of cars. Most of its suppliers offer terms of 30 days, and Ambroise tries to stay on good terms with its suppliers by paying on time.

Required:

a. What is the average time it takes Ambroise to collect its accounts receivable? How does that compare with the credit terms that the company offers?
b. What is the average length of time that it takes Ambroise to sell through its inventory?
c. What is the average length of time that it takes Ambroise to pay its payables? How does that compare with the credit terms it is offered?
d. The cash-to-cash cycle is the length of time from when a company purchases an item of inventory to when it collects cash from its sale, reduced by the days it takes to pay the related accounts payable. How long is Ambroise's cash-to-cash cycle?
e. Assume that Ambroise finances its inventory with a working capital loan from the bank. If Ambroise could improve its inventory management system and reduce the days to sell inventory to an average of 50 days, how much lower would the company's bank loan be?

AP12-13 (ROE, ROA, and gross profit)

The following financial information relates to Smooth Suds Brewery Ltd. (amounts in thousands):

	2014	2015	2016
Sales	$18,360	$25,840	$36,120
Average total assets	23,715	31,965	47,340
Average shareholders' equity	14,664	22,415	31,515
Net income	715	1,845	3,580
Gross profit	9,180	13,954	19,866

Required:

For each year:

a. Calculate the return on equity. Comment on the trend in this ratio.
b. Calculate the return on assets. Comment on the trend in this ratio.
c. Calculate the company's gross profit margin. Comment on the trend in this ratio.
d. Comment on the profitability of Smooth Suds Brewery Ltd.

AP12-14 **(Debt to equity, debt as a percentage of total capitalization, and interest coverage)**

Artscan Enterprises' financial data are as follows:

	2014	2015	2016
Income before depreciation, amortization, interest, and taxes	$1,650	$2,625	$3,300
Interest expense	150	340	435
Cash	50	115	225
Current liabilities (does not include any debt)	600	800	1,200
Bank loan payable (all long-term)	2,000	4,000	4,500
Shareholders' equity	4,250	5,500	7,250

Required:

a. Calculate the debt to equity, net debt as a percentage of total capitalization, and interest coverage ratios.
b. Comment on the solvency position of Artscan Enterprises.

AP12-15 **(Debt to equity, debt as a percentage of total capitalization, and interest coverage)**

Silver City Ltd.'s financial data are as follows:

	2014	2015	2016
EBIT { Income before depreciation, amortization, interest, and taxes	$6,900	$7,200	$5,700
Interest expense	380	340	280
Cash	200	260	310
Current liabilities (does not include any debt)	1,010	1,900	2,700
Bank loan payable (all long-term)	5,500	6,100	5,200
Shareholders' equity	6,500	6,900	7,600

Required:

a. Calculate the debt to equity, debt as a percentage of total capitalization, and interest coverage ratios.
b. Comment on the solvency position of Silver City Ltd.

AP12-16 **(Transaction effects on ratios)**

Two lists follow: one for ratios (including the ratio prior to the transactions) and another for transactions.

Ratios:

1. Current ratio, 1.2:1
2. Quick ratio, 0.6:1
3. Accounts receivable turnover, 12 times
4. Inventory turnover, 6 times
5. Return on assets, 10%
6. Return on equity, 15%

Transactions:

1. Goods costing $200,000 are sold to customers on credit for $380,000.
2. Accounts receivable of $140,000 are collected.
3. Inventory costing $110,000 is purchased from suppliers.
4. A long-term bank loan for $500,000 is arranged with the bank, and the company receives the cash at the beginning of the year.
5. The bank loan carries an interest rate of 18% and the interest payment is made at the end of the year. Assume no interest expense had previously been recognized.
6. The company uses $40,000 to buy short-term investments.
7. New common shares are issued for $250,000.

Required:

State the immediate effect (increase, decrease, or no effect) of each transaction on each ratio. You may want to format your answer in a table with the ratios across the top, and the transactions down the left side.

AP12-17 **(Asset investment effect on ratios)**

Beachwood Manufacturing Inc., a manufacturer of wood furniture in Nova Scotia, has approached you to make a private equity investment in the company. The owner has provided you with financial statements for the years ended December 31 and other relevant information. Selected data for the past three years are as follows:

In thousands $	2016	2015	2014
Cash	$ 5,900	$ 3,200	$ 1,450
Accounts receivable	8,800	6,800	6,200
Inventory	9,500	7,000	6,850
Property, plant, and equipment	20,300	15,000	15,500
Total assets	44,500	32,000	30,000
Current liabilities (does not include any debt)	14,000	13,000	12,500
Long-term debt	18,000	8,000	8,000
Total shareholders' equity	12,500	11,000	9,500
Sales revenue	50,000	48,000	45,000
Cost of goods sold	30,000	28,800	27,450
Earnings before interest and taxes	6,953	6,245	6,030
Interest expense	1,620	1,245	1,230
Earnings before taxes	5,333	5,000	4,800
Net income	4,000	3,750	3,600

Other information:

On December 30, 2016, Beachwood purchased the assets of another small furniture manufacturer as part of an expansion plan. Beachwood paid $10 million for the assets and financed them entirely by borrowing. Beachwood is seeking a private equity investor to invest $8 million and will use the proceeds to reduce the debt from the purchase. The $10 million purchase consisted of $2 million of accounts receivable, $2.2 million of inventory, and $5.8 million of property, plant, and equipment.

Required:

a. Start your analysis by reviewing the company's historical performance. Calculate and comment on the receivables and inventory turnover ratios for the three years. For 2014, use year-end values, not averages, for the assets in your calculations.

b. Next, review the solvency and profitability of the company. Calculate and comment on the debt to equity, interest coverage, return on assets, and return on equity for the company. For 2014, use year-end values, not averages, for the assets and equity in your calculations.

c. You realize that Beachwood bought a large amount of assets right at the year end and that those assets are included on the 2016 statement of financial position, but that the company has not used them yet to generate any sales. Therefore, including the assets in your values distorts your analysis. You decide to recalculate the turnover ratios and return on assets excluding the new assets. Comment on your results.

d. Finally, adjust the liability and equity side of the 2016 statement of financial position to see what it will look like once the company obtains the new equity financing and pays down the debt. Recalculate the debt to equity ratio and return on equity under the new capital structure. Comment on your results.

e. Assume that, as a result of the acquisition, Beachwood expects its sales revenue to grow at 1.3 times the growth experienced in 2016, while its gross margin percentage will remain constant. What impact would this have on the company's 2017 gross margin?

f. Comment on the usefulness of retrospective analysis and of using the financial statements alone to make investment decisions.

AP12-18 (Equity analysis ratios)

Two companies in the transportation industry had the following information:

	Company 1	Company 2
Basic earnings per share	$ 0.87	$ 0.67
Market price per share	$ 11.82	$ 25.26
Dividends per share	$ 0.475	$ 0.535
Cash flows from operating activities ($ thousands)	$64,621	$235,786
Net capital expenditures ($ thousands)	$ 6,155	$ 75,042

Required:

a. Calculate the P/E ratios for both companies and comment on which is more affordable from that perspective.

b. Calculate the dividend payout ratio and dividend yield for both companies and comment on the results.

c. Determine the net free cash flows of both companies. Comment on what these amounts represent.
d. What picture do you have of each company based on the financial information provided and the ratios you have calculated?

AP12-19 (Analysis of assets)

You have inherited money from your grandparents and a friend suggests that you consider buying shares in Galena Ski Products, which manufactures skis and bindings. Because you may need to sell the shares within the next two years to finance your university education, you start your analysis of the company data by calculating (1) working capital, (2) the current ratio, and (3) the quick ratio. Galena's statement of financial position is as follows:

Current assets	
Cash	$154,000
Inventory	185,000
Prepaid expenses	21,000
Non-current assets	
Land	50,000
Building and equipment	145,000
Other	15,000
Total	$570,000
Current liabilities	$165,000
Long-term debt	190,000
Share capital	80,000
Retained earnings	135,000
Total	$570,000

Required:

a. What amount of working capital is currently maintained? Comment on the adequacy of this amount.
b. Your preference is to have a quick ratio of at least 0.80 and a current ratio of at least 2.00. How do the existing ratios compare with your criteria? Based on these two ratios, how would you evaluate the company's current asset position?
c. The company currently sells only on a cash basis and had sales of $900,000 this past year. How would you expect a change from cash to credit sales to affect the current and quick ratios?
d. Galena's statement of financial position is presented just before the company begins making shipments to retailers for its fall and winter season. How would your evaluation change if these balances existed in late February, following completion of its primary business for the skiing season?
e. How would Galena's situation as either a public company or private company affect your decision to invest?

AP12-20 (Ratio analysis over time)

The following information comes from the accounting records of Hercep Ltd. for the first three years of its existence:

	2014	2015	2016
Statement of Financial Position			
Assets			
Cash	$ 22,500	$ 20,000	$ 25,000
Accounts receivable	67,500	50,000	145,000
Inventory	110,000	130,000	220,000
Capital assets (net)	430,000	450,000	500,000
Other assets	232,000	210,000	266,400
	$862,000	$860,000	$1,156,400
Liabilities and equity			
Accounts payable	$100,000	$ 50,000	$ 100,000
Long-term debt	200,000	250,000	500,000
Common shares	525,000	525,000	525,000
Retained earnings	37,000	35,000	31,400
	$862,000	$860,000	$1,156,400

	2014	2015	2016
Statement of Earnings			
Sales	$ 700,000	$ 800,000	$ 900,000
Cost of goods sold	(420,000)	(540,000)	(630,000)
Other expenses	(170,000)	(220,000)	(218,000)
	110,000	40,000	52,000
Income tax	(33,000)	(12,000)	(15,600)
Net income	$ 77,000	$ 28,000	$ 36,400

Required:

a. Based on above information, analyze and comment on the changes in the company's profitability and liquidity, in addition to the management of accounts receivable and inventory from 2014 to 2016.
b. Based on the above information, analyze and comment on the company's use of leverage from 2014 to 2016.

AP12-21 **(Ratio analysis of two companies)**

You have obtained the financial statements of A-Tec and Bi-Sci, two new companies in the high-tech industry. Both companies have just completed their second full year of operations. You have acquired the following information for an analysis of the companies (amounts in thousands):

	A-Tec		Bi-Sci	
	2016	2015	2016	2015
Cash	$ 10	$ 0	$ 25	$ 25
Accounts receivable	195	140	120	100
Inventory	130	100	110	100
Prepaid expenses	5	5	5	5
Capital assets (net)	350	300	230	160
Current liabilities	110	125	50	50
Long-term debt	200	220	0	0
Share capital—common shares	100	100	220	220
Retained earnings	280	100	220	120
Sales (all credit sales)	1,900	1,300	1,250	1,200
Cost of goods sold	1,250	900	910	900
Interest expense	20	22	–	–
Taxes (30%)	77	56	64	56
Net income	180	130	150	130

Required:

a. Calculate the following ratios for the two companies for the two years:
   i. Current ratio
   ii. Accounts receivable turnover
   iii. Inventory turnover
   iv. Debt to equity
   v. Interest coverage
   vi. Gross margin ratio
   vii. Net profit margin
   viii. Return on assets
   ix. Return on equity
b. Write a brief analysis of the two companies based on the information given and the ratios calculated. Be sure to discuss issues of short-term liquidity, activity, solvency, and profitability. Which company appears to be the better investment for the shareholder? Explain. Which company appears to be the better credit risk for the lender? Explain. Is there any other information you would like to have to complete your analysis?

AP12-22 (Compare ratios and comment on results)

Selected financial data for two intense competitors in a recent year follow (amounts in millions):

	Zeus Corporation	Mars Company
Statement of income data:		
Net sales	$3,350	$ 6,810
Cost of goods sold	2,980	5,740
Selling and administrative expenses	95	410
Interest expense	130	175
Other expenses	8	0
Income taxes	62	110
Net income	$ 75	$ 375
Statement of cash flows data:		
Net cash inflow from operating activities	$ 125	$ 260
Net increase in cash during the year	10	37
Statement of financial position data:		
End-of-year balances:		
Current assets	$1,020	$1,620
Property, plant, and equipment (net)	1,865	2,940
Other assets	720	1,020
Total assets	$3,605	$5,580
Current liabilities	$ 575	$ 830
Long-term debt	2,220	3,130
Total shareholders' equity	810	1,620
Total liabilities and shareholders' equity	$3,605	$5,580
Beginning-of-year balances:		
Total assets	$3,250	$5,160
Total shareholders' equity	750	1,245
Other data:		
Average net receivables	$ 350	$ 790
Average inventory	290	575

Required:

a. For each company, calculate the following ratios:
   i. Average collection period for receivables
   ii. Days to sell inventory
   iii. Current ratio
   iv. Net debt as a percentage of total capitalization
   v. Interest coverage
   vi. Return on assets
   vii. Return on equity

b. Compare the financial position and performance of the two companies, and comment on their relative strengths and weaknesses.

User Perspective Problems

UP12-1 (Use of ratios in debt restrictions)

Contracts with lenders typically place restrictions on a company's activities in an attempt to ensure that the company will be able to repay both the interest and the principal on the debt owed to the lenders. These restrictions are frequently stated in terms of ratios. For instance, a restriction could be that the debt to equity ratio cannot exceed 1.0. If it does exceed 1.0, the debt covered by the restrictions becomes due immediately. The other commonly used ratio is the current ratio.

Required:
Explain why the debt to equity and current ratios might be used as restrictions. How do they protect the lender?

UP12-2 (Cross-sectional analysis)

Required:
In using cross-sectional analysis to evaluate performance, what factors should an investor match in choosing companies for comparison? Why are these factors important?

UP12-3 (Understanding the business)

Understanding the nature of the business is important for analysts. It helps them interpret the results but it also helps them focus their analysis on the ratios that are key for the industry or strategy being pursued.

Required:

a. From the ratios discussed in the chapter, identify three ratios you think would be key measures of performance for a retail clothing business that operates inside malls.
b. Which ratios would be key measures of performance or efficiency for a hydroelectric utility?

UP12-4 (Use of ROA in performance measurement)

Management compensation plans typically specify performance criteria in terms of financial statement ratios. For instance, a plan might specify that management must achieve a certain level of return on investment—for example, ROA.

Required:
If managers were trying to maximize their compensation, how could they manipulate the ROA ratio to achieve this goal?

UP12-5 (Use of cash flow ratios)

There is judgement involved in preparing financial statements. For example, management must often estimate warranty expense and bad debts expense. Management may also need to select an accounting policy if accounting standards allow a choice. Ultimately, these estimates and decisions affect the determination of net income.

Required:
Do you believe that financial statement ratios using cash flows are more reliable than measures of performance that use net income? Discuss.

UP12-6 (Types of information)

A friend of yours has received a scholarship and wants to invest the funds for a year, because she earned enough money in her summer job to pay for her current academic year. She explains to you that she went to an on-line investing site that had lots of ratios calculated for companies and has selected the company with the highest ROE to invest in. She has asked your advice on if there is any information other than ratios she should be considering and what you think of her decision to select based on ROE.

Required:

a. Explain to your friend that, although ratio analysis provides a good indication as to a company's financial strength, there is much more information available that an informed investor should consider before making any investment decisions. Provide her with several examples of additional information to consider.
b. Comment on your friend's choice of ROE as the sole criterion.

UP12-7 (Using ratios to evaluate creditworthiness)

You are the lending officer in a bank and a new customer has approached you for a working capital loan. A working capital loan is intended to help a business finance the fluctuations in daily cash flows that arise from long cash-to-cash cycles in operating a business.

Required:
Explain how you would use the accounts receivable turnover ratio, inventory turnover ratio, and accounts payable turnover ratio to assist you in your analysis.

UP12-8 (Use of ratios in decision-making)

Managers, investors, and creditors usually have a specific focus when making decisions about a business.

Required:
Each of the following independent cases asks one or more questions. Identify the ratio or ratios that would help the user answer the question and/or identify areas for further analysis:

a. A company's net income has declined. Is the decrease in net income due to:
   i. a decrease in sales or an increase in cost of goods sold?
   ii. an increase in total operating expenses?
   iii. an increase in a specific expense, such as tax expense?
b. Is the company collecting its accounts receivable on a timely basis?
c. Does the company rely more heavily on long-term debt financing than other companies in the same industry?
d. In a comparison of two companies, which company is using its assets more effectively?
e. In a comparison of two companies, which company has used the capital invested in it more profitably?
f. Has the decline in the economy affected the company's ability to pay its accounts payable?
g. Has the company been successful in reducing its investment in inventories as a result of installing a new ordering system?

UP12-9 (Discuss value of comparability)

One enhancing qualitative characteristic that underlies financial accounting is comparability. As you will recall, comparability is the similarities of financial information between different companies, and consistency of the financial information produced by a company over time, that allows financial statement users to make meaningful and equal comparisons. Two of the many ways of achieving comparability for users are by limiting the number of different ways transactions may be recorded, and by specifying how assets, liabilities, equities, revenues, and expenses will be reported in the financial statements.

One argument against comparability is that it limits companies' ability to choose among accounting methods, and thus may result in financial reports that may not be agreeable to management or best suited to the particular circumstances.

Required:
Discuss the pros and cons of limiting accounting choices, with reference to the analysis of financial statements.

Reading and Interpreting Published Financial Statements

RI12-1 (Ratio analysis for public company)

The financial statements for **Danier Leather Inc.** are in Appendix A.

Required:
Use the financial statements to answer the following questions:

a. Calculate the following ratios for 2014 and 2013. For the 2013 ratios, use the year-end balance sheet amounts, rather than an average for the year.
   i. Gross profit margin
   ii. Net profit margin
   iii. Inventory turnover
   iv. Debt to equity and net debt as a percentage of total capitalization
   v. Return on assets and return on equity
b. Comment on Danier's profitability and use of leverage over the period.
c. Calculate and comment on Danier's current ratio and quick ratio for both years. What factor leads these ratios to be high for Danier? Why might your interpretation of its current ratio depend on if you were an investor or a creditor?

RI12-2 (Comparison of two companies in same industry)

The balance sheets and statements of earnings and loss for **Le Château Inc.** are in Exhibits 12-11A and B. In Canada, Le Château and Danier Leather are both in the fashion industry. Both companies manufacture and retail goods, although they sell in different segments of the fashion market. Danier operates in the niche segment of quality leather goods, primarily coats and accessories, whereas Le Château sells a wide range of clothing and accessories targeted to the young adult market.

EXHIBIT 12-11A **LE CHÂTEAU INC.'S 2014 CONSOLIDATED BALANCE SHEETS**

CONSOLIDATED BALANCE SHEETS

As at January 25, 2014 and January 26, 2013
[In thousands of Canadian dollars]

	2014	2013
	$	$
ASSETS		
Current assets		
Cash	**1,446**	1,783
Accounts receivable *[note 6]*	**1,476**	1,906
Income taxes refundable	**6,663**	3,211
Derivative financial instruments	**418**	215
Inventories *[notes 6 and 7]*	**124,878**	123,218
Prepaid expenses	**2,292**	1,890
Total current assets	**137,173**	132,223
Property and equipment *[notes 8 and 12]*	**69,870**	83,315
Intangible assets *[note 9]*	**3,815**	4,672
	210,858	220,210
LIABILITIES AND SHAREHOLDERS' EQUITY		
Current liabilities		
Bank indebtedness *[note 6]*	**30,767**	13,034
Trade and other payables *[note 10]*	**19,553**	20,718
Deferred revenue	**3,712**	3,558
Current portion of provisions *[note 11]*	**265**	228
Current portion of long-term debt *[note 12]*	**7,987**	9,844
Total current liabilities	**62,284**	47,382
Long-term debt *[note 12]*	**7,843**	14,290
Provisions *[note 11]*	**391**	530
Deferred income taxes *[note 14]*	**1,829**	2,298
Deferred lease credits	**13,412**	15,912
Total liabilities	**85,759**	80,412
Shareholders' equity		
Share capital *[note 13]*	**42,960**	42,740
Contributed surplus	**3,581**	2,664
Retained earnings	**78,253**	94,239
Accumulated other comprehensive income	**305**	155
Total shareholders' equity	**125,099**	139,798
	210,858	220,210

EXHIBIT 12-11B **LE CHÂTEAU INC.'S 2014 CONSOLIDATED STATEMENTS OF LOSS**

CONSOLIDATED STATEMENTS OF LOSS

Years ended January 25, 2014 and January 26, 2013
[in thousands of Canadian dollars, except per share information]

	2014 **$**	2013 $
Sales *[note 20]*	**274,840**	274,827
Cost of sales and expenses		
Cost of sales *[note 7]*	**101,770**	92,565
Selling *[note 8]*	**155,859**	155,561
General and administrative *[notes 8 and 9]*	**36,218**	35,847
	293,847	283,973
Results from operating activities	**(19,007)**	(9,146)
Finance costs	**2,714**	3,063
Finance income	**(13)**	(23)
Loss before income taxes	**(21,708)**	(12,186)
Income tax recovery *[note 14]*	**(5,722)**	(3,469)
Net loss	**(15,986)**	(8,717)
Net loss per share *[note 17]*		
Basic	**(0.59)**	(0.34)
Diluted	**(0.59)**	(0.34)
Weighted average number of shares outstanding	**27,288,766**	25,658,585

Required:

Use the information provided, the ratios you calculated for Danier Leather in problem RI12-1, and Le Château's financial statements to answer the following questions:

a. Prepare a common-size analysis of the statements of income (loss) for the two companies for both years. Why do you think the cost of sales percentages are so different for the two companies? In which areas does Le Château seem to have an advantage? In which areas does Danier have an advantage?
b. Compare the current and quick ratios for the two companies. Which company is more liquid? Are you surprised by the large difference between the current ratio and the quick ratio for the companies? Why or why not?
c. Compare the inventory turnover of the two companies.

RI12-3 (Ratio analysis for public company)

Big Rock Brewery Inc. is Calgary-based public company. The company is a producer of all-natural craft beers and cider. Its products are sold in nine provinces and three territories in Canada. The 2013 consolidated statements of income, financial position, and cash flows are shown in Exhibits 12-12A to C (amounts in thousands).

EXHIBIT 12-12A **BIG ROCK BREWERY INC.'S 2013 CONSOLIDATED STATEMENTS OF COMPREHENSIVE INCOME**

BIG ROCK BREWERY INC.
Consolidated Statements of Comprehensive Income
(In thousands of Canadian dollars, except per share amounts)

	Year ended **December 30, 2013**	December 30, 2012
Net revenue (Notes 3.2 and 4)	**$ 41,587**	$ 46,057
Cost of sales (Notes 5 and 24)	**20,260**	21,149
Gross profit	**21,327**	24,908
Expenses		
Selling expenses (Notes 6 and 23)	**12,910**	13,987
General and administrative (Notes 7 and 24)	**4,821**	4,945
Depreciation and amortization	**314**	358
Operating expenses	**18,045**	19,290

continued

EXHIBIT 12-12A BIG ROCK BREWERY INC.'S 2013 CONSOLIDATED STATEMENTS OF COMPREHENSIVE INCOME (continued)

	Year ended December 30, 2013	Year ended December 30, 2012
Operating profit	**3,282**	5,618
Finance costs (Note 8)	**9**	93
Other income	**286**	351
Other expenses	**109**	147
Income before income taxes	**3,450**	5,729
Current income tax expense (Note 9)	**2,485**	426
Deferred income tax expense (recovery) (Note 9)	**(1,586)**	1,168
Net income and comprehensive income for the period	**$ 2,551**	$ 4,135
Net income per share (Note 10)		
Basic and diluted	**$ 0.42**	$ 0.68

EXHIBIT 12-12B BIG ROCK BREWERY INC.'S 2013 CONSOLIDATED STATEMENTS OF FINANCIAL POSITION

BIG ROCK BREWERY INC.
Consolidated Statements of Financial Position
(In thousands of Canadian dollars)

	December 30, 2013	December 30, 2012
ASSETS		
Non-current assets		
Property, plant and equipment (Note 11)	**$ 35,142**	$ 35,277
Intangible assets (Note 12)	**108**	128
	35,250	35,405
Current		
Inventories (Note 13)	**2,983**	3,892
Accounts receivable (Notes 14 and 22)	**1,353**	2,358
Prepaid expenses and other (Note 15)	**754**	364
Cash	**2,317**	4,281
	7,407	10,895
Total assets	**$ 42,657**	$ 46,300
LIABILITIES AND SHAREHOLDERS' EQUITY		
EQUITY		
Shareholders' capital (Note 16)	**$ 100,109**	$ 100,109
Contributed surplus (Notes 16 and 17)	**892**	701
Accumulated deficit	**(71,043)**	(68,739)
	29,958	32,071
LIABILITIES		
Non-current		
Long term debt (Notes 18 and 22)	**–**	1,342
Share-based payments (Note 17)	**687**	238
Deferred income taxes (Note 9)	**4,745**	6,331
	5,432	7,911
Current		
Accounts payable and accrued liabilities (Notes 19 and 22)	**4,100**	3,978
Dividends payable (Notes 20 and 22)	**1,214**	1,214
Current portion of long-term debt (Notes 18 and 22)	**–**	700
Current taxes payable (Note 9)	**1,953**	426
	7,267	6,318
Commitments (Note 26)		
Total liabilities and shareholders' equity	**$ 42,657**	$ 46,300

EXHIBIT 12-12C **BIG ROCK BREWERY INC.'S 2013 CONSOLIDATED STATEMENTS OF CASH FLOWS**

BIG ROCK BREWERY INC.
Consolidated Statements of Cash Flows
(in thousands of Canadian dollars)

	Year ended	
	December 30, 2013	December 30, 2012
OPERATING ACTIVITIES		
Net income for the period	**$ 2,551**	$ 4,135
Items not affecting cash:		
Depreciation and amortization	**3,157**	3,228
Gain on sale of assets	**(13)**	(19)
Stock-based compensation	**640**	446
Deferred income tax expense (recovery)	**(1,586)**	1,168
Net change in non-cash working capital related to operations (note 25)	**3,148**	1,496
Cash provided by operating activities	**7,897**	10,454
FINANCING ACTIVITIES		
Dividend payments	**(4,855)**	(4,850)
Principal repayments of long-term debt	**(2,042)**	(641)
Cash received on exercise of options	**—**	131
Cash used in financing activities	**(6,897)**	(5,360)
INVESTING ACTIVITIES		
Purchase of property, plant and equipment	**(2,992)**	(1,487)
Purchase of intangibles	**(6)**	—
Proceeds from sale of equipment	**34**	19
Cash used in investing activities	**(2,964)**	(1,468)
Net increase (decrease) in cash	**(1,964)**	3,626
Cash, beginning of year	**4,281**	655
Cash, end of year	**$ 2,317**	$ 4,281
Supplemental cash-flow information		
Cash interest paid	**$ 52**	$ 103
Cash taxes paid	**958**	—

Required:

Based on the financial statements in Exhibits 12-12A to C, answer each of the following questions:

a. Calculate the following ratios for both 2013 and 2012:
   i. Current ratio
   ii. Quick ratio
   iii. Inventory turnover
   iv. Days to sell inventory
b. Comment on Big Rock's liquidity.
c. Calculate the following ratios for both 2013 and 2012, and comment on the changes:
   i. Return on assets
   ii. Return on equity
d. Comment on the use of leverage by Big Rock, using appropriate ratios to support your analysis.
e. Calculate Big Rock's net free cash flow for 2013 and 2012. What does this tell us about the company's financial flexibility?
f. What do you know about Big Rock given that its basic and diluted earnings per share amounts are the same?

RI12-4 (Ratio analysis for public company)

Cineplex Inc. is the largest movie exhibition company in Canada. It operates theatres in 10 provinces across Canada. The company's financial statements are presented in Exhibits 12-13A to C.

EXHIBIT 12-13A CINEPLEX INC.'S 2013 CONSOLIDATED BALANCE SHEETS

Cineplex Inc.
Consolidated Balance Sheets

(expressed in thousands of Canadian dollars)	December 31, 2013	December 31, 2012 (note 2)	January 1, 2012 (note 2)
Assets			
Current assets			
Cash and cash equivalents (note 6)	$ 44,140	$ 48,665	$ 50,145
Trade and other receivables (note 7)	100,891	77,278	70,473
Inventories (note 8)	7,234	5,193	4,124
Prepaid expenses and other current assets	6,838	3,047	3,727
	159,103	134,183	128,469
Non-current assets			
Property, equipment and leaseholds (note 9)	459,112	418,498	389,674
Deferred income taxes (note 10)	17,635	53,528	12,052
Fair value of interest rate swap agreements (note 4)	92	–	–
Interests in joint ventures (note 11)	44,359	41,623	26,163
Intangible assets (note 12)	113,601	78,460	84,379
Goodwill (note 13)	797,476	608,929	608,929
	$ 1,591,378	$ 1,335,221	$ 1,249,666
Liabilities			
Current liabilities			
Accounts payable and accrued expenses (note 14)	$ 157,333	$ 129,499	$ 115,076
Share-based compensation (note 15)	12,151	–	1,331
Dividends payable (note 16)	7,552	7,063	6,285
Income taxes payable (note 10)	2,656	13,654	17,485
Deferred revenue	136,373	106,253	93,955
Finance lease obligations (note 18)	2,394	2,222	2,411
Fair value of interest rate swap agreements (note 4)	635	513	565
Convertible debentures (note 21)	–	–	76,864
	319,094	259,204	313,972
Non-current liabilities			
Share-based compensation (note 15)	15,622	12,223	9,466
Long-term debt (note 17)	217,151	148,066	167,531
Fair value of interest rate swap agreements (note 4)	–	273	1,199
Finance lease obligations (note 18)	17,722	20,548	26,474
Post-employment benefit obligations (note 19)	6,522	6,274	5,688
Other liabilities (note 20)	170,125	141,319	103,727
Convertible debentures (note 21)	96,870	–	–
	524,012	328,703	314,085
Total liabilities	843,106	587,907	628,057
Equity			
Share capital (note 22)	853,411	847,235	764,801
Deficit	(107,323)	(102,547)	(140,469)
Accumulated other comprehensive loss	(1,715)	(1,142)	(2,723)
Contributed surplus	3,899	3,768	–
	748,272	747,314	621,609
	$ 1,591,378	$ 1,335,221	$ 1,249,666

EXHIBIT 12-13B **CINEPLEX INC.'S 2013 CONSOLIDATED STATEMENTS OF OPERATIONS**

Cineplex Inc.
Consolidated Statements of Operations

(expressed in thousands of Canadian dollars)

	2013	2012 (note 2)
Revenues		
Box office	$ 665,306	$ 638,296
Concessions	350,353	329,332
Other	155,608	124,873
	1,171,267	1,092,501
Expenses		
Film cost	346,373	331,281
Cost of concessions	74,693	68,398
Depreciation and amortization	70,890	62,163
Loss (gain) on disposal of assets	4,372	(2,352)
(Gain) on acquisition of business (note 3 d)	–	(24,752)
Other costs (note 23)	551,819	495,537
Share of income of joint ventures	(3,850)	(3,263)
Interest expense	10,743	12,585
Interest income	(307)	(205)
	1,054,733	939,392
Income before income taxes	116,534	153,109
Provision for income taxes		
Current (note 10)	3,608	31,436
Deferred (note 10)	29,369	1,189
	32,977	32,625
Net income	$ 83,557	$ 120,484
Basic net income per share (note 24)	$ 1.33	$ 1.98
Diluted net income per share (note 24)	$ 1.32	$ 1.97

EXHIBIT 12-13C **CINEPLEX INC.'S 2013 CONSOLIDATED STATEMENTS OF CASH FLOWS**

Cineplex Inc.
Consolidated Statements of Cash Flows
For the years ended December 31, 2013 and 2012

(expressed in thousands of Canadian dollars)

	2013	2012 (note 2)
Cash provided by (used in)		
Operating activities		
Net income	$ 83,557	$120,484
Adjustments to reconcile net income to net cash provided by operating activities		
Depreciation and amortization of property, equipment and leaseholds, and intangible assets	70,890	62,163
Amortization of tenant inducements, rent averaging liabilities and fair value lease contract liabilities	(6,735)	(5,033)
Accretion of debt issuance costs and other non-cash interest	2,001	562
Loss (gain) on disposal of assets	4,372	(2,352)
(Gain) on acquisition of business	–	(24,752)
Deferred income taxes	29,369	1,189
Interest rate swap agreements – non-cash interest	(939)	1,485
Non-cash share-based compensation	1,826	2,108
Accretion of convertible debentures	274	323
Net change in interests in joint ventures	(2,686)	4,356
Tenant inducements	5,417	7,615
Changes in operating assets and liabilities (note 26)	37,302	7,486
Net cash provided by operating activities	224,648	175,634

continued

EXHIBIT 12-13C CINEPLEX INC.'S 2013 CONSOLIDATED STATEMENTS OF CASH FLOWS (continued)

	2013	2012 (note 2)
Investing activities		
Proceeds from sale of assets	3,573	3,683
Purchases of property, equipment and leaseholds	(62,410)	(72,242)
Acquisition of business, net of cash acquired (note 3)	(238,338)	(2,811)
Net cash invested in CDCP	(50)	(438)
Net cash used in investing activities	(297,225)	(71,808)
Financing activities		
Dividends paid	(88,130)	(80,794)
Borrowings (repayments) under credit facility, net	70,000	(20,000)
Repayment of debt acquired with business (note 3)	(12,875)	–
Payments under finance leases	(2,277)	(2,104)
Proceeds from issuance of shares	–	501
Net proceeds from issuance of convertible debentures (note 21)	103,469	–
Deferred financing fees (notes 17 and 21)	(2,135)	–
Shares repurchased and cancelled	–	(1,786)
Repayment of convertible debentures at maturity	–	(1,123)
Net cash provided by (used in) financing activities	68,052	(105,306)
Decrease in cash and cash equivalents	(4,525)	(1,480)
Cash and cash equivalents – Beginning of year	48,665	50,145
Cash and cash equivalents – End of year	$ 44,140	$ 48,665
Supplemental information		
Cash paid for interest	$ 9,421	$ 10,293
Cash paid for income taxes	$ 14,148	$ 35,268

Required:

a. Assess the company's operating effectiveness by calculating and comparing the activity ratios for Cineplex for 2012 and 2013. (Note: use other revenues for the accounts receivable turnover ratio; use cost of concessions as cost of goods sold.)
   i. Based on those ratios, do you think Cineplex is operating more effectively in 2013? Support your conclusion.
   ii. What other information would you like to have to assess its management of receivables, inventory, and payables?
b. Assess the financial riskiness of the company by calculating and comparing the following ratios. Based on those ratios, do you think the financial risk on the company has decreased in 2013? Support your conclusion.
   i. Current ratio
   ii. Quick ratio
   iii. Debt to equity
   iv. Interest coverage
c. Calculate the company's profitability by determining the following ratios and comment on them:
   i. Net profit margin
   ii. Return on equity
   iii. Return on assets
d. Determine the company's net free cash flow for 2012 and 2013. Has this improved or worsened?

RI12-5 (Ratio analysis of a public company)

Required:

Choose a company as directed by your instructor and answer the following questions:

a. Using the ratios given in the text, prepare an analysis of the company for the past two years with respect to profitability, liquidity, activity, solvency, and equity analysis ratios.
b. Even though the ratios calculated in part "a" do not span a long period of time, discuss the company's financial health. Would you invest in it? Why or why not?

Cases

C12-1 Cedar Appliance Sales and Service Ltd.

Cedar Appliance Sales and Service Ltd. owns several retail and service centres in northern British Columbia. Financial ratios for the company for the years ended December 31, 2016 and 2015, are provided below. For comparative purposes, industry averages have also been provided.

Ratio	2016	2015	Industry Average
Current ratio	1.6:1	1.7:1	2:1
Quick ratio	0.75:1	0.80:1	1:1
Accounts receivable turnover	8 times	7.75 times	12 times
Inventory turnover	4.0 times	3.8 times	7.0 times

The company is in the process of opening two new retail outlets and will need to obtain a line of credit to finance receivables and inventory. To receive a competitive interest rate on its line of credit, it needs to ensure that its liquidity ratios are close to the average for the industry. In particular, the company would like to see the current ratio at 2:1. The company has hired you, an independent consultant, to suggest how it might improve its liquidity ratios.

In preparing your report, you have gathered the following additional information:

1. The company's credit terms to its customers are net 45 days; no discounts are provided for early payment.
2. The company policy is to pay accounts payable every 45 days regardless of the credit terms. Many supplier invoices offer discounts for payments within 30 days.
3. Cedar's policy is to keep high amounts of inventory on hand to ensure that customers will have maximum selection.

Required:

Propose several steps that Cedar Appliance Sales and Service Ltd. might take to improve its liquidity. All suggestions must be ethical.

C12-2 Christine's Yogourt Venture

Christine Wilde is considering opening a frozen yogourt store. One option is to purchase an existing independent store that is available for sale. The seller, Mark Preradovic, has operated the store for three years and has assured Christine that his location, although smaller than the average store, is an above-average performer for the industry. Mark has provided the financial data shown below for his outlet.

Mark's Yogourt Plus Store
Selected Financial Results

	Year 1	Year 2	Year 3
Store size: 1,200 square feet (110 square metres)			
Sales	$240,000	$280,000	$330,000
Gross margin	168,000	196,000	231,000
Other expenses	160,000	180,000	200,000
Net income	$ 8,000	$ 16,000	$ 31,000

Christine has approached you to help her decide. You find the following information on the website of Yogourt Yogourt, a franchisor of similar outlets:

- The average store is 1,500 square feet (140 square metres) and contains six yogourt machines, a topping bar, and seating for 20.
- Sales in the first year average $400,000 and $650,000 for a mature store. It usually takes three years for a store to mature.
- Gross margins on start-up average 70% and normally increase to 75% for established locations.
- Operating costs start at 50% and drop to 43% of sales for mature stores as the fixed costs are spread out.
- The initial investment for a 1,500-square-foot store is $350,000 for machines, franchise fees, and other capital costs, plus $50,000 for liquid assets including inventory.
- Franchisees are expected to invest two thirds of the required investment in equity and arrange to borrow the remaining one third.

You recall that in retail, a key statistic is sales per square foot and you make a note to yourself to factor the different store sizes into your analysis.

Mark is asking $400,000 for his store and explained to Christine: "I am offering you a great deal by just asking for the carrying value of the total assets. I just want to recoup my initial investment plus a little bit more for the time and sweat equity I have put in. I have done all the hard work getting the store established; it should be easy for you now."

Required:

a. Use financial statement analysis to evaluate the performance of Mark's store compared with the average Yogourt Yogourt franchise.
b. Based on Mark's most recent financial results and Christine's investment if she pays Mark's asking price, what would be her ROA and ROE compared with a start-up franchise?
c. What other factors would you want to consider before buying the store?
d. Do you recommend Christine purchase Mark's store? Why or why not?

C12-3 Hencky Corporation

The management of Hencky Corporation is developing a loan proposal to present to a local investor. The company is looking for a $1-million loan to finance the research and development costs of producing a revolutionary new wearable computer. Most of the loan proceeds will be spent on intangible costs, such as research salaries, and this will therefore be a very risky investment. Because of the risk associated with the project, the investor is requiring some assurance that the company is currently solvent and operating as a going concern.

As the accountant for Hencky Corporation, you have used the most recent financial statements to calculate the following ratios:

	2016	2015
Current ratio	1.8:1	1.7:1
Quick ratio	1.10:1	1.08:1
Accounts receivable turnover	10 times	11 times
Inventory turnover	6 times	5 times
Debt to equity ratio	25.2%	35.8%

Required:

Provide an explanation of how each of the above ratios should be interpreted and what they specifically tell you about Hencky's solvency and ability to continue as a going concern.

ENDNOTES

1. Adam Stanley, "Investing Clubs Put Real Money on the Line," *The Globe and Mail*, November 5, 2013; "MBA Students: Head of the (Asset) Class," *Canadian Business*, November 6, 2012; "The Desautels Capital Management Inc. Unearthed," *The Bull & Bear*, March 31, 2012; Paul Dalby, "MBA Students Start Fund with Their Own Money and Queen's Cash to Do Battle on Bay Street," *Toronto Star*, February 11, 2012; McGill University website, www.mcgill.ca; Queen's University website, www.queensu.ca.
2. Statistics Canada, "National Balance Sheet and Financial Flow Accounts, Fourth Quarter 2013," *The Daily*, March 14, 2014.
3. The market share information in this analysis was obtained from the historic prices section of Yahoo Finance's website (http://ca.finance.yahoo.com) and Stockhouse's price history website (www.stockhouse.com).

Specimen Financial Statements: Danier Leather Incorporated

This appendix includes a number of extracts from the 2014 annual report of **Danier Leather Inc.** These extracts provide an example of the financial reporting of a Canadian public company and are referred to throughout the text. The extracts include:

- management's statement of responsibility for the financial statements
- independent auditor's report to shareholders
- consolidated financial statements
- notes to the consolidated financial statements

Students are encouraged to refer to these financial statement extracts as they move through the text. These extracts provide additional context to help students develop an understanding of the material.

We thank Danier Leather Inc. for granting us permission to include these extracts in the text. The complete annual report of Danier Leather Inc. can be found on the company's website (www.danier.com) or on the Canadian Securities Administrators' SEDAR (System for Electronic Document Analysis and Retrieval) site (www.sedar.com) as well on the companion site for this text and in *WileyPLUS*.

MANAGEMENT'S RESPONSIBILITY FOR FINANCIAL STATEMENTS

The accompanying financial statements and other financial information contained in this Annual Report are the responsibility of management and have been approved by the Board of Directors of Danier Leather Inc. The financial statements have been prepared by management in conformity with International Financial Reporting Standards using management's best estimates and judgments based on currently available information, where appropriate. The financial information contained elsewhere in this Annual Report has been reviewed to ensure consistency with that in the financial statements.

Management is also responsible for a system of internal controls which is designed to provide reasonable assurance that assets are safeguarded, liabilities are recognized and that financial records are properly maintained to provide timely and accurate financial reports.

The Board of Directors is responsible for ensuring that management fulfills its responsibility in respect of financial reporting and internal control. The Audit Committee of the Board, which is comprised solely of unrelated and outside directors, meets regularly to review significant accounting and auditing matters with management and the independent auditors and to review the interim and annual financial statements.

The financial statements have been audited by PricewaterhouseCoopers LLP, the independent auditors, in accordance with Canadian generally accepted auditing standards on behalf of the shareholders. The Auditor's Report outlines the nature of their examination and their opinion on the financial statements. PricewaterhouseCoopers LLP have full and unrestricted access to the Audit Committee to discuss their audit and related findings as to the integrity of the financial reporting.

Jeffrey Wortsman
President and CEO

Bryan Tatoff, CPA, CA
Executive Vice-President, CFO and Secretary

INDEPENDENT AUDITOR'S REPORT TO SHAREHOLDERS

To the Shareholders of Danier Leather Inc.

We have audited the accompanying consolidated financial statements of Danier Leather Inc. and its subsidiaries, which comprise the consolidated balance sheets as at June 28, 2014 and June 29, 2013 and the consolidated statements of earnings (loss) and comprehensive earnings (loss), cash flow, and changes in shareholders' equity for the 52-week period ended June 28, 2014 and 52-week period ended June 29, 2013, and the related notes, which comprise a summary of the significant accounting policies and other explanatory information.

Management's responsibility for the consolidated financial statements

Management is responsible for the preparation and fair presentation of these consolidated financial statements in accordance with International Financial Reporting Standards, and for such internal control as management determines is necessary to enable the preparation of consolidated financial statements that are free from material misstatement, whether due to fraud or error.

Auditor's responsibility

Our responsibility is to express an opinion on these consolidated financial statements based on our audits. We conducted our audits in accordance with Canadian generally accepted auditing standards. Those standards require that we comply with ethical requirements and plan and perform the audits to obtain reasonable assurance about whether the consolidated financial statements are free from material misstatement.

An audit involves performing procedures to obtain audit evidence about the amounts and disclosures in the consolidated financial statements. The procedures selected depend on the auditor's judgment, including the assessment of the risks of material misstatement of the consolidated financial statements, whether due to fraud or error. In making those risk assessments, the auditor considers internal control relevant to the entity's preparation and fair presentation of the consolidated financial statements in order to design audit procedures that are appropriate in the circumstances, but not for the purpose of expressing an opinion on the effectiveness of the entity's internal control. An audit also includes evaluating the appropriateness of accounting policies used and the reasonableness of accounting estimates made by management, as well as evaluating the overall presentation of the consolidated financial statements.

We believe that the audit evidence we have obtained in our audits is sufficient and appropriate to provide a basis for our audit opinion.

Opinion

In our opinion, the consolidated financial statements present fairly, in all material respects, the financial position of Danier Leather Inc. and its subsidiaries as at June 28, 2014 and June 29, 2013 and their financial performance and their cash flows for the 52-week period ended June 28, 2014 and the 52-week period ended June 29, 2013 in accordance with International Financial Reporting Standards.

PricewaterhouseCoopers LLP

Chartered Professional Accountants, Licensed Public Accountants
Toronto, Ontario
August 13, 2014

CONSOLIDATED STATEMENTS OF EARNINGS (LOSS) & COMPREHENSIVE EARNINGS (LOSS)

(thousands of Canadian dollars, except per share amounts and number of shares)

	Years Ended	
	June 28, 2014	June 29, 2013
	52 weeks	*52 weeks*
Revenue	$141,930	$154,995
Cost of Sales (Note 13)	73,697	76,579
Gross profit	68,233	78,416
Selling, general and administrative expenses (Note 13)	79,086	76,620
Interest income	(118)	(236)
Interest expense	59	51
Earnings (loss) before income taxes	(10,794)	1,981
Provision for (recovery of) income taxes (Note 14)	(3,131)	570
Net earnings (loss) and comprehensive earnings	($7,663)	$1,411
Net earnings (loss) per share:		
Basic	**($2.00)**	**$0.34**
Diluted	**($2.00)**	**$0.33**
Weighted average number of shares outstanding:		
Basic	3,840,319	4,180,829
Diluted	3,948,336	4,323,619
Number of shares outstanding at period end	3,854,168	3,832,168

See accompanying notes to the consolidated financial statements

CONSOLIDATED BALANCE SHEETS

(thousands of Canadian dollars)

	June 28, 2014	June 29, 2013
Assets		
Current Assets		
Cash	$ 13,507	$ 24,541
Accounts receivable	638	1,197
Income taxes recoverable	3,461	358
Inventories (Note 5)	21,721	22,810
Prepaid expenses	643	803
	39,970	49,709
Non-current Assets		
Property and equipment (Note 6)	16,826	16,034
Computer software (Note 7)	1,459	1,143
Deferred income tax asset (Note 14)	2,374	2,163
	$ 60,629	$ 69,049
Liabilities		
Current Liabilities		
Payables and accruals (Note 9)	$ 9,185	$ 10,101
Deferred revenue	1,511	1,548
Sales return provision (Note 10)	94	99
	10,790	11,748
Non-current Liabilities		
Deferred lease inducements and rent liability	1,432	1,392
	12,222	13,140
Shareholders' Equity		
Share capital (Note 11)	11,772	11,533
Contributed surplus	1,040	954
Retained earnings	35,595	43,422
	48,407	55,909
	$ 60,629	$ 69,049

Contingencies, Guarantees and Commitments (Notes 16 and 17)

Approved by the Board of Directors
August 13, 2014

Jeffrey Wortsman, Director

Edwin F. Hawken, Chairman

See accompanying notes to the consolidated financial statements

CONSOLIDATED STATEMENTS OF CASH FLOW (thousands of Canadian dollars)

	Years Ended	
	June 28, 2014	June 29, 2013
	52 weeks	*52 weeks*
Cash provided by (used in)		
Operating Activities		
Net earnings (loss)	($7,663)	$1,411
Adjustments for:		
Amortization of property and equipment	3,517	3,149
Amortization of computer software	791	412
Impairment loss on property and equipment	663	327
Amortization of deferred lease inducement	(75)	(100)
Straight line rent expense	115	121
Stock-based compensation	209	131
Interest income	(118)	(236)
Interest expense	59	51
Provision for (refund of) income taxes	(3,131)	570
Changes in working capital (Note 15)	883	1,348
Interest paid	(107)	(12)
Interest received	133	244
Income taxes (paid) recovered	(183)	(664)
Net cash generated from (used in) operating activities	**(4,907)**	**6,752**
Financing Activities		
Subordinate voting shares issued	227	183
Subordinate voting shares repurchased (Note 11)	(275)	(11,399)
Net cash used in financing activities	**(48)**	**(11,216)**
Investing Activities		
Acquisition of property and equipment	(4,972)	(4,498)
Acquisition of computer software	(1,107)	(829)
Net cash used in investing activities	**(6,079)**	**(5,327)**
Decrease in cash	**(11,034)**	**(9,791)**
Cash, beginning of period	24,541	34,332
Cash, end of period	**$13,507**	**$24,541**

See accompanying notes to the consolidated financial statements

CONSOLIDATED STATEMENTS OF CHANGES IN SHAREHOLDERS' EQUITY

(thousands of Canadian dollars)

	Share Capital	Contributed Surplus	Accumulated Other Comprehensive Income	Retained Earnings	Total
Balance - June 29, 2013	$11,533	$954	$ -	$43,422	$55,909
Net loss	-	-	-	(7,663)	(7,663)
Stock based compensation related to stock options	-	209	-	-	209
Exercise of stock options	350	(123)	-	-	227
Share repurchases (net of tax)	(111)	-	-	(164)	(275)
Balance - June 28, 2014	$11,772	$1,040	$ -	$35,595	$48,407

	Share Capital	Contributed Surplus	Accumulated Other Comprehensive Income	Retained Earnings	Total
Balance - June 30, 2012	$15,040	$925	$-	$49,526	$65,491
Net earnings	-	-	-	1,411	1,411
Stock based compensation related to stock options	-	131	-	-	131
Exercise of stock options	285	(102)	-	-	183
Share repurchases	(3,792)	-	-	(7,515)	(11,307)
Balance - June 29, 2013	$11,533	$954	$-	$43,422	$55,909

See accompanying notes to the consolidated financial statements

NOTES TO CONSOLIDATED FINANCIAL STATEMENTS

For the Years Ended June 28, 2014 and June 29, 2013

(unless otherwise stated, all amounts are in thousands of Canadian dollars)

1. GENERAL INFORMATION:

Danier Leather Inc. and its subsidiaries ("Danier" or the "Company") comprise a vertically integrated designer, manufacturer, distributor and retailer of leather apparel and accessories. Danier Leather Inc. is a corporation existing under the Business Corporations Act (Ontario) and is domiciled in Canada. The Company's subordinate voting shares (the "Subordinate Voting Shares") are listed on the Toronto Stock Exchange (the "TSX") under the symbol "DL". The address of its registered head office is 2650 St. Clair Avenue West, Toronto, Ontario, M6N 1M2, Canada.

The Company's operations are focused on the design, manufacture, distribution and retail of leather apparel and accessories in Canada. As such, the Company presents one operating segment in its consolidated financial statements.

Due to the seasonal nature of the retail business and the Company's product line, the results of operation for any interim period are not necessarily indicative of the results of operations to be expected for the fiscal year. A significant portion of the Company's sales and earnings are typically generated during the second fiscal quarter, which includes the holiday selling season. Sales are usually lowest and losses are typically experienced during the period from April to September.

2. BASIS OF PREPARATION:

(a) Statement of Compliance

These consolidated financial statements have been prepared in accordance with International Financial Reporting Standards ("IFRS") as issued by the International Accounting Standards Board ("IASB") and using the accounting policies described herein. These consolidated financial statements were approved by the Board of Directors of the Company on August 13, 2014.

(b) Basis of Presentation

These consolidated financial statements have been prepared on a going concern basis, under the historical cost convention, except for the following items which are measured at fair value:

- Financial instruments at fair value through profit and loss; and
- Liabilities for cash-settled share-based compensation plans.

(c) Functional and Presentation Currency

These consolidated financial statements are presented in Canadian dollars ("C$"), the Company's functional currency. All financial information is presented in thousands, except per share amounts, which are presented in whole dollars, and number of shares, which are presented as whole numbers.

(d) Use of Estimates, Judgments and Assumptions

The preparation of these consolidated financial statements in accordance with IFRS requires management to make certain judgments, estimates and assumptions that affect the application of accounting policies and the reported amounts of assets and liabilities and disclosure of contingent liabilities at the date of the consolidated financial statements, and the reported amounts of revenues and expenses during the period.

Judgment is commonly used in determining whether a balance or transaction should be recognized in the consolidated financial statements, and estimates and assumptions are more commonly used in determining the measurement of recognized transactions and balances. However, judgments and estimates are often interrelated.

Management has applied its judgment in its assessment of the classification of leases and financial instruments, the recognition of tax provisions, determining the tax rates used for measuring deferred taxes, and identifying the indicators of impairment of property and equipment.

Estimates are used when estimating the useful lives of property and equipment and computer software for the purposes of depreciation and amortization, when determining the number of share-based payments that will ultimately vest, when accounting for or measuring items such as inventory provisions, gift card breakage, assumptions underlying income taxes, sales and use taxes and sales return provisions, certain fair value measures including those related to the valuation of share-based payments and financial instruments and when testing assets for impairment. These estimates depend upon subjective and complex judgments about matters that may be uncertain, and changes in those estimates could materially impact the consolidated financial statements. Volatile equity, foreign currency and energy markets, the potential illiquidity of credit markets and unpredictable changes in consumer spending have combined to increase the uncertainty inherent in such estimates and assumptions. As future events and their effects cannot be determined with precision, actual results may differ significantly from such estimates and assumptions.

Estimates and underlying assumptions are reviewed on an ongoing basis. Revisions to accounting estimates are recognized in the period in which the estimates are revised and in any future periods affected.

3. SIGNIFICANT ACCOUNTING POLICIES:

The accounting policies described below have been applied consistently to all periods presented in these consolidated financial statements.

(a) Basis of Measurement:

The consolidated financial statements have been prepared on a going concern basis, under the historical cost convention as modified by the revaluation of certain financial assets and financial liabilities (including derivative instruments) at fair value through profit and loss.

(b) Basis of Consolidation:

The consolidated financial statements include the accounts of Danier Leather Inc. consolidated with those of its wholly-owned subsidiaries, 1331677 Ontario Inc., Danier International Corporation and Danier Leather (USA), Inc. 1331677 Ontario Inc. was incorporated in Ontario, Canada on December 22, 1998 to hold vacant land next to the Company's Toronto head office. Danier International Corporation was incorporated in Barbados on April 7, 2006 to hold the international intellectual property of Danier. Danier Leather (USA), Inc. is currently inactive and was incorporated in Delaware, U.S.A. on September 8, 1998 to operate Danier stores in the United States, which operations have since been discontinued. On consolidation, all intercompany transactions, balances, revenue and expenses have been eliminated.

(c) Year-End:

The fiscal year end of the Company consists of a 52 or 53 week period ending on the last Saturday in June each year. The current fiscal year for the consolidated financial statements is the 52-week period ended June 28, 2014 and, comparably, the 52-week period ended June 29, 2013.

(d) Foreign Currency Translation:

Items included in the financial statements of each wholly-owned consolidated entity in the Danier Leather Inc. group are measured using the currency of the primary economic environment in which the entity operates (the "functional currency"). The consolidated financial statements are presented in Canadian dollars, which is the Company's presentation currency.

Accounts in foreign currencies are translated into Canadian dollars. Monetary financial position items are translated at the foreign currency exchange rate in effect at the balance sheet date and non-monetary items are measured at historical cost and are translated into Canadian dollars at foreign currency exchange rates that approximate the rates in effect at the dates when such items are transacted. Revenues and expenses are translated at the foreign currency exchange rate in effect on the transaction dates or at the average foreign currency exchange rate for the reporting period. The resulting net gain or loss is included as part of selling, general and administrative expenses ("SG&A") in the consolidated statement of earnings (loss).

(e) Revenue Recognition:

Revenue comprises the fair value of the consideration received or receivable for the sale of merchandise and services in the ordinary course of the Company's activities inclusive of amounts invoiced for alteration services and shipping. Revenue is shown net of sales tax and estimated returns.

The Company recognizes revenue when the amount can be reliably measured, it is probable that future economic benefits will flow to the Company and when specific criteria have been met for each of the Company's activities as described below. The Company bases estimates on historical results, taking into consideration the type of activity and the specifics of each arrangement.

Retail Sales

Revenue for merchandise sold to customers through the Company's stores is recognized at the time of purchase. Alteration revenue is recorded at the time the buyer takes possession of the merchandise.

Online Sales

Revenue for online customers is recognized upon estimated receipt of the merchandise by the customer.

Third Party Distributor

Revenue for merchandise sold through a third party distributor is recognized when the significant risks and rewards of ownership have been transferred to the buyer, which is at the time the distributor ships the merchandise to their customer.

Gift Cards

Gift cards sold are recorded as deferred revenue and revenue is recognized at the time of redemption or in accordance with the Company's accounting policy for breakage. Breakage income represents the estimated value of gift cards that are not expected to be redeemed by customers where the unredeemed balance is more than two years old from the date of issuance. Historically, breakage has not been material.

(f) Share-Based Compensation Plans:

The Company maintains an equity-settled Stock Option Plan and cash-settled Restricted Share Unit ("RSU") and Deferred Share Unit ("DSU") share-based compensation plans.

For the equity-settled Stock Option Plan, where options to purchase Subordinate Voting Shares are issued to directors, officers, employees or service providers (further details of which are described in Note 12(a)), the expense is based on the fair value of the awards granted, excluding the impact of any non-market service conditions (for example, continued employment over a specified time period). Non-market vesting conditions are considered in making assumptions about the number of awards that are expected to vest. The fair value of options granted is estimated at the date of grant using the Black-Scholes Option Pricing Model. The expense is recognized on a graded vesting basis over the vesting period of the stock options, which is generally three years.

When stock options are subsequently exercised, share capital is increased by the sum of the consideration paid together with the related portion previously added to contributed surplus when compensation costs were charged against income.

For the cash-settled RSU plan, where RSUs are issued to eligible directors, officers or employees and vest over a period of up to three years (further details of which are described in Note 12(c)), the expense is recognized on a graded vesting schedule and is determined based on the fair value of the liability incurred at each balance sheet date until the award is settled. The fair value of the liability is measured at each balance sheet date by applying the Black-Scholes Option Pricing Model, taking into account the extent to which participants have rendered services to date.

For the cash-settled DSU plan, where DSUs are issued to directors and vest immediately and can only be redeemed once the director leaves the Board of Directors of the Company (further details of which are described in Note 12(b)), the expense is recognized on the grant date based on the fair value of the award by applying the Black-Scholes Option Pricing Model. The fair value of the liability is measured at each balance sheet date by applying the Black-Scholes Option Pricing Model until the award is settled.

At each balance sheet date, the Company reassesses its estimates of the number of awards that are expected to vest and recognizes the impact of any revisions in the statement of earnings (loss) with a corresponding adjustment to equity or liabilities, as appropriate.

(g) Cash:
Cash consists of cash on hand and bank balances.

(h) Financial Instruments:
(i) Classification of Financial Instruments
Financial instruments are classified into one of the following three categories: fair value through profit and loss, loans and receivables or financial liabilities at amortized cost. The classification determines the accounting treatment of the instrument. The classification is determined by the Company when the financial instrument is initially recorded, based on the underlying purpose of the instrument.

The Company's financial instruments are classified and measured as follows:

Financial Asset/Liability	Category	Measurement
Cash	Loans and receivables	Amortized cost
Accounts receivable	Loans and receivables	Amortized cost
Payables and accruals	Financial liabilities	Amortized cost
Sales return provision	Financial liablilities	Amortized cost
Foreign currency option contract derivatives[1]	Fair value through profit and loss	Fair value through profit and loss

(1)The carrying value of the Company's derivatives are included in the consolidated balance sheet as accounts receivable (if the fair value is an unrealized gain) or payables and accruals (if the fair value is an unrealized loss).

Loans and receivables are initially recognized at fair value and then subsequently at amortized cost using the effective interest method, less any impairment losses recognized in the statement of earnings (loss) in the period in which the impairment is recognized. Financial liabilities are initially recognized at the amount required to be paid less, when material, a discount to reduce the payables to fair value. Subsequently, financial liabilities are measured at amortized cost using the effective interest method. Changes in fair value of financial instruments classified as held for trading are recorded in the statement of earnings (loss) in the period of change.

The Company categorizes its financial assets and financial liabilities that are recognized in the balance sheets at fair value using the fair value hierarchy. The fair value hierarchy has the following levels:

- Level 1 – quoted market prices in active markets for identical assets or liabilities;
- Level 2 – inputs other than quoted market prices included in Level 1 that are observable for the asset or liability, either directly (as prices) or indirectly (derived from prices); and
- Level 3 – unobservable inputs such as inputs for the asset or liability that are not based on observable market data.

The level in the fair value hierarchy within which the fair value measurement is categorized in its entirety is determined on the basis of the lowest level input that is significant to the fair value measurement in its entirety.

(ii) Transaction Costs
Transaction costs are added to the initial fair value of financial assets and liabilities when those financial assets and liabilities are not measured at fair value subsequent to initial measurement. Transaction costs are recorded in SG&A using the effective interest method.

(iii) Derivative Financial Instruments
The Company uses derivatives in the form of foreign currency option contracts and forwards, which are used to manage risks related to its inventory purchases, which are primarily denominated in United States dollars. All derivatives have been classified as fair value through profit and loss, are not designated as hedges, are included in the balance sheets as accounts receivable or payables and accruals, and are classified as current or non-current based on the contractual terms specific to the instrument. Gains and losses on re-measurement are included in SG&A.

(iv) Fair Value
The fair value of a financial instrument is the estimated amount that the Company would receive to sell an asset or pay to transfer a liability in an orderly transaction between market participants at the measurement date. These estimates are subjective in nature, often involve uncertainties and the exercise of significant judgment and are made at a specific point in time using available information about the financial instrument and may not reflect fair value in the future. The estimated fair value amounts can be materially affected by the use of different assumptions or methodologies.

The methods and assumptions used in estimating the fair value of the Company's financial instruments are as follows:

- The derivative financial instruments, which consist of foreign currency option contracts and forwards, have been marked-to-market and are categorized as Level 2 in the fair value hierarchy. Factors included in the determination of fair value include the spot rate, forward rates, estimates of volatility, present value factor, strike prices, credit risk of the Company and credit risk of counterparties. As at June 28, 2014, a $364 unrealized loss (June 29, 2013 – $822 unrealized gain) was recorded in SG&A for the contracts outstanding.
- Given their short-term maturity, the fair value of cash, accounts receivable, payables and accruals and sales return provision approximates their carrying values.

(i) Impairment of Financial Assets:
At each reporting date, the Company assesses whether there is objective evidence that a financial asset is impaired. Evidence of impairment may include: indications that a debtor or a group of debtors are experiencing significant financial difficulty; default or delinquency in interest or principal payments; and observable data indicating that there is a measurable decrease in the estimated future cash flows. If such evidence exists, the Company recognizes an impairment loss.

For financial assets carried at amortized cost, the loss is the difference between the amortized cost of the receivable and the present value of the estimated future cash flows, discounted using the instrument's original effective interest rate. The carrying amount of the asset is reduced by this amount either directly or indirectly through the use of an allowance account. Impairment losses on financial assets carried at amortized cost are reversed in subsequent periods if the amount of the loss decreases and the decrease can be related objectively to an event occurring after the impairment was recognized.

(j) Inventories:
Merchandise inventories are valued at the lower of cost, using the weighted average cost method, and net realizable value. For inventories manufactured by the Company, cost includes direct labour, raw materials, manufacturing and distribution centre costs related to inventories and transportation costs that are directly incurred to bring inventories to their present location and condition. For inventories purchased from third party vendors, cost includes the cost of purchase, duty and brokerage, quality assurance costs, distribution centre costs related to inventories and transportation costs that are directly incurred to bring inventories to their present location and condition.

The Company estimates the net realizable value as the amount at which inventories are expected to be sold, taking into account fluctuations in retail prices due to seasonality, age, excess quantities, condition of the inventory, nature of the inventory and the estimated variable costs necessary to make the sale. Inventories are written down to net realizable value when the cost of inventories is not estimated to be recoverable due to obsolescence, damage or declining selling prices. When circumstances that previously caused inventories to be written down below cost no longer exist, the amount of the write-down previously recorded is reversed.

Storage costs, administrative overheads and selling costs related to the inventories are expensed in the period in which the costs are incurred.

(k) Property and Equipment:
Property and equipment are recorded at cost less accumulated amortization and accumulated impairment losses, if any. Cost includes expenditures that are directly attributable to the acquisition of the asset. Borrowing costs attributable to the acquisition, construction or production of qualifying assets are added to the cost of those assets, until such time as the assets are substantially ready for their intended use. Qualifying assets are those assets that take longer than nine months to be substantially ready for their intended use. All other borrowing costs are recognized as interest expense in the statement of earnings (loss) in the period in which they are incurred.

Subsequent costs are included in the asset's carrying amount or recognized as a separate asset, as appropriate, only when it is probable that future economic benefits can be measured reliably. The carrying amount of a replaced asset is de-recognized when replaced. Repair and maintenance costs are charged to the statement of earnings (loss) during the period in which they are incurred.

Depreciation of an asset begins once it is available for use. The Company allocates the amount initially recognized in respect of an item of property and equipment to its significant parts and depreciates each such part separately. The depreciable amount of an asset, being the cost of an asset less the residual value, if any, is allocated on a straight-line basis over the estimated useful life of the asset. Residual value is estimated to be zero unless the Company expects to dispose of the asset at a value that exceeds the estimated disposal costs. Gains and losses on disposals of property and equipment, if any, are determined by comparing the proceeds with the carrying amount of the asset and are included as part of SG&A in the statement of earnings (loss).

The major categories of property and equipment, their methods of amortization and useful lives for the fiscal years ended June 28, 2014 and June 29, 2013 are as follows:

Building	25 years straight-line
Roof	20 years straight-line
HVAC equipment	5 to 15 years straight-line
Computer hardware	4 to 7 years straight-line
Furniture and equipment (non-retail)	5 to 7 years straight-line
Leasehold improvements, furniture and fixtures (retail locations)	Term of lease not to exceed 10 years

The residual values, useful lives and amortization methods applied to assets are reviewed annually based on relevant market information and management considerations.

Property and equipment is derecognized either upon disposal or when no future economic benefits are expected from their use. Any gain or loss arising on derecognition is included as part of SG&A in the statement of earnings (loss).

(l) Computer Software:

Computer software is recorded at cost less accumulated amortization and accumulated impairment losses, if any. Amortization commences when the computer software application is available for its intended use. Residual value is estimated to be zero unless the Company expects to dispose of the asset at a value that exceeds the estimated disposal costs. The residual values, useful lives and amortization methods applied to computer software are reviewed annually based on relevant market information and management considerations. Computer software costs are capitalized and amortized on a straight line basis over the period of its expected useful life which ranges from 4 to 7 years. The assets are reviewed for impairment whenever events or circumstances indicate that the carrying amount may not be recoverable.

Computer software is derecognized either upon disposal or when no future economic benefit is expected from its use. Any gain or loss arising on derecognition is included as part of SG&A in the statement of earnings (loss).

(m) Impairment of Non-Financial Assets:

Property and equipment and computer software with finite lives are tested for impairment at each reporting date and whenever events or changes in circumstances indicate that the carrying amount may not be recoverable. Events or changes in circumstances which may indicate impairment include: a significant change to the Company's operations, a significant decline in performance or a change in market conditions which adversely affects the Company.

An impairment loss is recognized for the amount by which the asset's carrying amount exceeds its recoverable amount. For purposes of measuring recoverable amounts, assets are grouped at the lowest levels for which there are separately identifiable cash flows (cash-generating units or CGUs), which is at the individual store level for the Company. The recoverable amount is the greater of an asset's fair value less costs to sell and value in use (being the present value of the expected future cash flows of the relevant asset or CGU). The Company evaluates impairment losses for potential reversals when events or circumstances warrant such consideration.

(n) Leased Assets:

Leases are classified as either operating or finance, based on the substance of the transaction at inception of the lease. Classification is re-assessed if the terms of the lease are changed.

Leases in which a significant portion of the risks and rewards of ownership are not assumed by the Company are classified as operating leases. The Company enters into leases of varying terms for the operation of its stores, which are accounted for as operating leases. Payments under an operating lease are recognized in SG&A on the statement of earnings (loss) on a straight-line basis over the term of the lease. When a lease contains a predetermined fixed escalation of the minimum rent, the Company recognizes the related rent expense on a straight-line basis and records the difference between the recognized rental expense and the amount payable under the lease as deferred rent, which is included in deferred lease inducements and rent liability on the balance sheet. Contingent rentals (rent as a percentage of sales above a predetermined sales threshold) are recognized in SG&A in the period in which they are incurred.

Tenant allowances are recorded as deferred lease inducements and amortized as a reduction of rent expense over the term of the related leases.

(o) Provisions:

Provisions represent liabilities to the Company for which the amount or timing is uncertain. Provisions are recognized when the Company has a present legal or constructive obligation as a result of past events, it is probable that an outflow of resources will be required to settle the obligation and the amount can be reliably estimated. The sales return provision primarily comprises customer returns of unworn and undamaged purchases for a full refund within the time period provided by Danier's return policy, which is generally 14 days after the purchase date. The sales return provision is estimated based on historical experience and, since the time period of the provision is of relatively short duration, the present value of the expenditure expected to be required to settle the obligation approximates the actual provision estimate. The provision is reviewed at each balance sheet date and updated to reflect management's latest best estimate. However, actual returns could vary from these estimates.

(p) Deferred Lease Inducements and Rent Liability:

Deferred lease inducements represent cash benefits received from landlords pursuant to store lease agreements. These lease inducements are amortized against rent expense over the term of the lease, not exceeding 10 years.

Rent liability represents the difference between minimum rent as specified in the lease and rent calculated on a straight-line basis.

(q) Income Taxes:

Income tax comprises current and deferred tax. The Company's income tax expense is based on tax rules and regulations that are subject to interpretation and require estimates and assumptions that may be challenged by taxation authorities.

Current income tax is the expected tax payable on the taxable income for the year using tax rates enacted or substantially enacted at the end of the reporting period and any adjustments to tax payable in respect of previous years. A weighted average of rates across provinces or categories of income is used if it is a reasonable approximation of the effect of using more specific rates. The Company's estimates of current income tax are periodically reviewed and adjusted as circumstances warrant, such as for changes to tax laws and administrative guidance and the resolution of uncertainties through either the conclusion of tax audits or expiration of prescribed time limits within the relevant statutes. The final results of government tax audits and other events may vary materially compared to estimates and assumptions used by management in determining income tax expense and in measuring current income tax.

In general, deferred tax is recognized in respect of temporary differences arising between the tax bases of assets and liabilities and their carrying amounts in the consolidated financial statements. Deferred income tax is determined on a non-discounted basis using tax rates and laws that have been enacted or substantially enacted at the balance sheet date and are expected to apply when the deferred tax asset or liability is settled. The effect on deferred income tax assets and liabilities of a change in tax rates are included in net earnings in the period that the laws have been enacted or substantially enacted. Deferred tax assets are recognized to the extent that it is probable that the assets can be recovered.

Estimation of income taxes includes evaluating the recoverability of deferred tax assets based on an assessment of the Company's ability to utilize the underlying future tax deductions against future taxable income before they expire. As described above, the Company's assessment is based upon substantially enacted tax rates and laws that are expected to apply when the assets are expected to be realized, as well as on estimates of future taxable income. If the assessment of the Company's ability to utilize the underlying future tax deductions changes, the Company would be required to recognize more or fewer of the tax deductions or assets, which would decrease or increase (respectively) the income tax expense in the period in which this is determined. Deferred income tax assets are recognized on the balance sheet under non-current assets, irrespective of the expected date of realization or settlement.

Significant judgment is required in determining the provision for taxation. There are many transactions and calculations for which the ultimate tax determination is uncertain during the ordinary course of business. The Company assesses the need for provisions for uncertain tax positions using best estimates of the amounts that would be expected to be paid based on a qualitative assessment of all relevant factors. However, it is possible that at some future date an additional liability could result from audits by taxation authorities. Where the final outcome of these matters is different from the amounts that were initially recorded, such differences will affect the tax provisions in the period in which such determination is made.

(r) Earnings Per Share:

Basic earnings per share is calculated by dividing the net earnings available to shareholders by the weighted average number of shares outstanding during the year (see Note 11(c)). Diluted earnings per share is calculated using the treasury stock method, which assumes that all outstanding stock options with an exercise price below the average monthly market price of the Subordinate Voting Shares on the TSX are exercised and the assumed proceeds are used to purchase the Company's Subordinate Voting Shares at the average monthly market price on the TSX during the fiscal year.

(s) Share Capital:

Subordinate Voting Shares are classified as equity. When Subordinate Voting Shares are purchased for cancellation, the carrying amount of the Subordinate Voting Shares is recognized as a deduction from share capital. The excess of the purchase price over the carrying amount of the Subordinate Voting Shares is charged to retained earnings.

(1) Accounting Standards Implemented During Fiscal 2014:
The Company adopted the following new accounting standards in preparing these annual consolidated financial statements:

(i) Financial Instruments – Offsetting Financial Assets and Financial Liabilities: The IASB issued an amendment to IFRS 7, Financial Instruments: Offsetting Financial Assets and Financial Liabilities ("IFRS 7") which was effective for annual periods beginning on or after January 1, 2013 and was adopted by the Company on June 30, 2013. Amendments to IFRS 7 increased the disclosure requirement related to offsetting of financial assets and liabilities. The implementation of IFRS 7 did not have a significant impact on the Company.

(ii) Fair Value Measurement: The IASB issued a new standard, IFRS 13, Fair Value Measurement ("IFRS 13"), which was required to be adopted for annual periods beginning on or after January 1, 2013 and was prospectively adopted by the Company on June 30, 2013. IFRS 13 provides a standard definition of fair value, sets out a framework for measuring fair value and provides for specific disclosures about fair value. IFRS 13 defines fair value as the price that would be received to sell an asset, or paid to transfer a liability, in an orderly transaction between market participants at the measurement date. The Company determined that the adoption of IFRS 13 had no measurement impact on the Company's consolidated financial statements. The Company has included the disclosures required by this standard in Note 18.

4. FUTURE ACCOUNTING STANDARDS:

A number of new standards, and amendments to standards and interpretations, are not yet effective for the year ended June 28, 2014 and have not been applied in preparing these annual consolidated financial statements. New standards and amendments to standards and interpretations that are currently under review include:

IFRS 9 – Financial Instruments
On November 12, 2009, the IASB issued a new standard, IFRS 9, Financial Instruments ("IFRS 9"), which will ultimately replace IAS 39, Financial Instruments: Recognition and Measurement ("IAS 39"). The replacement of IAS 39 is a multi-phase project with the objective of improving and simplifying the reporting for financial instruments and the issuance of IFRS 9 is a part of the first phase.

On November 19, 2013, the IASB published IFRS 9, Hedge Accounting, which is a part of the third phase of its replacement of IAS 39. The new requirements allow entities to better reflect their risk management activities in the financial statements. As part of the amendments, entities may change the accounting for liabilities that they have elected to measure at fair value before applying any of the requirements in IFRS 9. This change in accounting would mean that gains caused by a worsening in an entity's own credit risk on such liabilities would no longer be recognized in profit or loss.

Because the impairment phase of the IFRS 9 project is not yet completed, the IASB decided that a mandatory effective date of January 1, 2015 would not allow sufficient time for entities to prepare to apply IFRS 9. Accordingly, the IASB determined to apply a later mandatory effective date, which will be determined when IFRS 9 is closer to completion. However, entities may still choose to apply IFRS 9 immediately. IFRS 9 must be applied retrospectively; however, hedge accounting is to be applied prospectively (with some exceptions). At the present time, Danier does not expect to apply IFRS 9 earlier than the date required by the IASB. The Company is assessing the potential impact of IFRS 9.

IAS 32 – Financial Instruments: Presentation ("IAS 32")
The IASB issued an amendment to IAS 32 which provides further guidance on the requirements for offsetting financial instruments. The amendments to IAS 32 are effective for annual periods beginning on or after January 1, 2014 and must be applied retrospectively. The Company will apply IAS 32 beginning in the first quarter of fiscal 2015 and no significant impact on the consolidated financial statements is expected.

IAS 36 – Impairment of Assets: Recoverable Amount Disclosures for Non-Financial Assets ("IAS 36")
The IASB issued amendments to IAS 36 which reduces the circumstances in which the recoverable amount of assets or cash generating units is required to be disclosed, clarifies the disclosure required and introduces an explicit requirement to disclose the discount rate in determining impairment or reversals where the recoverable amount (based on fair value less costs of disposal) is determined using a present value technique. The amendments to IAS 36 are effective for annual periods beginning on or after January 1, 2014 and must be applied retrospectively. The Company will apply IAS 36 beginning in the first quarter of fiscal 2015 and no significant impact on the consolidated financial statements is expected.

IFRIC 21 – Levies ("IFRIC 21")
The IFRS Interpretations Committee ("IFRIC") of the IASB issued IFRIC 21 which addresses the accounting for a liability to pay a levy to a government. IFRIC applies to levy liabilities within the scope of IAS 37 – Provisions, Contingent Liabilities and Contingent Assets, and to levy liabilities when the timing and amount is uncertain. IFRIC 21 is effective for years beginning on or after January 1, 2014 and must be applied retrospectively. The Company will apply IFRIC 21 beginning in the first quarter of fiscal 2015 and no significant impact on the consolidated financial statements is expected.

A number of other standards have been adopted by the IASB but currently have no impact on the Company.

5. INVENTORIES:

	June 28, 2014	June 29, 2013
Raw materials	$ 1,026	$ 2,594
Work-in-process	198	222
Finished goods	20,497	19,994
	$ 21,721	$22,810

	Year Ended	
	June 28, 2014	June 29, 2013
Cost of inventory recognized as an expense	$ 73,084	$ 75,805
Write-downs of inventory due to net realizable value being lower than cost	$ 2,589	$ 1,632
Write-downs recognized in previous periods that were reversed	$ 9	$ 30

6. PROPERTY AND EQUIPMENT:

	Year Ended June 28, 2014							
	Land	Building	Roof	HVAC	Leasehold Improvements	Furniture & Equipment	Computer Hardware	Total
Cost								
At June 29, 2013	$ 1,000	$ 6,063	$ 308	$ 840	$ 22,679	$ 9,957	$3,348	$44,195
Additions	-	-	-	-	3,078	1,671	223	4,972
Disposals	-	-	-	-	(2,451)	(270)	(280)	(3,001)
At June 28, 2014	$ 1,000	$ 6,063	$ 308	$ 840	$ 23,306	$ 11,358	$3,291	$46,166
Accumulated amortization and impairment losses								
At June 29, 2013	-	$2,508	$216	$625	$15,322	$6,754	$2,736	$28,161
Amortization for the period	-	154	16	49	1,865	1,005	428	3,517
Impairment losses	-	-	-	-	661	2	-	663
Disposals	-	-	-	-	(2,451)	(270)	(280)	(3,001)
At June 28, 2014	-	$2,662	$232	$674	$15,397	$7,491	$2,884	$29,340
Net carrying value								
At June 28, 2014	$1,000	$3,401	$76	$166	$7,909	$3,867	$407	$16,826
Capital work in progress included above								
At June 28, 2014	-	-	-	-	$56	-	$81	$137

	Land	Building	Roof	HVAC	Leasehold Improvements	Furniture & Equipment	Computer Hardware	Total
	Year Ended June 29, 2013							
Cost								
At June 30, 2012	$ 1,000	$6,063	$308	$793	$22,208	$9,088	$3,386	$42,846
Additions	-	-	-	47	2,970	1,333	148	4,498
Disposals	-	-	-	-	(2,499)	(464)	(186)	(3,149)
At June 29, 2013	$1,000	$6,063	$308	$840	$22,679	$9,957	$3,348	$44,195
Accumulated amortization and impairment losses								
At June 30, 2012	-	$2,354	$201	$578	$15,875	$6,321	$2,505	$27,834
Amortization for the period	-	154	15	47	1,669	847	417	3,149
Impairment losses	-	-	-	-	277	50	-	327
Disposals	-	-	-	-	(2,499)	(464)	(186)	(3,149)
At June 29, 2013	-	$2,508	$216	$625	$15,322	$6,754	$2,736	$28,161
Net carrying value								
At June 29, 2013	$1,000	$3,555	$92	$215	$7,357	$3,203	$612	$16,034
Capital work in progress included above								
At June 29, 2013	-	-	-	-	$299	$19	-	$318

The Company conducted an impairment test for its property and equipment and determined that there were impairments at some non-performing stores in the amount of $663 for the year ended June 28, 2014 ($327 for the year ended June 29, 2013) and recorded in SG&A during the third and fourth quarters of fiscal 2014. The recoverable amount of the CGU was estimated based on value-in-use calculations as this was determined to be higher than fair value less costs to sell. These calculations use cash flow projections based on actual performance during the past 12 months which are then extrapolated over each CGU's remaining lease term and then discounted using an estimated discount rate. The key assumptions for the value-in-use calculations include discount rates, growth rates and expected cash flows. Management estimates discount rates using pre-tax rates that reflect a current market assessment of the time value of money and the risks specific to the CGUs. Changes in revenues and direct costs are based on past experience and expectations of future changes in the market.

The pre-tax discount rate used to calculate the value-in-use range is 12% (11% during the year ended June 29, 2013) and is dependent on the specific risks in relation to the CGU. The discount rate is derived from retail industry comparable post-tax weighted average cost of capital.

If management's cash flow estimate were to decrease by 10%, the impairment would have increased by $128 (unchanged for the year ended June 29, 2013). Similarly, if the discount rate were to increase by 100 basis points, the impairment would have increased by $36 (unchanged for the year ended June 29, 2013).

7. COMPUTER SOFTWARE:

	Year Ended June 28, 2014	June 29, 2013
Cost		
Beginning of fiscal year	$4,684	$3,994
Additions	1,107	829
Disposals	(752)	(139)
End of Period	5,039	4,684
Accumulated amortization		
Beginning of fiscal year	$3,541	$3,268
Amortization for the period	791	412
Disposals	(752)	(139)
End of Period	$3,580	$3,541
Net carrying value		
End of period	$1,459	$1,143
Beginning of fiscal year	$1,143	$726
Capital work in progress include at end of period	$2	$702

8. BANK FACILITIES:

The Company has an operating credit facility for working capital and for general corporate purposes to a maximum amount of $25 million that is committed until June 25, 2016 and bears interest at prime plus 0.75%. The Company also has a revolving term credit facility ("term capex facility") to be used exclusively for capital expenditures in the amount of $4 million that is committed until June 25, 2016 and bears interest at prime plus 0.75%. At the end of each quarter, repayments equal to 6.25% of the aggregate principal amount of all borrowings under the term capex facility must be paid.

Standby fees of 0.50% are paid on a quarterly basis for any unused portion of the operating credit facility and term capex facility. The operating credit facility and term capex facility are subject to certain covenants and other limitations that, if breached, could cause a default and may result in a requirement for immediate repayment of amounts outstanding. Security provided includes a security interest over all personal property of the Company's business and a mortgage over the land and building comprising the Company's head office/distribution facility.

The Company also has an uncommitted letter of credit facility to a maximum amount of $10 million and an uncommitted demand overdraft facility in the amount of $0.5 million to be used exclusively for issuance of letters of credit for the purchase of inventory. Any amounts outstanding under the overdraft facility will bear interest at the bank's prime rate. In addition, the Company has a US$4.05 million foreign exchange line available to hedge foreign currency exposure not exceeding 12 months. The foregoing facilities and exchange line are secured by the Company's personal property from time to time financed with the proceeds drawn thereunder.

9. PAYABLES AND ACCRUALS:

	June 28, 2014	June 29, 2013
Trade payables	$ 1,250	$ 1,840
Accruals	5,089	4,981
RSU/DSU liability	1,591	2,516
Commodity and capital taxes	891	764
Derivative financial instruments	364	-
	$ 9,185	$ 10,101

10. SALES RETURN PROVISION:

The provision for sales returns primarily relates to customer returns of unworn and undamaged purchases for a full refund within the time period provided by Danier's return policy, which is generally 14 days after the purchase date. Since the time period of the provision is of relatively short duration, all of the provision is classified as current. The following transactions occurred during the years ended June 28, 2014 and June 29, 2013, respectively, with respect to the sales return provision:

	Year Ended June 28, 2014	June 29, 2013
Beginning of period	$99	$124
Amount provided during the period	1,996	2,049
Utilized or released during the period	(2,001)	(2,074)
End of period	**$94**	**$99**

11. SHARE CAPITAL:

(a) Authorized
1,224,329 Multiple Voting Shares
Unlimited Subordinate Voting Shares
Unlimited Class A and B Preference Shares

(b) Issued

Multiple Voting Shares	Number	Consideration
Balance June 30, 2012	1,224,329	Nominal
Balance June 29, 2013	1,224,329	Nominal
Balance June 28, 2014	1,224,329	Nominal

Subordinate Voting Shares	Number	Consideration
Balance June 30, 2012	3,422,573	$ 15,040
Shares repurchased	(862,801)	(3,792)
Shares issued upon exercising of stock options	48,067	285
Balance June 29, 2013	2,607,839	$ 11,533
Shares repurchased	(25,000)	(111)
Shares issued upon exercising of stock options	47,000	350
Balance June 28, 2014	**2,629,839**	**$ 11,772**

The Multiple Voting Shares and Subordinate Voting Shares have identical attributes except that the Multiple Voting Shares entitle the holder to 10 votes per share and the Subordinate Voting Shares entitle the holder to one vote per share. Each Multiple Voting Share is convertible at any time, at the holder's option, into one fully paid and non-assessable Subordinate Voting Share. The Multiple Voting Shares are subject to provisions whereby, if a triggering event occurs, then each Multiple Voting Share is converted into one fully paid and non-assessable Subordinate Voting Share. A triggering event may occur if, among other things, Mr. Jeffrey Wortsman, President and Chief Executive Officer: (i) dies; (ii) ceases to be a senior officer of the Company; (iii) ceases to own 5% or more of the aggregate number of Multiple Voting Shares and Subordinate Voting Shares outstanding; or (iv) owns less than 918,247 Multiple Voting Shares and Subordinate Voting Shares combined.

(c) Earnings Per Share

Basic and diluted per share amounts are based on the following weighted average number of shares outstanding:

	Fiscal Year Ended	
	June 28, 2014	June 29, 2013
Weighted average number of shares for basic earnings per share calculations	3,840,319	4,180,829
Effect of dilutive options outstanding	108,017	142,790
Weighted average number of shares for diluted earnings per share calculations	**3,948,336**	**4,323,619**

The computation of dilutive options outstanding only includes those options having exercise prices below the average market price of Subordinate Voting Shares on the TSX during the period. The number of options excluded was 111,200 as at June 28, 2014 and 26,200 as at June 29, 2013.

(d) Issuer Bids

During the fiscal year ended June 29, 2013, the Company announced its intention to commence a substantial issuer bid (the "Offer"). The Offer was formally commenced on October 24, 2012 by filing and mailing a formal offer to purchase and accompanying circular, pursuant to which the Company offered to purchase for cancellation up to $10 million in value of its Subordinate Voting Shares from shareholders for cash by way of a "modified Dutch Auction" at a range of Offer prices between $12.55 and $13.30 per share. The Offer expired on November 28, 2012 and a total of 1,748,470 Subordinate Voting Shares were validly deposited and not withdrawn under the Offer. Pursuant to the terms of the Offer, the Company determined the purchase price to be $12.70 per share. As the aggregate value of Subordinate Voting Shares deposited under the Offer exceeded the $10 million maximum value of consideration payable by the Company pursuant to the Offer, a pro-ration factor of 0.9852 was applied to deposited Subordinate Voting Shares (except for odd lot deposits, which were not subject to pro-ration), and the Company repurchased for cancellation 787,401 Subordinate Voting Shares at a purchase price of $12.70 per share. Approximately $3,460 of the purchase price, representing the average paid-in value of the shares, was charged to share capital, and approximately $6,913, which included the excess paid-in value of the shares as well as the transaction costs (net of tax) associated with the Offer, was charged to retained earnings.

During the past several years, the Company has from time to time received approval from the TSX to commence various normal course issuer bids ("NCIBs"). On February 12, 2014, the Company announced that the TSX had accepted a notice of its intention to proceed with its seventh NCIB (the "2014 NCIB"). Pursuant to the 2014 NCIB, the Company may purchase for cancellation up to a maximum of 145,496 Subordinate Voting Shares. The maximum number of Subordinate Voting Shares that may be purchased pursuant to the 2014 NCIB represents approximately 10% of the "public float" of the Subordinate Voting Shares outstanding as at the date of the notice of its intention to proceed with the 2014 NCIB. The 2014 NCIB commenced on February 14, 2014 and will terminate on February 13, 2015, or on such earlier date as the Company may complete its purchases under the 2014 NCIB.

The following Subordinate Voting Shares were repurchased for cancellation under the Offer and NCIBs then in effect during the years ended June 28, 2014 and June 29, 2013, respectively:

	Fiscal Year Ended	
	June 28, 2014	June 29, 2013
Number of shares repurchased under Offer	-	787,404
Number of shares repurchased under NCIBs	25,000	75,400
Amount charged to share capital	$111	$3,792
Amount charged to retained earnings representing the excess over the average paid-in value	$164	$7,515
Total cash consideration	**$275**	**$11,307**
Income tax related to Offer that was recorded directly to Shareholders' Equity	-	$92

12. SHARE-BASED COMPENSATION:

The Company's net share-based compensation expense recognized in SG&A related to its stock option, RSU and DSU plans is presented below:

	Fiscal Year Ended	
	June 28, 2014	June 29, 2013
Stock option plan expense	$209	$131
RSU plan expense	296	693
DSU plan expense	(157)	75
	$348	**$899**

The carrying amount of the Company's share-based compensation arrangements including stock option, RSU and DSU plans are recorded on the consolidated balance sheet as follows:

	Fiscal Year Ended	
	June 28, 2014	June 29, 2013
Payables and accruals	$1,591	$2,516
Contributed surplus	1,040	954
	$2,631	**$3,470**

(a) Stock Option Plan

The Company maintains a Stock Option Plan, as amended, for the benefit of directors, officers, employees and service providers, pursuant to which granted options are exercisable for Subordinate Voting Shares. As at June 28, 2014, the Company has reserved 525,100 Subordinate Voting Shares for issuance under its Stock Option Plan. The granting of options and the related vesting periods are at the discretion of the Board of Directors, on the advice of the Governance, Compensation, Human Resources and Nominating Committee of the Board (the "Committee"), at exercise prices determined as the weighted average of the trading prices of the Company's Subordinate Voting Shares on the TSX for the five trading days preceding the effective date of the grant. In general, options granted to officers, employees and service providers under the Stock Option Plan typically vest over a period of three years from the grant date and expire no later than the tenth anniversary of the date of grant (subject to extension in accordance with the Stock Option Plan if the options would otherwise expire during a black-out period).

A summary of the status of the Company's Stock Option Plan as of June 28, 2014 and June 29, 2013 and changes during the fiscal years ended on those dates is presented below:

	June 28, 2014		June 29, 2013	
		Weighted Average		Weighted Average
Stock Option	**Shares**	**Exercise Price**	**Shares**	**Exercise Price**
Outstanding at beginning of year	277,900	$6.45	357,767	$7.14
Granted	85,000	$11.29	26,200	$12.97
Exercised	(47,000)	$4.83	(48,067)	$3.80
Forfeited	(28,100)	$10.68	(58,000)	$15.85
Outstanding at end of year	287,800	$7.73	277,900	$6.45
Options exercisable at end of year	185,332	$5.60	232,966	$5.37

The following table summarizes the distribution of these options and the remaining contractual life as at June 28, 2014:

	Options Outstanding			Options Exercisable	
Exercise Prices	# Outstanding	Weighted Average Remaining Contactual Life	Weighted Average Exercise Price	Shares	Weighted Average Exercise Price
$3.15	83,600	4.3 years	$3.15	83,600	$3.15
$6.25	50,000	4.0 years	$6.25	50,000	$6.25
$7.80	28,000	2.6 years	$7.80	28,000	$7.80
$8.68	15,000	2.8 years	$8.68	15,000	$8.68
$10.99	25,000	9.6 years	$10.99	-	$10.99
$11.21	25,000	9.6 years	$11.21	-	$11.21
$11.56	35,000	9.3 years	$11.56	-	$11.56
$12.97	26,200	8.6 years	$12.97	8,732	$12.97
	287,800	5.9 years	$7.73	185,332	$5.60

During the year ended June 28, 2014, the Company granted an aggregate of 85,000 stock options with exercise prices ranging from $10.99 to $11.56 per stock option (June 29, 2013 – 26,200 stock options were granted with an exercise price of $12.97 per stock option). The estimated fair value at the date of grant for the options granted during the year ended June 28, 2014 was between $3.74 and $4.10 per stock option (June 29, 2013 – $6.57 per stock option). The fair value of each option granted was estimated on the date of grant using the Black-Scholes Options Pricing Model with the following assumptions:

	Year Ended June 28, 2014			Year Ended June 29, 2013
Grant date	Oct 30, 2013	Feb 7, 2014	Feb 12, 2014	Feb 7, 2013
Number of options granted	35,000	25,000	25,000	26,200
Expected option life	5 years	5 years	5 years	10 years
Risk free rate	1.7%	1.6%	1.6%	2.0%
Expected stock price volatility	36%	36%	36%	38%
Dividend yield	-	-	-	-
Estimated forfeiture rate	0%	0%	0%	0%
Share price at grant date	$11.56	$11.21	$10.99	$12.97
Weighted average fair value of options granted	$4.10	$3.82	$3.74	$6.57

The risk free rate was based on the Government of Canada benchmark bond yield on the date of grant for a term equal to the expected life of the options. Expected volatility was determined by calculating the historical volatility of the Company's share price over a period equal to the expected life of the options. The expected contractual life was based on the contractual life of the awards and adjusted, based on management's best estimate and historical redemption rates. The estimated forfeiture rate was estimated based on forfeiture rates for options granted between January 2007 and December 2013.

The Black-Scholes Option Pricing Model was developed for use in estimating the fair value of traded options, which have no black-out or vesting restrictions and are fully transferable. In addition, the Black-Scholes Option Pricing Model requires the use of subjective assumptions, including the expected stock price volatility. As a result of the Company's Stock Option Plan having characteristics different from those of traded options, and because changes in the subjective assumptions can have a material effect on the fair value estimate, the Black-Scholes Option Pricing Model does not necessarily provide a reliable single measure of the fair value of options granted.

(b) Deferred Share Unit Plan

The cash-settled DSU Plan, as amended, was established for non-management directors. Under the DSU Plan, non-management directors of the Company may receive an annual grant of DSUs at the discretion of the Board of Directors on the advice of the Committee, and can also elect to receive their annual retainers and meeting fees in DSUs. A DSU is a notional unit equivalent in value to one Subordinate Voting Share of the Company based on the five-day average high and low board lot trading prices of the Company's Subordinate Voting Shares on the TSX immediately prior to the date on which the value of the DSU is determined.

Upon retirement from the Board of Directors, a participant in the DSU Plan receives a cash payment equal to the market value of the accumulated DSUs in their account. The fair value of the liability is measured at each balance sheet date by applying the Black-Scholes Option Pricing Model until the award is settled.

The following transactions occurred during each of the years ended June 28, 2014 and June 29, 2013, respectively, with respect to the DSU Plan:

	Year Ended June 28, 2014	Year Ended June 29, 2013
Outstanding at beginning of year	83,136	103,920
Granted	-	-
Redeemed	-	(20,784)
Outstanding at end of period	83,136	83,136
Danier stock price at end of period	$9.41	$11.31
Liability at end of period	$782	$940

(c) Restricted Share Unit Plan

The Company has established a cash-settled RSU Plan, as amended, as part of its overall compensation plan. An RSU is a notional unit equivalent in value to one Subordinate Voting Share of the Company. The RSU Plan is administered by the Board of Directors, with the advice of the Committee. Under the RSU Plan, certain eligible officers, employees and directors of the Company are eligible to receive a grant of RSUs that generally vest over periods not exceeding three years, as determined by the Committee. Upon the exercise of the vested RSUs, a cash payment equal to the market value of the exercised vested RSUs will be paid to the participant. The market value is based on the average daily closing prices of the Subordinate Voting Shares on the TSX immediately prior to the applicable payment date. RSU expense is recognized on a graded vesting schedule and is determined based on the fair value of the liability incurred at each balance sheet date until the award is settled. The fair value of the liability is measured by applying the Black-Scholes Option Pricing Model, taking into account the extent to which participants have rendered services to date.

The following transactions occurred during each of the years ended June 28, 2014 and June 29, 2013, respectively, with respect to the RSU Plan:

	Year Ended June 28, 2014	Year Ended June 29, 2013
Outstanding at beginning of period	174,605	167,536
Granted	45,000	46,600
Redeemed	(91,647)	(36,063)
Forfeited	(4,569)	(3,468)
Outstanding at end of period	123,389	174,605
RSUs vested at end of period	14,785	39,331
Liability at end of period	$809	$1,576

13. AMORTIZATION AND IMPAIRMENT LOSS:

Amortization of property and equipment and computer software and impairment loss on property and equipment, included in cost of sales and SG&A is summarized as follows:

	Year Ended June 28, 2014	Year Ended June 29, 2013
Cost of sales	$165	$168
SG&A	4,806	3,720
End of period	**$4,971**	**$3,888**

14. INCOME TAXES:

The Company's income tax expense is comprised as follows:

	Year Ended June 28, 2014	Year Ended June 29, 2013
Current tax expense		
Current period	($2,856)	$746
Adjustment for prior years	(64)	(14)
Current tax expense	($2,920)	$732
Deferred tax expense		
Recognition and reversal of temporary differences	($158)	($156)
Changes in tax rates	(6)	(7)
Adjustment for prior years and other	(47)	1
Deferred tax expense	($211)	($162)
Total income tax expense	**($3,131)**	**$570**

The Company's effective income tax rate consists of the following:

	June 28, 2014	June 29, 2013
Combined basic federal and provincial average statutory rate	26.5%	26.4%
Current year losses applied to prior year	2.6%	-
Non-deductible expenses	(1.1%)	4.2%
Future federal and provincial rate changes	0.1%	(0.3%)
Adjustment for prior years	1.1%	(0.7%)
Other	(0.2%)	(0.8%)
	29.0%	28.8%

Deferred income tax asset is summarized as follows:

	June 28, 2014	June 29, 2013
Amortization	$1,190	$1,041
Stock based compensation	421	667
Deferred lease inducements and rent liability	380	369
Federal and provincial tax credits	308	-
Other deferred expenses	75	86
	$2,374	$2,163

15. CHANGES IN WORKING CAPITAL ITEMS:

	Year Ended June 28, 2014	Year Ended June 29, 2013
Decrease (increase) in:		
Accounts receivable	559	(680)
Inventories	1,089	2,081
Prepaid expenses	193	(53)
Increase (decrease) in:		
Payables and accruals	(916)	(60)
Deferred revenue	(37)	85
Sales return provision	(5)	(25)
	$883	**$1,348**

16. CONTINGENCIES AND GUARANTEES:

(a) Legal proceedings

In the course of its business, the Company from time to time becomes involved in various claims and legal proceedings. In the opinion of management, all such claims and suits are adequately covered by insurance, or if not so covered, the results are not expected to materially affect the Company's financial position.

(b) Guarantees

The Company has provided the following guarantees to third parties and no amounts have been accrued in the consolidated financial statements for these guarantees:

(i) In the ordinary course of business, the Company has agreed to indemnify its lenders under its credit facilities against certain costs or losses resulting from changes in laws and regulations or from a default in repaying a borrowing. These indemnifications extend for the term of the credit facilities and do not provide any limit on the maximum potential liability. Historically, the Company has not made any indemnification payments under such agreements.

(ii) In the ordinary course of business, the Company has provided indemnification commitments to certain counterparties in matters such as real estate leasing transactions, director and officer indemnification agreements and certain purchases of non-inventory assets and services. These indemnification agreements generally require the Company to compensate the counterparties for costs or losses resulting from legal action brought against the counterparties related to the actions of the Company. The terms of these indemnification agreements will vary based on the contract and generally do not provide any limit on the maximum potential liability.

17. COMMITMENTS:

(a) Operating leases:

The Company leases various store locations, a distribution warehouse and equipment under non-cancellable operating lease agreements. The leases are classified as operating leases since there is no transfer of risks and rewards inherent to ownership.

The leases have varying terms, escalation clauses and renewal rights. Minimum lease payments are recognized on a straight-line basis. Leases run for varying terms that generally do not exceed 10 years, with options to renew (if any) that do not exceed five years. The majority of real estate leases are net leases, which require additional payments for the cost of insurance, taxes, common area maintenance and utilities. Certain rental agreements include contingent rent, which is based on revenue exceeding a minimum amount. Minimum rentals, excluding rentals based upon revenue, are as follows:

Not later than one year	$10,978
Later than one year and not later than five years	$30,740
Later than five years	$14,793
Total	$56,511

Minimum lease payments and contingent rentals recognized as an expense are summarized as follows:

	Year Ended June 28, 2014	Year Ended June 29, 2013
Minimum lease payments	$11,875	$11,550
Contingent rentals	$289	$292

(b) Letters of credit:

As at June 28, 2014, the Company had outstanding letters of credit in the amount of $7,146 (June 29, 2013 – $8,743) for the importation of finished goods inventories to be received.

18. FINANCIAL INSTRUMENTS:

(a) Fair value disclosure

The following table presents the carrying amount and the fair value of the Company's financial instruments:

			June 28, 2014		June 29, 2013	
	Classification	Maturity	Carrying Value	Fair Value	Carrying Value	Fair Value
Cash	Loans and receivables	Short-term	$13,507	$13,507	$24,541	$24,541
Accounts receivable	Loans and receivables	Short-term	$638	$638	$375	$375
Payables and accruals	Financial liabilities	Short-term	$8,821	$8,821	$10,101	$10,101
Sales return provision	Financial liabilities	Short-term	$94	$94	$99	$99
Derivative financial instruments[1]	Fair value through profit and loss	Short-term	($364)	($364)	$822	$822

(1) Included in payables and accruals for the fiscal year ended June 28, 2014 and included in accounts receivable for the fiscal year ended June 29, 2013.

The fair value of a financial instrument is the estimated amount that the Company would receive to sell an asset or pay to transfer a liability in an orderly transaction between market participants at the measurement date. These estimates are subjective in nature, often involve uncertainties and the exercise of significant judgment and are made at a specific point in time using available information about the financial instrument and may not reflect fair value in the future. The estimated fair value amounts can be materially affected by the use of different assumptions or methodologies.

The principal methodologies and assumptions used in estimating the fair value of the Company's financial instruments are as follows:

- The derivative financial instruments, which consist of foreign exchange contracts, have been marked-to-market and are categorized as Level 2 in the fair value hierarchy. Factors included in the determination of fair value include the spot rate, forward rates, estimates of volatility, present value factor, strike prices, credit risk of the Company and credit risk of counterparties. As at June 28, 2014, a $364 unrealized loss (June 29, 2013 – $822 unrealized gain) was recorded in SG&A for the foreign exchange contracts outstanding.
- Given their short-term maturity, the fair value of cash, accounts receivable, payables and accruals and sales return provision approximate their carrying values. There were no transfers between Level 1 and 2 during the year.

(b) Financial instrument risk management

Foreign Currency Risk

Foreign currency risk is the risk that the fair value or future cash flows of a financial instrument will fluctuate because of changes in foreign currency exchange rates. The Company purchases a significant portion of its leather and finished goods inventory from foreign vendors with payment terms in U.S. dollars. The Company uses a combination of foreign exchange contracts and spot purchases to manage its foreign exchange exposure on cash flows related to these purchases. A foreign exchange contract represents an option with a counterparty to buy or sell a foreign currency to meet its obligations. Credit risk exists in the event of a failure by a counterparty to fulfill its obligations. The Company reduces this risk by mainly dealing with highly-rated counterparties such as major Canadian financial institutions.

During the years ended June 28, 2014 and June 29, 2013, the Company entered into foreign exchange contracts with Canadian financial institutions as counterparties with U.S. dollar notional amounts as listed below. Foreign exchange contracts outstanding as at June 28, 2014 expired or will expire at various times between July 3, 2014 and April 24, 2015 and the foreign exchange contracts that were outstanding as at June 29, 2013 expired or will expire between July 8, 2013 and August 29, 2014.

	Year Ended	
	June 28, 2014	June 29, 2013
Notional amount outstanding at beginning of period (US$000)	$32,700	$21,000
Notional amount of foreign exchange contracts entered into during the period (US$000)	21,800	38,200
Notional amount of foreign exchange contracts expired during the period (US$000)	(29,000)	(26,500)
Notional amount outstanding at end of period (US$000)	$25,500	$32,700
Maturing in less than 1 year (US$000)	$25,500	$29,000
Maturing from 1 to 2 years (US$000)	-	$3,700
Fair value of foreign exchange contracts — gain/(loss) – (CDN$000)	($364)	$822

As at June 28, 2014, a sensitivity analysis was performed on the Company's U.S. dollar denominated financial instruments, which principally consist of US$1.7 million of cash, to determine how a change in the U.S. dollar exchange rate would impact net earnings. A 500 basis point rise or fall in the Canadian dollar against the U.S. dollar, assuming that all other variables, in particular interest rates, remain the same, would have resulted in a $62 decrease or increase in the Company's net loss for the year ended June 28, 2014.

Liquidity Risk

Liquidity risk is the risk that the Company will not be able to meet its financial obligations as they become due. The Company's approach to managing liquidity risk is to ensure, to the extent possible, that it will have sufficient liquidity to meet its liabilities when due. As at June 28, 2014, the Company had $13.5 million of cash; an operating credit facility of $25 million and term capex facility of $4 million that are committed until June 25, 2016; and a $10 million uncommitted letter of credit facility which includes an uncommitted demand overdraft facility in the amount of $0.5 million and an uncommitted foreign exchange credit line in the amount of US$4.05 million related thereto. The credit facilities are used to finance seasonal working capital requirements for merchandise purchases and other corporate purposes. The Company expects that the majority of its payables and accruals and deferred revenue will be discharged within 90 days.

Interest Rate Risk

Interest rate risk is the risk that the fair value or future cash flows of a financial instrument will fluctuate because of changes in market interest rates. The Company's exposure to interest rate fluctuations is primarily related to cash borrowings under its existing credit facility, which bears interest at floating rates, and interest earned on its cash balances. The Company has performed a sensitivity analysis on interest rate risk at June 28, 2014 to determine how a change in interest rates would have impacted net loss. As at June 28, 2014, the Company's cash available for investment was approximately $13.5 million. A 100 basis point change in interest rates would have increased or decreased net loss by approximately $0.1 million for the year ended June 28, 2014. This analysis assumes that all other variables, in particular foreign currency exchange rates, remain constant.

Equity Price Risk

Equity price risk is the risk that the fair value or future cash flows of a financial instrument will fluctuate because of changes in market equity prices. The Company's exposure to equity price fluctuations is primarily related to the RSU and DSU liability included in payables and accruals. The value of the vested DSU and RSU liability is adjusted to reflect changes in the market value of the Company's Subordinate Voting Shares on the TSX. The Company has performed a sensitivity analysis on equity price risk as at June 28, 2014 to determine how a change in the price of the Company's Subordinate Voting Shares would have impacted net loss. As at June 28, 2014, a total of 123,389 RSUs and 83,136 DSUs have been granted and are outstanding. An increase or decrease of $1.00 in the market price of the Company's Subordinate Voting Shares would have increased or decreased net loss by approximately $0.2 million for the year ended June 28, 2014. This analysis assumes that all RSUs and DSUs were fully vested and all other variables remain constant.

Credit Risk

Credit risk is the risk that a customer or counterparty to a financial instrument will cause a financial loss to the Company by failing to meet its obligations. The Company's financial instruments that are exposed to concentrations of credit risk are primarily cash, accounts receivable and foreign exchange option contracts. The Company limits its exposure to credit risk with respect to cash by investing in short-term deposits with major Canadian financial institutions. The Company's accounts receivable, excluding derivative financial instruments, consist primarily of credit card receivables from the last few days of the fiscal period end, which are settled within the first few days of the new fiscal period. Accounts receivable also consist of accounts receivable from distributors and corporate customers. Accounts receivable are net of applicable allowance for doubtful accounts, which is established based on the specific credit risks associated with the distributor and each corporate customer and other relevant information. The allowance for doubtful accounts is assessed on a quarterly basis. Concentration of credit risk with respect to accounts receivable from distributors and corporate customers is limited due to the relatively insignificant balances outstanding and the number of different customers comprising the Company's customer base. Credit risk for foreign exchange option contracts exists in the event of a failure by a counterparty to fulfill its obligations. The Company reduces this risk by mainly dealing with highly-rated counterparties such as major Canadian financial institutions.

As at June 28, 2014, the Company's exposure to credit risk for these financial instruments was cash of $13.5 million, accounts receivable of $0.6 million and foreign exchange option contracts that had a notional value of US$25.5 million.

19. CAPITAL DISCLOSURE:

The Company defines its capital as shareholders' equity. The Company's objectives in managing capital are to:

- Ensure sufficient liquidity to support its current operations and execute its business plans;
- Enable the internal financing of capital projects; and
- Maintain a strong capital base so as to maintain investor, creditor and market confidence.

The Company's primary uses of capital are to finance non-cash working capital along with capital expenditures for new store additions, existing store renovation or relocation projects, information technology software and hardware purchases and production machinery and equipment purchases. The Company maintains a $25 million operating credit facility, a $4 million term capex facility and a $10 million uncommitted letter of credit facility which includes an uncommitted demand overdraft facility in the amount of $0.5 million and an uncommitted foreign exchange line in the amount of US$4.05 million related thereto, that it uses to finance seasonal working capital requirements for merchandise purchases and other corporate purposes. The Company does not have any long-term debt and therefore net earnings generated from operations are available for reinvestment in the Company.

The Board of Directors does not establish quantitative return on capital criteria for management, but rather promotes year-over-year sustainable profitable growth. On a quarterly basis, the Board of Directors monitors share repurchase program activities. Decisions on whether to repurchase shares are made on a specific transaction basis and depend on the Company's cash position, estimates of future cash requirements, market prices and regulatory restrictions, among other things. The Company does not currently pay dividends.

Externally imposed capital requirements include a debt-to-equity ratio covenant as part of the operating credit facility. The Company was in compliance with this covenant as at June 28, 2014 and June 29, 2013. There has been no change with respect to the overall capital risk management strategy during the year ended June 28, 2014.

20. RELATED PARTIES:

Key management personnel are those individuals having authority and responsibility for planning, directing and controlling the activities of the Company, including members of the Company's Board of Directors. The Company considers key management to be the Company's Board of Directors and its five most highly compensated executive officers. Compensation awarded to key management included:

	Year Ended	
	June 28, 2014	June 29, 2013
Salaries and short-term benefits	$2,090	$2,000
Termination benefits	457	-
Share-based compensation	249	810
	$2,796	**$2,810**

The Company's subsidiaries are described in Note 3(b).

21. EXPENSE ANALYSIS:

Selling, general and administrative expenses include the following:

	Year Ended	
	June 28, 2014	June 29, 2013
Selling expense	$60,168	$60,464
General and administrative expense	18,918	16,156
	$79,086	$76,620

Selling expense comprises costs incurred to operate the Company's stores including wages and benefits for store management and staff, rent and occupancy, advertising, credit card fees, amortization of store property and equipment and computer software and other store operating expenses.

General and administrative expense includes the cost of design, merchandising, sourcing, merchandise planning, marketing, store administrative support, finance, loss prevention, information technology, human resource and executive functions.

22. EMPLOYEE BENEFITS EXPENSE:

Selling, general and administrative expenses include the following:

	Year Ended	
	June 28, 2014	June 29, 2013
Wages, salaries and bonus	$27,523	$27,783
Short-term benefits expense	4,125	4,295
Termination benefits	783	237
Share-based compensation	348	898
	$32,779	$33,213